THE SURVIVAL OF THE SOUL

THE SURVIVAL OF THE SOUL

and
its Evolution after Death
Notes of Experiments

by

PIERRE-EMILE CORNILLIER

www.whitecrowbooks.com

The Survival of the Soul and its Evolution after Death

Original Copyright © 1921 by Pierre-Emile Cornillier.
This Copyright © 2017 by White Crow Productions Ltd. All rights reserved.

Published and printed in the United States of America by White
Crow Books; an imprint of White Crow Productions Ltd.

For information, email White Crow Books at info@whitecrowbooks.com.

Cover Design by Astrid@Astridpaints.com
Interior design by Velin@Perseus-Design.com

Paperback ISBN 978-1-78677-031-8
eBook   ISBN 978-1-78677-032-5

Non-Fiction / Body, Mind & Spirit / Death & Dying / Parapsychology

www.whitecrowbooks.com

CONTENTS

PROLOGUE

My home library contains hundreds of books, journals and other documents dealing with psychical research, old and new. This 1921 book somehow escaped my attention until recently when I noted that Dr. Robert Crookall, a botanist and geologist who authored 14 books on psychical matters during the middle of the last century, named it as his favorite among his many references. Upon reading that, I went in search of the book, found a rare copy, and plunged into it. Like Crookall, I rank it number one. It explains so much that other authors didn't or couldn't.

Books by William Stainton Moses and Allan Kardec offer much as to how the spirit world works, but I think Pierre-Emile Cornillier has outdone even them with this book. Why it has not survived as a classic in the field, as their books have, is a mystery to me. My attempts to find anything to discredit Cornillier have turned up nothing.

Cornillier (1862 – 1933) was not a scientist or scholar, at least in the strict sense of those words. He was an artist who had an interest in psychical research when, in 1912, he realized that Reine, an 18-year-old model he had been employing for several months, had psychic abilities of some kind. Although a student of agnostic philosopher Herbert Spencer, Cornillier had closely followed the psychical research of the time and had been an observer at some séances. On a November afternoon, when it became too dark to paint, Reine asked Cornillier if they could experiment with table tipping, something he had mentioned to her. He somewhat reluctantly consented and they sat facing each other at a small table. They sat for a full hour and nothing happened. They were about to give up when they heard cracking noises and the table swayed to the right and to the left, then tapped clearly several times. Familiar with this phenomenon, Cornillier noted that the taps were spelling out letters. After some confusion and repetition of the message, Cornillier understood that he was to hypnotize Reine. Although he had never hypnotized anyone before, he had observed the process and decided to give it a try. It worked, but Cornillier was reluctant to go too far with it and was concerned about bringing Reine back to consciousness, so he quickly brought her back to full awareness. He decided to wait until after Reine's next modeling session with him to further experiment.

It was on November 29, 1912 that Cornillier recorded his first real success in what amounted to clairvoyance by Reine. After she was in "hypnotic sleep," he asked her to visit his apartment, on another floor of the building, and she, never having been in the apartment, provided an accurate description of the layout. Further experimentation involved communication with some apparently low-level spirits, but a "high spirit" named Vettellini emerged in the ninth séance and continued on as Reine's primary guide, the 107th and final séance in this book taking place on March 11, 1914. Publication of the book was delayed due to the outbreak of the Great War and the recovery period following the war.

The usual procedure was that Reine would be "magnetized" and placed in the trance state, then after some wait she would begin communicating with Vettellini and relay what he had to say back to Cornillier. If Cornillier had questions, he would put them to Reine, who would repeat the question back to Vettellini, then give his response. When Reine returned to normal consciousness, she had no recollection of what was said or had taken place while she was in the trance state. On some occasions, Vettellini would take her to distant places, and she would report back to Cornillier on what she had seen or with whom she had met. On one occasion, near the end, Vettellini apparently took possession of Reine, as the voice heard by Cornillier was much deeper and not hers. On some occasions, Reine would write what Vettellini had to say by means of automatic writing. A number of sessions were preceded by table messages in which Vettellini gave special instructions on how to proceed that day, or to communicate that the "fluid" was not strong enough that day.

There were several contacts with deceased old friends and acquaintances that were evidential to Cornillier, his wife, and some visitors, but Reine's mediumship is not about evidence, per se, as it was with most of the pioneering researchers. Cornillier was more interested in learning how things worked in the spirit world. They discussed the nature of the spirit body, how spirits awaken on the other side, what they look like, their faculties, grades of consciousness among spirits, activities in the spirit world, spirit influence on humans, God, reincarnation, astral travel, difficulties in communication by high spirits, deception by inferior spirits, premonitions, dreams, time, space, animal spirits, materializations, apparitions, cremation, and other concerns that Cornillier had about the non-material world.

What was evidential to Cornillier is that Reine was a "simple child" in her conscious state, with no prior knowledge of the things she related in some detail and without hesitation in the trance state. Of this as well as her sincerity and integrity he had absolutely no doubt. In his Conclusion, he recognizes that his book will not appeal to the "scoffers," as his faith in Reine's character was such that he "refrained from establishing a so-called scientific control over my medium." He points out that scientists of the highest reputations, mentioning Crookes and Richet, have taken every possible precaution, and yet their skeptical peers have questioned their methods and objectivity while heaping abuse upon them.

This book is for the open-minded reader who recognizes or is prepared to recognize that there are many difficulties and distortions in spirit communication. To quote Cornillier:

> "Reine – and this must not be forgotten – does not hear in words the substance of what she repeats. She translates into words the vibrations that convey Vettellini's thought, and as her education is extremely meager, and her vocabulary limited, her interpretations may occasionally be inexact. Conscious of her difficulties, Vettellini, in certain cases, gives her the precise words, which she then repeats mechanically, without comprehending. And this is another source of error. The rectification is always made in a following séance, but sometimes long after; for, oftener than not, it is an unexpected question which reveals that the transmission has been imperfect." (p. 66)

I recommend that the reader begin with the Conclusion of the book on page 387 in order to get a feel for Cornillier's intelligence, if not brilliance, and his scientific acumen. Be prepared to be overwhelmed, and if you know someone approaching this life's end, pass the book on to him or her.

~ Michael Tymn, author of *The Afterlife Revealed*, *Resurrecting Leonora Piper*, *Dead Men Talking*, and others.

July 19, 2017

INTRODUCTION

"Not as adventitious therefore will the wise man regard the faith which is in him. The highest truth he sees he will fearlessly utter; knowing that, let what may come of it, he is thus playing his right part in the world—knowing that if he can effect the change he aims at—well; if not—well also; though not so well."

This inspiring principle of the great philosopher Herbert Spencer has persuaded me to publish the notes which compose this book, though they may be received with scorn by the general public and possibly, even, with commiserating stupefaction on the part of my friends. It is true that for the latter my long-time interest in psychical research is no secret, for I have constantly studied the different interpretations of the various phenomena, occasionally experimenting myself and keeping informed, as far as possible, of all that is accomplished in this field. Even a certain few among them, know that six or seven years ago I published an essay with the object of popularising the admirable doctrines of Cosmosophy.[1] But in all these circumstances I have adopted the attitude of an attentive spectator, glass in hand, tranquilly regarding the scene from his allotted place. Then, all of a sudden I found myself on the stage—author and actor at the same time. There was no premeditation about it. My first step was all unconscious, and this is how it came about Early in the year of 1912, I

---

[1] Cosmosophy is an occult doctrine, exteriorized by the Maitre S. U. Zanne for few students in Paris, from 1899 to 1906.

xi

received a visit from a young girl sent me by the sculptor D., to whom I had applied for a model. As the child was interesting and serious, I employed her regularly; and little by little, in the course of the sittings, remarking her courage and delicacy in struggling with rather miserable conditions of existence, I came to have a real esteem for her.

Reine had been posing thus for several months in my studio when, one day, she discovered on my writing table one of those glass balls which are used for crystal-gazing, and asked what its use might be. I explained briefly that certain people, by looking fixedly at the ball for a few moments, could fall into a sort of half-sleep, and sometimes even had curious visions. She was so interested that I allowed her to carry it home to experiment for herself. Three or four days later, when she came to pose again, she brought the crystal back to me, greatly disappoint-ed. She had seen absolutely nothing, and the fact annoyed her for, as she said, she would like so much to see. And it seemed to her that she *ought to see*. If she kept on trying, did I think perhaps it would come? I told her to keep the ball during the summer vacation, if it interested her, and to look at it occasionally for ten or fifteen minutes at a time. As a matter of fact, instances are known where people have had vi-sions only after long efforts.[2] I told Reine this might be the case with her, adding that, personally, I had never obtained the least result with the crystal, though I had had success in certain other experiments.

Reine questioned me almost with anxiety. She was wholly ignorant of such phenomena, but clearly my words awakened in her some in-tense and mysterious sensibility. She repeated her desire to assist at some experiment,—oh, only to see a table move! ... Did I think it was possible? I promised her that some time next winter, some day too dark for work, we would try our hand at typtology.

The summer passed. In October I returned to Paris, resuming work with Reine soon after my arrival. The good child brought me back the wretched ball. She had put her eyes out over it and had seen just nothing at all but the tears of fatigue which she shed. I set my crystal back on its shelf and, giving the matter no further thought, we took up again our normal sittings for the picture upon which I was then working. But one November afternoon, about half-past two, the light grew so faint that I was forced to abandon all idea of painting. Reine had not forgotten my promise and, to my great embarrassment, recalled it to me. Though

---

[2] See "Les Annales des Sciences Psychiques," March, 1905, Dr. Edmond Waller: "Une aventure de Vision dans le Cristal."

I had no valid objection to offer, ... a certain sense of the ridiculous constrained me. Finally, however, I decided to accede to her request.

Indifferently I cleared a small table, and we took our seats opposite each other, she, serious as a Pope, I, feeling at heart rather foolish. Hands on the table, we waited ... ten minutes ... twenty minutes. Not a quiver. Our failure began to be rather vexing, for I had assured her that this experiment always succeeded. Judging from certain indications, I had suspected that Reine might have the mediumistic faculty, and I was surprised at not seeing the smallest manifestation of it. I decided to persevere for forty minutes and then if nothing happened, to abandon the game. There had been some cracking noises, it is true, and that obscure working in the wood which all operators know, but there was nothing definite and I left the table at the hour agreed, secretly pleased to be liberated from a situation which had become absurd.

Standing there, and rubbing my stiffened hands, I began to suggest some explanation when suddenly glancing at the table, I felt a strange unreasonable impulse to return to it; and abruptly I said to Reine: "We will try again ... for ten minutes."

Almost immediately there were cracking noises, the table swayed to the right, to the left, and finally tapped clearly several times. I watched Reine narrowly; she, at the same time was vigilantly surveying me. Observing the position of her body and feet, and convinced that she had no part in these movements, I began to note the letters of the alphabet corresponding to the number of taps. First came my name: "Cornillier;" then these words: "Reine to sleep." Surprised, I asked for a repetition of the message, and this time, with more politeness and better grammar, the table tapped: "Monsieur Cornillier, make Reine sleep."

This was astonishing. My experiments in psychical phenomena had never yet led me into this special domain.

Never in my life had I hypnotized anyone, never had I dreamed of hypnotising anyone; and of the methods employed to produce hypnosis, I knew only what my reading and my observations at two séances had taught me. I stared blankly at the child:

"Curious! ... Would you like me to try? You're not afraid?"

"Oh no, Monsieur Cornillier, not with you. Try."

So then, mustering my slight and scattered memories, I set to work to apply them. Soon—and almost to my dismay—I saw the eyes of my little model first grow red and watery ... then the lids flutter ... and finally close. In appearance she slept! But was she really sleeping?

Quite abashed at my success, and prudent by nature, my first thought was to test my talent in the contrary direction. To provoke sleep is not the whole trick. I was frankly anxious when I blew on her eyes, and made a few passes to awaken her; but Reine came back to her senses all right—and so did I! After telling her what had happened, I added: "I think I could perhaps make you sleep, but first you must understand what hypnotic sleep is, and then, if you wish, we will try again." After some simple explanations, she assured me that, if it interested me in the least, I had only to go on, her confidence was complete, and she would be overjoyed to take part in real experiments.

Some days later, when our sitting was finished, we returned to the table, which, this time, moved at once and tapped the words: "Make Reine sleep."

Determined to find out what this persistence meant, I installed the young person in a comfortable chair and proceeded to mesmerize her methodically and with great prudence, asking constantly how she felt, observing her respiration, etc. At the end of a quarter of an hour she seemed to be sleeping profoundly. But, again, could I be sure it was hypnotic sleep? Was she just taking a good nap? Or, could she be simply fooling me? To set these doubts at rest, I quietly took a pin and pierced the fleshy part of Reine's hand. Not an eyelash quivered; there was no interruption in her respiration; no slightest sign of pain. Lifting the eyelids, I remarked the revulsion of the eyeballs.

No further doubt seemed possible; it was after all hypnotic sleep. In her response to some questions I put to her, I noticed an alteration in her voice and a curiously childish accent in her replies. Then I tried several suggestions which she accepted: a small bottle of turpentine became an exquisite perfume, a piece of chalk turned into a bunch of violets, etc.

Nevertheless, I reflected that all this might, in truth, be simulated. Something still more convincing was needed. Taking a tone of authority, I ordered her to go down, in thought, to the apartment below, where she had never been. (My studio is on the sixth floor, and we occupy the apartment of the fifth floor which has no communication with the upper story.)

After evident effort, Reine announced in a feeble voice that she was in the room underneath the studio. I told her to look around and give a description of what she saw. She seemed really to see and even gave precise details, describing ivory brushes and other toilet articles on a table, remarking an oval glass, two small portraits of myself on the mantel-shelf, and various other objects, precluding all possible confusion of this room with any other.

I was deeply interested, for, were it only a case of mind reading, the experiment was no less valid. Several incidents followed: I asked her to grow a little older and see her future life, etc., etc. Then deciding to halt there, I, with considerable anxiety, began the passes to waken her, asking myself what I should do if she should not waken. But again little Reine came back quite easily, gently rubbing her eyes, still a bit sleepy, but evidently all right, and without the least remembrance of her experience. I took good care not to enlighten her. Beyond the mere fact of her having been asleep I only told her that she was possibly a good subject for experiment and that, if she wished, we would try again occasionally, after our sitting, to see what came of it.

As she was leaving, I gave her only the ordinary remuneration for the sitting, thinking that if she had Machiavellian designs it would be well to discourage them promptly.

Much interested now, and keen to pursue the study of this phenomenon, I decided to seek the approbation of my wife: first, because this tête-à-tête between an artist and a sleeping model was, at the least, unusual, and then, too, because I considered it necessary to have a witness who was less sympathetic than I to this kind of investigation. My wife filled these conditions. Anglo-Saxon, of positive temperament, she had passed an appreciable part of her life under materialistic influences, and although she had never in any way opposed my researches, she had always refrained from taking part in them. She listened to me calmly, without manifesting the hostility which I felt was in her mind. At heart, she deplored my interest in these questions but consented nevertheless to assist at the next séance, since I wished it.

When the moment came to operate before her I was absurdly nervous, feeling her disapprobation and finding myself absolutely grotesque with my passes and my gestures. Under these circumstances it is scarcely surprising that sleep came slowly. It was little short of thirty-five minutes before I dared to renew the pin test. As Reine endured it without flinching, my confidence returned, but alas! Not one of my suggestions met with response.[3] The pencil that I baptized violets persisted in remaining pencil, and several different objects refused all temptations to transform themselves under the quite unmagical influence of my

---

[3] Through inexperience I had unwittingly pushed the degree of hypnosis beyond the point of suggestibility.

will. Reine investigated them with her hands, scrutinized them with her closed eyes, and very gently said: "But no, it is not a peach—it is a cork." What stupid stubbornness!

Secretly annoyed, I risked another test, asking my wife to hand me a letter that was lying on my work table. This I placed in Reine's hands, telling her to press it against her forehead, to discover its author, to go to his house, and to describe him and his occupation at that moment. After visible efforts, punctuated by long sighs, Reine announced that she saw him. He was, she declared, in his house; it was like a studio, a sculptor's studio. He was there in a gray blouse, wearing slippers, and working on a man in clay. Then suddenly she cried: "But I know him! It is the artist who sent me to you. It is Monsieur D." This was exact. The description continued, more and more interesting, for Reine's tone changed. She spoke in a man's voice, hoarsely, and with an automatic articulation. Her words fell swift and sharp as a hatchet, and when I enquired the dimensions of the statue, the reply "Seven feet two inches" was flung back at me before I could achieve my question.

My wife was no longer indifferent. She stood very close now, carefully observing the medium.

(I may as well say at once that I went the following day to see the sculptor D., whom I had not met since the preceding spring, and in the course of conversation made a point of discovering his occupation of the day before, at the hour of Reine's sleep, the costume he was wearing, etc. Reine's description was exact in every particular—the dimensions of the statue, the mood of the artist, the discouragement he felt. From my house in the rue Guénégaud she had seen, and with the most complete precision, what was going on in a little street in Montmartre.)

To return to our experiment. When I had exhausted my inquiries about D., I told Reine to come back to my studio, and, wishing to crown my triumph, ordered her to go down to the apartment on the fifth floor and into the back room. What, I asked her, did she find there?

Not only did she see immediately that it was a bath room, with the various accessories in their relative positions, but her description proved that she saw by herself and not through the picture existing in our minds. For, astonished that she did not mention the window, I drew her on to speak of it, but my discreet suggestions had no effect, and I finished by saying impatiently: "Yes, yes—but there is a window. Don't you see it?" After a moment's silence, she seemed to look about attentively, then said: "No, there is no window; there is a curtain." Now, as it was already dark, the room had been lighted, and a heavy curtain drawn across the window; this I verified after the séance. The same thing happened with regard to the fire: she obstinately refused to see a fire, though she said she felt the heat of the hearth. Going downstairs later I remarked that the fire was, in fact, very low; no apparent glow was left in the stove, but there was still emission of heat.

Another excursion into the future followed. Then, à *propos* of nothing, Reine, repeating certain phrases she had already used, declared that she saw a "Spirit" there, who wanted to direct her. It was he who had manifested his presence when she spoke in that rough voice, and it was he who had told me to make her sleep, etc., etc.

Despite these last assertions, the success of the séance certainly authorized me to continue. My wife immediately agreed to this.

Tranquillized on this point, and sure of having an impartial witness at my side, I rarely failed, from this time onwards, to hold a séance of hypnosis after my work was over ... counting always on marvels in advance.

But alas! I had soon to sing another note. The third, the fourth, the fifth séance gave nothing of any value. Reine slept as before, but she seemed to have lost all lucidity. Spirits, the famous "Spirits," had invaded her mind, and what she now said had the characteristic marks of spirit communications in general. It is true there were interesting details. Ignorant of everything concerning psychical phenomena, as well as of the spirit-theory, she had spontaneously seen a smokelike form coming out from her body, which was, she declared, *much more herself than the body sleeping in the chair.* She has also noticed tiny blue flames escaping from my fingers when I magnetized her; besides possessing a precise view of her own internal organs which she described. Of course all these visions represented ideas quite unsuspected by the humble little model in her ordinary life. But for one curious or interesting statement we had to put up with ten stupidities—silly lies, she angrily said, told her by mean little spirits who surrounded her, mocked her, and whose dupe she surely would never be.

I was discouraged. So then, I said to myself, it is always the same story. One seems to get hold of one thread in the labyrinth of the psychical world, then suddenly the thread breaks, and once more one is groping obscurely through blind alleys that lead nowhere.

But all at once, at the sixth séance, something happened. In a written communication[4] followed by an oral one, given in a tone of marked

---

[4] These written communications are explained in the text.

authority, I was informed by the force, whatever it was, which produced the phenomena, that I was on the wrong road and that I would never obtain anything of value if I did not change my tactics. A contract was then proposed to me: If I consented to renounce all questioning of the medium, and to conform to the instructions given me, "Superior Spirits" would come and take direction of the séances, and I was promised remarkable results. But I was warned that patience was essential. I must hypnotize Reine by other methods (which would be indicated to me), and allow her to sleep, neither questioning her, nor demanding any manifestations, for a certain number of séances. "Spirits" would thus be able to take advantage of her sleep to develop her mediumistic faculties.

The proposition was made with such clearness and precision that, consumed with curiosity, I promptly accepted it. I agreed to follow exactly the instructions given me. In hypnotizing Reine, I promised to use the method prescribed. But for my part, I exacted that the mysterious other party to the contract should be faithful to his engagement.

He was faithful.

As I had been led to expect, the seventh, eighth, and ninth séances offered no great interest, though each had its special incidents, as will be seen in the text. I did as I was told, asking no questions other than those concerning Reine's sleep. At the eighth séance the order came to suggest to the medium that she must remember what she saw and tell me about it when she wakened. This suggestion however aroused no response. When she came out of her sleep, Reine had no remembrance whatever of what had happened.

I had, however, given evidence of patience and good faith, and in the tenth séance my recompense came. The medium received the order to explain to me *during her sleep* what she was doing and seeing. And regularly from this time on, we assisted, my wife and I, at a truly prodigious phenomenon: *the development of a medium by forces clearly exterior to herself, and her education by indisputably intelligent entities,* whom, for convenience and clearness, I will henceforth call *Spirits,* thus according them the quality which they claim for themselves—that of *Spirits who have lived on earth in human form, and who are continuing their evolution after death.*

Each successive séance brought fresh proof of the logic of this training which the Spirits imposed upon Reine. They evidently had a definite aim and used the most rational methods to attain it. No more incoherence, no more lies; the exercises proceeded in a preordained progression, one step led to the next, and all held together.

Henceforward my notes must reveal the character of my research and the development of the facts and ideas transmitted.[5] Prodigiously interested, I wrote them down immediately after each séance, and while still under its impression. I hope and believe that the reader will feel the sincerity and the desire for accuracy which runs through them all. I publish them as they were written, voluntarily retaining the errors and contradictions[6] which may provide an easy triumph for the sceptical, but which will enable those who are unprejudiced to judge the question as it was presented to me—complete in all its elements. I have suppressed only incidents without interest, tedious repetitions, or communications of too intimate a nature for publication. In regard to this point, I shall inevitably be charged with a lack of delicacy, or at least a lack of taste, in introducing here the personality of people who have been dear to me and whose eternal rest I shall be told I should not have troubled. While appreciating these sentiments thoroughly, I have, nevertheless, ascribed to certain communications the authorship claimed for them, fearing, otherwise, to destroy their evidential value. The psychological manifestations which constitute individualities, presented by this young girl of no instruction, will be the more convincing when it is known that I find in them illuminating and revealing signs of people to whom I am bound by blood or affection. In many cases I have been obliged to struggle against a personal repugnance and do violence to my own sentiments, in order that what I believe to be a truth—more important surely than any private considerations— might reveal itself.

After having read this account of the debut of my experiments with Reine, there are two points which I hope the reader will retain in his memory—important points, which will aid him in forming an opinion:

    1. The indisputable sincerity of the medium.
    2. Her disinterestedness.

---

[5] The first eight or nine séances will, however, be made clearer by what has been stated in this preface, for, according no great importance to my experiment in the beginning, I noted only the chief points without taking pains, as I did later on, to express the exact character of the communications.

[6] These errors and contradictions are, moreover, often rectified or explained in the course of following séances and sometimes even at a distant date. To form an opinion, the reader should make careful note of this fact.

Reine's sleep, beyond any doubt, is hypnotic sleep with all its characteristic and unmistakable symptoms. Her unconsciousness is absolute; once awake, she has no recollection whatever of what she has said or done during her hypnosis.[7]

In addition to this undeniable fact, which of itself would suffice to establish the first point, I must add a few words concerning the character and the morality of the child. I have known her for more than two years, and we have observed her constantly and carefully, my wife and I, for a year and a half. During this long period I have held approximately three séances a week with her, lasting from four to five hours each time. More than this, she spent several weeks with us in the country, seldom separated from us and treated like a child of the house. Submitted to constant observation—shy and reserved at first, all confident during the latter period—she has uniformly manifested the same straightforward, frank, and delicate nature; and the proofs which we have of Reine's honesty in normal life strengthen and corroborate the conviction which we have of her sincerity in her abnormal life.

Her disinterestedness would, if one refuses to accept the explanation which she herself gives in a state of hypnosis, be incomprehensible; for not only does she derive no pecuniary advantage from these séances, but she has thereby suffered loss from a professional point of view. As a matter of fact, she was forced, by reason of the great fatigue which they entailed, to abandon all posing, and as compensation I gave her but a very trifling sum.

It seems obvious therefore from these considerations that if Reine had a genius for deceit sufficiently developed to fabricate all that these notes contain, she would unquestionably have contrived séances of greater profit to herself.

P. E. C.
Paris, April 21, 1914.

---

[7] It is by this book that she is going to learn—quite like any other reader—the strange adventure of her mysterious life, and there are moments when I ask myself rather anxiously what the effect may be.

Reine in 1912

FIRST SÉANCE

Friday, November 29, 1912

Today I succeeded in completely hypnotizing the little model Reine C. having made last week a voluntarily abandoned effort which convinced me of the possibility of the phenomenon. She undoubtedly possesses the faculty of clairvoyance, for immediately on the expression of my wish, she seemed to see the apartment on the fifth floor, and gave me quite characteristic details of its arrangement.

I also asked her to grow a little older and describe to me her future. She sees herself in a small two-roomed apartment—a bedroom and a sort of office; a closed door, through which she cannot pass, she thinks may be the door of a little kitchen? This lodging is in the quartier des Ternes, in a small street leading from the rue de Courcelles. She sees herself there, very clearly, and she is unquestionably at home; her hat is hanging there on the wall. She sees her husband[8] in the office, writing and taking notes. She will be happy in this place, but it is not for her immediately; first, she must find the pennies.

---

[8]   Reine, who has the air of a child of fifteen, but who in reality is eighteen years old, was married a few months ago to a modest young bank clerk.

SECOND SÉANCE

Friday, December 6, 1912

Today I have more difficulty in making Reine sleep—probably because of my wife's presence. Sleeping, she does not yield, as in the first attempt, to my suggestions, but cutaneous insensibility is complete.

I try for evidence of psychometric and clairvoyant power, by placing against her forehead a letter from the sculptor D., and in a few moments she describes explicitly the author of the letter and his occupation ... "With some clay, he is making a man." She appears to be really there in D.'s atelier, and sees him working and grieving over this figure of a man, "who is picking apples." The figure is 7ft. 2in. in height. There is something the matter with it. "Tell him it is not right here"—(she points to her own hip)—"*here—the torso*," etc., etc.

I drop D., and ask her to go again to the apartment on the fifth floor. She describes the bathroom very exactly. She appears really to see it herself, and not in any way to be accepting my thought-images or suggestions. For example, in spite of my insistence, I cannot make her mention the window; but she discovers the curtain which, as was proved later, had been drawn over the window. She perceives the fireplace, but refuses absolutely to see the fire, though she feels the heat of the stove which (the fact is verified) emits at that moment absolutely no light. While in my mind I see two chairs, she sees only one, but that one she describes correctly (a round seat of unusual form, etc.).

Again I question her about her future, and again she distinctly sees herself in the little two-roomed apartment, quartier des Ternes:—"In the bedroom there is an armoire à glace—just the kind I like!" (This with emphasis and joy.) She locates the lodging exactly: "When you leave the 'métro,' it is the fourth little street, as you go toward the lower end of the Avenue des Ternes." She does not see the name of the street, but it is the seventh house (or the number 7). She makes a touching reference to her husband whom she sees there working, and whose sentiments she analyses with surprising penetration; he is no longer at the bank, he is the secretary of a business man, or lawyer.

It is difficult to express the emotion and color of this scene. Reine's efforts to see and describe, her unexpected attitudes, and even their very awkwardness, all combine to give conviction of the reality of her visions.

A curious fact is the invention of a "Spirit" who, she affirms, is there, and wishing to direct her. She sees him, hears him, and speaks with him. His name is Fernand Kerloz. From time to time, he manifests himself orally, through her; and at those moments her voice and expression become hard and imperious. It is he who, in the beginning, told me (by means of the table) to make Reine sleep. He seems to want to take possession of her, and she does not care for this idea: she is worried.

A tranquil waking. She feels rested and happy.

THIRD SÉANCE

Friday, December 13, 1912

(Reine ill with grippe)

As in the preceding séances, we begin first by the table, which, after six or seven minutes, rises and taps softly, but with a rather different movement. I ask if it is Fernand Kerloz. "No," replies the table, "Fernand is not free. I come to replace him." Upon this I decide to put Reine to sleep at once. The table asks me to wait.

Communications of no interest follow, and, after a few moments, I install the child in her big chair.

When she is sleeping, I hand her a letter and a pair of sleeve links belonging to C. (who died some six or seven years ago) and ask her to give me news of him. We wait. Finally she speaks:—"It's all dark, and there's no one here to help me. Fernand will not come. He is being punished ... because he did not speak the truth. He's a liar. The 'High Spirits' forbid his coming today, but he will be here at the next séance." She says that everything is confused. She will certainly see nothing today, but I must not be discouraged by that; she is not well, and then, too, she is not very strong yet (psychically). Oh, she sees plenty of Spirits around her—it is they who told her about Fernand—but they are little inferior things, no better, she says, than herself. After a pause, a more important one approaches her, an old man with a long white beard (I think that she imagines it is C.). He speaks very softly ... and says that he knew the person who wore those sleeve links. He recognizes

4

them, and twice repeats that he has seen their owner wearing them. His own name is Pierre Hamonot. He lived in le Hâvre … died some six years ago, while travelling. He says that the person we want will surely come, but later on. The medium must have the force necessary to go to find him, etc.

I distract Reine from this subject by speaking of her health. She admits that it is not good, perceives her internal organs, examines them closely; describes the bronchial tubes as a little inflamed on the left; says that she must take a potion (an extract of tar) and be cupped. But, no, she *will not* be cupped! That leaves ugly marks and would prevent her posing. No! She will use mustard plasters—one on the chest, one on the back. Her bronchial tubes are affected, it is true, but it is nothing. On Monday she will be all right again.

Questions about what she sees provoke nothing interesting at first (she refers to the "inferior Spirits" who are still there, surrounding her). But suddenly, spontaneously, she perceives her own astral body, which she describes as *a smoke body, somewhat larger than her real one, and quite luminous. It makes the same movements and gestures that she makes.* And at the same time she sees herself sleeping in the big chair, and sees me also, very distinctly. Blue flames come out from my fingers, and from my eyes as well, but these are less strong. I do not magnetize her enough, I am afraid of hurting her … (she smiles) … She is almost as strong as I … *and she sleeps because she chooses to sleep!*

Then I make her select an envelope from amongst four which I have prepared. Each one of them contains a letter. She picks up one (naturally, I do not know which letter is contained in it) and immediately announces that it comes from a lady—"an elderly lady, living in Paris … in a hotel, not an ordinary hotel (for travellers), but a whole big house belonging to her, rue de la—." Then she can see no more. "It is a lady who does not do anything, but she works hard just the same."[9] She will do better at another séance … when she will be stronger and more trained. It will come quickly now: we have only to continue.

I ask if another than I could develop her better. "Oh, yes, later on—but now it is you who are needed. Later, however, an enormous force will be required, for I myself am very strong, quite as strong as you are."

I hand her another envelope, taken at random. She says that it comes from an artist, a painter (verified after the séance). She would like to describe him, but she sees nothing herself, and warns me that she is

---

[9]   All this is accurate, including the beginning of the name of the street: "de la."

only repeating what the little Spirits tell her, and she has not the smallest confidence in them: "They are laughing at us—mocking us. Keep your letters. I will be more capable soon."

My wife had come into the room silently. After some moments Reine (in answer to my question) perceives her presence, and remarks that she should be very careful just, now, for she too runs the risk of *grippe*—from now until Thursday. "Watch her well. She must avoid a chill." Then suddenly, à *propos* of an insignificant reflection—"I'm like that here, but before ... I was different." "What do you mean by that?" "Oh, in another life I was," etc., etc. And she explains that, long ago, she lived in Italy, in Milan. It would seem that I, too, have been here on earth very often before, and that my wife and I have known each other in a preceding existence, not the last one, when I was alone, but the one before the last: "Oh, she was a wicked one then!"

I am about to close the séance and begin to waken her, when she sits up brusquely to remind me that I must watch over Madame Cornillier carefully for the next five or six days.

I forgot to note this fact in its order: In the course of the séance I placed on her knees a board, on which sheets of paper were fixed by drawing pins, and put a pencil in her hand. In a few moments the pencil began to scratch, the paper in such a way that I supposed she was only making senseless scrawls, and so asked for a simple signature. Immediately she went through the gesture of writing and flourishing, but so vigorously that I was not surprised to hear her exclaim: "But you're hurting me! Don't be so stupid!" When I asked her what had happened, she said that the Spirit who had informed her several times, "the one who is not serious, who laughs," had seized her hand and made it move so fast and tremble so much that she was frightened. Taking the paper to the light, I saw two well-written sentences: "You must look out for your health." "Pray for me," and a signature, "Henri Morin," underlined by a vigorous and dashing flourish.

Reine wakens easily, feeling well and rested.

FOURTH SÉANCE

December 18, 1912

(Miss H. is present.)

Aless interesting séance. At the end, a curious incident which, to have weight, should be verified.

About four o'clock we go to the table. "Fernand" quickly manifests his presence. He did not come to the last séance, and he will not stay long at this one; he is punished. I do not insist on this point, but ask rather for information and proofs. Banal result: he declares himself incapable of reading a word in a magazine lying on my work-table. Sudden silence. The table does not budge.

I proceed to magnetize Reine. Nearly twenty-five minutes pass before she is sleeping.

Asleep, she says that she sees Fernand near her, that he goes away ... giving place to Henri Morin and other inferior little Spirits. I get nothing of any interest, nothing precise. Henri Morin cannot answer my questions, and says that he is not allowed to.

Then I try sending Reine to a lodging in the court, which had been occupied by a person who disappeared three weeks ago, and of whom there is no trace. Reine seems to have obeyed me and to be in the little apartment, says that she feels death there; a woman, a needlewoman—she embroidered. She went away with someone, then fell ill. She is dead. Indecision, contradictions, nothing satisfactory. Reine says that she does not see for herself; it is Henri Morin who communicates this information, and she cannot rely upon what he says, for he is an inferior Spirit, and a stupid one—a common kind of person who plays jokes. Fernand is at least superior to him. We would better wait for him; he will come back Friday probably.

Abandoning this inquiry, I return to the question of the astral body, and ask her to describe exactly what she observes in her own case. She says that out from her whole body, but chiefly from her head, there comes a sort of mist or vapour that collects above her, forming into a shape, which is attached to her mouth by a-something which she compares to a ray of sunlight filtering through a room. Her spirit is in the upper part where the matter is at once condensed and more luminous. *"And that,"* she says, *"is my real self—the one that thinks and wills. The body in the chair is only an envelope."* (She compares it to the skin of an orange in relation to the pulp—"the good part," as she expresses it.) She declares that she will be able to move about in this vaporous body of hers, come and go at will, but not today; for the atmosphere is full of mean little Spirits who form a barrier to hold her back, and she has not yet force enough to order them about, as she will certainly do later on.

She sees these Spirits as glimmering lights, as a luminous mist, more brilliant in the upper part; and it is only when they come near to her that they assume a human form, or rather a human head. This is the case with Fernand Kerloz, whose handsome head, she says, is definitely formed—a pale face with black hair and beard, while his shoulders and torso are vague.

I ask Henri Morin, who seems still to be present, if he will write the name of the place where he died. He accepts, and I give pencil and paper to Reine, who writes immediately. When she has finished I beg Morin to copy the ninth line of a review that lies open on the table, and again the pencil moves vigorously. Then suddenly Reine announces: "He has gone!" Another Spirit approaches, seizes her hand, she says, writes at length, then signs.

I try to make her describe the authors of different letters which I hand her, but with no success. She hesitates, fumbles about, is vague, seeming to listen nervously to something that I do not hear, and says angrily: "Those mean little Spirits who are nothing and who are trying to fool me." As the incoherence continues, I decide to finish this monotonous comedy, and begin the passes to waken her, when, suddenly seizing my hands, she tells me to wait. A new Spirit wishes to communicate. And immediately, with evident excitement, Reine speaks:—

"Yes ... Yes ... He says that he has revelations to make ... something that happened a long time ago to an uncle of my Armand (Reine's husband). This uncle (his mother's brother) left Corsica for America, where he went into business with another Corsican who had accompanied him. After several years, the partner came back to France on a business trip, and during this time a revolution, or a kind of revolt, broke out in America, in the State, or the plantation, where the uncle had remained. He was killed, and the partner, on his return to America, appropriated the uncle's entire fortune, destroying all papers and traces. Then he established himself in Paris, in great luxury, and had a son who is now deputy, etc., etc. He will give me details and proofs at the next séance."

I ask if he will not write a precise accusation. He seizes Reine's hand violently (she says) and writes: "Monsieur, Monsieur F. stole three millions from Monsieur T., saying that he died leaving nothing." Then he adds by the mouth of the medium: "Armand should go to see him. He feels remorse, and something could be gotten from him."[10] "Never will Armand go!" protests Reine.

"Then you should go yourself. He is sorry. He will make reparation."

Upon this, I waken her. She comes back to consciousness rather slowly, and complains of feeling tired.

Then I read the communications written during the séances. To my first question Henri Morin has written that he died in Tours—"*au Portillon, 14, Montée des Fours* à *chaux.*" I ask Reine casually if she knows the "Portillon" quarter in Tours. She looks astonished and says that it is there that she lived with her family. I ask if she knew the Morin family. Her surprise increases. Of course she knew the Morin family—the children and the father. The father is still living. They were of the working class, and in comfortable circumstances. "And Henri Morin—who was he?" I abruptly ask. Reine thinks he was the grandfather ... but she never knew him, and knows nothing about him; he died a long time ago.

The second reply written by the so-called Morin, in answer to my request that he should write the ninth line of the review, is: "I don't know how to read. *Vous m'embêtez.*"

The following communication, from a new Spirit who signs "Lucien," is an instruction for the training of the medium: "Reine, you should

---

[10]   The full names were given; but as, later, I had some reasons for believing that the people in question really do exist, I prefer to suppress them here. (See 79th Séance.)

sleep every day. Ask for the crystal ball, and take it home with you. I would also like you to try to write every day."

Questioned about the "American uncle," Reine says that she knows her husband had an uncle who went to the United States a long time ago—"Oh, before Armand was born"—and he must have made a fortune there, for he wrote to his family that when he came home they would not need to work any more. But he died over there, and the family never heard anything more about him. He left nothing—no papers, no money. This is all she knows. And she knows it very indifferently.

FIFTH SÉANCE

December 21, 1912

(S. O. is present)

A dull séance, but giving one precise fact.

On her arrival Reine says that the evening before, when alone in her room, she had tried to see if she could make the table move, and to her great surprise it had tapped: "Reine, you will not sleep tomorrow. Cornillier will not have fluid enough."

Disregarding this warning, we go to the table first, as usual; but it absolutely refuses to budge. This is most annoying, for I had invited my friend S. O. to be present, and it is stupid to have brought him here for nothing.

After waiting nearly forty minutes, I make up my mind to try to hypnotize Reine. Everything seems to go normally. She falls into a sort of torpor quite rapidly, but in spite of her own good will and my great effort, she does not reach the point of insensibility, and after about an hour's struggle, quite exhausted, I capitulate.

Because of S. O.'s presence we once again try the table. Almost at once Fernand announces himself. I ask for a demonstration that will prove his independence of the medium: for example, will he tell us the exact time by my watch, which is lying on the table twenty feet away from us all? An instant, and the table taps: "Nine minutes to six." My wife rises to verify this statement and announces: "It is seven or eight minutes to six." This lack of precision comes from the fact that the face of my watch is gold, and the minute divisions, merely engraved, are difficult to decipher. Moreover, as about a minute had been spent for the table to spell out the answer one may say that the hour has been quite accurately given. S. suggests that we can hear in the studio the clocks outside in the neighborhood striking the hour, and that possibly the medium has unconsciously recorded the time? (This seemed a perfectly just criticism and I had accepted it at its value, when, after dinner, I noticed that my watch was ten minutes in advance of the clocks of *la Monnaie* and *l'Institut*, and that it was not the correct hour that had been given by the table, but really the hour registered by my watch.)

I propose another experiment: to count the money in my purse. Fernand accepts the proposition, makes a mistake and insists that it is correct. When I prove his error he retorts: "Oh, one can't always be serious!"

As he pretends to come from Spain, I ask him to say a few words of Spanish to S., who knows that language. The table taps "Hombre gracia." *Hombre* is too well known to have any value, and *gracia* seems not to be Spanish ... He then says that he will speak by the voice of the medium later on—after eight séances.

SIXTH SÉANCE

December 23, 1912

The table is slow to communicate and makes several efforts before succeeding. Finally, however, conversation begins by means of a more abrupt and noisier tapping than that to which we are accustomed. It cannot be Fernand. "No," says the table, "Fernand is engaged in another séance, and will not come today; but Reine will sleep just the same." Following the instructions given me[11] I begin to provoke sleep with the crystal ball, completing the hypnosis by magnetizing—thus saving strength. Though seeming to sleep well, Reine is in a kind of torpor, says that she feels heavy, heavy, and sees nothing but a thick, black fog. After a moment, however, she distinguishes a Spirit—the one who manifested by the table—a woman. "Why,—it is Fernande! She says she is Fernande Raymond ... but I can't say I really recognize her!" I ask who Fernande Raymond may be, and Reine says she is a young girl whom she knew when she herself was a little girl, and who died a long time ago. But I don't recognize her—she is so changed. She says she has come just to see me, of her own free will. I ask Reine to find out if she would like to help us, and upon her assent, I beg her to give some reliable information concerning the young needlewoman who has disappeared. Reine transmits her words languidly, and with considerable difficulty. Fernande asserts that the woman really went off with someone, and then, when this someone abandoned her, she had

---

[11] In a precedent séance by the Spirit Lucien.

drowned herself in the Rhône at Bordeaux. When I remark that the Rhône and Bordeaux do not go very well together, a discussion ensues between Reine and the Spirit Fernande, and I hear the former making excuses. Turning to me, she says that the mistake was hers, she had misunderstood; it was not the Rhône, it was the Garonne, but it was at Bordeaux. The young woman arrived there rather late in the evening. Coming out from the station, she went to a hotel on the right-hand side of the square—*Hôtel de la Gare*, where she stayed one night, having no other luggage than a small handbag. It was just outside of the city that she jumped into the water. Her body was carried off by the current. Nothing of her was left, not a trace. She will never be found[12] ... I try to get something more, but it is so slow in coming, and so indefinite that, worn out, I turn to other subjects, asking Reine to analyze some letters. But she declares that everything is black, she sees nothing and feels heavy, so heavy that she cannot even rise (meaning her astral body). Meanwhile I had asked to see Pierre Hamonot, and now Reine says that he is there. I beg him to write his name exactly and to give us some more information about my friend C. Reine writes at length, then says that Pierre Hamonot goes away.

Reine's condition today discourages me. She seems to lose, more and more, her lucidity of the first séances. She is really heavy, dull, almost crushed; her speech is thick. The séance drags along lamely. Deciding that I was wasting time, and that it were better to arrest an effort that led to nothing, I am on the point of waking her, when, suddenly, she seems to shake off her torpor, pulls herself together, arid, as though impelled by an outside influence, she speaks all at once with a quite unexpected precision and clearness:

"Monsieur Cornillier, if you want really interesting phenomena, you must change the method entirely. I am not well directed. That is why we have no success. I am not strong enough to act by myself: I cannot disengage myself, and I do not see clearly. If you want to succeed, you must stop all questions. Magnetize me vigorously and long, suggesting at the same time that I hear and perceive nothing of the outside world. Isolate me, in fact, and let me sleep at least three-quarters of an hour, without trying to obtain any phenomena. Then waken me gently. The superior Spirits will take advantage of my sleep to train me. They will

---

[12] I wrote to the hotel, but the letter was retrned to me by the Post Office. There is no *hôtel de la gare at Bordeaux* ... ? Actually no trace has yet been found of this woman who disappeared a year and a half ago.

bring me to the point where I shall be capable of serving as an instrument to them, and, also, where I shall be able to see for myself. It must be like this for several séances, and after that you may begin again with your questions."

I am stunned by her tone of authority.

She resumes: "Do not forget what I say. It is most important. Otherwise we shall accomplish just nothing at all. Later you will be given a more efficacious method for hypnotizing me. But for the moment use the crystal to begin with, and then magnetize me a long time. The Spirits will do the rest."

Keenly interested by her air of command, I reply that I accept the proposition ... temporarily. I will ask no more questions, will conform exactly to the prescribed conditions and I will be patient, if in this way a result may be obtained. It is agreed.

I waken her. She is extremely tired.

I then read the communication written by Pierre Hamonot. It is the initial idea, the original source of the words that the medium has just pronounced with such authority. No answer to my question about C., and signed "Pierre Hamelot."

SEVENTH SÉANCE

December 25, 1912

(I am alone with the medium)

I conform exactly to the instructions given, beginning first by the table, which moves after a long wait, and then simply to say: "Make Reine sleep at once." I install her in her armchair, give her the crystal ball, and, finally, magnetize her. In half an hour she is sleeping profoundly. I leave her and wait rather anxiously for three-quarters of an hour, when I waken her gently. She comes back to consciousness quite naturally, without shock, without fatigue, and says that her sleep has been quite different from that of the other séances.

The table stands near. I tell Reine to put her hands on it, and, placing my own on it at the same time, I ask if the séance has been properly conducted. The table taps: "Yes, all right. Till Friday."

Until Friday, then.

EIGHTH SÉANCE

December 27, 1912

Acurious séance, interesting and unexpected.

We begin with the table, which has still another movement. Evidently the motive power is not the same. A new method for provoking sleep is given: I am told to make the passes with the right hand only, pressing my thumb upon the forehead in a special way, to speak to the medium in a low voice, from time to time, and when she no longer replies, to let her sleep until she wakens naturally.

I set to work, and this time she is sleeping in a quarter of an hour. I leave her lying back inert in her chair, and proceed to draw at some distance from her.

Twenty-five minutes pass. Suddenly there is a certain agitation in the armchair—a whispering—and movements. I go nearer to observe her. She is excited, gesticulates, speaks ... listens attentively, makes more gestures, then finally seems to acquiesce. It is as though there were people around her; she is talking with them, or she is dreaming? Now her hands reach out in evident search of something. It is the table. She places her right hand upon it, flat, as though expecting it to rap; in a moment she adds her other hand. The table cracks and oscillates; but it is badly placed, quite on one side. So I arrange it conveniently in front of the medium who—sleeping profoundly—tranquilly proceeds to make it talk for me. The raps fall regularly, and I begin to spell. It is a message for me, but a long one, and I get mixed up, confound the letters, etc. Deliberately, then, I rise to find paper and pencil, placing them in Reine's hands without uttering a word. She examines the pencil with her fingers ... examines the paper ... and then begins to write, she writes ... writes, turns the sheet, and, when the other side is covered as well, hands it to me and indicates by a gesture that she wishes another one. This I give her ... and still three more. She appears to write under dictation, listening first, then transcribing. Once she turns and says imperiously: "Not so fast!" Finally she signs and hands me the last sheet; then she rises, lifts the table, places it back where it was, on one side, and comes to throw herself down again in her chair—motionless.

After some moments of perfectly tranquil sleep, she wakens naturally.

I examine the written pages. The first is advice to the medium, and a warning to me that I must magnetize her in another way. Then follows an appreciation of the trouble I am taking to develop Reine's mediumistic faculties, with an added word of thanks, and the assurance that before long I shall have valuable results. And the communication terminates with this: "That Fernand is not a good Spirit. We have taken Reine under our direction. Even this first time she was able to talk with us. Today she will remember nothing, but next time she will." The last page is a recommendation that, in magnetizing the medium, I suggest that she must remember all that she sees during her sleep, and that she must tell me about it when she wakens.

It is signed: "Frank Hermann."

NINTH SÉANCE

December 30, 1912

(I am alone with the medium)

Séance quasi null ... though not without interest. One must indeed be patient.

We begin with the table (which serves only to concentrate us a little), but very soon I abandon it and proceed to magnetize the medium according to the new method indicated by Frank Hermann. Reine is sleeping in twenty minutes, but I have the impression that she is not sleeping as she should. Her face has not its habitual childlike expression; nevertheless, as she does not reply to my question, and as she has lost cutaneous sensibility, I leave her, having ordered her to remember what she sees, and to tell me about it when she wakens.

After about half-an-hour she comes back to her normal state, and when I ask her what happened during her sleep she replies that nothing at all happened. She saw nothing except a kind of flames ... and butterflies; but as in an ordinary dream, without special character. She is sure that she has neither done, nor felt, anything unusual.

Somewhat disappointed, I tell her to come to the table, hoping for an explanation of the fiasco. The table begins to spell with its usual and inevitable slowness. Impatience ... confusion ... So I ask if Reine could not just as well write (in her present normal state—awake). The table says "No." Then I ask if she could transmit the desired explanation in writing, were I to re-magnetize her. The table says "Yes," and the brave little thing consents to begin again. This time ten minutes suffice, and she sleeps well. I hand her paper and pencil. She scribbles five or six pages, evidently under dictation. In due time, she wakens naturally ... rather tired.

The writing—this time signed "Vettellini"—is an explanation of my failure and advice as to how to correct the deficiency of my fluid-ic force. The entire communication is clear and perfectly reasonable.

I have only to conform to these instructions and be patient.

We will see at the next séance.

TENTH SÉANCE

January 1, 1913

We begin at four o'clock with the table, which glides and drags over the floor, without rising or tapping. I have the impression that it would be better to magnetize Reine at once. As she has forgotten to bring her crystal ball, I make her look fixedly at a small object in white porcelain, and when her eyelids begin to droop and redden, I make the passes according to the last directions—first chasing away the fluid from the arms and legs with my left hand, then magnetizing the head with my right. When she seems almost asleep, I speak to her with authority, ordering her to disengage herself, to remember all that she sees or hears, and to tell me about it on waking. Then I leave her.

About a quarter of an hour later, hearing a restless movement, I go back to observe her, and, much to my dismay, find on her face a terrible expression of fear and anguish. She looks all around her, first ... then down below, and with a sort of terrified astonishment, exclaims: "But it is Paris! It is all Paris. Oh! Oh!" Then silence. She sways a little from right to left, making slow gestures, and finally leans back in her chair—motionless.

I leave her alone again for ten or fifteen minutes, when suddenly she straightens up and calls: "Monsieur Cornillier ... listen." Her hands reach out to find me. "I must tell you all about it. They want me to tell you at once—before I am awake—everything that I have seen, as it is better that I should remember nothing when I waken," and with anxious volubility she explains that, little by little, she has disengaged herself; her spirit went out of her body; her sleep has been profound this time, and she was able to rise easily quite a distance.

Without knowing how it happened, she found herself above the house where, she says, she was seized with mortal fear—she was sure she was lost! But the Spirits, who were all around her, helped her, held her up, led her on higher—very high—and carried her over Paris—over all Paris!—telling her to look, to observe, but not to speak. "It is too soon for me to ask questions. I haven't force enough yet. I have to use all my strength just to get out of my body and rise. I will learn to fly in this way. If it had not been for the Spirits and their aid, I should have been obliged to come back at once."

Then follows a long description of these Spirits who surrounded her: "They have no body. First I saw glimmering lights coming and going; then these lights, this sort of luminous smoke, slowly took shape. They held me up just by surrounding me—more and more of them—more and more closely. And I saw Paris—the houses, the streets, the crowds of people—everything! Oh—but it is astonishing! Oh, if everyone could know it! ... First of all, everybody—everyone, you understand—has a double. All the people who are moving about, walking, talking amongst themselves, coming and going, all, are surrounded by, or followed by, their double. Usually, it comes out only a little, and all around them. Sometimes, but not so often, it is quite half outside, and stands above them. It is this double which is the thought, the consciousness. No, it is not the consciousness, *it contains the consciousness,*" etc.

I do not note all that was said on this subject. Moreover, as information, it is familiar to all who have made a study of occultism; but what gives it particular flavour is the accent of sincerity, the emotion, with which she speaks, and also because it comes from this little Reine, a nice child in her normal state, but quite a simple child.

She declares that, after a few excursions of this sort, she will see for herself what exists, and may be observed; or, she will inform herself through Spirits; and that she will even be able to enter into relations with the doubles of living beings.

She adds, too, that when, finally, she is able thus to liberate herself, and when her astral body acquires the strength to direct itself unaided, her physical body will lose all apparent signs of life: "You will notice that I become pale, grow perfectly cold; my hands will be icy; I shall not seem to breathe. And as I manifest some anxiety for her health, she interrupts with: "Oh, no, you. mustn't worry—there is no danger.

The moment there is danger my double will instantly come back. It has to be like this."

She is convinced that it is the Spirit Vettellini who is going to take her in hand. He is evidently the only one who took shape enough to be recognized another time, and it was he who forbade her to ask questions, and he who gave her the order to report everything to me before waking. I tell her, then, to thank this "Vettellini" ... and ask him if I must let her waken naturally. "Nor for I am very tired. Waken me." This I do. She remembers nothing, says she feels as though she had been, far, far off—a little as though she had taken a very long walk.

Certain details in her description of the astral bodies of living people should be noted. She sees them as different and distinctive, in density, color, and attitude, as each individual is. The color red seems to indicate, for Reine, a heavy material substance, to be inferior; while the superior and more ethereal double is bluish or whitish. The facility in disengaging itself which this substance possesses, would seem to be in direct proportion to its degree of evolution. Its attitude may be calm and dignified, or agitated and careless. And sometimes, too, it seems to struggle with the material body, to try to resist, it.

ELEVENTH SÉANCE

January 3, 1913

This séance, as might be expected, is only a repetition of the last one, but with certain variations.

Reine sleeps a long time—about three-quarters of an hour—and tranquilly, without words or gestures. Finally, she sits up straight, seeks for me with her hands like a blind person, and meeting mine, begins by verifying me, so to speak. Then she reports: "Monsieur Cornillier? Ah! ... Well, here I am! I've been a long way off! And now I must tell you what has happened." She begins her account, calling attention constantly to the difference between this excursion and that of Wednesday. In the first place she went out voluntarily this time, and by the window. The Spirits, only one of whom she recognized—Vettellini—were waiting to escort her off and exercise her.

She did better this time. And at a given moment Vettellini said to her: "Reine, try to go alone now—without help." He spoke severely, and with authority. She was frightened—frightened to death, feeling sure that she was not strong enough to go alone. When I ask what would have been the consequence of this fear and lack of strength, had she been alone, she replies: "Oh, I would have come straight back to my body ... and wakened. You, too, have done better today," she adds, "the fluid that you sent me during my sleep helped me constantly, gave me new force." (I had, as a matter of fact, returned several times to magnetize her while she was sleeping.) "But, you know ... it's something fearful! ... And I'm not a coward, either! But just imagine being carried

24

off like that by all those people who have only their heads! And some-times even hardly that! They are really only a kind of shining smoke, but in order to make me understand better and be willing to go with them, they put on their heads! Vettellini is an old man with a gray beard and long hair; looks severe. Oh, that one will never mislead us. He's the right kind." And she goes on, describing the itinerary followed, etc., etc.

I ask further details about the astral body, and, after confirmation of what has already been said, I brusquely interrupt: "And animals—have they, too, a double?" She gives a rather hesitating "Yes," seeming to look back, to recall. "Yes—but it is not at all the same thing. There is a certain kind of light around the horses and the dogs ... yes; but it cannot be compared to that of human beings. It's another thing—quite another thing." She says that in going to sleep she felt as though thousands of infinitesimal cords were pulling her and trying to carry her off.

When her story is finished I ask if the Spirit Vettellini is present, if she sees him. Upon her affirmation, I ask if he, Vettellini, can read my thoughts; if he knows the motives which impel me to continue these experiments, if he can understand my aim, my purpose. Reine seems to listen an instant, then exclaims: "But certainly he knows! Other-wise, he never would have come! They sent little ones at first—those inferior ones—to see what you were wanting to get in these séances, if it were just curiosity. But when they were sure of your intention, then they came. Vettellini is a high Spirit. He will direct the séances and will help you. He knows that you, who believe in survival, have no need of proofs, but that for others proofs are necessary ... and he will help you to get them," etc.

Finally she gives me an order for herself, which I must repeat to her when she wakens. Every day she must auto-hypnotize herself by means of the crystal ball. This is a purely gymnastic exercise, she will probably see no result. But it is a means of obtaining a more rapid and complete fluidic intoxication when I magnetize her. She should always have at hand a pencil and paper, the latter firmly fixed to a board, in case she should need to write.

Informing me that there will be a séance next Monday, she then says I must waken her.

TWELFTH SÉANCE

January 8, 1913

Down with *grippe*, I was obliged to give up the séance of last Monday, and, in notifying Reine, I told her that, at the séance she would have alone in her room, she must ask her Guide if I would be able to magnetize her the following Wednesday. Today (Wednesday) she brings me two pages written in complete unconsciousness on this same Monday. She had hypnotized herself by means of the crystal ball, and, while sleeping, had evidently turned the sheet of paper herself, replacing the drawing-pins which fastened it to the board; for both sides of the sheet are covered with writing. The communication—which she has not read—approves of my having postponed the séance till today, and then announces for the following night a "sortie" of Reine's astral body—"which she will consider a dream; of which she will understand nothing whatever; but in which you will recognize our presence."

This fluidic "sortie," which Reine relates on arriving, is another aerial promenade above the streets of Paris, at about eleven o'clock in the evening. She speaks of it as a strange, intense dream which she recalls with great distinctness. (From this moment on, my moral conviction has grown more and more confirmed that Reine rigorously respects the promise she has given me in regard to her mediumistic writings. As soon as she wakens, she folds, them and places them in an envelope to bring to me.)

We begin the séance. Reine sleeps easily and longer than usual. When she gives her report, it is of another excursion where she has been obliged to have greater initiative. There is a regular progress. The voyage this time is at a higher altitude, in that region where the Spirits of average evolution abound. To exercise her courage and give her confidence in herself, Vettellini abandoned her when she was still some distance away and forced her to come home alone. She was obliged to cross over the Seine, and declares that she was frightfully worried for fear she would fall into it!

In the course of her recital I can get no explanation of the statements she makes, for the reason that she has come home alone. To my questions she answers very simply: "Ah, that I don't know. Vettellini is not here, I can't ask him."

A new detail. Since Monday, when she looks into the crystal ball to hypnotize herself, Reine sees in it the face of an old man who gazes at her fixedly with brilliant and severe eyes, and it is these eyes that hypnotize her. (Vettellini?)

THIRTEENTH SÉANCE

January 10, 1913

A most interesting séance, but difficult to record, for it is in the tone of voice, in the accent of sincerity, the attitude, in short, in the thousand and one little details accompanying Reine's narration, that a great part of the interest lies. The progress is regular and extraordinarily methodical. Not the least incoherence. It is evident that the Guide has a definite aim in view, and is master of the best means of attaining it.

Upon her arrival, Reine says that she was informed by the table that she must not come yesterday, because she was not well enough; and that she also had the order to eat very little before coming today. This did not rejoice her, but, nevertheless, she has obeyed, taking only a cup of broth and an egg for her déjeuner.

I put her to sleep by the usual method and wait ... resuming the passes, however, from time to time. She is somewhat agitated, and seems to suffer; an exclamation of pain escapes her occasionally. I catch the words: "Oh, no! ... no, it is too high! Ah, it is cold! Ah!" This lasts for about half an hour, when, finally, she seems to be back here, calm, and talking with ... the invisible. Someone is certainly explaining a new system for hypnotizing her—her attitudes and gestures show it most clearly. This mute scene is extremely interesting. At last, when she thinks she has quite understood, her hands seek mine, and she begins at once to communicate the instructions she has just received. And it proves to be what it appeared to be—a new method for provoking a more profound hypnosis: a series of nine successive acts (which I note under dictation) that will cause a more complete disengagement of her fluidic body, and render it almost totally independent of its physical organism which will seem, momentarily, almost like a corpse.

She has again eaten too hearty a déjeuner. When she wakens I must give her the order to take only one egg before coming here next Monday. She does not find this in the least amusing, but she will obey.

And then she begins to talk about her excursion. It is quite a new one. She went higher than ever before, and she has acquired two new faculties. First, to instantly transport herself to a place merely by wishing to be there. Second, to understand Vettellini by the vibrations of his thought, and without the intervention of words. It is he—Vettellini—who taught her this. It was at his order that, being above the *Sacré Coeur*, Montmartre, Reine thought of and willed to be in the *parc Monceau* (she says she chose that place because she has always loved it), and, without understanding how it happened, she found herself there at the very instant her wish was formulated. It was also to obey Vettellini that she tried to comprehend his unspoken thoughts: "Ah—that, you know, is no small thing! ... I got it at last, but it took some work! And now I shall be able to understand him without his ever having to say a word!"

The "Maître" was much pleased. She says she went out twice without finding him. He was there all the time, but he watched her without manifesting his presence. He wanted to see if she would be courageous. The first time she was timid; but she went further the second time, when she met two Spirits who offered to escort her back. But she had no confidence and told them that she would find her own way home. Vettellini praised her for this, saying that those inferior Spirits would only have tried to make her lose her way, and the result for her would have been a big headache when she wakened.

She gives various descriptions of what she has seen, very precise and clear descriptions, and with many curious details. There should have been a stenographer present, or, better, a phonograph, to catch the accent, and emotion.

Vettellini informed her that he would take her out for another excursion this coming night, when she is sleeping, and also on Saturday and Sunday nights.

On Monday we will have a séance here, with the new method of hypnotizing.

FOURTEENTH SÉANCE

January 13, 1913

Reine arrives with no special report to give. Nothing unusual has happened; she has had no dream. She has tried to write, tried to put herself to sleep, but without results. She has only felt extremely tired each morning when she wakened, as though she had spent the whole night running about.

In mesmerizing her I scrupulously follow the instructions given; but the result is not what it should be, and several times I repeat anew the succession of passes, from beginning to end. I watch her closely, touch her hands and arms, and remark that she has not become cold as was expected. From time to time she makes a brusque movement, mutters to herself and seems irritated. "But, no!" I hear her say, "It's raining; too wet. I'm cold!" Then she settles down again, sleeping calmly for about a quarter of an hour.

Finally a change of attitude and expression, and certain gestures, announce her return. She pats her sleeves and skirt, seeming to examine them to see if they are wet. Then she falls at once into mute conversation, making expressive signs, shaking her head, discussing, protesting, and even rebelling. We can easily guess the subject of the disagreeable conversation from her pantomime, and the words that escape her. It is a question of meals. She still eats too much. She should eat nothing, or next to nothing, for déjeuner—and that, too, every day. Here she rebels; this is really too much to ask! (Her voice rises and is hard). But evidently there is an Authority that knows how to impose itself, for I hear Reine capitulate and promise—none too amiably—to obey. Then there is talk of the séances, of the new method employed, and of what she must repeat to me, etc. All this lasts a long time, and is very vivid.

At last the moment for transmission arrives, and, as usual, she hunts for me by reaching out her hands, finds comfort in the contact with mine (by this time she is very cold) and begins her report at once.

She says that she went out easily today, for her sleep was profound, but she came back immediately because it was raining.[13] Starting off a second time, she went a little further, above *la Monnaie*; ... but it was wet everywhere, she was afraid of being completely drenched, so back she came again, and, this time, with the intention to stay. Vettellini then suddenly revealed himself, ordering her out again, and to her pro-testations, "I'll be wet," "It's raining," etc.—which we had heard—he had answered, most severely, that Spirits need not fear the rain, and what she had to do was to obey at once. Then they started off together.

And here she raises a rather subtle point. She says that in her last excursions she was persuaded that she was going quite alone, without aid; but that this was not the case. In order to give her confidence, Vet-tellini had allowed her to believe that; but he was helping her all the time, without her perceiving it. Only today did he inform her of this, and she, stung in her pride, had resolutely said: "Let go, then! I want to do it alone." She was sure, at first, that she was going to fall, but she backed the effort with all her pride ... and held steady. The "Maître" was satisfied.

I curtail the description of the promenade to note a few more points which are especially interesting. Vettellini has gone to take her out in the night, just as he said he would, but he prevents her having any recollection of these prodigious trips (when she is awake) because her normal life would be disturbed by it: "I could think of nothing else, you understand: I would imagine myself an extraordinary person—queer. It would quite upset me. So Vettellini cuts off all souvenir."

She continues: "He comes often, when I am unoccupied, to train me—to exercise me (her hand expresses trituration), but he does not allow me to perceive it. This evening, when I am sleeping, he will come to take me out; and tomorrow, before I go to bed, he will come to make me write. Don't forget to tell me, when I waken, that tomorrow evening I must settle myself at the table with the crystal ball, and some paper and a pencil. He will make me write something that is going to happen

---

[13] Correct.

31

soon: it will be a prediction, and I am to bring it to you. You will keep it, so that you can verify it. At the next three séances I am to go out again with Vettellini, but at the fourth one, Wednesday, I shall not go out. He will teach me to see all sorts of things here around me—objects, people, you and Madame Cornillier, what you have in your pockets, what is hidden in a desk, in a box, etc; and to read writings. Oh, that, you know, is much more difficult! I shall make a lot of mistakes, of course, but Vettellini wishes it, and he will teach me. He also wants me to make you perceive my presence, that is, the presence of my astral body. You will feel something touching you. You will hear someone walking about, you will notice that certain little things are out of place, etc., etc. The room must be darkened for that: I shall then have more force."

After some explanation of certain points, she tells me to waken her, but before beginning the passes, I must make a strong suggestion that she shall have no headache, for she begins to suffer from the big effort she has made to understand Vettellini, who no longer speaks to her in words—whose thoughts she is now obliged to penetrate.

I follow the instructions, and she wakens rested and tranquil.

FIFTEENTH SÉANCE

January 15, 1913

I wait for Reine impatiently, anxious to know what she wrote yesterday at home, and am quite disappointed when she has nothing to show me. Nevertheless, she slept as she was ordered to do; but on the paper that she had prepared there was merely a senseless scribbling and the word "Monsieur."

She sleeps promptly. Her hands and forearms become completely cold, but the head remains warm and living.

At the end of half an hour she moves slightly, seems to listen, ... then abruptly rises. She goes directly to my work-table, takes up two pencils, hunts for, and finds, the usual drawing board and some paper, and, returning to her chair, makes ready to write—evidently under dictation.

She writes at length, with intervals of mute conversation. Finally she hands me the written pages, goes to put back the pencils and board where she found them, seats herself again, and reaches out to find me.

First of all, she says that if she wrote nothing at her house yesterday, it was because Vettellini preferred that no one could suspect that she had taken cognizance of the communication ... and he decided to transmit it to her in my presence today. I must read it at once.

I find that it is the announcement that he, Vettellini, and they, the Spirit-Directors, are going to use the little Reine as scribe in an important work, a complete book, in which will be revealed the mystery of Death and Birth, and of life in the Au-Delà ("Beyond"). To accomplish this, they are going to put her into a special nervous state. A few days hence, and, gradually, she will seem anxious and excitable; and whenever she finds herself alone, she will have an overpowering impulse to scribble things on bits of paper. But she will be so ashamed of this that she will not dare to mention it to anyone. She will conceal it until the day when, resisting no longer, she will come to confess to me. And when this happens, I must take great care not to warn her of what is going on: *I must answer her indifferently*. This, in order to avoid all accusation of suggestion, all possible argument that the idea of writing a book had been provoked in her. In the written communication Vettellini adds that he is prepared to give fuller explanations, if I do not clearly understand.

I confess that I am none too well pleased with the scheme. In the first place, communications of this kind—revelations made by Spirits—never have weight; for even if the substance has a real value, nothing can prove it: it is easy enough to attribute them to the imagination of the medium. Then, too, the fact that the autonomy of the child is to be profoundly disturbed, and her health attacked by this work seems to me not legitimate. What compensation can she possibly have for this? And, as to our séances here—what will be their utility?

Vettellini charges Reine to say that our séances here will continue along the lines already determined, that is, in ever closer efforts to obtain proofs of survival after death. He seems to understand the indispensable necessity of facts, and spontaneously proposes the following test experiment: that someone who is dead and who is unknown to us, and to the medium, shall come to give proofs of identity that may be verified. The book which they are planning is a work apart, and will interfere in no way with my investigations.

Reine adds: "But I must reach the point where I can go to get the disincarnated Spirits, bring them here, and transmit to you their communications. Vettellini is training me for this; it will surely come. Later on, too, Vettellini will be able to speak to you through my organism." Here she bursts out laughing. "It will be funny, you know, when he does that, for he has a grave, deep voice, his gestures are austere ... I can't see exactly what he is going to do with this little me—with my voice and my hands!"

Extremely interesting explanations of this phenomenon of momentary possession follow, and the séance is closed by Reine's remark that it is impossible for Spirits of such high evolution as Vetellini to provoke material phenomena (levitations, contacts, presentation of objects, etc.)—"It is only the inferior ones who can manifest themselves in this way, because they are more material, more dense. The high Spirits are so different from us in constitution that our perceptions cannot grasp them. When they have need of reaching us, they are obliged to use inferior Spirits as intermediary instruments."

Reine wakens easily and feels perfectly well.

I should note that Vettellini informs me that Reine will write all the substance of the book. It is through her that the revelations will be made, but she will not be capable of classifying them. The task of revising and editing will fall to me.

SIXTEENTH SÉANCE

January 17, 1913

A long séance, every incident of which should be recorded—words, inflections of voice, attitudes and gestures, even the mistakes of the medium and her rectifications, which so considerably enhance the value of the scene—all should be given in detail. Unhappily I can note only the chief elements.

After a moment at the table (which recommends me to draw all the curtains, to have the least possible light), I begin to mesmerize Reine, insisting upon the pressure of the wrists, as has been advised.

In about half an hour she begins to speak aloud, making remarks about what she perceives. Apparently she is here, in the studio, seeing Vettellini and other Spirits. Her attitudes and movements clearly testify that she is examining and analyzing several invisible entities that are moving about the room, rising and descending in the atmosphere. She tries to touch them, to grasp them; is vexed that she does not succeed.

After a while she quiets down, and falls into an attitude of direct conversation. It is with Vettellini that she speaks, and this time all her questions, the answers, and her reflections, are spoken aloud, so that we can easily follow the dialogue. When she does not understand readily, she repeats her question or the answer that has been given, insisting upon an explanation comprehensible for her. She is not satisfied with mere words; she intends to know what they mean, and argues with Vettellini, nags him, until he has given her satisfaction. It is altogether astonishing to see the child's persistence, the consciousness she has of her own incapacity to comprehend certain words or ideas, and the way in which she then surmounts the difficulty by finding for herself the illuminating image that expresses an analogy.

The scene lasts fully three-quarters of an hour. From time to time we all laugh together at her amusing phrases. She grows more famil-iar, and confesses to Vettellini that she was very much afraid of him at first, but today she has seen him laughing twice; and now she knows that he is good. They talk more as friends, but it is distinctly as iron-pot and earthen-pot friends. Occasionally she draws back with precipita-tion: "Ah, no! You must not be angry. It isn't my fault if I haven't bet-ter manners. The idea! You know perfectly well it is not just curiosity. I'm obliged to understand in order to repeat it to Monsieur Cornilli-er." And then, adroitly, she takes another way of finding out what she wants to know. It is most interesting to follow this long scene, but it finally comes to an end. I hear her thanking Vettellini and saying *au revoir*. Now she reaches out to find me, and proceeds at once to tell me everything that has happened to her, perfectly unconscious that we have been able to follow her dialogue.

I will note only the essential points. What most impressed me is an explanation about the clothing and accessories with which Spirits pro-vide themselves—an explanation which, thanks to Reine's persistence, became gradually clear and logical. It was brought about by Vettellini's saying that, soon, she could see her grandfather. Reine exclaimed: "Is that true? Will it really be my grandfather? Will I recognize him? Will he have his big hat? And his blouse?" Upon her Guide's affirmation, she pursued: "But no, Vettellini, look here, that's not possible! He will not have his big hat. Where would he get it? He's dead. Dead men hav-en't hats; and there are no shops where they could find them. So, then, it isn't possible." Vettellini evidently reiterated the statement that her grandfather would have the object in question, for Reine insisted upon understanding how that could be, and finally succeeded in obtaining the following explanation: When Spirits are in the normal conditions of astral life, they have—at least for Reine in hypnosis—the aspect of glimmering lights with a brilliantly luminous centre, which is the psy-chic centre. But when they wish to manifest themselves to living be-ings, they assume, in order to be recognized, the physical appearance which was theirs on earth, and they can show themselves in the cos-tume which they habitually wore and with all the accessories that made part of it. These costumes and accessories do not exist substantially:

it is only an image of them, created by the thought and intention of the Spirit, which exists. And it is this mere subjective image which is caught by the brain of the living being for whom the impression is destined. This is one case. But there is another.

In special circumstances, or in mediumistic séances, an objective image may be created—a materialization; and that is quite a different phenomenon. Just as the Spirit, who wishes to manifest himself, takes from the medium the organic elements necessary to give a certain consistency to his fluidic body and render it perceptible to our human senses, so, if he has need of a drapery, a costume and accessories, he must find in the immediate ambiance analogous objects—really existing draperies, costumes, and accessories—from which he can extract the elements to fabricate the costume in which he wishes to appear; *and whose substantiality will be in proportion to the quantity of substance he has borrowed from these objects.*

This is perfectly clear and logical, conforming possibly to what has already been advanced on this same subject, but, given by the little Reine with such precision and authority, the exposition is impressive.

It is evident that Reine now has complete confidence in her Guide, and she wishes to be assured that he will always be present at the séances:—"You're coming each time now, aren't you? You will not fail? ... Oh, of course I mean except when you're sick!" Here she listens, and after an instant, laughs outright: "No, of course not. I was stupid. You cannot be sick. Well ... let me tell you that's what I call luck!"

I felt sure that the austere Vettellini was laughing with her. He speaks again about her health. At the last séance he gave a prescription for her rheumatism. One of the ingredients, *la calmine*, was entirely unknown to me as it was to Reine, and I was rather uneasy about it. But it seems to have had good effect. Today Vettellini warns her that she is to take it only every other night.

Reine says that today she has seen, much more distinctly, both Vettellini and the group of Spirits that accompany him. She could distinguish and analyze them with much more precision than before.

Vettellini came to take her out in the night and will henceforth come regularly to train her in this kind of exercise. To her question: "But why do I not remember something of these promenades?" he evidently replies that she must not remember, for she murmurs: "Ah ... yes ... I would be frightened. It would upset me. I could think of nothing else!" An evident fact. And it is the second time that this answer has been given, for Reine has already asked why she had no recollection after waking.

She is again admonished not to eat at noon, for it is at that hour that her Guide works over her to make her supple—from noon till four o'clock. After that hour she may take anything she wants. She must obey him in this, or she will be punished.

During this colloquy Reine is not conscious of my presence, nor of the fact that she is talking aloud. She confesses to Vetellini that she is ashamed of her writing—all crooked, and so many faults! Could he not manage to write himself or guide her hand (here she makes the gesture) instead of dictating to her? Apparently he says no, for the child exclaims: "But why? I see your hands—they are there! Why don't you want to use them?" And Vettellini replies (we gather this from what Reine repeats) that he is of too high an evolution, too different from us in substance, too far from our physical world, to perform material actions; that he could only accomplish them through other Spirits inferior to him and more substantial than he.

The group of Spirits that Reine saw so clearly today seem to be under his orders, for we hear her say: "Then you are the chief? They are obliged to obey you?" His answer seems to be: "My evolution is higher. I am above them."

SEVENTEENTH SÉANCE

January 22, 1913

We had no séance Monday, Reine having caught cold, which degenerated into a congestion, because she stupidly drank two glasses of very cold water in the night, when she was feverish. However, she came today, not well by any means, but able, none the less, to give us a remarkable séance, of which my meager notes can give no adequate impression.

I begin by the table, which tells me to change the position of the armchair, so that Reine may be more in shadow, and gives a new order for magnetizing which I scrupulously observe.

After sleeping calmly for three-quarters of an hour, she moves slightly and begins to hold converse with her Guide. This time no words are uttered. It is her attitudes, her gestures, and the changing expression of her face that betray what is going on. Suddenly she examines her hands, points questioningly to her ring, and, evidently in obedience to an order, draws it from her finger. An instant later the necklace she is wearing suffers a like fate. We follow the scene attentively without understanding it. ... She draws off to one side of the chair, making herself as small as possible, and, arranging the cushions, seems to offer a place to someone ... Now she has a guest; there is no doubt of it. She is evidently discussing with someone; she listens, ... then some words become audible, and we are in the secret. She is being scolded by Vettellini for her stupid imprudence with the cold water. We hear her admit her fault and try to excuse it; but she is so distressed by the rebuke that the tears run down her face. We see her reach out with a beseeching gesture as though to ask pardon, and suddenly with infinite grace she grasps the hands that evidently are extended to her and smiles—a delicious smile of relief—a happy child who has been forgiven! Later in the séance she tells us that Vettellini threatened to leave her forever.

Now she turns happily to me to say that Vettellini wants to know if I have some questions to put to him.

First I inquire about Reine's health. He answers at length, giving a complete regime which she must follow minutely.

Then I ask about her grandmother (her father's mother), who, it seems, is very ill in Tours. Vettellini says that he will inform himself and give Reine news tonight. He cannot take her with him; she is not strong enough to go so far; but he will go and report the conditions.

Here follows the announcement of certain changes in daily happenings, that will be interesting to verify: the artist M., for whom Reine is posing regularly, will have *grippe*, and she will be obliged to give up her sittings with him. Her husband will find two new clients for the bank. She will find a new apartment soon and move into it, etc.[14]

I take advantage of Vettellini's mood to obtain more interesting information:

Why in the first two séances has Reine shown faculties superior to those of the following ones? She was able, at first, to move from one place to another, to go far, even, and to make precise descriptions; whereas, now, none of this is possible for her, and she has need of her Guide's assistance merely to go out of the studio. Why is this?

Vettellini replies that in the beginning Reine did not act alone. It was the Spirit Fernand Kerloz, inferior, malicious, but strong, who manifested himself. He had acted very cleverly to gain our confidence, giving exact information at first, in order to establish his influence, then lying and deceiving us, only to quicken our interest again by giving a successful experiment. If Vettellini had not interfered he would have gained the medium entirely, would have led me on, and, without doubt, would finally have succeeded, if not in fooling, at least in disgusting me.

We must not believe, however, that Fernand Kerloz and other inferior Spirits have acted independently and done as they chose. In reality Vettellini was there, watching the course of events, judging the motives, and the purpose of my investigations, "And now," says Reine,

---

[14] All these small predictions were exactly realized.

"he has assumed the direction.[15] Little by little he is teaching me how to use my faculties of medium. He promises nothing that he will not fulfil. Never will he deceive us. Everything which he says we should attain, we will attain, but slowly; for it depends upon me, and only me ... and it will be some time before I am able to move about everywhere, to see, to understand ... to penetrate the Au-Delà and report to you my astral perceptions." To my question, what will be Reine's chief faculty? Vettellini answers that communication with disincarnated Spirits will be easy for her ... and the production of materialized phantoms, as well. Disincarnated Spirits will be able to use her organism and write directly by her hand. She will no longer be obliged to write under dictation, of which she has such horror.

We return now to the question that occupied the last séance, the costume of Spirits—for Vettellini wishes to complete his information by the exposition of a third case. (The first being the projection of an image, created by a Spirit, to subjectively influence the brain of a subject; the second being the relative materialization of costume or accessories, obtained by extracting certain elements from analogous objects existing in the environment.) The third case—which Vettellini declares possible—occurs when a Spirit, in materializing, has been able to reach a nearly normal ponderability: he then has the possibility of using for his momentary needs the objects themselves, draperies, costumes, accessories, which are at hand in the environment. Having a quasi-normal force, so to speak, he can pick up a hat, wrap himself in a scarf, seize a cane, etc., etc. Duly certified evidence of such cases does exist, as a matter of fact.

The whole series of phenomena touching this interesting question of the costumes of Spirits is, in this way, rationally explained.

---

[15] It is interesting to follow the change of tone in the communications since Vettellini's advent. At the debut, whether by the table or by writing, they had the ordinary character of Spirit messages. For example, we were told to praise God, and "Pray for me" came several times by the table and by writing. In short, the tone that prevailed was religious at one moment, at another, libertine. But as soon as Vettellini announced his presence, this phase disappeared entirely. There are now only precise, positive statements, stripped alike of religious sentimentality and malicious irony. The substance of what is now transmitted seems to proceed from a high intelligence that does not lose itself in mysticism, nor waste itself in vain words ... We will see.

Various amusing scenes in the course of the séance: For example, à *propos* of the regime, Vettellini orders cod liver oil. Reine fights like a little fury. All possible reasons are invoked: it is too nasty; it will be very bad for her digestion; it will certainly make her ill; it is much too expensive. She defends herself as best she can, and, finally, we see her smile and make the gesture of caressing the hand of her invisible doctor, exclaiming at the same time: "Ah, that is really good of you, Vettellini. You see, you're not so bad after all!" Questioned, she explains that Vettellini has made a concession: she shall take only a teaspoonful of the detestable stuff, instead of the tablespoonful that was first imposed.

Another gay laugh, and further thanks: Vettellini sees that she is not quite strong enough to fast in the morning. So then she has the right to a cup of bouillon with five cents worth of hashed beef in it, one egg, and a very small piece of bread. Great joy.

And here we have the explanation of the scene at the debut of the séance when Reine took off her ring and necklace. Her Guide wants her to try at home, occasionally, to project her double. She must darken the room, concentrate her thought, and violently will a certain action on a distant person or object; making at the same time the gesture corresponding to this action (for example, pinching, kissing, pulling hair, touching a bell, upsetting a vase, etc.). It is a training exercise which will give no immediate result, but whose benefit will appear later on, when, in hypnosis, she will have to produce a similar phenomenon. And she is expressly warned that before beginning this exercise she must remove her rings and necklace—any metal object, in fact, that she has about her. Also, this same precaution should be taken each time I magnetize her—hence the gesture which I could not understand.

A modification is again made in the last method for hypnotizing Reine. It is noted.

EIGHTEENTH SÉANCE

January 24, 1913

Reine's cold has developed into bronchitis. She looks really ill.
I consult the table, which instructs me to magnetize her just the same, it will in no way affect her health; and while she is sleeping, I am to suggest an unusual act or gesture which she must perform when she wakens—this, merely as an exercise.

I put her to sleep. The poor child, coughing incessantly, and burning with fever, is quite pitiful to see. I anticipate failure. But no, she falls into deep hypnosis, and, after a short interval of calm, begins to move restlessly, muttering to herself and gesticulating. Finally she rises and walks up and down the studio. She seems to see forms and shapes—counts eleven of them; disputes about color; the color red which she attributes to something is evidently contested. Not red? … After a little fuss she ends by admitting that it is only reddish.

We have no idea what it all means.

She acts as though she were surrounded by Spirits. Evidently some of them touch her, pinch her, she is not at all pleased with these familiarities and complains: "It's horrid when they touch me! … . They're cold … ugh! … they feel just like snails.[16] And I'm afraid they'll leave marks

---

[16] January 21, 1914. This evening Mr. Guillaume de Fontenay, in a conference given for the *Société des Sciences Psychiques*, referring to the phenomena obtained by Madame Bisson with her medium Eva, said that he has several times touched the substances that emanates from the medium, and that the

on me—black and blue spots. I won't have it, Vettellini! Yes, yes, I know they're not wicked since they are with you, but, just the same—I don't care for them!" She seats herself in a small chair, jabbering all the time, but after a few moments goes back to her habitual place, without interrupting her reflections. Vettellini cuts this short, however, by telling her to ask me if I have any questions to put today.

Naturally I speak first of Reine's health. He says that she is quite seriously ill and that she must go at once to a doctor. He would indicate the treatment himself, but there is need of remedies which a chemist would not give without a doctor's prescription. When she wakens, I must insist upon the importance of care. Vettellini says that he really saved her after she took that ice-cold water, but he cannot cure her. She must have serious care, must stay in bed for several days, till Wednesday at least. We cannot have a séance before Friday.

I ask about a dream that Reine related when she came in today. On Wednesday night she saw her grandmother in her house in Tours, and they talked together. Her grandmother did not seem to be dying. She saw her in a familiar costume, with a special kind of headdress, etc. I ask Vettellini if, contrary to what he had thought, he had after all been able to take Reine to see the old lady. He says no, that he went alone; that he projected an image of Reine on the brain of the grandmother, who thought she saw her grandchild and talked with her; that then, coming back to Reine, who was sleeping, he recreated this scene and projected it on her brain. Reine supposed she had dreamed it. He adds that the grandmother will die before long, and that then she will be able to come and be recognized by her grandchild. From now on till her death, he will continue to project the image of Reine on the brain of the old lady who will believe her really present, and will talk to her. The people surrounding her will notice it, and will consider it a hallucination.

Now Reine reports what happened at the beginning of her sleep today. Being ill she could not do very much. It means a stupid interruption in her progress, she says, but not a setback, since she has been magnetized. Not to lose ground, she must be magnetized regularly. As Vettellini could not take her outside today, he made her observe, in the studio, the different categories of Spirits:

---

impression was that of touching snails. The similarity in the comparison proceeds evidently from a similarity of sensation.

First, those that are reddish—*not red* (we are reminded of her discussion on his subject). These are inferior Spirits whom she must always avoid.

Second, those that are blue, but a special blue—pure azure, luminous, intense. These are of high evolution, friend-Spirits, whom Vettellini will send from time to time, to help and teach her. These she may, and even must, follow. Their blue is not at all like that of the doubles of living beings, nor is it like that of ordinary Spirits which is, relatively, rather dull and grayish. No: the blue of Vettellini's followers is a pure, intense splendour!

Finally, a third category of Spirits made themselves visible for Reine. These were white—shining, golden white. And radiant with emotion the child says: "Monsieur Cornillier, you could never imagine what these Spirits are ... they are the Spirits of children who died at birth—of children who never lived at all. Having done no wrong, they had not to suffer, nothing to redeem."

This, I confess, shocks me. I ask Vettellini why these Spirits did not assume the color corresponding to their degree of evolution, since, given the law of reincarnation, they could not stay in this particular class (that of children who died at birth), which is only accidental, and which does not imply a special plus-value. They are, after all, disincarnated Spirits, each with his own personal degree of evolution, and it would seem that, logically, each should have the color corresponding to the evolution acquired at the last incarnation.

The answer was rather labored, due both to the complexity of the question (which evidently touches a principle of high importance), and to the physical condition of the medium, who transmits with difficulty. It was also unexpected. "These white and luminous Spirits are not white and luminous because they died at birth. They died at birth because they had completed the cycle of their terrestrial evolution and had obtained the maximum benefit that incarnations on your earth can give. They will never again reincarnate. And their color does correspond to their real degree of evolution."

I ask what could possibly be the advantage of mere foetal life to Spirits of this high grade. Vettellini replies that it is not easy to explain this point to me at the moment; the question is involved in many others which I must understand first: but, briefly, this uterine life is the final proof, the last accent of earthly suffering, which achieves their evolution. When I ask to what this condition leads, what may be the future of these high Spirits, he repeats that I must wait; there is much to learn before I can understand that subject. He will speak first of the laws of Death and Birth, but methodically, and little by little, we will approach other questions of highest import: "Although human intelligence," he adds, "can understand astral life only within certain limits."

These white and luminous Spirits are, it seems, rare, and Vettellini has allowed Reine to see them (or to perceive their projected image created by him?) only that I might learn of their existence.

I speak of the blue Spirits. The Maître explains that it is in this category that missionaries are to be found, the Messiahs, who voluntarily come back to incarnate on earth, choosing lives that serve as high examples. The white Spirits cannot furnish such teachers and leaders, for they are no longer in the physico-chemical conditions necessary for terrestrial incarnation.

Before closing the séance, I refer to the experience of Colonel de Rochas, who cured the wound of one of his mediums by magnetizing her exteriorized astral body in the spot corresponding to the wound of her physical body, and I ask if this is a possible case. Vettellini affirms that the case is possible, on condition that the medium is so developed that her astral body may be entirely independent of her physical organism which, at that moment, must be as dead. The operator magnetizes the astral body (the double), which, under his influence, creates the curative vibration and develops its power of modifying the conditions of the physical organism.

Before waking Reine, I suggest that just before leaving today she shall light a lamp with a match taken from the writing-table.

This suggestion was punctually executed and greatly to Reine's embarrassment. It was interesting to observe the struggle between this imperious desire, which she could not resist, and the habitual reserve of her attitude in our house.

NINETEENTH SÉANCE

February 7, 1913

(The sculptor W. is present)

Two weeks without a séance. Reine has been seriously ill, and I, too, have been down with *grippe*. But yesterday Reine was notified by the table that we could resume work today.

In all these fifteen days she has had only one incident of interest. Once, in the middle of the night, but when she was quite awake, she saw a blue light moving slowly to and fro, standing quite still, then quivering; and finally, this light, little by little, transformed itself into a head and shoulders; the body remained vaporous. It was Vettellini. She says that she then felt and, understood, rather than really saw, that he held a letter which he was trying to make her read. This letter, she was convinced, came from me and announced that I, too, was ill, and that we would not have our regular séance. She could not succeed in really reading this, but she understood perfectly the signification of the scene.[17]

---

[17] One may ask how Reine, awake, could recognise Vettellini, since I have never told her anything that occurs during the séances. It is by the table and the séances of training at her house that she has become conscious of the existence of a guide and director in our experiments. And the first time that she saw in the crystal ball the head of an old man, she immediately understood that it was he. Then, again, I, of course, transmit to her the advice and orders that Vettellini gives me during her hypnotic sleep regarding her

I had, in fact, written that very evening to inform her of my indisposition, and she received my letter the following morning.

We begin with the table, which is slow to move, but finally says that I may hypnotize Reine without fear.

She sleeps quite as usual, it seems to me. But, after ten or fifteen minutes, she moves a little, listens, replies by signs, and then—evidently following an instruction—her hands seek me and she says that she is not magnetized enough, that I must repeat the passes on her temples for a few moments, so that she can understand Vettellini more readily. She has lost ground. She is heavy and I, too, have lost. My fluid is less strong than it was.

So, then, I resume the passes of the temples and brow. After a few moments she is visibly more alert, and prepared to communicate with the Invisible. But she does not speak; the conversation is indicated by gestures and attitudes up to the moment when, again by order of her Guide, she asks me what I wish to know today.

Immediately I speak of her health, which alarms me, for she is looking really ill. Vettellini admits that she is extremely delicate and must take many precautions. He gives instructions which I must transmit to her, awake. He says that he watches over her constantly and each day helps her as far as his power goes. We may arrange for the three séances a week, but the night before each one he will notify her whether or not we are able, each of us, to support it without too great fatigue.

He seems perfectly informed of my condition, and remarks that I take good care of myself.

To my inquiry, he says that certainly we have lost time, but this will affect only Reine's secret writing. So far as the séances here are concerned, we shall promptly recover the lost ground.

It was really he, Vettellini, who manifested himself one night to Reine, when she was awake. He was trying to make her see the letter which I had written her. Their fluidic association, the ties that now exist between them, are such that she perceives his presence readily; even awake she can see him, for her sensibility has developed considerably.

He says, too, that I, on my side, when I am in good condition, should from time to time concentrate my thought on Reine (when I am at home,

---

health, etc., and speak openly of his part in our investigations. She knows then that he exists, and that he is interested in us, *but nothing more.*

and preferably in the evening), willing her to execute an act or gesture formulated by me. This is for the purpose of developing my influence over her. A few exercises of this kind, and I shall succeed.

Here I beg to revert to a point that came up in the last séance—the presence of Spirits seen by Reine—and I have the satisfaction of hearing my own supposition confirmed. The red (inferior) Spirits and the blue (superior) Spirits were really substantially present. But Vettellini could not ask the presence of the high white Spirits for the sole purpose of showing them to Reine. So, he had merely created a subjective impression of them for her astral perception. This sufficed to inform us of their existence.

He adds some interesting details about these white Spirits. It is absolutely impossible for them to reincarnate on earth. They can no longer live in the physico-chemical conditions of our planet. But they can have a guiding influence over us by indirect means—in using the blue Spirits as intermediaries, for example. For serious reasons, in important cases, they can manifest themselves by creating an image perceptible to a sensitive; an image representing either their own personal form or the form of another being whom they wish to impress upon the percipient. This would be an explanation of certain apparitions, angels and various personages, whose real existence may be doubtful or legendary. It would seem that they use this means to attain a special end, to modify an existing current of ideas, etc., etc.

Reine now gives a brief report of what she had done during her sleep today. Vettellini took her out for a promenade, but nearer the ground this time, so that he might teach her how to distinguish the different kinds of people. It was quite a new exercise for her. She had to perceive in detail the characteristic dissimilarities in people, so that she would be able to inform me when I should ask her.

Vettellini interrupts to say that in the following séances, when Reine is sleeping, I must return several times to the hands, making over and over again the prescribed gestures in their proper order. She must become cold: it is absolutely necessary. Otherwise the material phenomena promised are out of the question. First the hands must grow cold, then the arms, and finally the whole body.

He announces that the grandmother (in Tours) has had another attack. A letter informing Reine of this is waiting for her at the *poste restante*, and when she wakens I must tell her to go to claim it. The old lady will soon be taken to the hospital.[18] Her death is not immediate, but is approaching.

Various small counsels for Reine's practical life follow: The sculptor B., who has been employing her, is vexed with her; she must no longer count upon him; he will not engage her. T., the painter, will make her an offer for a long term. This she must not accept, for he would not pay her; but she must refuse politely, giving the pretext that she is engaged by other artists.[19]

Before waking the medium, I must suggest to her that care of her health is most important; also that she must stop worrying over the small troubles of her life.

---

[18] All this happens exactly. Reine found the letter waiting for her at the post office and a few days later the grandmother was carried to a hospital. (To avoid importuning visits, Reine had not given her address to her family in Tours. All communication from them came through the *poste-restante*.)

[19] Proved correct.

TWENTIETH SÉANCE

February 10, 1913

A simple séance today, and meager in incident, but it has filled us with compassion.

Hardly are we seated at the table when it begins to rise and fall violently and in a wholly unusual way. At the same time I feel on my hands, not the customary cold air, but a veritable wind. Then nothing further: no movement at all for eight or ten minues. We conclude that all the fuss was probably made by a stray Spirit who had wandered in,[20] and wait for other developments. Before long the soft and rapid tapping of Vettellini begins, telling us to stay at the table for awhile, in order to concentrate our fluids. After a few moments the order is given to begin the séance.

This time I force the dose to my utmost, repeating again and again, the finger pinching and the wrist pressure, even after Reine seems to be completely magnetized. She sleeps a long time, quite motionless, her hands are icy, the forearms very cold, but the head is burning. I notice the anxious expression of her face.

Suddenly she sits up and in a hoarse voice demands pencil and paper. Then she listens long and with great concentration, several times

---

[20] Vettellini informs me later that it was he who had sent us this Spirit, capable of making strong material demonstrations, but that we discouraged him by our attitude. I remember that, as a matter of fact, I made Reine remove her hands from the table, withdrawing my own at the same time, feeling sure that it was an inferior force that was manifesting.

stretching her hands towards Vettellini, as though asking him to magnetize them. Finally she begins to write ... then stops to listen, turns again to write, breaks off to lean towards Vettellini, then, nervously, resumes writing again. Her face is tense with anxiety. Her left-hand points to her breast as though designating herself ... and we see that she is weeping.

She hunts evidently for a handkerchief. My wife presses her own into the little hand. She wipes her eyes, but weeps still, weeps silently, stricken by a profound emotion. It is pitiful to see. (I infer that Vettellini has announced the death of her grandmother.)

Suddenly she draws a big line across the paper and begins to write again. At last she makes a signature, hands me the pencil and falls back in the chair, exhausted.

I remove the writing-board from her knees, and wait near her. Finally she leans forward, reaches for my hands and murmurs: "Monsieur Cornillier, Vettellini has nothing to say. He has written ... You will read. The séance has been better than he expected, in my present condition, for I am ill. Nothing happened today. I did nothing—saw nothing. Only we have made up our lost time. Moreover you are stronger than before your *grippe*, your fluid is more powerful. Vettellini has written a new method for you—so that I may grow absolutely cold. I am ill now, but will be better soon, and the phenomena that have been promised will be realized. Vettellini says so!"

I ask if, really, she will be all right again soon, and the ambiguity of her reply strikes me—"Yes, yes—I will be better; well enough for the séances. But—you know ... I am sick. Oh, it will not affect our work, only it will take much longer, because Vettellini is obliged to look out for me a little. But the result will be the same. *We will surely succeed.*" (This with great emphasis.) "But as to me ... I am sick."

I ask what made her cry. She seems not to remember, says: "Cry? ... I don't know ... It was—oh, it is written!"—You have forgotten?—"Yes, yes." A vague sadness persists, but she does not understand why. I foresee a drama, and as she asks me to waken her, I suggest with force that, when she wakens, she must feel happy and confident in the future. And, as a matter of fact, when she comes out of the hypnosis, she laughs gaily, chatters a while, and then goes home contentedly.

I now read the communication giving a new method for mesmerizing. The tone is confident, the purpose clear, coherent and positive. Vettellini seems perfectly sure of what he affirms—but without boasting or exaggeration. And it is in the same serious tone that he adds: "... so much the more, that she will die very young ... And it is also why she will succeed in giving you remarkable results. Do not speak of this to her, I beg of you. Moreover, it is preferable; ... her place is not on earth." This, then, is the explanation of the child's tears and emotion. Writing under dictation, she has been conscious of the terrible menace. Poor little Reine!

I am told to make the room perfectly dark at the next séance, but I may use a red lantern, so arranged that the light does not strike the eyes of the medium.

TWENTY-FIRST SÉANCE

February 12, 1913

This séance has been different from the others, without great evidential interest perhaps, but marking a new orientation in the research.

I begin by taking no end of trouble to darken the atelier, and all in vain: there are too many windows and openings through which the light can filter.

The table moves promptly and gives some orders for the séance. Reine seems to sleep immediately, but in spite of continued passes and finger pinching, she does not become cold. For three-quarters of an hour we wait.

Finally she moves, seizes first my hands, then my head, which she turns in the direction on the couch, and pointing towards it says: "Look ... You will see." I look, look ... and see nothing. She says that Vettellini is trying to make me see him in the form of a small light, a tongue of blue fire. She sees it very distinctly, ... and I, too, ought to see it. Evidently, however, the light is not sufficiently materialized, for I distinguish nothing, and after a hopeful moment we abandon the effort.

Reine tells us what has happened. Sleep has come more rapidly to-day, but she did not grow cold because she has fever. For the first time there have been three distinct phases in her sleep, instead of the usual two: First, a dead sleep—the beginning of the cataleptic stage. During this phase she had no consciousness nor sensibility of any kind.

Second, a conscious sleep—during which she could see, act, and move about. (It was then that she turned my head toward the divan and said "Look!")

Third, the stage in which she now is—where she is less lucid in regard to astral conditions, but where she can talk with me, explain what she has seen, give my questions to Vettellini and transmit to me his replies.

Vettellini decides that we will henceforth hold our séances in the little salon, where we can have complete obscurity. The red light is allowed. He hopes to draw from Reine and myself the substance necessary to make himself perceptible to my senses. I must succeed in seeing him.

I ask Reine if she had any unusual sensation yesterday at six o'clock. (I had attempted suggestion at a distance.) But, no, she has felt nothing at all. And with singular authority she explains that, as conditions are at present, I shall not succeed in this experiment: "Though your fluid-ic force has grown so much stronger of late, a still far greater force is needed. The fluid that you send out with all your will has to cross a big space full of countless currents, some of them absorbing and weaken-ing—and after a while your fluid falls to zero. You must gain in power ... and I in sensibility. It will come. But for the moment try direct sug-gestions when I am in hypnosis—things that I must realise at a given time. You will succeed in that all right."[21]

Of no thrilling interest, the séance nevertheless abounds in amus-ing incidents, and the play between Vettellini and Reine is captivating. The Maître is evidently a very susceptible personage, and this gives rise to scenes of inimitable spontaneity, excited words, and hot replies.

Before leaving, Vettellini again lays stress upon Reine's ill health. I must tell her to stop the arsenic. She must eat more, she is by far too run down. It is he who has stimulated her appetite these past few days, and she must do all she can to profit by it ... etc., etc.

---

[21] Subsequently I made any number of such suggestions, and Reine always executed them at the moment fixed, but the phenomenon is so well known that I did not trouble to note it.

TWENTY-SECOND SÉANCE

February 14, 1913

Reine arrives early and announces that she had a long communication on Wednesday, at home, telling her to be here at three o'clock today, to begin at once with the table, continuing till quarter to four; and at four o'clock to sleep. In this communication (by the table) Vettellini also told her that she must rest for ten days, otherwise she risks a severe illness. She must go to bed early, rise late, take plenty of nourishment and moderate exercise in the open air. She must not pose. The only interruption to be made in this life of a convalescent is the usual séance here. The gallant child protested—and still protests—for it happens that she has plenty of work just now. But Vettellini formally insisted.

Confident in her sincerity, I comfort her and tell her to obey. We will see that she is able to observe the program.

Three o'clock. We go to the table, which, after giving a long regime for the medium, begins to make various and violent movements, greatly to Reine's delight. She has never seen anything like it before.

Four o'clock. We are installed in the little salon; obscurity almost complete; red lantern. I proceed in due form and have the impression that all is well. Reine sleeps at once, and profoundly, becoming unusually cold. I move around her chair, renewing the passes from time to time and reiterating the order to liberate herself.

Suddenly she straightens up, her arms flung out in fright, seeming to be seized by a spectacle of horror. The red lantern and a slight infiltration of daylight allow me to follow her gestures, and the expression of her face. She gives a piercing cry of terror: "Ah ... ah ... but this is frightful! frightful! It's hideous! ... Oh, just look how they fight!—These men—massacre! ... what carnage! ... Dead men heaped these horsemen—oh, what a terrible battle! ... blood everywhere—and fire! Oh, it's fearful! ... What a wounded ... and fire on all sides—death and fire. Cities are crumbling away! ... Even from the heavens flames and shell are falling! Ah ... here are trains crowded with men going to the frontier. Oh, the horses! thousands of them that they are pushing and stuffing into fourgons ... And trains ... and trains, no end of them ... countless ... all packed with soldiers ... And all that is going to kill! Everything in flames! Whole forests and entire cities ... all the country ... All is devastated! ... Nothing but death and desolation on every side. Oh, how hideous! How hideous! ... Ah ... Ah ... Ah!"

And the poor child falls back in her chair, writhing and gasping at this vision of terror, her contracted hands now clutching at mine, now trying to cover her eyes.

But the appalling scene rolls on in all its horror.

From time to time she interrupts her ejaculations to explain that it is a succession of images which she is seeing. It rolls before her terrified eyes exactly like the cinematograph, she says. It stretches to the infinite horizon, the entire earth ... the sky itself—all is murder, ravage, destruction. It is not France alone. It is Europe ... All the nations of Europe ... and the colonies, as well. The conquered peoples are in revolt ... All kill, and burn, and pillage!

France has resisted a long time. She is the last to be caught in the disaster ... but it is inevitable.

Then, suddenly, different images sweep in: The government is changing ... has changed—the Republic is overthrown. It is a prince—an exiled prince. Reine sees him distinctly and describes him: "... high forehead, hollow at the temples; dark, deep-set eyes; big, black moustache; looks hard ... hard." He will be well received. Everyone detests the Republic, accused as cause of all the trouble.

Again the vision changes. Another dreadful scene and even more intense—"But ... it is Paris? ... Yes, it is Paris that is burning ... *Paris!* ... and they are all fighting ... They are all killing each other. There's nothing left! Whole quarters are wiped out. Nothing but ruins, fragments of smoking walls still standing. Dead bodies in heaps. Blood everywhere. And famine, too—no bread even ... Those who have not been killed die of hunger!"

"Paris is besieged—not by strangers, by the French. It is the Revolution—the people have risen ... They satisfy their vengeance by destroying everything ... attack everywhere ... whole quarters are gone ... The Champs-Elysées wiped out."

Another vision of the Prince ... who establishes order. He gives bread. The war is finished ... but no one knows how to begin again. Discouragement on all sides. He—the Prince—will find the means ("and yet," she remarks, "he hasn't a penny now!") They are two brothers ... There is jealousy. Each tries to eclipse the other. "It is the married one who wins out. His wife is beautiful ... I see her; she is tall ... Yes ... Yes ... it is He." And, in a decided tone, she adds: "He's a Napoleon."

I try to make her fix the epoch of this disaster. She hesitates, and says: "It is so intense ... it is near ... quite close at hand. The year cannot pass without it ... They will try to avert it ... but they can only retard it ... And to retard it too long would make it more terrible, for that will give the revolutionary spirit time to organize and begin the revolt first. And if that should happen," cries Reine in terror, "*it would be the end of us*, for war here amongst the French would give all facility to the others. *Oh, they must not have the time!*"[22]

I importune Reine with questions. She turns from her vision of terror, to listen to Vettellini, and transmits his words:

"The war in the Balkans has spread throughout all Europe. France has resisted as long as she could. Poincaré has done his best, but he can only struggle to hold the ship, he cannot control the tempest. He will be overwhelmed. All France is tearing herself to bits. The movement is already on foot. At this very moment there are conspiracies on all sides: Bonapartists, who are seeing their exiled Prince right here in Paris; other partisans of other princes; socialists, anarchists—all of them detesting each other, and each one working for his own interests."

It is the *hallali* of France! Treason, espionage, villainy—Reine-Vettellini touches all sides of the question, entering into details of government and police, characterizing the temperaments of the different peoples engaged in war, etc., etc. "In Russia, an orgy of disorder in the

---

[22] All this, and a number of other remarks already noted, would seem to indicate that destiny is not ineluctable. A prediction, a reading in the Astral, is often only a judgment based upon signs which, at the moment of reading would indicate a certain state of affairs, but which may nevertheless undergo modifying influences. This will be seen in communications which follow.

military organization ... in Germany, the hatred of the working-class for the Kaiser, their desire for a Republican Government. The future of William II. is dark, ill-omened. He is marked." (She seems at a given moment to see him prisoner of his own people.)

She cannot, however, see clearly the destiny of the nations. I push her in this sense, but she says that she cannot make out the consequences of this war, in comparison with which the wars of the past were mere child's play. Nevertheless, she does not see France completely invaded. All the horrors seem to take place near the frontier. The hatred is such, each side realizing that it is the crucial struggle, that they fall upon each other in frenzied rage. Entire cities are destroyed in France, but she does not see the armies of the enemy completely mastering our country. Here, in Paris, it is the French who are killing each other—and in other cities, as well, it is only the French.

Then comes an appreciation of the actual moment: "oh, any number of people hate the present regime without daring to say so! But all of a sudden they will show their hands. Even now posters are ready—gotten up in most flamboyant style and ornamented with huge portraits of their Prince. On the eve of the great movement, in a single night, the walls will be covered with them ... and the feeling against the Republic will be so great that all will approve."

Then another scene: "Spies everywhere. What a crowd of them! And the kind, too, whom you would never suspect: people of standing, people of influence—generals, even—are spies! They are all working together, big and little, for their nation." (Germany.)

"At sea, too—the battle is raging. Ah, we are not fortunate at sea ... no. But the English. Yes, they show up magnificently!"

With this extraordinary cataclysm of humanity, a formidable cataclysm of the elements seems to be mingled—geological convulsions, eruptions, floods—as though Earth had gone mad, contaminated by man.

Vettellini, whom I harass with questions, cannot—or will not—satisfy me. He says that all is confused and upside-down in all the nations: nothing is certain. And then, too, this is not the war of a day. It lasts ... it lasts so long that, in the distance, nothing is clear.

However, France seems to live through the terrible catastrophe. She exists. Regenerated by this tempest of fire and blood? There is ambiguity, a voluntary mystery, in Vettellini's words ... He will say no more ... for fear of being mistaken, is it?—Or fear of overwhelming us?

Suddenly Reine falls back in her chair and lies there like a corpse.

It is evidently a sleep of repose that is given to her—for four or five minutes. Gently, little by little, she seems to come back to another state. We hear her speaking very low; then, evidently by Vettellini's order, she hunts for the crystal ball (fallen beside her in the chair), looks at it with closed eyes, and quietly, in a happy voice, begins to speak: "How lovely! ... And so calm. Oh, how good the sun is! ... And that adorable sky! ... Oh, and that blue, that blue! Why, it goes forever—as far as I can see. What is it? Is it the sea? ... I never saw it. I can't be sure ... But yes, it must be the sea ... It is all wavy lines and silver fringes. Oh, how beautiful it is ... and so calm!"

The contrast is most impressive. We understand, even before Reine's question, that Vettellini is tranquillizing her spirit after the shock of her vision of terror. She asks: "Why am I here where everything is so good?" When Vettellini tells her it is to rest her eyes, she is astonished and asks why her eyes should be rested. He says that she cannot, she must not remember; but that I must. The vision was for me, and I must make note of it.

And then he explains to me directly, through Reine, that this tragic vision must be considered as a prediction. He was not to have given it for several weeks yet, but the conditions of hypnosis were so favorable today that he took advantage of it. His first intention had been to make the communication in writing, but it would have been too long and less impressive than in giving the child the direct vision and letting her tell it as she saw it.

In the course of our talk I am led to ask what Reine is—or rather, what Reine's spirit is—from the point of evolution. A long and interesting reply, too long to be given in detail. Reine is far above her present social condition. She has already had many lives on earth. This one, which will be short, is perhaps the last one. She might come back once more—but only for an apparition. Speaking for herself, Reine explains her situation, but with great reserve: "In suffering all my miseries here, I am refining. Death no longer frightens me; we are friends now," ... etc.

I ask if we cannot acquire conscience and evolution through happiness as well as through suffering. Vettellini admits that this is possible, but adds that the soul capable of gaining through happiness is already of high evolution; the average soul is unable to understand it.

A word is dropped that brings me to the question of cremation. Vettellini considers that from the terrestrial point of view—the hygienic—it is a good thing; but, as he seems to have a reservation on the subject, I insist and obtain the following details:—"The Spirit whose body has been cremated, becomes at once liberated and independent. This may be an advantage, if he is sufficiently evolved, but for an average evolution it is not the case. By cremation he has lost his point of attachment to the world to which he belongs; he has lost his anchor, so to speak, he is a balloon without ballast. Whoever has no further need of the Earth may be incinerated; but whoever must return for another life here, or who would wish to come back from the Au-Delà to aid those whom he has left here, should choose burial.

Here certain incidents lead me to say that if I could only succeed in seeing Vettellini, I might, perhaps, be able to make a portrait of him from memory. The suggestion is more adroit than I had dared to hope. The Guide betrays himself a little by saying that this would be all the easier for me that I had known him in my childhood. Discreetly, I try to pump him, but obtain only a confirmation of the statement ... It was in my childhood that I knew him. Later he will reveal his identity completely.

Here Reine maliciously gives a description of Vettellini's appearance, and the pantomime which follows shows plainly that he refuses to be analyzed and examined for this purpose. (The figure which she portrays, however, suggests no one whom I ever knew, or, at least, no one whom I recollect.) He cuts the incident short and resumes control of the situation by forcing Reine to admit that she broke the rules this morning. She neglected her regime. I must scold her well when she wakens.

It is the spontaneity of these scenes that I would wish to give ... But how? The séance has lasted from four o'clock till seven.

A detail. In the preceding séances, in the studio, Vettellini has always stood on the right of Reine. In the little salon the big armchair seems to take up a good deal of room, and there is less space on the right. Wishing to speak to her Guide, Reine looks for him in his usual relation to her, but appears not to find him. She hunts around and evidently sees him at her left, for she leans over on this side, and conversation begins between them. But she is uncomfortable, nervous ... and, all of a sudden, she interrupts with: "Oh, Vettellini, this won't do at all! Come over here on my right. It's more natural for me that way." She taps the arm of the chair, and leans over it in her usual position, saying: "that's it! I prefer it that way. I'm more comfortable. Stay on this side now."

TWENTY-THIRD SÉANCE

February 17, 1913

To day's séance is in a way the complement of Friday's, being a more general view of the extraordinary cataclysm seen from a higher point.

Out of the disorder of the inspired vision, out of the confusion of the successive images, often inadequately transmitted because of Reine's limited vocabulary, this is what I have been able to gather:

The frenzied spirit of massacre and destruction has spread from Europe to Asia. The oriental countries under the yoke of the white race are all in revolt—Indo-China, Annam, Tonkin, and British India. These thousands of subjugated peoples, in insurrection, would be a sufficiently formidable foe for Europe, already occupied and harassed. But the occasion is too tempting to the innumerable yellow hordes, whose pride has so often been insulted, whose deepest sentiments have been so constantly outraged. Crouching and cowering, they have waited for their moment. It has come: All China rises. In a sort of animal revendication of justice, she bears down in countless numbers upon the Europeans, and rolls over them—a living sea of vengeance. No warning, no menace. The perfected arms with which occidental commerce, in its greed, has furnished them, count little in the issue. They crush by mere force of numbers. They roll in and engulf. Japan, cousin by race and son by civilization, is with them, aids and sustains them. The yellow race sweeps over all Europe ... Annihilating it? ... In any case they terrorize it. All that has been taken from them they take back. Their reprisals are complete. Their vengeance is satisfied.

Africa is shaken and convulsed. America also. The upheaval is so prodigious, the ruin so appalling, that Reine struck by the exaggeration, seeks a cause higher than that of human atrocity. It is not only the cruelty of men, nor the obstinate incomprehension of their established Societies that will provoke this cataclysm. It is the cyclic law of transformation: it is sidereal evolution. An evolutionary cycle is drawing to its close. The most evolved race must disappear; this is the natural law. Three hundred years from now, or thereabouts, geological convulsions, earthquakes, volcanic eruptions, floods, the submergence of old continents and the appearance of new ones, are destined to destroy in great part this country and its people. By a sort of dumb instinct they are precipitating their destiny and rendering it even more cruel!

I have tried to express the lyrical and inspired character of Reine's visions, but it is better to give the dry analysis of this séance whose significance was first expressed in a symbolic phrasing difficult to imagine:

Sleep is long in coming, and Reine does not grow cold. But at last she is motionless in her chair, breathing regularly and appearing to sleep comfortably for about three- quarters of an hour, after which she begins to be agitated. She seems to be observing curious scenes, speaks in a low voice, listens, and mutters unintelligibly. Finally she calls me: "I am tired, oh, so tired! Vettellini took me far away, but ever so far—across the sea—through most extraordinary countries. I saw such peculiar people, whose hair was braided—yes, in braids." And she gives a description of the people and the scenes that Vettellini made her observe in this distant foreign country, before conducting her to another one, still farther off. And there she saw another kind of people, equally strange, but different—very dark and clothed in brilliant stuffs. And they, too, had gold, sacks of gold, which they were burying in the earth feverishly, furtively, and with great mystery. And here she is back again from this long, long voyage! It was China, first; then India—the Hindus. (These names she gets from Vettellini, and only after great effort.) These people are all amassing gold, which, later on, soon even, will be needed in their revolt against their oppressors—the white men. "This is what Vettellini wanted to show you. Revolt is being prepared in every direction. They are collecting and hiding gold because with gold they can get arms and foment massacres." ... And off she flies on her prophetic steed again, touching foot to earth from time to time, to comment on social and political conditions altogether beyond her comprehension.

I have the impression that Vettellini does not wish to say what he foresees—the ruin of our country; its fatal end. With infinite sadness Reine says only: "Our race has gained what it had to gain; its evolution is finished. In any case it was destined to disappear soon. It is horrible and stupid, but they are going to anticipate their fatality!

It is also the end of the German Empire ... the death or disappearance of their Kaiser and his house ... the federation of the German States," etc., etc.

Weary with these terrific subjects, I propose that Reine should try to find again the blue sea and sky that the crystal ball revealed to her in the last séance. She returns to it easily, and gives a new description of its enchantment. I try to learn the name of this paradise. She leans towards her Guide, listens an instant and says: "It is Brittany." —Ah? What part of Brittany?—Same play of attitude, then a burst of unexpected joy: "Why, Monsieur Cornillier, he says it is where you go! ... Oh, it is lovely there. Such sun! ... So warm! ... And Vettellini talks to me there in the rocks!"

The séance closes with this happy impression. I waken her.

I will introduce here a communication given later on (in the thirty-fifth séance), because it is, in a way, the complement of this one, modifying, as it does, the prediction relative to the extinction of our race:

I say to Vettellini:—The French race is an old one, and the French people have attained a high degree of civilization; consequently they must disappear. Well and good. But, just the same, it is a very small minority that is so civilized, as all that, Vettellini! The immense mass seems hardly to have attained a level of evolution that would justify this wholesale liberating catastrophe. Is everyone, then, to benefit by the acquisition of conscience in so small a unit? Does solidarity of race exist to this extent? "No," replies Vettellini, "those who have not reached the necessary degree of evolution will simply continue their lives of incarnation, first in what remains of France, and, after that, in other countries—England, Russia, Germany."

I ask if the order of the disappearance of other nations can be foreseen. Without affirmation, Vettellini says that, after France, Spain and Italy will be destroyed by floods, volcanic eruptions, earthquakes. Then it will be Germany's turn. England and the United States will persist a long time ... though a part of the English coast—that which faces France—will be destroyed at the same time that our country is destroyed, but the catastrophe for them will be limited. China, too, will persist. (This is contrary to the theory of Cosmosophy, which foresees the extinction of the yellow race long before that of the white.)

The world centre of political power will pass in the future from Europe to Asia ... etc., etc.

Note:

It is evident that the information given in any one séance should not be regarded as final and definite. From the very conditions of transmission, errors will occur. Reine—and this must not be forgotten—does not hear in words the substance of what she repeats. She translates into words the vibrations that convey Vettellini's thought, and as her education is extremely meager and her vocabulary limited, her interpretation may occasionally be inexact. Conscious of her difficulties, Vettellini, in certain cases, gives her the precise words, which she then repeats mechanically, without comprehending. And this is another source of error. The rectification is always made in a following séance, but sometimes long after; for, oftener than not, it is an unexpected question which reveals that the transmission has been imperfect.

I hope the reader will take this important point in consideration. Later, if it is possible, I will establish a definite synthesis of Vettellini's teachings.

TWENTY-FOURTH SÉANCE

February 19, 1913

Reine is ill—fever, suffocation, etc. After a communication received by her yesterday, we need not use the table today, as she will sleep at once. She also reports a clear and precise vision in the crystal ball, a vision that rather worries her. She saw herself propped up in bed by pillows and holding a baby in her arms—a little girl, dark, and whose hair was already quite long. Is it an annunciation?

I begin magnetizing her at four o'clock and, immediately, she starts off for the land of mystery. She does not grow cold, is feverish, but the sleep is calm and lasts a long time. Finally, towards five o'clock, she begins to speak, unintelligibly at first, then more and more explicitly, repeating her own questions as well as the replies given by her Guide, and articulating so carefully that I conclude she is made to do this in order that we may clearly understand everything.

It is a communication on Life and Death that Vettellini gives her. Stripped of the dialogue, so spontaneous and picturesque, and which stenography alone could adequately render, here is the substance of her transmission:

Terrestrial life (incarnation) is an ordeal imposed upon us for our evolution. During this life we may be influenced by Spirits superior or inferior, as our own tendencies and aspirations determine. We attract or repel the good or the bad by our very way of being and thinking. In short, each one creates his own astral society.

The Spirit protectors (or stimulators) are themselves under the direction of others, still more evolved, who seem to have a certain power of modifying human destinies; and these, in turn, are subject to an order that is higher still. (So, then, it would seem that a very precise hierarchy exists in the astral plane?) It is a noteworthy fact that Reine tries several times to use the term *God*. But each time she retracts it, and evidently under Vettellini's correction. We hear her saying: "Ah ... well, whatever is above us ... what governs." At a given moment she turns towards him and says: "But you, Vettellini, you, who are a high Spirit, haven't you ever seen God?" After listening, she murmurs, "Yes ... Yes ... I see. Even beyond the very highest,—beyond the white ones— there are still others ... and even these are led and directed by Spirits higher than they!"

Death is predetermined. Sickness and accident are the means used by the Spirit-directors for the accomplishment of destiny. Life sometimes defends itself vigorously against death, particularly in the case of inferior beings who intuitively dread the mystery. But Spirit-messengers are there, awaiting the release of the soul and, when the hour comes, aid and, if need be, force the escape.

The soul is then conducted before an assembly of high Spirits—the white ones—who recognize the degree of evolution. If this evolution is slight, the soul will wander about in our atmosphere for a longer or shorter period, reviewing his earthly life, taking cognizance of his responsibilities and learning to develop his own conscience by observing, from the other side, the struggle of living beings. In all this he will at first be guided by the higher Spirits; then alone, or surrounded by those of his own evolution, he will wander through space—indifferently, lamentably or joyfully, as his level determines—until the moment, more or less remote, when the Spirit-directors will send him back to Earth again for a new incarnation, for another beneficent experience.

If the disincarnate soul has already attained a superior evolution, he may become a Spirit-director himself, or he may voluntarily accept another reincarnation for a definite purpose—a sacrifice that will carry him on still higher in the scale of evolution.

Spirits like Vettellini come back to earth for such purposes only. But, normally, it is by astral activity that they attain a superior state: they become white Spirits—relatively sovereign judges for all that concerns terrestrial affairs. White Spirits, they continue their evolution and pass into another sphere, unknown and incomprehensible to us, and of which Vettellini refuses to speak, at least for the moment. (I gather, however, that in this other sphere, or, more exactly, in this new state—for it does not seem to be reincarnation on a star of higher plane—the Spirits are entirely above and beyond all terrestrial interest; it is too insignificant, they have outgrown it.)

Reine comes back to her normal state of hypnosis—the second state. She talks familiarly with Vettellini, finds that he has said a great deal too much—never will she be able to tell it all to Monsieur Cornillier. When he says that he has made her speak aloud so that I might assist at their conversation, she is stupefied and expresses: strong doubts as to the veracity of the statement. Resolutely she informs him that she is going to find out about it. Leaning towards me she asks, in a whisper, if she has really been repeating what has been said between them ... Vettellini means it? ... He's not mocking her?

Several times during her long talk with the Maître who, today seems to stand on her left (later on I understand why), Reine has glanced to her right, and a little above her, tipping back her head and puckering her brow, as though examining something up there. Having observed this play, I am not surprised to hear her allude politely to "this gentleman (ce Monsieur) who is here." Later on, referring to the same presence, she says more indifferently, "this man here" (ce garçon-là). At the moment I understand nothing, but the explanation comes in time. Vettellini says that to satisfy my wish for material phenomena—such as his evolution prevents him from producing himself—he has brought an inferior Spirit who, with a little training, will be able to provoke them: lights, noises, transportation of objects, etc.

Reine again examines the newcomer with cold attention then, turning around to Vettellini, remarks sternly and with conviction: "I must say he's ugly! ... Why must he be so ugly, Vettellini? ... Couldn't you find someone a little less ugly than that?" This is so unexpected and so comical that we shake with laughter. Evidently Vettellini replies that beauty has no importance in the question, for we hear her persisting: "No ... but he's really too plain. He's the limit ... And then, you know—blondes! ... I've no use for them ... I can't bear the sight of them! But just look at him, Vettellini, with that outlandish nose ... all twisted! The idea! ... Good? Well, I should think he'd better be—with a head like that! H'm ... do you think he's reliable, Vettellini?—He's not a liar? ... Well, I suppose I've got to speak to him. What's his name? ... Say it again. Jani ... Jan ... ah, Jeanik! ... Well, it suits him; ... with that name and that head I must say he's complete." And with a final withering glance at the gentleman in question we hear her muttering: "Oh, no, all the same!—he's too ugly!"

But she seems somewhat appeased when she understands that Jeanik will not speak with us, that he is there solely to execute material phenomena, and that she must invoke him for this purpose and command him. We may begin to experiment at once.

I darken the room completely. We wait for about ten minutes. Reine, taking her new role seriously, orders with authority: "Jeanik, make a light. Stronger!

Better than that, Jeanik! Now, a rap. Louder!" Save one clear rap—coming, seemingly, from the wall—nothing is precise enough to be of value: vague lights, uncertain phosphorescence, etc. It seems there is also a third Spirit present, who is superior to Jeanik, and destined to serve as intermediary in mixed phenomena. In spite of her efforts, Reine cannot perceive him; but she takes pains to inquire if he is as ugly as the other one, and sighs with relief when Vettellini assures her that he is more presentable: "I can't help it, I do not like ugly people ... Oh, that Jeanik!"

We resume conversation, and I try to clear up the contradiction which seems to exist between the announcement of the advent of the "Prince" who is to re-establish order and create a new France, and the predicted destruction of our country. Vettellini explains that the establishment of order in France, bleeding and ruined, will be relative. The Prince will be at the head of a reduced and diminished nation. He will try to build it up again, and, relatively to the epoch of terror and desolation which will have preceded his advent, he will, as a matter of fact, bring about a certain prosperity. But it will be a respite only. The inexorable law of evolution is in force.

I ask about Reine's health, and this brings me naturally to speak of the vision she had yesterday morning in the crystal ball. The Guide says that it is an annunciation. Reine will have a little daughter. Soon? Vettellini is prudent. It might be a year and a half from now ... two years? Perhaps he does not want to frighten her. Suddenly I notice that Reine is overcome with emotion—What is the matter?—Trembling, and with an accent of ineffable tenderness, she says in a low voice: "Monsieur Cornillier, she is there. Vettellini leads her by the hand—my little daughter!" The scene is the more interesting in that, in her normal life, Reine professes an indifference to children.

Vettellini has created the image as a prediction and possibly also to prepare the poor child to carry one burden more.

When she is awake Reine questions me about her vision. In spite of my rather vague reply, she appears transformed, already a happy and a jealous mother!

An incident. The Maître is not always patient. He is frequently irritable when asked to repeat certain statements that have not been understood, or when we appear sometimes to doubt them. Often Reine's hand reaches out in his direction, seeming to touch him imploringly, seeming to want to calm him, and we hear her protesting:

"Come, come, Vettellini, you mustn't be angry. You fly out like a shot!" Today when he explained that Spirits can continue their evolution in the astral, that they can acquire new qualities, etc., we hear Reine murmur: "Yes, yes, I see. Well you know, Vettellini, it wouldn't be a bad idea for you to acquire a little patience. It's a good chance. You'd better not let it slip!"

It must be remarked that Reine, a timid and unassuming little person in ordinary life, has in hypnosis a singular authority and vivacity. She frankly attacks Vettellini, argues with him fearlessly, and accepts his explanations only when she finds them adequate. It is curious to observe her. Day before yesterday she suddenly interrupted him in the midst of a reply: "But look here, Vettellini, since what you are revealing to us now has always existed, and since there have always been Spirits, why is it that it is only in the last few years that you have manifested yourselves? How does it happen that Spirits like you have not come before this to talk to the people on earth and teach them all these things?" (The child shows her ignorance in supposing that spirit-manifestation is recent, but in this she is only sharing the error of the majority of people who ignore the importance that mediumistic phenomena have had in history—under other names—and the uninterrupted continuity of manifestations of the "Au-Delà" in Time and Space). Vettellini's answer was fitted to Reine's comprehension; he could not give a lecture on the history of occultism. "If Spirits—who have, indeed, always existed—have begun to manifest themselves only in these latter days, it is because formerly people were so ignorant, were so fixed and narrow in their religious convictions, that they would have attributed all such phenomena to the Devil; and the people who were used as instruments in such manifestations would have been considered sorcerers, and would have been tortured or burned in consequence."

Another time she interrupts him: "But how does it happen that we remember nothing at all of our former lives? That's too bad, Vettellini—it's awkward!" ... "To remember all the mistakes of other lives, all the situations one has been in, all the experiences through which one has passed, would render the new life insupportable, impossible. One would be too unhappy. It is better that each life presents itself as something quite new, quite simple, uncomplicated by memories, if the reincarnated Spirit is to extract all its advantage. But those who have attained a certain degree of evolution have, as a matter of fact, intuitions, souvenirs of the past," ... etc., etc.

TWENTY-FIFTH SÉANCE

February 21, 1913

Compared with the preceding séances this one seems: rather colorless; it is an exercise more than anything else.

We begin directly with the magnetizing. Reine sleeps rapidly, and is quiet for about three-quarters of an hour, when she straightens up in her chair to say that Vettellini wishes us to work with the table, as it will serve to concentrate our fluid. Jeanik is there and must be trained to his work; we must not hesitate to command him, he is a workman, and is there to obey orders.

I draw up the table, and we sit before it nearly an hour, quickly obtaining strange swaying movements, but not at all what I ordered—a frank levitation of the four feet. We must begin again. It is a bore; but the Maître says it is the best possible gymnastic, and that when we have once succeeded, we will pass immediately to other things. He gives us the cheerful order to stay at the table two hours next Monday, hoping thus to finish the drudgery once for all.

The second half of the séance is more interesting. Vettellini proposes to clear up any obscure point in his last communications.

Resuming, then, the subject of incarnation, I ask at what precise moment the Spirit is imprisoned in the body. A considerable number of observations, made by mediums, tend to the supposition that sometimes the Spirit is not definitely captured before the child has attained the age of four, five or even seven years. What truth is there in this? And what may be the reason of the difference in epoch?

Vettellini replies that the complete capitation of the Spirit by the body occurs *generally* at the moment of delivery, but that from the moment of conception, and throughout all the time of pregnancy, there has been an intermittent penetration of the Spirit into the organism in course of human formation. The Spirit comes to prepare his dwelling, so to speak, to give the cachet of his own personality, thus modifying the maternal work and that of organic heredity; and, at the delivery, he definitely imprisons himself—or is imprisoned—losing all consciousness, all memory of anterior states. This is the general law. But what has been observed by psychics (mediums) is equally true; for when the child is destined to die young—a destiny which denotes an already high evolution and consequently a clear consciousness in the reincarnating Spirit—the complete capitation, the total imprisonment, is never achieved. The obscurity on this point, then, is cleared up.

I return to the question of the judgment of souls by the tribunal of the white Spirits, and confess that I find it unpleasantly akin to our own terrestrial idea of social order. How is it that the classification of Souls is not accomplished automatically? In his last life, a Spirit has gained a given degree of evolution, independent of all judgment of other beings, be they never so superior. Where there is judgment, there is, inevitably, the personal element. This Tribunal, is it, then, an institution created by the Spirits, established and constituted according to their ideas— and hence open to discussion? Or is it the function of a higher Law?

Vettellini replies that, first of all, we must remember that the necessity of expressing the conditions of astral life in terms created for terrestrial relations—in human language—cannot fail to give rise to confusion and mistakes. And then, too, it is not a judgment, as we understand that word, that is pronounced by the white Spirits, not a condemnation or acquittal,—no. The Soul having left his body, after death, is conducted into the presence of these high Spirits that he may acquire consciousness of his responsibilities in his past life. *It is his own conscience that makes the classification.* In other words, passing before the white Spirits is like passing before a mirror: the Soul sees himself as he is.

It is a difficult question to fathom because of our inability to conceive a condition of matter different from that in which we live, but Vettellini promises a fuller exposition later on. We must wait.

Speaking of cremation, I ask the Maître if it does not render reincarnation more difficult, and, since the complete destruction of the body has cut off all ties to earth, what is its effect upon inferior Spirits who, in accordance with the general law, should return to earth speedily? He says that capitation is certainly more difficult for them; and often, unless they are aided (according to their merit) by the protecting Spirits, they wander about for a long time before finding favorable circumstances.

I turn to another subject. From the point of view of evolution, what is a medium? Reply: Mediumistic faculties are altogether independent of the soul. They are derived entirely from the physico-chemical constitution of the organism. Consequently, all degrees of evolution may be found in mediums. Certain people may possess the organism of a medium, and, at the same time, a spirit that rebels against the employment of such faculties, and they live and die without suspecting their own powers in this direction. This aptitude of the organism is readily perceived by the disincarnate who, if they are inferior, almost always try to take advantage of it to manifest themselves more or less properly. But in such cases—exception made for the manifestations having a probative value despite their vulgarity—the Spirit-Guides are there to maintain order.

The interesting point for me is that the spirit has no part in mediumship.

I speak of Reine's health, which is better just at present. Vettellini says that she may begin again to pose. There is also question of a complementary method for provoking a more profound sleep. And then Reine suddenly begins to speak on her own account and with that authority and ease which is sometimes hers, she calls attention to the fact that she was colder today: "You must have noticed it? But it is still not enough. I must be just like ice, otherwise we'll never get anywhere, Jeanik and that other one are going to help me. Vettellini can do nothing for us in this kind of work. It is you who must act. Those two there are inferior Spirits and you will command them. You alone will be master," etc. And she explains at length the manner of procedure necessary for success. Remarkable, the abnegation of this child, her absolute devotion to the purpose of these dances; and incomprehensible, if one rejects the explanation given. She speaks of herself as a simple instrument that must be refined to perfection ... and this with a clear comprehension of her role.

I am on the point of waking her when she brushes my hand aside, straightens up, listens, then says, rapidly: "Monsieur Cornillier, Vettellini says that you are sick—yes, sick. You have caught cold again. You must not go out. Keep warm. Take that medicine again ... you know? Be careful."—This evening I am forced to admit the truth of the impeachment.

Towards the end of the séance Reine sees a luminous head in the atmosphere. After looking at it for a few seconds, she says it is her mother. We all have the same thought: probably something serious has happened—an accident ... or death? Vettellini, whom I consult, says it is not so grave as that. It is he who has created this image as a reproach to Reine for not having been to see her mother for two weeks, and I am to scold her a little for this when she wakens.

TWENTY-SIXTH SÉANCE

February 24, 1913

(I am alone during the first part of the séance)

Reine comes in at two o'clock,—in better health, more buoyant. We set about the irksome task of the table, persisting during a good long hour, with no other result than crackings, violent movements, and some vague glimmers of phosphorescence on our hands, or on the centre of the table. Out of all patience, I cut short this tedious gymnastic to magnetize Reine, already so sleepy that she does not even hear my preparations. I work over her for a long time, adding the complementary method prescribed in the last séance, and, when the moment is auspicious, order her spirit to go into the studio and describe what I have arranged there for this purpose. She goes, but with so much difficulty that I ask if she is in the condition necessary to obey my orders. She tells me tersely, and in a hoarse voice, to continue the passes, adding, "I am sleeping well, but not deeply enough." Finally, she says I may stop. She is more liberated, and perhaps will be able to see better.

I order her to go back to the studio and look on the writing table. Does she find anything unusual there? At expense of great effort she discovers three playing cards that I had pulled from a pack and thrown down without looking at them. She tries to name them but hesitates, sees nothing clearly, is not sure; and, rather awkwardly, gives a vague description, which I find to be false at the end of the séance. Suddenly, her manner changes, her attention is all alive. She declares that she sees a fire—"a big fire, flames are bursting out everywhere! ... Here are the firemen! Everybody is looking," ... etc.

I try to get precise indications as to the quarter of the city and the building that is burning, but obtain only the statement that it is a big building not far from *la Place de la République.* (It was about half-past four.)[23] She sees nothing more: says that she is back here.

I resume the passes, and when the hypnosis seems at the right point, send her imperatively to 86, rue de Miromesnil, telling her to enter an apartment of the fourth floor and describe what she sees there. As she does not know the street, I give directions. She reaches the house, takes the staircase (which she herself discovers in the court), and, at my formal order, enters the apartment. She sees the hall clearly, and is attracted to the room on the right, which she describes accurately, remarking a big writing-table, pictures on the wall, etc.; but it is only later that she discovers a man seated at the table and writing—"a big, strong man, ... with a beard, ... and who wears eyeglasses ... or is it spectacles? Oh, he's a big man—powerful."

She cuts off her description with an exclamation: "But I know who he is! It's the gentleman who was here that day when we were at the table and the time by your watch was given!" Bravo. It is indeed to my friend S. O. that I have sent her, and Reine has recognized him though she has seen him only once, at that unsuccessful fifth séance, the twenty-first of December.[24]

Just here the bell rings. Not wishing to open the door to a stranger, I take advantage of Reine's condition to discover who the visitor may be. Quickly I order:—"Reine, come back immediately. Are you here? Then go to the door and see who has rung."—"Must I go outside?"—"Yes, outside. Be quick. Look."—A second of suspense, then she whispers gaily: "It's Madame Cornillier."—"You are quite sure?" "Ha! Yes!" I open the door to my wife.

This incident having brought Reine to a less profound state of hypnosis, I tell her to get into communication with Vettellini that he may clear up certain points that remain obscure for me.

First, I would like to know if the length of each individual life is determined at birth. "No," says Vettellini, "except in the case of children

---

[23] The newspapers of the next day made no mention of a fire in Paris.

[24] A note relative to this visit will be found at the end of the Thirty-third séance.

destined to die young. But for those who are to have a normal life the date of death is determined in the course of their existence, and even by the course of their existence. Their development of consciousness may advance or delay the fatality which, in any case, can be foreseen a long time before it occurs."

I ask if Reine is right in affirming that to die in infancy is a sign of fairly high evolution.—"Yes, certainly." I remark that there are children who die between five and ten years of age who seem to be mentally inferior and who are sometimes even idiots. "That is true," replies Vettellini, "but it is merely an inferiority of the organism, it has nothing whatever to do with the Spirit who, indeed, in many cases, has a dull consciousness of imminent death, and does not take the trouble to ameliorate his instrument of expression."

If to die in infancy is a sign of high evolution, does that imply that death in age shows an inferiority of the Spirit? "Not at all. Generally speaking, inferior Spirits should have a long life, to give all possible chances for their evolution. But a high Spirit may also attain an advanced age—and for various reasons: for instance, if he has a role to fill, an aim to accomplish, teaching to give; if he is a cause of evolution to those around him, or, even, merely for his own benefit."

The accidents which suddenly cut off life, are they always determined beforehand? Is it not sometimes a question of chance?—"Never. They always occur at the date and under the conditions determined."

Those whose existence is a long physical agony, do they in this way expiate faults or crimes committed in a former life?—"Yes, always. It is the result of past acts. It is the redemption—which sometimes they themselves have chosen ... as expiation."

I come to the question of suicide and try to obtain the assurance that under exceptional circumstances it has its excuse.—"There is no excuse for arresting life—one's own, or that of another. They who have killed themselves are reprobate, as are all murderers and assassins, as is even the judge who inflicts a death sentence." Here Reine gives an interesting appreciation of this question of capital punishment. Vettellini considers it as another crime—for which, in a relative degree, each public officer is reponsible, be he judge, juror, or hangman. They will bear the consequences *until they come to understand that one may not arrest a life in its course.* Never. Never. He even goes so far as to say that it is wrong to neglect one's health, and the care of one's body. One should keep one's instrument in the best possible condition.

I turn again to the question of cremation, not yet quite clear. Can it possibly be just that those who have been cremated, either without their consent, or voluntarily, believing it best, should suffer from the fatal function of a law of which they were ignorant? "On principle, no one may be punished for an act that he has committed through ignorance," replies Vettellini. "There is no question of expiation, no painful remorse for people in this case; but they will nevertheless be retarded, because of certain physico-chemical difficulties, in their reincarnation. But the white Spirits appreciate the circumstances and modify the application of the law in consequence."

Here I ask if I was wrong to leave the table before the time prescribed—explaining how annoying it is to sit in the dark for an hour or so, holding on to a piece of unstable furniture. He says that it was because he saw my great desire for material phenomena that he had recommended this exercise, and had sent his aids—Jeanik and the other one. As a matter of fact, it is hardly possible to get what I want except with a group of assistants forming a chain, etc., etc. If we wait for the complete development of Reine's faculties, she herself will realize such phenomena; but for that she must reach the point of catalepsy. Until she becomes lifeless and cold as death, we shall obtain nothing in this direction. Today the sleep has been profound, but not sufficiently profound to allow her double to obey me instantly. I should begin earlier, magnetize her gently and slowly (not to fatigue myself), but during a very long time, and without questioning her. After several such séances she should obey me, as my own thought obeys me. I must work especially on her head, inhibit her will and substitute my own. For instance, today, when I sent her into the studio, she calmly strolled outside on her own errands. It was then she saw the fire—which Vettellini says really existed. He repeats and affirms that I shall get marvelous results with Reine, but I must have patience: her health worries him; she is better, but she must continue to take great precautions ... and this she does not always remember.

This last reflection provokes one of the scenes, so impossible to describe, and so convincing that we always regret being the only observers of them. There is a discussion between them—a violent one. At first we catch only a few sharp disjointed phrases, it is more by her gestures and expression that we understand her anger. Evidently she flatly refuses to obey, turns her back abruptly on Vettellini and sulks. Too angry to be silent, however, she flings about in her chair again, only to repeat that she does not want to, and she won't! But probably the Maître knows how to make use of a fit of temper, for there are signs of capitulation; she yields ... on one point only. Reluctantly turning to me, she confesses that the last two days she has not taken her cod liver oil ... But this is not enough. Vettellini insists. No, and no! She will not and she will not! And the scene of fury begins all over again. I urge her then to make a clean breast of it, just to get out of trouble, and suddenly she breaks down. She did not breakfast this morning, but it was not her fault, she had no money (*pas des sous*). This time all is confessed. Only, she hears Vettellini laugh, and once again turns her back on him—wounded and angry. But evidently his charm is irresistible, for, like a child tired of sulking, she laughs herself and makes peace.

TWENTY-SEVENTH SÉANCE

February 26, 1913

(Mlle. D. is present)

I foresaw that this séance of training would be of no great interest. My orders were to assume more and more control of Reine's will, by magnetizing her as long as possible, and to exact nothing from her; and I made every effort to accomplish this end.

Reine arrives late, miserable in health and much affected by a family scene. (In the last few years her father has become an inveterate alcoholic.) Nevertheless she sleeps rapidly and during one hour and a half I continue to magnetize her.

Finally she sits up and informs me in a tired voice that she has been outside—without doing much of anything. Her head was completely empty, as it should be, she had slept profoundly; but her body was still too living—due to her state of health. Vettellini made her look at different scenes, in order to habituate her to observe with precision. I ask if one of the scenes which she describes— a snow-covered country, where bears are playing about— has any signification. Vettellini says not, only an exercise, an image which he created for the purpose of training her astral sight to notice details.

Reine speaks of the cataleptic state which she should attain as soon as her health permits: "When the condensation of my double is accomplished, I shall lose weight and even seem to grow smaller. It is then that disincarnated Spirits—Vettellini or others—will be able to use my organism to communicate with you. If they speak, you will hear their voices, the gestures will be their gestures. They will also be able to use my fluidic substance to materialize and make themselves visible."

I turn again to the question of children predestined to an early death. In certain almshouses, such as Bicêtre for example, four or five hundred little children may be found together, all idiots or deformed, destined to die, between three and twelve years of age. Must we then believe that all these pitiful creatures are highly evolved beings? The answer is precise:—"They are all Spirits of about the same degree—and of a fairly high degree. At the moment of their reincarnation they were conscious of the fate ahead of them. They accepted without revolt—sometimes voluntarily choosing it—this painful destiny, for the purpose of more quickly attaining a superior degree of evolution."

I ask if in the entire existence of a being,—that is, throughout the succession of his periods of incarnation and disincarnation,—the earthly period may not be considered the most difficult to endure, the time of hard labor and painful effort; and the period in the Astral as the time of harvest, good or bad, according to the work accomplished, but, in any case, a repose? The answer is affirmative. "Earth is hard labor, struggle and suffering. The Astral may be a happiness, but in every case it is a respite, a truce, and the ..."

"Vettellini wants me to tell you to look at your lamp!" exclaims Reine. Amazed by this absurd interruption, I nevertheless jump in the direction of the red lantern, to find that it is smoking frightfully. Lowering the wick, I ask her: "But did the odor inconvenience Vettellini?"—"Oh, no—he says it was on account of the ladies. He warned me a few minutes ago that your lamp was smoking, but I did not understand what he meant; so then he insisted."

Our amusement breaks the thread of my ideas.

I explain to the Guide how useful it would be to have an exact and clear prediction from him—one that would be realized at an early date. It would add considerable weight to the value of the tragic visions which he has already given us. He promises to try to satisfy my wish.

This brings me to ask: what is the basis upon which Spirits establish a prediction of future events? Reine transmits that when there is merely question of the future of an individual, Spirits can first enter into relation with his double, during his sleep, and thus obtain many indications for a prognosis. But all events exist in the astral long before their realization on earth; and Spirits are able to take cognizance of them by reading the mysterious signs of currents and fluids, more or less correctly, according to the acuity of their perceptions, and the competence of their judgment,—which is always determined by their degree of evolution.

This explanation is purely verbal. Our human intelligence cannot conceive of currents and fluids that contain or express ... future events. But what do we understand of the phenomena that we witness each day of our lives?

TWENTY-EIGHTH SÉANCE

February 28, 1913

I t was understood that Reine would come at two o'clock today, and I have everything ready to begin promptly.

At three she is not here. Half-past three, ... four, ... and she does not come. I am impatient and displeased; but, finally concluding that she is ill, I put my room in order again.

But at half-past four she appears—a humble and embarrassed Reine. She explains that she had a quarrel with her husband this morning, and, to vex him, she went herself to the lavoir to wash their linen; it took a long time, she finished only at three o'clock. Not daring to come at that hour, she had begun to work at home, when she felt an irresistible impulse to place her hands on the table, which immediately tapped: "Cornillier displeased. Go at once." She argued that it was too late, but the table tapped again, very savagely: "Cornillier impatient. Go." And she started off, frightened to death at the idea of being scolded.

We begin the séance at once. She sleeps rapidly. During a full hour I continue the passes, then I leave her.

Towards six o'clock she begins to move a little; seems to see apparitions. Then, sitting up straight, she makes a sign to someone on her right to pass to the left. Some words she lets fall make us understand that it is Vettellini with whom she is speaking. He was in his usual place, on the right, but Reine's right side and arm are so bruised by the unusual exercise of rubbing and beating that she tells him it will be easier for her to lean toward the left. This arranged to her satisfaction, a perfectly normal conversation begins between them. Reine relates what she has done, and receives advice and some criticism of her conduct. She plagues Vettellini, rebels against his authority, stings him a little ... and finally settles down to a serious talk. All this is so natural, and so real, that one has the conviction that her interlocutor is present there in fact. At a certain moment she is stirred by an emotion roused by a reference to her father, and a truly touching and pitiful cry reaches our hearts.

Reine perceives that Vettellini is perfectly informed of all that she does, and even to the smallest detail. Later on she says: "Why, he watches me as a cat watches a mouse!" They speak of the artist M. with whom Reine, it seems, has definitely broken—thus justifying her Guide's prediction. And this gives rise to a second prediction, a valuable one—if realized—because of its special form. The painter M. had engaged Reine for three sittings, but as he was sick the first two and unable to work, he refused to pay her for them. She is too proud to insist and exact her due, but she is vexed and distressed—"for, you know, fifteen francs lost ... that counts!" Now Vettellini says to her: "Don't worry about that, Reine. M. will be sorry he did that; *and next Tuesday he will leave with your concierge an envelope containing two five-franc pieces, and a line asking you to resume the séances.*" (Today, Friday, there is no indication of such an intention on the part of M., but above all there is no possibility of foreseeing this special manner of paying his debt.) Reine exclaims: "But Vettellini—those ten francs, do you think I should keep them? I didn't work, you see. H'm? ... Yes, of course I know he engaged my time, but just the same, are you quite sure they *belong* to me ... ? *May I spend them, Vettellini?*"

It is after this that the incident of her father is placed. She has once more tried to save him by making her mother take him back home again, by giving him money, finding him a situation, etc., etc., all which efforts were vain. After two weeks of abstinence, the passion resumed its sway and it became necessary to once more tie up his bundle, and send him out to bear alone the burden of his miserable life. All this we learn from her talk with Vettellini, who admonishes her to think no more about him. But the tears run down her poor little face, she explains and protests. Finally we hear her implore: "Oh, Vettellini, promise me that you will watch over him—that you will help him a little? He's going to suffer so dreadfully when he realizes that he has failed again. And ... see that he has bread—just bread, Vettellini! ... and the nights—don't let him be cold, ... *don't let him sleep out of doors!*" The poor little thing continues to supplicate between her sobs.

Another scene helps us to forget our emotion. Reine remarks to her Guide, that he is very nice today. He has not scolded her. It makes her very happy when he is friendly like that. He evidently replies by some reference to his age, for Reine exclaims: "Too old! You are too old? Just listen to that, will you! ... Well, Vettellini, let me tell you, I like it better that way. Yes, I do assure you, Vettellini, it's more tranquil like that. At least we can be good comrades." Then to a remark which I do not catch she retorts: "Oh, yes, you're much pleased with yourself for being a Spirit, I see that, but one of these days I'll be a Spirit myself!"

They say *au revoir.* Reine then reaches out to find me, that she may recount the principal things she has seen and done, wholly unconscious that we have been able to follow her all this time.

TWENTY-NINTH SÉANCE

March 3, 1913

We begin about four o'clock. Reine is in better health and gayer than usual. She sleeps promptly. I continue my passes as usual, interrupting them to rest, resuming them again. At a certain moment she lifts her head, listens, then suddenly sits upright, stretching out her left hand in my direction and seeming to show me her ring. As she has been told to put aside any rings or objects in metal during her séances, I understand the gesture and remove her wedding ring; then she holds out her right hand for the same operation, and falls back in her chair.

After a rather long sleep, she starts nervously and answers quickly, as though someone had called her. I conclude from her attitudes that she hears someone speaking but cannot see him. It is not Vettellini, and this astonishes and worries her. The new arrival must announce something that does not please her, for she questions him with evident anxiety. She begins now to distinguish his form and color. It is a white Spirit. He speaks with such authority that she is a little frightened. She sees no face; only a cloudy form, tall, important, and white,—a wonderful, pure and luminous white, which ravishes her still when, later on, she gives me the description. He has come to tell her that Vettellini will not appear during the next séances. It will be better for her. She counts too much on his aid.

Reine lays the situation before me: "I'm not a bit of a coward, you know, but, just the same, when I feel this cold creeping over me, this ice penetrating all through me, I am afraid, and unconsciously I arrest the disengagement of my fluidic substance. But I must become just like a corpse, you know,—it is necessary. Feel that; (she holds out her arm) even now I am cold to my very bones, but it is not enough—and I am frightened ... and then I get Vettellini to help me, and talk with him a little, just put off the moment of complete disengagement. Oh, you know, it's enough to frighten anyone ... But I have got to conquer that fear!"

The child is so discouraged by the announcement that she is not to see Vettellini, that she asks the white Spirit to let him come at least to-day,—just a little while,—just a minute? She supplicates, insists, then finally rebels. It is a curious scene. Even before this high authority Reine does not capitulate. *She wishes to see Vettellini. She will see him!—and today!* Without any promise, the white Spirit turns away, and, in spite of her emotion, Reine cannot help exclaiming at his marvelously luminous whiteness as he disappears by the window.

But immediately her anxiety prevails. She looks about on all sides ... "Vettellini?" She lifts herself in her chair, peers around, stands up, turning her head in every direction, scrutinizing the corners of the room, trying to penetrate space. Then, bursting into tears, she finally flings herself down: "Vettellini ... Oh, Vettellini!" I'm afraid she will break with sobbing.

A sudden cry of joy. She reaches her hands to the left. He is there. Ah! ... She breathes again. She tells him to come over to the right,—"It's better here"—makes room for him in her chair, but he does not accept the offer, holding himself outside as usual. She begins at once to tell him what has happened but interrupts herself: "You're laughing! Ah, you know all about it? Well, it's a pretty mess! Of course you're coming just the same? What? ... Disobey? No,—no, of course not. We'll, do it, certainly we'll do it, only—(coaxingly) you are coming just the same, Vettellini,—tell me! And then, you know, Mr. Cornillier wouldn't like it at all—he has to ask you questions!" It is not the first charming scene we have witnessed between them.

The Guide confirms the necessity of leaving Reine and myself to work our way alone, for the moment. It must be so. But he will be present without manifesting himself, and after two or three séances he will come back and resume his talks.

Then he gives some information—a veritable prediction, in fact, which I am to note with care: Tomorrow Reine's mother will receive a letter announcing that her own mother is very ill, and, if she wishes to find her alive, she must come immediately. Reine and her mother have had no relations with the old lady for several years past.

Vettellini affirms that, in spite of the material difficulties that seem to exist, Reine's mother will go, will be absent three days, and that the old lady will not die this time. This will happen later,—towards Easter. Reine remarks that her mother will not have permission to absent herself, for her employers are exceedingly severe, and, as she has no money, she certainly will not go. "You will see," replies Vettellini. Then he confounds her by saying that he is perfectly aware of her intention to stop the cod liver oil. He tells me to watch her and, if need be, scold her.

The séance is closing and Reine remembering that she is not to see her "grand ami" for several days, begins again to grieve. She looks at him with affection, speaks of his appearance, remarks his beautiful hair and asks if she may touch it. He refuses, but she risks a little hand just the same: "Oh! ... why, it's real! It feels just like hair!" she exclaims in delight.

At the moment of waking her she asks me if I am sure I have not forgotten the way to do it. I have already laughed at her fear of being stuck in the Astral, saying it would not be such a great misfortune, people did not seem to be so badly off there. "No,—but you see I wouldn't have my Armand," was her reply.

THIRTIETH SÉANCE

March 5, 1913

I was hoping to learn today if the prediction concerning the artist M. had been realized. It is a fact. Everything has happened as Vettellini announced it. *Yesterday, Tuesday, M. deposited with Reine's concierge an envelope for her. This envelope contained two five-franc pieces.*

The first part of the second prediction has also been realized. *Reine's mother received yesterday a letter from Vierzon saying that her own mother was very ill and that she must come at once if she wished to find her living.* She obtained from her employers permission and the necessary advance to leave Saturday evening. They allow her Sunday no longer. Vettellini predicted an absence of three days. We will see.

Today I begin earlier, having an engagement at six o'clock. The sleep seems good, but Reine does not grow as cold as at the last séance. I force myself to intensify the passes. Suddenly she springs forward, seeming to suffocate. She tries to speak, but only stammers unintelligibly. For a second she listens, then indicates by gestures that I must disengage her chest, and especially her heart—which, in truth, is hardly beating. She is stifling. I work quickly, and little by little she grows easier, breathes more freely, and finally is delivered from an anguish in which I have most acutely shared for several moments.

She begins by saying that she has done almost nothing. She went out three times, wandering about at hazard, surprised to find herself alone, and, at moments, lacking strength to go further. Once, she went into a fine house, mounted the staircase, knocked at the door, and then came back here ... like that, without knowing why. (This must have been the result of an order to go and see my friend O., which I gave in magnetizing her). At another moment she found herself in the Luxembourg gardens and she describes the Carpeaux fountain, which she has never seen, and which interested her greatly. Her hands and feet have not become cold; but, on the contrary, her chest, "way inside," was like ice; and her heart almost stopped beating. She was frightened! ... I see that she was not conscious of the orders that I gave in magnetizing,—probably because of her fright in finding herself alone. I recall to her the incidents of the last séance and assure her that Vettellini was undoubtedly watching over her all the time, invisible himself, because he wishes her to rely upon her own efforts. Seeing her comforted and confident once more, I decide to push the exercise no further today and begin the passes to waken her.

But her hand arrests me sharply. She looks eagerly to the right and utters a cry of pure joy: "Ah-ha! It is you! Oh! Monsieur Cornillier, he is here,—Vettellini!" and, alive with emotion, Reine leans forward, grasps and caresses invisible hands, laughs and babbles like a child wild with joy: "Ah, well,—this is a surprise! Ah? ... Yes? ... We were so good? Ah, yes—not to ask questions ... and not to try to make you come! And so you come to please us? ... Ah, well—*we are pleased!*" and, charmingly, she turns to associate me in this rejoicing. I must admit that we, too, are smiling.

Vettellini says that all has gone well. He was there watching her, ready to intervene if need be. It was he who communicated that I must disengage her heart. It was he, too, who made her come back from her excursions, "because," explains Reine, "he says you have to go out at six o'clock." (I had not mentioned this fact to her). I have the feeling that we are watched and guarded ... and that Reine risks no harm under these conditions. Finally they say "au revoir," and I waken my medium.

THIRTY-FIRST SÉANCE

March 7, 1913

Today we have made a step forward. Reine has obeyed me and, quite unaided, has gone where I wished to send her.

We begin at three-thirty, and an hour later I order her to go to O.'s house, rue Miromesnil. After a moment I question her. She replies that she has obeyed me, but that she is back here again because she could not pass through the door of the apartment; she had not enough strength. She heard voices of people talking inside, but she did not know how to enter. So then she came down over the stairs again, following a gentleman who came out from an apartment on the second floor, and, not knowing what else to do, she accompanied him a little while; but finally, feeling tired, she came back here.

I begin again the magnetizing, and, when she seems to have absorbed a good dose of fluid, renew my order, but more imperiously this time. The second attempt is more successful. She enters the apartment and finds O., whom she recognizes, seated at his desk. He is not alone. A lady is there, in an armchair on the right; her costume is simple and dark. I ask for details, but Reine sees masses without distinguishing the details. She sees the movement of O.'s lips, hears a murmur of voices, but cannot catch the words. The conversation ceases. O. bends his head as though reflecting, then turns to write. The lady waits.[25] But Reine loses force, the scene grows dark, she wants to come back and does not

---

[25] See note at the end of the Thirty-third Séance.

know how to do so. I indicate the means, and after a few instants she announces that she is here—just above her physical body.

Noticing her fatigue, I am on the point of waking her when she seems to perceive something of interest.

It is a light in the room which grows bigger and more precise, begins to look like a cloudy form, she says. A head forms in the upper part of it. She seems to feel rather shy of it, but I encourage her to go nearer and find out what this cloud is. After some hesitation she obeys and says it is a woman's head, very beautiful,—with long red hair. Then she gathers courage and questions the apparition, who replies: "Pray for me,"... and "Be good." I remark that we can pray for her to better advantage if we know who she is. "Jeanne," she replies. I insist, and she gives her family name, Kemikow (or Kcmirow). Her given name is Jane, not Jeanne. She is Russian. She comes here sometimes because she is happy here. I try to have something more, but Reine says she has disappeared.

My medium is much pleased: "you know, that is good. I saw her all by myself! I have worked alone today. It is good!" Suddenly the cry of joy: "Vettellini!" He too is pleased. We have only to persevere. I must insist next time, and send her back to the same place until she is able to see details. After that I must send her further, and still further, training her in this way until she obeys me immediately and completely. He tells me how to direct her without fatiguing her so much. Then a discussion ensues between them. He wants her to tell me something that she does not care to talk about. It is a little trouble with a neighbor who tries to borrow money from her. Vettellini says that when Reine wakens I must warn her against the woman, with whom she must have no further relations.

I waken her after ordering her to come here tomorrow evening (during her natural sleep, that is, in a sortie of her astral body), at ten o'clock, to observe what we are doing. She is so tired that she falls into a doze immediately, but in a quarter of an hour is herself again.

THIRTY-SECOND SÉANCE

March 10, 1913

T he work is slow, but Reine certainly sees with more precision
and rapidity.

I magnetize her for a long time before sending her on her
habitual visit to my friend O. She obeys me at once without hesitation,
says she sees O. in his office, writing. He is alone. "The letter he is writing is not a friendly letter; it is like ... lawyers' letters. It is important." I
try to discover the general object of the missive, but she sees, only the
preoccupation of the writer, notices the paper, says it has an engraved
heading, distinguishes the lines perfectly well, but cannot read them.
I tell her to manifest her presence. She tries, says that she is making
the furniture crack, is turning around him, touching him. Without being sure of it, she thinks he is conscious of something unusual, for he
stops writing to look around. I tell her to make his eyeglasses fall. She
concentrates all her force, her hand makes a swift, short gesture, and
she bursts out laughing: "It's done! It fell!"—You are sure, Reine, absolutely sure, that you made the eyeglasses fall?—"Oh, yes, I know I did!
He picked them up, and fixed them on his nose again. Oh, yes, they
fell all right, but he doesn't know I did it!" I tell her to do it again. She
tries once more, visibly making a great effort, sighing and trembling:
"No—I cannot; he put them back too firmly. The first time I could do
it because he had been wearing them a while, and they slipped easily—but now they are well fixed." She says that he is getting ready to go
out. She tries to attract his attention, thinks he is vaguely conscious of

something unusual. He rises, opens a door ... But Reine sees nothing more, her force is exhausted. I order her to return here.[26]

What about my order for Saturday night? She says that at ten o'clock Saturday evening she suddenly fell into hypnotic sleep (her words are "into a sleep like this one now") and found herself here in the little salon, but hearing strange voices she had not dared to enter the studio; so she seated herself on the chair near the window and through the half opened door she saw there were some people with us—ladies and gentlemen.[27]—But why did you not come in? We were there; and expecting you.— "Yes, I know, but I was afraid they would see me."— But what difference would that make? You would have been well received.—"Oh, but—(Reine seems confused) I was in my nightdress."

She goes on to say that after watching us for some time she went down to the fifth floor, where she first inspected the dining room, and then Madame Cornillier's room. (And here her astral visit, which up to this time might have been purely imaginary, assumes character: for Reine does not know this room, yet she describes it very exactly, furniture, bibelots, the brushes and toilet accessories in ivory, etc., etc. She mentions a large reproduction of my picture *Le Pelerin* at the head of the bed, and a marine sketch on the side, and a portrait of me in an oval frame. All the details are exact.) Then she came back to the sixth floor, saw we were drinking something, and not knowing what more to do, she went home.

Spontaneously she adds: "Vettellini helped me in all this, I would not have had force enough alone. He opened my eyes. When I was home again he made me pass from hypnotic sleep into natural sleep, and I did not waken until morning."

My wife, obliged to go out, has said that she would try to be back in time to help with an experiment, but she does not come. Impatient, I ask Reine to try to find her and tell me if I may expect her soon. She is about to obey when I see a joyful smile and hear her mumbling to herself. It is Vettellini who appears. He says that Madame Cornillier is coming; she is in the street now, she will be here in two minutes. And, indeed, my wife arrives almost immediately.

I ask her to go into the room behind the studio, there to make some gestures (which only she will know) and to pronounce aloud, and several times, a number,—any number. I will send Reine's double to observe

---

[26] See note at the end of the Thirty-third Séance.

[27] A fact. But Reine knew nothing about it.

the scene. I magnetize Reine more deeply, then send her into the room mentioned. She finds the door of this room closed. (Correct.) In obedience to my order she enters, but everything is black, she distinguishes nothing and says that we are both too tired. Finally, however, she perceives a form, "It is a woman,—a tall woman." All of a sudden she recognizes the person.[28] "Why, it is Madame Cornillier." She sees her two hands stretched far apart and holding something, (correct) but cannot say what it is. She hears her speaking, but cannot catch what she says. I insist, but with no better success. The experiment is null, or almost so. I call Reine back.

Vettellini warns me that tonight and tomorrow I shall be very tired, for Reine has taken much of my force today. He says I must take a stiff drink and something to eat immediately after the séance, and adds that I ought to be pleased, for the little that Reine did at O.'s house was done with rapidity and decision.

I take advantage of Vettellini's satisfaction to ask for a prediction that would fill all requirements. Will he tell me, first, if the three years' service law will be voted? Second, at what date? Third, by how many votes? After a moment he says that he believes he can do this. On Wednesday he will have Reine write his answer.

Here he gives us other information, unimportant it is true, but whose realization would nonetheless have an evidential value. This evening Reine will receive a letter from her mother, who left Saturday night to pass Sunday at Vierzon, Vettellini having said that she would be absent three days. This letter announces her return tomorrow (Tuesday) night, which makes exactly the three days. Reine will have a surprise; her mother will bring her some apples. As to her father, he has not left Paris. Reine draws back in dismay. Vettellini tells her to fear nothing, he will prevent him from going to see her.[29]

---

[28] It must be remembered that Reine in hypnosis sees nobody but me. She becomes conscious of the presence of my wife only when I put them into relation with each other.

[29] Although Reine's father remained in Paris for more than a month after this date, he made no attempt to see his daughter, whereas usually he went to her often for assistance.

THIRTY-THIRD SÉANCE

March 12, 1913

The realization of the small events predicted by Vettellini in the last séance must first be noted. On Monday evening Reine did receive a letter from her mother, announcing her return on the following evening, making exactly the period of absence predicted, and, on arriving at the station where Reine was awaiting her, she joyfully presented her daughter with a basket containing eight fine apples. The grandmother is still living. In short, *all has happened as it was foretold.*

We begin at the usual hour. I feel in good form, and magnetize deeply. Thinking Reine in the proper condition, I try to send her once more to O.'s house. But I obtain no reply whatever, nor any sign of obedience; so I continue the passes a while longer, then order her more imperiously. She appears to be bewildered and as though returning from a long distance; her voice is faint when she says that she is going where I sent her.

After a time she announces that she sees O. at his desk; he is preoccupied and annoyed; his hands are clasping his head. Now he begins to write,—on the same paper as before; he uses purple ink. Reine tries to manifest her presence by making his eyeglasses fall again, but has no success. She passes into an adjoining room where she says she hears a voice. Here we have a slight discussion about the plan of the apartment. I thought Reine had made a topographical error but am obliged to admit that it is I who am mistaken. In this room, which she calls a sleeping-room (*chambre* à *dormir*), a lady is standing—a tall lady, dressed in a black or dark blue tailor suit, with a white chemisette. She is not wearing a hat, etc., etc.

Suddenly conscious of great indiscretion, I call Reine back, deciding to abandon this imprudent investigation until I shall have the assent of the victim, at least.

The nerveless attitude of the medium surprised me, for I myself felt unusual vitality today. She seems dull and heavy. I cannot understand it. I am about to send her on another excursion when she begins speaking in a low voice. Evidently her Guide is present. Immediately I inquire the reason of the failure and learn that it is my own stupidity. Reine was plunged in profound hypnosis. Never before has she attained that degree. And I should not have insisted when she did not reply to my first order. *She was beginning to see things and beings of another plane.* To obey me, she came back, all influenced still by the etherean atmosphere. Thus, quite unintentionally, I have cut off *a new phenomenon and one of infinitely higher import than our habitual experiments.* My brusque recall has startled and troubled Reine and is the cause of her apathy and indecision.

I ask how I am to know when to give orders and when to wait. Vettellini tells me to call her softly three times. If she does not reply, I am to continue the passes, enjoining her at the same time to observe more and more precisely whatever she may be seeing at that moment. As soon as her observation is made, she will come back of her own accord to recount it; and when this is done, I may send her off on an excursion for my own purposes.

Spontaneously Reine asks for writing materials. She writes: "The law of three years will be voted March 25, 1913." So far so good, but I wish to know by what number of votes. It is absolutely necessary if the information is to be considered of transcendental origin. One might foresee the date and the result of the vote; but the date, the vote, and the number of the majority vote, make a platform difficult to upset. Vettellini says that he will give the rest on Friday. (I silently reflect that the twenty-fifth of March will be the Tuesday after Easter. The deputies will undoubtedly take the Easter vacation, and it is highly improbable that the law will be voted that day.)

Thinking of an unhappy cousin, who has been in a hospital for over a year now, I ask what insanity really is? Vettellini answers that insanity exists because the Spirit has abandoned the body; that the intermittent states of madness and reason come from the fact that the Spirit has abandoned the body, or has again returned to it. This is, after all, rather evident, but leads, little by little, to an unexpected statement: "A new faculty," says Reine, "will develop before long in certain specially good mediums. They will be able not only to hear the words of a person with whom they are conversing, but they will at the same moment penetrate his thought." There will thus be two versions of the phenomenon of a thought that is exteriorized in words: First, the intrinsic thought, second, its translation into words. Reine—this ignorant and unlettered person—explains to us that thought, which takes form in the brain under the impulsion of the Spirit, is distorted by language. In almost every case its expression in words is only a loose and unfaithful translation. There will be, in the future, a possibility of psychological analysis that will have enormous value. "That is new," says Reine, "it has never yet been realized by a medium, but it will come soon."

I prepare to waken her, but she says she is not obliged to go home early because her mother is coming to prepare the dinner. But Vettellini informs her that her mother will not come tonight. "Oh, yes she will," retorts Reine, "the dinner is for her. It's her anniversary. She wouldn't miss it!" But Vettellini repeats that she would do better not to count on it: "She will not be able to leave this evening. She will be kept."

Reine is already displeased, but she grows furious when Vettellini adds that she also need not count upon posing tomorrow for the prince de L. who has engaged her for several sittings. "He will send you word this evening not to go tomorrow."—"I shall have a letter?" "No, not a letter," explains Vettellini, "he will send his *garçon d'atelier* to inform you. He will ask you to postpone the sitting till Saturday. But think no more about him; he will not employ you." Poor Reine is vexed. It is not every day one poses for a prince!

When she is awake I tell her what Vettellini has said, but she is confident. "That cannot be so. It's all arranged with my mother. The dinner is for her. She has permission to come."

March 14. All happened as Vettellini stated. Neither mother nor prince for the poor little Reine.

Verification of Reine's Four Visits at the House of My Friend O.

Circumstances are such that it is only on the fifth of January, 1914, that I go to see O., to try to ascertain whether or not he was at home the afternoons of February 24, and March 7, 10, and 12 (1913), between four and five o'clock.

I had little hope that O. could give me precise information, for he is frequently absent, and eight long months have passed since these visits of Reine. But it was perfectly easy for him to give me an absolutely certain reply on this point, first, by consulting a memorandum book of 1913, second by opening his letter press, where he found the copies of business letters written at these dates, thus establishing his presence in his office on those afternoons. On the other hand, the lady discovered there by Reine is the stenographer who goes to O.'s office regularly every day, staying a longer or shorter time as need be. She removes her hat in another room before coming in to take down his letters, and she always sits in the chair where Reine perceived her. Naturally, I was unaware of her existence.

Without wishing to exaggerate the value of these four experiments, they nevertheless constitute—and especially when taken in connection with other similar demonstrations—a serious basis for belief in the positive reality of Reine's astral visits.

THIRTY-FOURTH SÉANCE

March 14, 1913

We begin at three-thirty. I magnetize as has been indicated, and then in a low voice speak Reine's name three times. At the third call she mutters a little. Concluding that I may command her, I send her to the house of friends in Passy—giving her, as usual, the itinerary to follow. She enters the apartment easily enough, notices the arrangement and mentions characteristic details; finds no one present except a servant, who is cleaning silver in the kitchen. All that she describes is exact as to form, but the color is not correct. It is the value of the tones and the degrees of light that strike her attention.

Once more I am struck by the fact that her descriptions do not conform to the ideas or images that are existing consciously in my mind. If this is mind-reading, it is nevertheless strange that never, never, does she read a thought of which my mind is conscious, or one which is held in my normal memory; and that she discovers only impressions or memories which I ignore, and which are quite contrary to the habitual character of my observation. As a matter of fact, when she describes a place that I know, she never mentions the details that I have in my mind.

I make her come back to try another experiment with my wife, whom I again ask to go into the room behind the atelier, sending Reine's double to observe her. An indifferent result,—a little truth with many hesitations and inaccuracies. Reine deliberately affirms that a red scarf is green, but she easily sees form and motion; she perceives the vibrations of speech, yet cannot seize the words. In short, nothing remarkable is obtained, but a certain particularity in her observation gives hope that the training will lead to good results.

When her astral body comes back, she asks for writing materials. Vettellini is evidently dictating. She listens, writes, interrupts to stretch her head in his direction, and again her pencil scratches the paper. Then she says that Vettellini, fearing that she may make a mistake in writing figures, asks her to speak aloud what he has just made her write. It is the number of the votes for the three-years' service law: "Tuesday, March 25, 1913, the law of three years will be voted by 410 or 430 votes. There may be a delay, on account of the Easter vacation, but in that case I will warn you." And he adds, "I cannot be more definite, for at the last minute certain deputies will change their vote."

I am far from satisfied, and say so. The prediction, as it stands, might be made by any one at all familiar with the political situation. Impossible to make use of it as an example of transcendental knowledge.

Disappointed, I turn to another subject. Can a table move without the presence of a Spirit? Answer: "It is perfectly possible. But for that the vibratory conditions of the people gathered around the table must be in harmony, so that, united, their fluid may have a force that will dominate terrestrial attraction. In these circumstances a table may move and rise. He adds that it would even be possible to get replies, to establish a sort of conversation if, the people present being of the same mentality, there should be produced, by the amalgam of their fluids, a potential force representing the average of their combined mentalities. This force might seem for a few moments to have an independent existence and could make replies; which replies, it must be remembered, could never be any other than the combined ideas, conscious or unconscious, of the group.

A similar phenomenon may occur in automatic writing, when the Spirit of the medium who is writing—being partially disengaged—may reply to his own thoughts and questions.

At this moment I have a great desire to know Vettellini's view of certain family questions, and, to feel quite free, I ask my wife to leave me for a few moments alone.

She leaves the room, and I explain the case which preoccupies me, asking for an opinion—for advice. To my stupefaction the reply is neither a counsel nor an opinion: it is a complete exposition of the moral development of each person concerned, a profound and close analysis of our characters and of the situation. Reine transmits with volubility.

It seems that Vettellini is informed of our most intimate relations. He knows the characters, the tendencies, the temperaments, their mutual action and reaction, and their antecedents! My surprise changes to emotion, for his analysis is far more searching than my own, and his revelations exceed my judgment.

A small fact, of interest to me, has been confirmed. Last night about eleven o'clock, just after I had gone to bed, I distinctly saw (in the dark) a luminous spot at the foot of my bed. It lasted perhaps a second; then, an instant later came an exact and strange impression of vibrations of air whirling about me. I was sitting up to examine the luminous spot, and there is no doubt as to the objectivity of these two sensations.

When she came in today, Reine told me that she had gone to sleep last night concentrating all her will in the wish to send her double to see me. But she had no impression either of success or of failure. She slept well and remembered nothing. Now, during her hypnosis, I question her on this subject, and she replies that she came here about eleven o'clock, went to my room and tried to manifest her presence. She says that I certainly was aware of it, but only for a moment, although she stayed there a long time trying to impress me again.

The séance has been varied, but nothing in these notes can give an adequate idea of the relation between Reine and Vettellini, of the confidence which now exists between them, the respectful friendship that flashes now and then into a teasing mood; the tenderness, the sudden irritability, the cajolery of Reine, her mischievous malice, her gravity;—Ah, what marvelous play it is!

THIRTY-FIFTH SÉANCE

March 17, 1913

Acurious séance of unexpected interest.

Reine sleeps quite as usual, but just as I decide to cut short the passes and send her off on an excursion, I notice that she is grimacing and muttering with anxiety. Not wishing to interrupt, I defer my order and wait, my right hand resting on her forehead.

In a few moments she pushes my hand aside, sits upright and reveals by her gestures and attitudes that she is witnessing an impressive scene. She mumbles and mutters to herself; we seize the words: "What eyes,— what awful eyes! Fearful!" Then she leans over and says in a very soft whisper, as though speaking in someone's ear: "Then— it's a secret meeting? Yes, I understand." Little by little, thanks to the jumble of words and phrases which escape her, I come to understand that she is assisting at a secret gathering of revolutionists—socialists, anarchists, agitators, etc.,—assembled there to take measures to prevent the passing of the three-years' law. The meeting is held in a sort of subterranean hall having two exits, one of which is a cellar that gives on to a stretch of waste land, while the main, and obvious, door opens into a mean little alley-way. It is in the Ivry quarter. Reine has been carried there by Vettellini who explains to her the purpose of the gathering and the trend of the violent discussions. She cannot understand the words herself, perceiving only the vibrations of sound; but the tragic aspect of the crowd, the ferocity of their faces, terrifies her. She would like to be almost anywhere else. With an accent that betrays small confidence, she keeps saying: "Yes, yes, I understand, but—what if we just moved on, Vettellini?" And later, "Aren't we going now? It's suffocating here—such filthy air! And then you know ... I don't think it's so very amusing! ... They frighten me, those people. Come on, Vettellini,—let's just slip out, eh?" In spite of the drama that is passing, her nervousness is irresistibly comical.

Later, she explains that there are no seats in the hall, no furniture whatever—just four grimy walls; some boards, placed across two stumps, serve as platform to the speaker, and that is all. Their violence is extreme. Riots and all kinds of disturbances will be organized before the law comes up for vote; and if it is passed, then crime and assassination will follow. They are determined to prevent its execution. Oh, there will be a lot of trouble, it will be a hot and dreadful moment—blood will flow! ("What if we just slipped out now, eh?")

While Reine is giving her report of it, I wonder if the scene may not be an image that Vettellini has created, to illustrate the attitude of the working classes. To my inquiry she says that she does not know, for she cannot distinguish the difference between an image and a reality. She will ask her Guide. This is his curious reply: "I did indeed actually carry Reine (her astral body, while she was sleeping) to witness this gathering which took place late on Saturday night. She was really present there, and saw for herself exactly what she has just described to you. But, on her return home, she continued her night of natural sleep, and completely forgot the whole scene. So then, for your information, today, I have simply made the image of the scene pass before her identically as she had witnessed it. I have made her live over again, one by one, the moments she passed in that place last Saturday night."

This leads me to ask if it is impossible for our human intelligence to understand how future events can pre-exist in the Astral. Vettellini replies that for the moment he cannot explain the mechanism to me, but that I shall gradually become acquainted with other phenomena that will naturally and logically lead to a comprehension of this one. He promises it. Here Reine, speaking for herself, announces that it will be she, and not Vettellini, who will make me to understand the law of this phenomenon. "You see, Vettellini could not make it clear to you, if he were to try to explain a fact so far beyond our usual conceptions. It is too far away from us, all that. He sees it from the other side, but he cannot hand it on to us, because there are no words in our language corresponding to it. But he will make me experience the phenomenon, and I will translate it, as well as I can, into our own words. Vettellini says it will be possible because in this, as in all other phenomena, known or unknown to us, there is a logic which can be reduced to a form comprehensible to our human brain."

She goes on to say that even already she knows something about it herself: "They are not, as you seem to think, images that exist in the Astral.—No, they are *waves* that keep following one after the other,—*fluids*, which the high Spirits perceive and analyze. Oh, I shall understand it all in the end, but there are heaps of things I must see first."

To change the subject I ask Reine what she did on Sunday night.—"I came here."— "What do you mean by 'here!' I did not feel your presence."—"Oh, I surely came, but after the fatigue of my day at Meudon I had no force left. I went to the fifth floor and sat there by the door, on a big trunk covered with huge nails[30] waiting till I should get strength to manifest myself. But I could not ... and after a long time, I went home."

I ask Vettellini if in the course of one of Reine's astral visits here, her double could not enter into conversation with mine. By concentrating my will at the moment of sleeping I might possibly provoke the disengagement of my double. "He says that this is perfectly possible, we might make the experiment, but it will be a great fatigue for me. Moreover, in his program of future communications, he has reserved a place for this very question, which is far more important than I suspect. As a matter of fact, not only can the astral body of a person sleeping go to converse with another astral body, but more than that, by following a special training, he may be able to secure information and proofs concerning life in the Astral *and retain it integrally in memory.* He affirms that it is a question of training. It will be possible to be quite independent of mediums, and to acquire directly for oneself, and by oneself, knowledge which, at the present average of evolution, can be obtained only through an intermediary—who, in many cases, transmits but a mangled version of the information received. This will be one of the most important acquisitions of mankind in the future. By their own powers people will secure indubitable proofs of the soul's survival."

A perplexing point. It has seemed to me that in her fluidic promenades Reine has an exact perception of forms and values, but not at all the vision of color. Is this a lack of force? Or is it the rational consequence of her state? Vettellini says that this non-perception of colors comes from the conditions of her hypnotic state. Her spirit, disengaged, distinguishes lights and shades, but color vibrations affect it indifferently. Sometimes it perceives the complementary color. But this special vision may be developed by training.

---

[30] Exact—an old oak chest.

THIRTY-SIXTH SÉANCE

March 19, 1913

When Reine is thoroughly magnetized I call her three times, and, as there is no response, I continue the passes, giving her no order other than to observe carefully what she is seeing and report it to me faithfully at the end. After about fifteen minutes she stirs a little, shivers, hunts for my hand and, with considerable difficulty, begins to speak.

She says she is tired—oh, very tired!—she went up so high. Yes, today she felt herself attracted towards the clouds, through which she had passed, only to go on further still,—oh, high, high up! And then, suddenly, she found Vettellini, who was waiting there to show her the inhabitants of that big ethereal space. It is crowded with Spirits, and he wanted Reine to observe them in their normal life and under their natural aspect, when no terrestrial influence affects them. Reine tries to give me a description, but it is not an easy task. With her astral senses she has seen substances and matter that our corporal eyes could not perceive, and her meager vocabulary can give no adequate expression of her visions. The terms, which she finds with greatest effort, do not in the least satisfy her.

The space in which she found herself was filled with Spirits of various evolutions, whose grade she immediately recognized by their color. There were none there, however, of very low evolution and few of very high. The low ones stay in our terrestrial atmosphere, while the very high ones withdraw to spaces far distant from our planet. She was in a region where an honorable average is maintained.

The word "sparks" does not satisfy her,—nor "flames," nor "gleams," nor "phosphorescent clouds," nor "tongues of fire." No, nothing is just right. Evidently our language cannot depict it.—The general form of these lights seems to be oblong; their dimension, about that of a large hand. These luminous forms contain the Spirit—the consciousness, the will, the whole potential force of the being—and they intercommunicate by emanation, by vibratory impressions.

Reine talks at length about them, but without great clearness,—which is perfectly comprehensible. Vettellini is there, aids her a little, corrects her sometimes, adds a detail or a new bit of information which frequently Reine cannot transmit, telling me "There's no word for that." He makes me understand, however, that the highly evolved Spirits who are in these regions are passing through a phase which will advance them still further in the hierarchy of evolution.

I gather also that in these superior degrees the notion of "evil," as we conceive it on earth, no longer exists. But it persists after death in Spirits of inferior evolution, *who retain in the Astral their habitual mode of thought.*

Vettellini also made Reine assist at the creation of images and scenes by means of which the Spirits sometimes, subjectively or objectively, impress those who are incarnate. From her description, the method of procedure would seem analogous to that which is employed when a Spirit creates the idea or image of garments and accessories (of which a rational theory is given in the sixteenth séance). It is merely a much more complicated operation in proportion to the complexity of the images or scenes desired; and one which often requires an organized band of workers, who gather up the essential, material elements that constitute these images, which are afterwards projected in the physical plane.

All this may be of indifferent interest to those who read it in cold print. One should hear Reine and witness her amazement when she sees—or believes she sees—these extraordinary activities of astral life.—"And you have no idea how clever they are, those Spirits!" she exclaims in excitement, "crowds of them are working at that—going to and fro all the time to get bits of the people and the things they need to make their pictures with!"

Abandoning these speculations, I ask Vettellini what exactly takes place when, following his instructions, I make the passes along Reine's arms and body, chasing away the air that surround her, so to speak. This is his reply:

The fluidic body slightly exceeds the contour of the material body, forming in this way a kind of aura. To induce hypnotic sleep in Reine, and to make her cold, I must drive her fluidic or astral body from her physical body; and the more complete this disengagement is, the more profound will be her state of hypnosis. The passes of expulsion that I make along the arms, chest, legs, etc., serve to separate and push away from her physical body that portion of her double which already lies outside it—the aura. This aura, once separated, goes immediately to join the main mass of her double, which has condensed at some distance from Reine, and which has disengaged under the influence of my will in my first profound passes.

As Reine's astral body leaves her, my own replaces it and, following the direction that hers has taken, goes finally to join her double, thus adding my energy to hers. First it is my aura that goes to her from the tips of my fingers; then follows a small portion of the mass of my double. Reine says: "You must reach the point where you give me about three quarters. Just now you are giving only one quarter, perhaps. But each day you send a little more, and soon the quantity will be sufficient for you to control and command me as though I were yourself. Naturally, this is a fatigue for you, but it will not really affect your health. There is, of course, a certain loss of substance; all that you give will not come back to you; just as I, too, leave some of myself in the course of my excursions. But this force is quickly regained. After a few hours of rest we are about normal again."

Here I ask if auto-magnetization is possible. Vettellini understands by this that I am thinking of the yoga practice, the voluntary provocation of the "sortie" of the astral body, and replies by explaining the training necessary to acquire it. But I have no such ambition. I merely wished to know if by intense concentration, one could arrive at a curative modification of one's self, correct a certain feebleness of will, for example; mitigate nervous troubles, or physical ills of any kind.

Vettellini says that good results can certainly be obtained in this direction and that he will give me a progressive method if I wish.

The political situation, so intense just now, forms the subject of my last inquiry. Vettellini says that it is impossible to know what will happen, so complex are the elements and so varying from day to day. It is the most dangerous crisis that France has known for many a year and it is the beginning of the troubles announced. He sees only one fact written with precision in the Astral: Poincaré will last no longer than November, 1913. Here Reine exclaims sharply: "That's no kind of a prediction! Why, I said that to Monsieur Cornillier myself before the séance!" She is indignant that Vettellini should do no better than she, and continues rather irritably: "How do I know it? Well, how can I know it? I haven't read it, and I haven't heard it. Talking with Armand, this morning, I thought if the three-years law passes, they'll make Poincaré resign—or they'll finish him somehow; and when I came in today, I said so to Monsieur Cornillier. You'll have to do better than that, Vettellini,—I don't call that a prediction!"

The good Vettellini takes his medicine tranquilly, satisfied to repeat, "A note must be made of it. Poincaré will last no longer than November, 1913." He adds that in November the war will be virtually engaged, ... begun, or on the point of beginning. I am a good deal of Reine's opinion. It is not a prediction, that!

THIRTY-SEVENTH SÉANCE

March 21, 1913

A good séance of information. I decided to send Reine to visit a maternity hospital and give a description of what she observed there. The experiment has succeeded. Reine has seemed to really see, and has replied clearly to my questions concerning the relations existing between the Spirit in course of incarnation and the mother. She spoke with such decision and authority that I supposed she was inspired by her Guide. But no, she energetically maintained that it was she herself, she all alone, who was observing and reporting. "I am more sure of what I am telling you than I could be of anything told to me, even by Vettellini,—and you know my confidence in him. But this I see and know by myself. It's as true as truth."

Sleep is normal. The body grows cold. I call Reine three times. At the third call she groans and says feebly that she is ready to go where I wish. I have chosen the "Refuge Maternel" for the experiment and give her the itinerary without letting her know, of course, the character of the house nor the purpose of her visit.

After a few seconds she says she is in a house; in a room, where women are seated, working, sewing, etc. These women are all in different stages of pregnancy. (I was surprised at what she said, for I had supposed she would see a dormitory with women in bed, before or after confinement. It was only later, when I went to inform myself, that I found Reine had made no mistake. I learned that confinements do not take place in the "Refuge." Women are received there, where they are given some light work to do,—sewing, making layettes, etc.,—and two days before the probable date of delivery they are sent to another house for their accouchement. The point is interesting.)

I order Reine to take all the time necessary to observe carefully, and try to perceive the captured Spirits in course of incarnation. After some moments of examination she begins to speak. Her information comes in some disorder due for a large part to the surprise of her observations and the unexpected questions with which I pursue her. I will not attempt to reproduce the curious dialogue but will give only the conclusion that may be drawn from it, as a theory of the process of incarnation.

The sexual act is really the snare in which the Spirit is caught.[31] Whether in complete ignorance (the case of inferior Spirits), or whether in conscious purpose (the case of superior Spirits), he is captured; and henceforth he belongs to the earth. During the first two or three months he is relatively free, and it is only occasionally that he comes to visit his house that is building; but, as time advances and his dwelling takes form, his visits become more frequent. He comes to give his measures, to intimate his desires, to make, in short, his own personal imprint. Towards the seventh month he takes possession of his little body, establishes himself in it, and makes it his. From this time on he rarely leaves it and, finally, at the moment of delivery, becomes its definite prisoner; not only because of his intimate union with the organism, but also because his own individual conscience, memory, etc., is completely veiled and stupefied by the physico-chemical condition in which he is plunged.

This is the general rule. But the rule has various readings and diverse modes, whose causes we must investigate.

An inferior Spirit, captured by chance (or, rather, submitting to higher forces which he does not comprehend) may indolently accept the imprisonment or, on the contrary, he may struggle like an animal held in leash, escaping as often and as far as possible, returning only during the months preceding the deliverance; it depends upon his force of reaction,—his individuality and character. But if he does not come in time to fashion and prepare his dwelling place, he runs the risk of finding one inadequate to his needs; there will be faults in the construction; a lack of harmony between the house and its tenant. (This

---

[31] This statement is not absolutely exact, but as precise corrections are to be found later on, I leave the passage as I understood it at the time.

lack of correspondence between Spirit and organism, which results from the indolence or the resistance of an inferior Spirit, must not be confounded with an infirmity accepted or imposed, as expiation, or as means of refining and developing sensibility).

A highly evolved Spirit may sometimes consciously and voluntarily incarnate, choosing his progenitors. He knows the law of reincarnation, knows that it is beneficent, and submits to it with resignation; for this suction of spirit by matter, this slow absorption of the conscious into the unconscious is painful. It is in itself a rude ordeal, sufficient sometimes to crown an evolution.

As has already been said, stillborn children are always of high evolution, as are also those who die in premature accouchement. (Reine remarks: "After the seventh month the individual exists; to destroy him is a criminal act, and those who do destroy are responsible.")

Children who die young are also superior Spirits. Often complete imprisonment in the organism does not take place for them. Knowing their destiny, they do not take the trouble to form their dwelling, leaving the organism to live a merely animal life (when life is to be so short that it plays no part in the ordeal).

There are, however, beings,—but this is rare—whose physical development is never achieved, and who grow old in a state of idiocy. This would seem to be a horrible expiation, ... the redemption of tragic faults in a precedent life? ... "It is perhaps," says Reine, "the most bitter of all expiations, for these Spirits are conscious. They do not inhabit their bodies completely, they are simply attached to them, and so retain a part of consciousness which causes them acute anguish. We must be kind to these people and help them, but without commiserating them, for that merely aggravates their suffering."

I ask Reine if in a maternity hospital, such as this to which I have sent her, the Spirits in course of incarnation have intercourse amongst themselves.—"No, the fact of their capture isolates them, veils their astral perceptions; they do not perceive each other."

Such is the theory that Reine's observations, and her innate knowledge, have allowed me to establish on this subject.

Now I ask her to come back and try to give a manifestation of the presence of her fluidic body in the room where we are. She seems to work with the best possible will, but to no effect. Decidedly she is not a medium for material phenomena. There are signs of impatience ... I do not insist.

I put various questions in regard to her double, questions that give rise to a discussion with Vettellini. First, by what part of her physical body does the mass of her fluidic body make its exit? She answers that it comes out from "all over": "Tiny infinitesimal parcels escape from all over my body like a foam or mist, and go immediately to form themselves into a mass at some distance from me." I refer to a number of observations that would establish the fact that the double leaves the body at a certain point,—the side, the heart, the solar plexus, the head? She says this may be true, but exceptionally; a medium may have a resisting organism, but with a weak point, an open door, through which the double passes.—Where does the double enter the body again?— "By all the pores of the body, along the whole surface ... just as it went out."—It would seem that sometimes it enters at the nape of the neck!—"Yes, exceptionally, and the reason is the same as for its exit at a certain point."

Finally I come to speak of the experiments of certain savants, made by means of two mediums, one observing the other. The observing medium sees the double of the other one coming from his body by two distinct outlets, and condensing to form two columns, one on the right and one on the left of the subject observed; the right column generally blue in color, the left red. In continuing the magnetization, these two columns reunite and the phantom then forms in normal volume and outline. This description provokes the stupefaction of Vettellini, who protests roundly, and asks how it could possibly be so. "The fluidic body has its own color corresponding to its evolution. It may be red or blue,—but not both at the same time. And why these two columns? It is absurd!"

I cite my authorities, which are weighty ones; ask if there might not be a question of positive and negative polarity, speak of the magnetic emanations coming from each hand, of the loadstone whose positive pole is seen blue by psychics, while the negative pole is seen red, etc., etc. But he is in no way influenced, and affirms that M. de Rochas and others have misinterpreted certain phenomena; that their conclusions are incorrect. He thinks that he, Vettellini, ought to know something about it! Never has he observed an anomaly like that in the Astral. How could it be so—logically? And he winds up by declaring that in the Au-Delà phenomena have their logic just as they have on earth. I insist no further, promising myself to return to this point from another direction.

We pass to the explanation of a tale Reine told on her arrival today, when she was still under the influence of an extraordinary impression:

Last night, about one o'clock, having risen to draw water from the tap on the staircase, she perceived, on coming up the stairs, a gray vapor, which feebly lighted the space around her, and which had the rough outlines of a huge body. She did not think too much about it, but went quickly to bed again and fell asleep. During her sleep, she suddenly became conscious that a cloudy form, surmounted by a head, was looking at her, and she wakened to find the form in question standing at the foot of her bed. The head and face grew more and more precise; the expression became smiling and kind. She noticed all the details of face and head. It was that of a woman about fifty years old, thin, emaciated by illness; ardent black eyes; very black hair—braided; a black handkerchief tied around her head, peasant fashion; and—characteristic detail—a big black braid had escaped from the head-dress, and, falling heavily, stood out clearly against the gray and cloudy substance that formed the shoulder.

Reine, completely awake by this time, was already feeling a little frightened; but when she saw the form lean over and approach her face to kiss her, she had a violent emotion, and throwing herself back on the pillow, she hastily pulled the clothes tight over her head in wild fear. Her husband awoke and asked what the trouble was. She answered "Nightmare," but she knew well enough it was not nightmare; it was real. Such was her story. I asked if the phantom resembled her grandmother. She said that she was only ten years old when she left her grandmother, that she had detested her and had forgotten all about her. She thinks, however, that she wore the peasant coif, and she knows that she had black eyes.

Vettellini, to whom Reine now turns for explanation, knows better than she what has happened. "Yes, it was the Grandmother in Vierzon." "Dead?" I ask. "No, not dead, but in a sort of stupor which allows her spirit to leave her. She ardently wished to see her grandchild and kiss her before dying. That is why she came." Reine does not seem particularly touched by this tardy tenderness, and still less so when Vettellini informs her that the old lady will come again. On Sunday Reine will receive a letter from one of the family, giving information about her. She will die soon. I ask Vettellini if he cannot give me the date and hour of her death, but he says he cannot, adding rather vaguely that it might be about Easter.

We speak then of Reine's astral visits here in the evening. On Wednesday evening, about eleven o'clock, I distinctly saw, first, a very beautiful and strong phosphorescence, vibrating, followed by another less vivid, and, finally, a spark. On Thursday evening, nothing. She assures me that she came nevertheless, and tried to make the same manifestations.

Here Vettellini observes that to succeed she must eat nothing, or near-ly nothing for dinner,—as was the case on Wednesday. When she eats heartily she is too heavy, and does not disengage sufficiently.

Before waking her, I order Reine to come to the studio tomorrow evening about eleven o'clock (her double). Two or three friends anxious to know the history of our experiments are to dine with us. She must try to make some small manifestation of her presence,—a light, ... a noise, ... ring a bell. She says she will do her best to satisfy me.

THIRTY-EIGHTH SÉANCE

March 24, 1913

An interesting séance, in spite of the fact that the sleep was not very profound. Later on, Vettellini says that the atmospheric conditions were not favorable. But, though Reine's body did not become as cold as it should, I have obtained two quite different proofs of clairvoyance, one of which will be valuable if I am able to verify it. Valuable, too, the discussion with Vettellini on the subject of astral emanations, where it is once more proved that Reine does not adopt my ideas and beliefs as hers, but on the contrary expresses her own independent opinion, or, at least, one that is beyond my control.

On her arrival, she tells me that last evening after dinner, in her mother's room, she felt so weary that she had to throw herself on the bed. Once there, she fell into a sort of dull heaviness—retaining consciousness, however—her eyes wide open, hearing, understanding, but totally incapable of speaking or moving. Suddenly she saw me coming out from the shadow at the foot of the bed, my head well formed and very vivid, but the body in a kind of smoke. She looked at me for a few moments, then everything disappeared and the feeling of heaviness left her. She affirms that she certainly was awake and that certainly the apparition was objective. (Her words are "outside of me," "there before me.")

Of Saturday evening and night she has no recollection, no special impression.

When Reine is thoroughly magnetized I send her to R.'s house, Boulevard Montparnasse, ordering her to enter by the window, as I myself am unable to direct her by the staircase which is rather complicated. She enters the apartment easily, but once there seems confused and troubled; she sees nothing but black. Finally, little by little, she perceives that she is in the salon and describes it. First, on the left (entering by the window) she notices a "frame"—"a portrait of a woman, half-length."[32] But her attention is attracted to a strange piece of furniture which she hesitates to name. She never saw one like that before. It is a piano, but a mighty queer one. It's too big! (A concert grand.) She sees a table with books on it, a fireplace, and, on the mantelpiece, big vases. Then suddenly she discovers books, oh, any number of books, rows and rows of them!

There is no one in the room ... or in the apartment, through which I make her pass. She counts three rooms and a small kitchen; two of these rooms give on to the boulevard, with a view of the cemetery; the other one and the kitchen are in a sort of back wing and look out upon small buildings, she says. In "the room for sleep" she notices another portrait of a woman, but of an older woman; and this one also is half-length. She describes the dining room tritely. But suddenly she has the conviction that the people who live here are musicians. "It is full of music here." She sees, it is true, sheets of music and books of music, but her conviction does not come from that; *it comes from the special vibratory condition of the atmosphere.* She is not at all happy in this house; she feels horribly oppressed and depressed; she wishes I would call her back.

When she is here, I hand her a box that is closed, wrapped in paper and tied with string, and in which, this morning, I placed three objects: a brass barometer shaped like a watch, the little black wooden cup which is the support of her crystal ball, and a small bronze lizard. I order her to see what the box contains. She puts it on her lap, folding her hands around it, and remains like that, motionless, for a few instants. Then she describes the barometer: "it is like a big watch. It has a glass—and needles that point." Bravo! Then she sees something that is black. She sees it perfectly well, but cannot understand what it is. I insist. But in spite of her efforts she cannot classify the object, cannot make out "what it is for." When the idea occurs to me to change the relative positions of the objects in the box by shaking it lightly, she suddenly recognizes her support for the ball: "Why, that's mine! I see it very well now. It's the thing that holds my crystal ball. I couldn't make

---

[32] Exact—a reproduction of *la Joconde*. I did not know it was there.

it out because there was something else hanging on to it that length-ened it out, and I thought it was all one thing." This would show that she was not reading in my thought, but really saw the objects exactly as they were placed; and, judging from one or two remarks, her dou-ble seems to have really penetrated inside the box. After the second effort she fell back with a sigh of exhaustion: "Ah ...! I can tell you it's not easy to get into such a little box as that!"

I do not insist for the third object. Reine is too tired. I tell her to rest a little and then we will talk with Vettellini.

Returning to the subject of the last séance, I ask what it is that de-termines sex. Is it the incarnating Spirit? Is it the mother? The father? Or does it depend upon the physiological conditions of the moment? Has the alimentation of the mother an influence, as is pretended by some specialists?

Reine's language is limited in scientific terms, and she speaks with reserve on this subject, but here is a brief summary of Vettellini's reply:— The incarnating Spirit has nothing to do with the question of sex; no more has the physiological condition of the mother. Sex is determined by the semen of the male. The foetal formation is feminine when the semen has a relatively feeble vibration, masculine when the vibration is strong. And no influence in the course of pregnancy can change it.

I refer to artificial fecundation and ask at what moment, in such a case, the Spirit is incarnated. Reply:—The Spirit is captured the moment the spermatozöon penetrates the ovule. This process of fecundation is detrimental to the offspring, offering, as it does, the worst possible conditions for foetal formation, the orgasm being, if not an indispen-sable, at least a favorable condition of procreation.[33]

Having re-read the experiments of Colonel de Rochas and others, touching the question of the color of fluidic emanations, I express my conviction of the value of their opinion. But Vettellini makes no con-cession. He does not doubt the good faith of the experimenters, and is even convinced that before long, when they will have experimented further, and with other methods, they will recognize their error.—"The astral body has a mode of vibration which produces a corresponding color. This color is an expression of its state of being and of the densi-ty of its substance. How, then, should there be two colors at the same

---

[33] These questions are treated more completely later on.

moment? It can change in time; having been red, it may become blue. But it is quite impossible that it should be blue on one side and red on the other."

I speak of the portrait which I mean to try to make of him, after the descriptions that Reine has given from time to time. The idea pleases him and he says that he will help me.

He says that it was really my double that Reine saw Sunday evening, when she was lying on her mother's bed, that the lethargy in which she had fallen came from a spontaneous sortie of her own, and that, thus, she had come to make me a visit, as is her habit almost every evening at that hour; that I was sleeping, and my double had disengaged itself and was wandering about the room, and it was then that Reine's double saw me. Vettellini adds that I have the habit of disengaging myself now, and that sometimes I go far and acquire ideas by which I unconsciously benefit.

Concerning Saturday evening (when some friends came to hear about my experiments with Reine), Vettellini says that it was he who prevented Reine from coming. The atmosphere was not favorable. And Reine says: "A good dinner is one thing, a talk about the Au-Delà quite another. It would be as well not to mix such different interests." As a matter of fact, I had my lesson on Saturday evening.

April 10. My friend R., to whose apartment in the boulevard Montparnasse I had sent Reine, came in to see me today, and I asked him to read my notes on this subject. He says that the descriptions given by Reine are exact, save in one point: the apartment has four rooms instead of three. There was no one at home the afternoon of March 24. Certain details are exact: the portraits, the piano, the books, the view from the windows, etc.[34] Madame R. is a musician of talent, who studies and practices her art as a professional.

---

[34] I know the salon of this apartment, but vaguely. The only impression that persisted in my memory was that of books.

THIRTY-NINTH SÉANCE

March 26, 1913

This is the first time (since the debut of my séances) that I have wished to evoke a disincarnated Spirit whom I have known in life. After reflection, my choice fell upon C. L.—one of the few people whom I have known in conditions sufficiently intimate to judge, who seemed to me of superior evolution. Unhappily, I found no letter from him amongst my papers, and I have only a meager guide for Reine—some verses written by him fourteen years ago, à *propos* of my picture "La Douleur."

But first I must speak of Reine's surprise when she came into the studio and found herself face to face with the portrait of Vettellini. She knew nothing of my attempt, since no reference had been made to it except in her hypnosis. My canvas—already the head has a perfectly precise character—was placed as is any other portrait upon which I am working, and which she usually regards with more or less indifference. I was curious to see if this one would provoke any special remark or attention as I carelessly led her into the studio.

Ah, I had not long to wait! Reine stopped short before the canvas like one frozen. Then dazed, lost, she turned to me.—"Why! .... How did you get it? ... Where does it come from? ... It is Vettellini!" Not an instant of hesitation. Immediate conviction. "It is Vettellini ... " And I am quite as astonished as she!

We talk it over a little. I take note of certain criticisms pronounced in a tone of voice so special that I conclude it is her Guide who inspires them.

Finally we begin the séance. When the moment comes I hand her (folded) the paper on which C. L. has written his lines, telling her to find the author and bring him back here with her.

She sits a long time, pressing the paper against her forehead. Finally she says, slowly: "It is a man who wrote this letter. He is dead. There is hardly any fluid left ... It is very difficult to find him." ... Nevertheless, I gather that she has started off. We wait ... wait.

A curious change occurs in Reine's condition—something altogether new. She tries to speak, her words are detached, come slowly and after infinite effort; but it is rather her mind that seems stupefied—overpowered; the enunciation is clear. She says: "The person who wrote the letter is coming. I went to find him. The letter and your appeal attract him ... He is here now, but I do not see him, I only feel his presence. He cannot manifest himself yet ... Wait ... I see only a sort of white cloud with two brilliant spots. He is doing all he can to make me see him. No, he cannot." I ask why. She does not know why—not force enough, probably. I insist: she must enter into relation with him—ask who he is. But she seems crushed, wiped out. Never before have I seen her like that. She looks intently at a point in space, above her head. The scene lasts a long time. Suddenly she demands paper and pencil and begins writing—evidently under the inspiration of the Spirit—stopping to listen intently from time to time, explaining that she does not seize his thought, asking him to formulate it more clearly, to begin over again, etc., etc.

She has finished and turns to me, saying, "This is certainly the Spirit who wrote that letter, but he is so high, so far beyond our conditions that it is almost impossible to understand him. He is higher than Vettellini. He will use Vettellini as intermediary. He would like to help us, ... but how is it possible? He is cut off from earthly ties. He has no means of intercourse with us—so far from him. To communicate these few lines, he has brought many forces into play." He leaves. Reine's eyes follow the wake of his passage. She seems exhausted.

Wishing to go on with the training already begun, I try again the experiment of vision of things in a box. Reine sees nothing at all at first, but after long effort she discovers keys, then "something in iron"; she insists upon the iron. I do not know what has been placed in the box.

Opening it, I find a thimble, a knife, and a bunch of several small keys. I try another similar experiment, but she sees black and nothing but black. Then I make her rest.

After a few moments we resume. I ask to speak with Vettellini. Will he tell us something about the Spirit who came today? Vettellini confirms the summary explanation given by the Spirit himself. It was really the one whom I had invoked—the one who had written the verses[35]—but he is of such high evolution that he has absolutely no possibility of direct communication with us. He has expressed the wish to help us through Vettellini. He would be able to manifest himself directly if Reine should reach such a degree of hypnosis that she could abandon not only her material body, but her astral body as well. For at his stage of evolution, even the astral body that we know about no longer exists.

Already he has conversed with Vettellini who (under his influence, it seems to me) now tells me that once again we must change the method of magnetizing—and, also, the tendency of our experiments. The crystal ball is to be suppressed; I must insist longer upon the fingers and, above all, on the head, according to definite instructions. When Reine is sleeping deeply, I must ask her gently what she sees, repeating the passes if she makes no reply. When she sees something, I must ply her with questions, persistently, till she answers with extreme precision. When she sees nothing, I must decide what I want her to do, and state it in a low voice.

Here Reine, her habitual vivacity returning, adds that the real nature of her mediumistic gift is established. She will be valuable above all for visions in the Astral. All astral life and its various phenomena, the evolution of Spirits, their hierarchy, the mysterious law which binds them, etc.—this is her true and proper power, and I should direct my investigations accordingly. She says that a gift for medicine might also be developed in her.[36]

I remark that this tendency of her mediumicity is exactly the one that interests me most, and that, personally, I am happy to turn my investigations in this direction, but that no matter what result is obtained, it will have not the slightest value for the skeptical. For them, we must have phenomena that admit of control, and information, and which are susceptible of test. Reine answers: "But who can do more, can do less—probably. You see my mediumicity is developing slowly, and first because of my health. But we are being very carefully helped. The Spirits want me to reach the highest possible degree of vision.

---

[35] These shades in words have a value. Reine, in speaking for herself, calls the paper which I placed in her hands "the letter"; but when she transmits for Vettellini she says, "the verses."

[36] This "gift for medicine," it is explained in a later séance comes from the fact that in a former life Reine made a study of therapeutics.

They are training me for vision in the Astral; they wish it to be that way. They know."

Vettellini harks back to the question of health. This gives rise to a scene of such vivid play that it is impossible to doubt the real presence of the Maître. The portrait is discussed. He seems pleased with it, but for greater accuracy suggests certain modifications, and says that to-night he will show himself to Reine in the costume which he habitually wore. Reine craftily tries to extract some information that will reveal his quality and calling, but Vettellini astutely avoids the snare. He says what he intends to say and not a word more. We gather, nevertheless, that he was a lover of the Arts, especially painting. And this is all we get.

I make no attempt to give the amusing repartee, the malicious teasing that crops out continually in the course of their dialogues. It is inimitable. The affection that exists between them now is a very real one.

This is the communication from the Spirit C. L., as written by Reine:—*"Pierre, I cannot appear to you, having liberated myself; that is, having entirely separated myself from mortals. I can do nothing more amongst you. It would mean too great a loss of force for the medium, as I would have to take possession of her body, for I myself no longer have one. I could help you with Vettellini as intermediary."*

FORTIETH SÉANCE

March 28, 1913

On arriving, Reine tells me that last night, when she was awake, she saw Vettellini in a special kind of costume—a black velvet coat and waistcoat—and that he threw back his head to show his collar and the high-cut of his waistcoat which his beard concealed. He is broad shouldered and slender; looks tall. His hands are delicate and exquisitely kept.[37] I take note of these details and will try to give their expression in the portrait.

Reine is again suffering from a severe cold, coughs and has fever, but seems in good spirits just the same. I put her to sleep by the new method, and, in spite of her incessant coughing, bring her quickly to the desired point of hypnosis, without, however, obtaining a marked degree of cold. After repeating several times the question "What do you see?" I receive the answer that she is looking into a big room, a kind of dormitory with beds on each side. It is a hospital; sick people are there, lying in bed, or sitting up. I tell her to try to understand what she sees, and why she is there, for I myself have no idea about it.

After a rather long moment she announces that she knows. "I am where you wanted to send me, but you would not ask Vettellini because you thought it too personal a question. I am in the hospital where your cousin is." This is truly remarkable. My cousin J. was placed in a *maison*

---

[37] When she is awake, it is generally only the head of Vettellini that is well formed for Reine: the shoulders are vague, and the body inexistent.

de santé more than a year ago, and often, in the course of these experiments with Reine, I have thought of using her to obtain some information about his condition and the probable outcome of his trouble. But considering it, as she says, a question of personal interest, I have always stifled my desire without mentioning it to anyone.

She hunts throughout the big room for my unhappy friend but does not find him. (How she reached that room she does not know.) I ask my wife to find one of his letters and place it in Reine's hands to facilitate her search. She wanders through the establishment, traversing many rooms, but without success. Then, suddenly, she finds him. Yes, it is surely he. He is in a room all by himself. (Verified). He is lying down, sleeping. Reine sees his astral body standing just above him and remarks: "Oh, his spirit is already quite independent! It will not be long now. He is a sort of grayish-blue, the color of a moderate evolution but nothing really high yet. He has a good start—that's all."

To my inquiry, she says that he is not very unhappy. When he is violent, it is the body which, no longer directed by the spirit, is excited and influenced by low Spirits, who play with and abuse the organism without a master. The only moment when he really suffers is when his spirit comes back to his body for a few moments and he becomes conscious of his pitiful condition.[38] He then has moments of tragic anguish which cause a new crisis, and his spirit again escapes. Even now he is intractable, but he will become more and more violent in these crises. He must be carefully watched for he will be dangerous, etc.

I ask Reine to enter into communication with his double. She says she will try, and after a moment says that he responds. He seems to understand what she explains to him—his condition and situation. (My cousin had made a study of occultism during several years under the direction of S. U. Zanne). She will write what he wants to say to me. I give her the necessary materials, and she writes six or seven lines, then suddenly jumps back in her chair, looking all around her, to the right, to the left, with a stunned and bewildered air. She says that she all at

---

[38] When the spirit comes back into the body, he forgets the astral life and is conscious only of his incarnated state. Whatever may be the reason of this oblivion of astral life, we are forced to admit its reality since we can verify it experimentally. As a matter of fact, Reine manifests it at every séance when, passing from one degree of hypnosis, into another less profound, she loses all recollection of what she has seen and heard in the more profound sleep; and finally, on waking, has no longer the least consciousness of what has passed in her astral excursion.

once found herself back here ... and she does not know why. She supposes that J. must have wakened in a crisis, and that she, frightened, flew back here immediately to protect herself? Vettellini confirms this, later on adding supplementary details about my poor friend's condition. He thinks that J. may live five or six months longer.[39] There is no possibility of recovery. Nothing to be done. It is well for him to be where he is. He would be dangerous at home. He is in good hands.

It is he, Vettellini, who conducted Reine to the hospital. Knowing, as he did, my desire, and the reason for my silence, he had wished to gratify me.

This is the communication from my cousin:

"I long to be liberated from my body, to pass into that Au-Delà of which I have glimpses,—but alas! I have yet to suffer. Do not believe that (I am) too unhappy,—no; for my spirit is almost always absent. Do not grieve; my troubles will come to an end, and then I shall be happy."

I now ask Vettellini to explain a point of extreme interest to me. The Spirit C. L., evoked in the last séance, seemed to say in his written message that he no longer had an astral body. What is the reason of this?

Vettellini replies that after a time (which is variable) passed in the Astral, when a Spirit has attained a very high degree of evolution and has never again to incarnate on earth, he loses his astral body which is only the intermediary, the medium, between him and his organism. This fluidic substance returns to terrestrial matter, and the Spirit conserves only an ethereal envelope, of so subtle a density that it is imperceptible, not only to the incarnated, but even to the disincarnated of average evolution.

This is the case of the Spirit C. L. So then, if he should wish to manifest himself to us by means of Reine's organism, the first essential would be that she should be in a state of complete catalepsy, that is, that her astral body should have absolutely and completely left her physical body. After this, under the influence of prolonged magnetization, the spirit of Reine will in turn disengage from her astral body, which thus evacuated, will be able to receive the spirit of C. L., who, now in possession of the essential intermediary, will be able to use Reine's organism to communicate with us.

I ask if Reine's spirit, thus completely liberated, runs no risk of accident. Vettellini declares that it is indeed a most delicate and perilous

---

[39] The end came five months and a few days later.

operation, but which will be without danger if we realize it; for he, Vettellini, and, if need be, another Spirit will watch over Reine while the Spirit C. L. is occupying her astral body. He says moreover that it is not her spirit that will be in danger, but her terrestrial life; for her physical body will be momentarily open to the influence of lower Spirits who might penetrate it and provoke terrible troubles, causing even the rupture of the cord that unites it to the fluidic body.

An idea altogether new to me is developed in the case of C. L. Although recognizing the fine intelligence of my old friend, and convinced of his superiority, I am nevertheless astonished to find him of so high an evolution. His earthly life, which I knew well, was certainly a valiant one, conducted with courage and tenacity of purpose; but ... it was not exactly an edifying life. That interesting and intelligent man had many weaknesses... Then ... what?

Vettellini replies that, as a matter of fact, C. L. was not remarkably evolved at his death; he had a good start without being superior. But for those who have attained this degree there is possibility of evolution in the Astral. The disincarnated Spirit may decide whether he will come back to earth to continue his development slowly, or whether, on the contrary, he will choose to refine himself in and by the ordeals of astral life, which Vettellini can, not now explain but which admit of rapidly attaining a high spirituality. If the Spirit disdains his earthly souvenirs and is resolved to break all earthly ties; and if, on the other hand, he does not shrink from the astral test, he will rise at once to the rank that this supreme detachment from terrestrial interests wins for him.

This illuminates the message dictated by C. L.:—"*Having liberated myself, that is, having entirely separated myself from mortals,*" etc.

Impossible to note all the talk, alas! ... too many pages would be needed; but I must not forget to mention a precise affirmation made by Vettellini namely, that in the Astral a Spirit of high evolution can take cognizance of all his precedent lives, can have a full and comprehensive view and understanding of his entire evolution. To my remark that this must be prodigiously interesting, he answers with a certain melancholy: "It is not always very ... pretty"—"Pretty?" says Reine, "why not pretty?"—"Oh, there are lives, or parts of lives that are not agreeable to recall—they are too ugly."

The discussion of Reine's health provokes this exclamation: "Oh, my Vettellini, you really ought to cure me! If you could only know how I suffer!—and all the time!" But after listening an instant, she turns to me with entire resignation: "He says he cannot. I must suffer. It is my lot. It has to be that way for my evolution."

In a moment, however, she is gay again, chaffing him about his prediction of the death of the grandmother she loves so little,—whose death was announced for Easter. "*Towards* Easter," corrects Vettellini.—"Well, it's a good whole week late, my old Vettellini, and that's too much for a prediction. Can't you come any nearer than that? Why, yes, of course one may make a mistake,—at least we may. But you, a Spirit? Oh, la—la, *my* Vettellini!"

FORTY-FIRST SÉANCE

March 31, 1913

Reine sleeps easily, grows cold from the very beginning of the passes, and then, to my surprise, returns to an almost normal temperature. Later on I learn that Vettellini, finding her in bad health, has arrested the chilling of the body.

At the end of an hour I question her. No reply. Reiterating my call after a few moments, and her silence still persisting, I then gently formulate an order. Placing in her hands a letter and some sleeve links coming from my friend C.,[40] who died several years ago, I told her, without comment or explanation, to find the Spirit whose fluid impregnates these objects.

We wait some time. Then Reine stirs and seems to be speaking with the invisible. She shows the sleeve links, holds them out to someone, points to me, handles the letter, and finally addresses me directly: "It is very difficult, Monsieur Cornillier; the fluid vibration left in these things is so feeble that I cannot perceive it. But Vettellini came to help me and he has gone now to find the Spirit. There is not a particle of fluid in the letter ... and very little in the buttons." Here Reine is evidently interrupted by some invisible person, for after listening she turns back to me again: "Vettellini comes to say that there is no trace left of this Spirit. Nothing remains by which to find him. What was done with his body, then?"

---

[40] This same experiment was tried in the third séance, December 13, 1912, but with no result.

This is interesting. As a matter of fact C. was cremated. "Ah, well, that explains it—that is why it is so difficult!" exclaims Reine, "Vettellini will start again. Oh, he will make out all right; but I never would have been able to."

More moments of waiting, then the same scene over again. Vettellini returns again to ask how long ago C. died. He has looked first amongst the inferior Spirits, my friend is not there; nor is he amongst the blue. Then Vettellini addressed himself to the white Spirits and was told that the one whom he was seeking had reincarnated. "It is strange," he adds, "and rare, after so short a period in the Astral" (six years). He is going back, he wants to find out all about it, to please me. But it is not easy.

Again we wait, talking a little, expecting Vettellini's return at any moment, but he does not come, and we begin to find the time long. Reine is visibly bored and jerks out crossly, "But what on earth is he doing?" My wife is shivering, and I am not so very amused myself.

As a distraction I propose an experiment. Reine will tell me how much change I have in my purse. After a mistake she says six francs, which is correct, but without value, because she took the purse in her hands. I place my pocket-book in her lap. She sees in it a photograph of Madame Cornillier and some visiting cards: exact, but probable also. She then discovers "a paper with little drawings on it—figures of women;" exact—a fifty-franc bank note.

And still Vettellini does not come. Reine grows more and more enervated: "But where do you suppose he is? What can he be doing all this time?"

We wait three-quarters of an hour. My wife, worn out, leaves the room.

Suddenly he is here. "Ah well, my Vettellini, you certainly take your time!" cries Reine, all joyful again. "It is difficult to find a Spirit in such circumstances. I wanted to be sure and I am now." And he explains that he has not himself seen the one who has reincarnated, but he has obtained the details from Superior Spirits. C. reincarnated about eighteen months ago, but not for a long life. He will die soon now. It was he himself who chose his fate in order to hasten his evolution which was already of a good degree; but he had still to live once more in the flesh, and he had preferred to do it at once, and with suffering, to gain a corresponding benefit. He is actually an infant nearly a year old.

Vettellini

I ask if Vettellini can tell me where he is, and in what family. "Here in Paris—yes." Reine begins to hesitate, her face grows sad. "Monsieur Cornillier, he is not very happy." "You mean that he is amongst poor people?" "Oh, yes!" "In a miserable family—bad?" "Worse than that. He hasn't any family at all. He was abandoned by his mother. He is in the Foundling Asylum. But he will die soon now—and he will have gained much!"

After some talk about the way in which Vettellini obtained this information, we change the subject.

"The portrait, Vettellini!" says Reine suddenly, "what do you think of the portrait?" He makes some legitimate criticism, very charmingly ... "for I have two eyes that are alike—or at least they were alike when I was on earth." "Well, upon my word," exclaims Reine sarcastically, "he proposes to be handsome!" Vettellini says that, unknown to me, he has helped, and will still help me in the execution of the portrait.[41]

---

[41] The portrait—a reproduction of which is found in this book—was executed with the greatest facility but without the least consciousness on my part of any abnormal aid. I quite simply tried, first, to make the portrait of

He will try to show himself to me in a dream which will rest in my memory.

The long absence of Vettellini in his search today leads me to ask how Spirits perceive time. What is the notion, the sensation, of time for them? The reply is long: Time does not exist for Spirits; they do not perceive its duration; the past, the present, and the future co-exist, etc. After the spending of many words on one side and the other, we are obliged to recognize that the conception of the non-existence of time is beyond our powers, necessarily inexplicable in terms of our language, and vain to discuss.[42]

I prefer to know if inferior Spirits can have an influence on their superiors—if not individually, then by uniting their vibratory force, for example. "Were all of them to unite together," replies Vettellini, "it would avail nothing. *Superiority is effective the instant that it is conscious.*"

Referring to the Elementals, I ask if they are the Spirits of animals. "Yes, they are the Spirits of animals. They sometimes hover about you, and may be used as instruments by Spirits of low order." What is their evolutive possibility? The reply interests me, particularly because of its conformity to cosmosophical teaching. Summed up, it is as follows:— Animals evolve the same as we do. Everything in nature evolves. We have been animals. But a cat or a horse does not become a man on our Earth. After successive reincarnations, by means of which an animal has gained all that can be gained in his class, he migrates to another planet, where he will acquire the vibratory condition that is necessary before he can incarnate in the higher form, and thus continue indefinitely the march of evolution.

The question of water diviners (dowsers) has been much agitated of late, and while we were waiting for Vettellini's return today, I spoke to Reine about it and was surprised to find that she seemed quite sure of the importance of the hazel-rod in the experiment. I said nothing at the time, but now tell her to ask her Guide what a water diviner really is. She listens attentively, and immediately says that she was altogether

---

the person whom Reine had described to me, and, then, to conform to the criticism which, in the course of the work she either made herself or transmitted to me from her Guide. This execution of a portrait without any material document is unique in my professional experience.

[42] Note 4 in the Appendix gives a modification of this statement which, I understood later, had been badly transmitted by Reine and falsely interpreted by me.

mistaken: "Vettellini says that it is a special sensitiveness in the man himself, that the hazel-rod has nothing to do with it. Substances throw out radiations; the spring-finder is a being specially sensitive to these radiations, which affect him differently according to the difference of their nature—running water, metals," etc.

I then speak about the propagation of our convictions. What is Vettellini's opinion in the matter? His opinion is that it is perfectly useless to try to convince people: "When they are ready, they come to the question of themselves. Otherwise, it is a waste of effort. Even positive proofs have no weight. Nothing is ever proved to those who do not understand. Time will do the work."

Before waking Reine, I give her the order to go to bed early tomorrow evening, and, during her natural sleep, her astral body must disengage itself and come here—not to make a manifestation this time, but to observe. And on Wednesday at our séance, she will tell me what she has found here. We will have some friends dining with us. She must observe closely and tell me exactly all about it. She seems to hesitate: "But ... then I must come in ... and listen? I'd never dare to!"

"Reine, you will come, and you will come and sit next to me. I invite you. You will be a guest." Her face lights up with joy: "Oh ... a guest? Ah, yes, I'll come!"

FORTY-SECOND SÉANCE

April 2, 1913

We begin in the usual way. Reine sleeps profoundly. I have decided to send her, this time, to observe her grandmother—the one she loves—who is in a hospital at Tours.

I give my order and very soon she says that she has arrived at the hospital. She hunts for her grandmother, whom she finds in the garden, walking alone and talking to herself, and who is wearing not the costume of the other pensioners but her own usual clothes. Reine does not see her spirit, thinks it must be inside. (This would imply that her grandmother is not very near her end, and also that she is of rather inferior evolution). I order Reine to make her presence felt. She tries, but the good woman perceives nothing at all.

She then gives a precise description of the surroundings, description which I omit, not having been able to verify it. The question of the costume, however, was proved to be exact. The women who are received in this house are, as a rule, clothed in a certain uniform, but I knew later, through a letter from one of the family, that in this case the rule had not been enforced, owing to a small pension which the family paid for her,—a fact of which her granddaughter was completely ignorant.

I bring Reine back,—maintaining the same degree of hypnosis. In my hand I hold a small magnet so that only the two extremities are perceptible. What does she see? At first she sees nothing. She takes my hand, passes her fingers over the two tiny magnetized surfaces that are uncovered, and seems to experience a strange sensation. Then she perceives little sparks, "lights such as Spirits have," she says. Noticing at this moment that the sun is shining through the curtains I rise to arrange them that the room may be dark again, and again I present the magnet to Reine's examination. Immediately she sees little red flames and little blue flames coming from the poles. She amuses herself by touching it lightly with her fingers. It seems that the magnet attracts them, and they stick to it. The sensation is not agreeable. She tries to understand about it and after a while finishes by saying: "You know, it is just like when you pick up little things with a magnet." The interesting point for me is that she has distinctly seen blue emanations and red emanations. I will keep this in reserve for Vettellini. Today I have a question of more importance, and when Reine tells me that he is there, I ask it:

Does individual consciousness become more and more individual in the course of evolution? Is the Spirit always consciously himself and the same? Or, on the contrary, as certain doctrines teach, does individual consciousness, by the very fact of evolution, become absorbed in a kind of universal consciousness,—evolution thus arriving, in fact, at the slow destruction of individuality?

After the usual acute attention Reine turns to me: "Monsieur Cornillier, Vettellini affirms that individual consciousness can but grow greater and greater as evolution progresses. All that is gained and conquered by a being, defines and strengthens his individuality. It is his,—and for himself. The blue Spirits are more individual than the gray; the white more individual than the blue; and above the white, *the still higher Spirits are still more themselves.*"

To these grave words the Maître must have added some rather sharp appreciations of the people who maintain the contrary opinion, for the child dared to say: "Vettellini, you are really a little severe. Why are you indignant with those people? ... They too are trying to find the truth."

Vettellini has seemed astonished at the rapid reincarnation of my friend C.; so I ask now what is the average period passed by a Spirit in the Astral before his return to earth. Answer: The length of time varies and, usually, it is in relation to the degree of evolution,—the inferior Spirits reincarnating after a period of from fifteen to twenty years in the Astral; those of higher degree, after about forty years. This is, of course, an average. But there are frequent modifications, the sole purpose of which is to hasten evolution. Certain tasks, missions and roles, voluntarily accepted, may intervene to advance or retard the reincarnation. The directing Spirits always conduct by the shortest route.

I close the séance by asking what should be done with the body after death,—cremation or burial? Vettellini prefers burial: "One may, for different reasons, wish to keep in touch with friends on earth, wish to reserve the possibility of returning and of influencing. Then, too, if the organic decomposition is painful for the Spirit, he has at least the benefit attaching to this last trial. Cremated, one is free, it is true, but free as a balloon without ballast. Intercourse or contact with those on earth becomes almost impossible, and reincarnation much more difficult. It is better not to be cremated."

I am about to waken Reine when I remember the "invited-visit" I had ordered her to make here last evening in astral body, and bluntly inquire: "Well, Reine, what about last evening?"—"Ah, well, I should think so!" she sharply retorts. "I was angry enough! I came twice, Monsieur Cornillier, *and there was no one.* The first time it was half-past nine. I came straight in here; it was all black, so, thinking I had come too early, I left. At half-past ten I came back. Still nobody, and no light. I looked about everywhere—and I was pretty mad! Then I went to the fifth floor, to Madame Cornillier's room,—no one. Then I was afraid there had been an accident or something, and I stayed wandering about in the two apartments a long time, terribly worried, ... and finally I went home. And you know it was that worry which wakened me, and kept me from sleeping the rest of the night.[43] In my normal state I do not know that this was the reason, but now, in hypnosis, I do know it." This is extremely interesting. I had ordered Reine to come and observe us in the atelier last evening, as we expected friends for dinner. But at the last moment a telegram announced that they could not come, and we suddenly decided to go to the theatre. I have never doubted the reality of the visits that Reine pretends to make in astral body, but here is a quite unexpected backing to my conviction.

---

[43] When she came in today Reine reported that after a first short sleep she had wakened and had not been able to sleep again during the whole night.

FORTY-THIRD SÉANCE

April 4, 1913

The usual preparation.

When Reine is sleeping I send her to find the Spirit of a young engineer, an acquaintance of mine, who died three or four years ago. She finds him and brings him here, but his presence gives nothing of interest to report, other than Reine's rather subtle appreciation of the case. Noticing that the Spirit replies with bad grace to my questions, I express astonishment. She explains: "He was more amiable on earth, you say? Of course. He had an organism of excellent quality, he succeeded admirably in all he undertook, and he felt important. Now that he is disincarnated he cannot enjoy finding himself less than he had supposed. If we were inferior to him he would be more agreeable, but, as it is, he feels humiliated and vexed. That is why he is so sulky."

After this excursion I propose another, more amusing for the medium,—to make a call upon Armand (her husband) in the office where he is working. This visit provokes a number of precise observations, only one of which I will note as it is all that I have been able to verify. Reine sees her husband leave the clerk's office and pass into another one, where a gentleman sits alone. There he takes some papers, which he carries back to place in a pigeon hole just above his desk. (It was confirmed that this happened at the exact moment when I sent her to the office.)

Recalling Reine, I try to get her to read a line written in large letters and placed on a table a few feet behind her. Complete failure. (It is, however, I who wrote the phrase in question, and she could have read it in my mind, were that her method of vision.)

I give her a box closed and tied together. It contains three objects. She sees one of them (a box of matches), but declares that she cannot make out the others. Then I try with all my will to impose upon her the image and the word collar,—one of the two objects which she cannot distinguish; but with absolutely no result.

After these exercises I ask to talk with Vettellini. Is there, for Spirits in the Astral, a rhythm of work and rest, analogous to ours on earth? After a period of activity, is there relaxation, repose? Are they ever tired? Vettellini replies that the idea of fatigue does not exist in the Astral. In the accomplishment of a work, efforts, and even painful ones, may be necessary; but when the task is finished there is only a suspension of activity, not a period of repose—which would be useless since fatigue, as we know it, is unknown to them. Moreover, it would be impossible to describe their various conditions and sensations in terms of our language. He goes on to say that often Spirits form groups, based on their affinities, for the purpose of working together on a common task. I ask if this does not give rise to a divergence of opinion, at times, or to rivalry between the groups. Answer:

As soon as a high degree of evolution is attained, by that very fact complete harmony exists. This does not conflict with the principle of individuality, but judgment about the work to be accomplished cannot differ. The ideal is the same. The work is subdivided into tasks which each group strives to achieve; the means of achievement never fall under discussion. In the lower spheres of astral life, on the contrary, antagonisms inherent to terrestrial life continue to exist. Each Spirit conserves his traits of character and opinions. Social, political, and religious questions are still subjects of controversy: passions are not vanquished. This is why, in Spirit communications, all opinions and all points of view are manifested. Certain Spirits are perfectly sincere in asking that prayers be made for the repose of their souls, or in begging gifts of money for the Church. There are others who wittingly deceive, either by vice, or merely as a joke for their own amusement. Dead, they understand no more than they understand when living, *and even sometimes much less.* If, for example, their organism has been of excellent quality, they find themselves impoverished in abandoning it.

The talk continues. I speak of Buddhism, of the Mahatmas, etc. Vettellini considers the Buddhist doctrines as expressing the needs of a race totally different from our own,—doctrines which, in consequence, can be of no benefit to us; but he speaks of the Mahatmas with great reverence. We touch upon Behäism and other sects, issues of Christianity. In all religions Vettellini finds good discipline and principles of conduct helpful to people who have not yet gone beyond a certain level; but he proclaims the necessity of complete liberty for the individual who has become master of himself.

And with this he leaves us.

I am about to waken Reine, but, as she does not seem tired, I take advantage of the absence of her Guide to complete the experiment with the magnet. I present my two open hands, placed vertically before her, and ask: "What, exactly, do you see?" She examines them.—"But ... I see little flames coming out of your fingers." I ask her to describe these flames precisely: She then declares that she distinctly sees blue flames coming from the finger tips of my right hand, and yellowish red flames from the finger tips of my left hand. I make her repeat and confirm her observation. Then I tell her to look at my eyes—"Your eyes too project flames, but they look blue for both eyes." Afterwards she observes my nasal respiration, and here again sees little blue flames coming from both nostrils. Here, then, is a poser for the good Vettellini. (The subjects of Colonel de Rochas see the same difference of color in the effluvia emitted by the eyes, the nose and the hands—blue and red in the three cases.)

FORTY-FOURTH SÉANCE

April 7, 1913

This séance has been of intense interest. Our one regret is that we were alone to witness it.

On her arrival Reine relates a number of small incidents. First, strange souvenirs of the night—an important conversation with someone—was it Vettellini? Was it I? She cannot say. Then yesterday, in her usual promenade in the woods of Meudon, she felt herself pulled for a moment in a direction quite opposite to that which her husband had taken, but she did not yield to this influence because he was already so far ahead of her. Finally, coming home, as she sat leaning over the side of the boat, watching the play of the water, the head of Vettellini rose suddenly from the foam. She was so startled that she threw herself backwards, falling on Armand, who was more than surprised. "Vettellini laughed as though it were a good joke," said Reine. And she adds that it is the first time she has seen his white teeth.

I begin magnetizing at the usual hour, asking myself what I shall have her do; hesitating between an excursion into the high astral spaces and the evocation of my paternal grandfather, with whom—after my own impressions and the stories that have been told me—I fancy I have affinities. Deciding for the latter experiment, I place in Reine's hands the only objects in my possession that have belonged to him—a pen-and-ink drawing of a boat, on a detached leaf of an account book, and a little apron of the Rose Croix order of freemasons—telling her merely to go and find the Spirit to whom they have belonged, and to bring him here. Reine examines the objects attentively, finds the fluid stronger in the apron and says she will go to find the Spirit who owned it. During her search I concentrate my thought upon my grandfather, and call him.

After a few moments she returns to say that she has not found him in Paris, and asks where he died. "In Nantes."—"I will go there, then, but where is it? ... I don't know." For a moment it seems difficult to explain to her. But as she knows Tours, I order her to transport herself there and, once at Tours, she will find the Loire and follow it down; she will see two large towns—Saumur and Angers—these she will pass by, and the third city will be Nantes. I send her there with all my force.

Very soon she says she is in Nantes. She will go to the cemetery to find the fluid. I give her the direction.—"Oh, it's a beautiful cemetery—so many fine chapels! Full of Spirits—crowds of them! No, he's not here. There are only red ones down here. I must go higher." After an error, promptly recognized, and caused, she says, by a similarity of fluidic vibration, I advise her to ask information of a blue Spirit. She appears to acquiesce but has a preoccupied air as though trying to understand something that baffles her. She touches first my hand and then the little apron; comes back to my hand again; compares and analyses her impressions of each; and, after two or three repetitions of this examination, I hear her mumbling: "But? ... H'm ... No, it's not the same, but there's the same in each ... *Some* of it is the same ... How queer!"

My interest is keen, but I give no sign of it, encouraging her simply to find the person who has worn the apron. Suddenly she cries: "Ha! ... I have him!"—You are sure, Reine, that it is he?—"Oh, yes, ... Must I bring him back with me." In a few moments he is here; Reine announces him.—Ask him if he recognizes me.

Immediately she is smiling: "He says, Yes, it is Pierre," and her smile grows charming; she is going to tell me something agreeable, something happy. But suddenly she stops, her expression grows grave, she lifts a small and menacing finger to the Spirit, who seems to be just opposite and a little above her: "You are sure you are telling the truth? It's not a lie ... h'm?" She leans towards me to speak, hesitates again, and returns to the charge, "You are sure? You're not lying? It is really the truth?" Finally her smile comes back. She is convinced. "He says he is your papa." (I silently assume that Reine has meant to say "your grandfather!")

To my question, what is the color of this Spirit? she gives a little shrug:—"Oh, he is, grayish, ... not red, no, ... bluish-gray."—Ask him if he recognizes these things. Did he make this drawing? Has he ever worn this apron?—Reine consults the Spirit, then shakes her head: "No. They don't belong to him—those things."

An intensely interesting moment follows, when Reine again silently examines and compares the three fluids—that of the object, that of the Spirit present, and my own. Then she says: "It's queer, you know,—They are not the same, no ... but they are so much alike! However, your fluid and the fluid in these things are much nearer each other. That of your 'papa' is different but he has a lot of the same, too!" And, after some questioning, I finish by understanding that it is indeed my father, and not my grandfather, who is present.

I inquire why my father was in Nantes, when he had died in Paris. He replies that he is often in Nantes. He was born there,[44] and there he constantly returns. I ask for details about his children, which he gives correctly, adding certain personal appreciations, perfectly coherent. Then I refer to my grandfather—his own father—who, he tells me, is a very high Spirit. Can he, and will he, go to find him? He will,—for me. Here Reine, who seems to consider him a child and treats him as such, says: "Hurry along then, or I'll go myself."

During the absence of this Spirit, Reine prattles about Nantes, which she had never seen before, and where, in passing, she has noticed many astonishing things ... "But the funniest thing of all is the little white head rigs of the women, and their hair pulled back so tight—like that." She flattens her own hair back with both hands and laughs so gaily that we laugh with her, amazed that she had had time to notice this and several other characteristics of the streets of Nantes.

But waiting is hard work. Reine grows restless.—"I'm going back there. He is too slow. Send me again, Monsieur Cornillier." I magnetize her a little more and send her. Immediately she is there. This time she evidently passes by the quays, for she sees immense ships, remarks with astonishment the big yards whose use she cannot imagine, as she has never before seen a big sailing ship.

At last she finds the two Spirits and brings them back with her. "There they are, both of them. And it is really your grandfather this time. Oh, he is a beautiful blue, your grandfather! Ah, yes, he is high,—very! ... But of course he knows you! He comes here often, he is happy here. He has followed you all your life and helped you all he could."

I put some questions, of interest to myself only, and then ask how it happens, since he loves me and comes here sometimes, that he did

---

[44] Correct.

not respond at once to my appeal. He explains that he was too far away, too high; my call was dissipated before it could reach him. He is very occupied. He belongs to one of those groups (to which reference has been made in other séances) who are engaged in a special task of their own choosing. He has preferred to continue his evolution in the Astral rather than come back for another incarnation: "It is more difficult, *but for souls of fine temper.*" (This expression is characteristic of my grandfather) "it is more attractive than a new life on earth." He says he has a painful souvenir of the earth; he suffered too much there; but he is happy now, having freely, and in full consciousness, chosen his way of evolution, etc.

Here follows a talk (concerning his family) whose chief interest lies in its unexpectedness and in the fact that his opinion is exactly opposed to that which I should have attributed to him.

He adds some general remarks:—A Spirit, such as he, cannot come into our terrestrial atmosphere without considerable discomfort. He is obliged to assume a heavy material envelope which seriously incommodes him; so that he must feel there is real utility in the effort, and find a valuable compensation for it in the reaction which he obtains from those whom he comes to see. And I must also understand that, in the Astral, family ties no longer count, they no longer exist. *The affinities of Spirit are the only ones that endure.*

I ask if I may evoke him, sometimes ... for advice and aid. He says that he will always come, and gladly; for that matter he frequently passes here, unknown to me. Is there anything at all that I could do for him—or, at least, to please him? "No, you can do nothing for me, but when I am gone you must talk to this one" (indicating my father who, it seems, is still waiting there in the corner); "him you can aid. Do it." And Reine repeats imperatively, "*He wishes, he commands, that you talk with your papa.*" He leaves us. Reine's lifted face follows him as she says "*Au revoir.*"

Then I turn to my father, saying that I will do anything in my power to help him. What would he like me to do?

The reply transmitted by this sleeping child (wholly ignorant of any family differences that may have troubled me in the past) is so extraordinary as a synthetic expression of facts and characters, so psychologically illuminative of the sentiments which the contact of our two individualities had created between my father and me, that I esteem it a proof of identity equal to a material proof. Evidently—and I realize this perfectly—it is a purely personal conviction. No one but myself can accept it. I will give only the opening phrase of the reply to allow the reader to infer the probative value of the communication:

"First, he asks you not to judge him so severely" ... falls gravely from Reine's lips.

Then she goes on to express his thoughts and desires. And when she has finished transmitting she explains to me, of her own accord, the condition in which he is. "He is not bad, you know, but he is not strong; his ideas are confused. He sees his father, so high, and then his son who, though not a Spirit, seems to be above him. He wants to understand about it. He has the best possible will, but he doesn't know what to do. ... In any case, he should not reincarnate now, he is too weak; he would begin the same kind of life right over again." And, turning from me, Reine addresses him with authority:—

"Above all things, you must not come back to earth, I see you are thinking about it. You have good souvenirs of the earth, you! But you are not strong enough yet to make a good life; you would fall right back into the same faults ... You must grow a little in the Astral before coming again, and for that you must avoid the red Spirits ... and you must not frequent the gray ones like yourself, either. Go with the blue ones; oh, not the blue blue! But ... they must be bluer than you are. It's the way for you to get on. It's the best way to understand."

Wishing to close the interview, I promise my father to ask Vettellini the best way of helping him in his evolution; and this provokes a further transmission of intimate thoughts, most interesting to me, which result in his asking to come back often. He says that he comes sometimes on his own responsibility, for he knows that he cannot hurt us, and that, on the contrary, he can be helped by the radiations here. It is good for him. He will be happy if I think of him, call him, and talk with him sometimes. He will go now, back to Nantes, where, he says, many things that he loved attract him. And he leaves us.

This long scene has taken much time, but I ask the medium if her Guide is there. I have some questions for him. Vettellini manifests himself, taking his habitual place.

I want first to settle the point about the color of the effluvia, but scarcely have I begun to formulate my question when Reine interrupts me:—"Monsieur Cornillier, Vettellini is just waiting to speak to you about that. He was mistaken. And his mistake came from the fact that he has never been interested in investigations of that nature; and, always seeing the fluidic bodies in the Astral, where each has only one color, he affirmed it to be true. But, disturbed by your remarks, he has since informed himself and ... you are right; and the authorities whom you quote are right too." And Reine transmits an explanation which may be resumed as follows:

The fluidic body which generates magnetic effluvia is influenced by two distinct elements: the spirit and the organism. The first determines the blue color in the effluvium and the second determines the red color. In practical experiments these two elements can separate momentarily and reunite again to form the complete fluidic body. It must be noted that the relative quantity of each element is in accordance with the evolution of the individual: in inferior people there is a preponderance of red, for example; higher in the scale of evolution there is a tendency to the equalization of the two colors; and finally, as the spiritual qualities predominate, the blue asserts itself. And in this latter case there may be an inversion in the sortie of the fluid, the blue substance coming from the left and the red from the right side, etc.

At the death of the body, and after a lapse of time varying in accordance with the degree of evolution, that portion of the fluidic body which is organic in origin abandons the disIncarnated Spirit and re turns to reform new combinations on the terrestrial plane, leaving the more subtle and etherean element to form the only envelope the Spirit needs in the Astral.

To a question from me, Vettellini specifies that this coloration of organic fluids has a different cause from that of inorganic effluvia (magnets, etc.)

This point cleared up, I ask for an explanation of the mechanism of suggestion, of thought-transmission and of telepathy. Since all these phenomena exist, how is it that never, *never*, can I transmit to Reine (in séance) an idea, an image, or a word, present in my mind,—and this in spite of all my will to do so, at times? I have innumerable examples of her absolute refusal to accept my suggestions.

Reine answers for herself, aided now and then by Vettellini:—"Monsieur Cornillier, you will never succeed in that with me, and the reason is quite simple: it is impossible because our two spirits are of equal force. The transmission of thought, imposed, or suggestion by authority, is effective only from superior to inferior. If you had a medium of feeble will, or one open (by reason of inferiority) to every influence, you could make her see, feel, or say anything you wished. But with me this is not possible: we are working together as equals. I obey you, certainly I do; but that is quite another matter. You tell me to see what there is in a closed box, and I try. But it is I myself who must see. *My spirit knows that for the experiment to be of value, it is the spirit that must see. Never will I accept your thought or suggestion. You will never be able to make me."*

She goes on to explain with extreme lucidity that what we call mind-reading, suggestion, thought-transmission, telepathy, visions, objective hallucinations, clairvoyance, etc., proceed, all of them, from one or two main causes. First: A brain in the active state sends out concentric waves which can be perceived by a brain in the passive or receptive state. (The principle of thought-transmission, telepathy, etc.)

Second: Under the influence of an impression generally, but not necessarily, intense, there is a liberation and projection of the fluidic body, which goes to manifest itself to a passive percipient: that is, to a person whose mind is in the receptive state. (The principle of visions, objective hallucinations, etc.) Also, the passive may become active, and procure information for himself—whether it be, says Reine, by reading the elements, or by projecting his fluidic body to observe the conditions about which he washes information. (The principle of mind reading, clairvoyance, etc.)

Finally, disincarnated Spirits—whether from interest in one who is incarnate, or for another reason—may assume the role of informers and transmit to a percipient ideas or images of existing realities, or even create symbolic signs for his enlightenment.

Reine terminates by saying that of course all these phenomena, when spontaneous, are possible between people of equal or unequal force, but that in experiments that are intentional, such as ours, the transmission of imposed thought, or even involuntary suggestion, can have effect only from a superior to an inferior force.

The serious questions are exhausted, and I ask Vettellini's opinion of his portrait. He makes one or two small criticisms, but says that it now needs very little alteration. He has tried to materialize at night for me, but even with Reine's help he could not succeed; it requires too much force.

Reine then tells me the cause of her painful impression of the past night,—of a conversation which she only vaguely remembers when she is in her normal state. Vettellini went to her place to bring her here (to help him in materializing for me). Arriving in my room, they perceived a Spirit near the fire place.—"A small grayish- blue light, poor and trembling." Reine was so frightened that she started to fly off, but Vettellini held her back. He had recognized the Spirit. "Monsieur Cornillier," says Reine sadly, "it was the one I went to see in the hospital, you know, ... your cousin. Yes, it was he. Vettellini recognized him, and we talked with him. He wanted to come to see you, and he got here all right: but that was all. He was not able to see you. He is too heavy,—and too weak; everything looked black to him; and he did not know how to get back to his body. We helped him. First we showed him where you were, made him see your bed, etc., and then we took him home. He would have lost his way, you know. He would have wandered about until his body was seized by another crisis. He got home all right, but I was terribly frightened." And she adds, "It's beautiful where he is, you know,—a fine park; and there are summer-houses in the great garden, and splendid alleys and walks, with plane trees,—oh, it's beautiful!"[45]

Then Reine explains the attraction she had felt during her walk in the woods of Meudon, Sunday. It was Vettellini who was trying to lead her to a spot where she could find cuckoos! She had been hunting them all afternoon; her gleaning was small, and Vettellini wanted to show her a little glade full of them, but she had not understood. "And just think, in my whole day I had found only two! It's too bad to have missed them! And, you know, it was really Vettellini I saw, when I was looking at the water," she exclaims excitedly. "He wanted to make me laugh, but I was paralyzed with fear!" ... Leaning toward the spot where her Guide must be, she protests: "You know, my Vettellini, not quite so suddenly another time? You should prepare me a little to see you—You understand, ... it frightens me to death when I am awake."

But I must cut short this extraordinary fairy tale without dwelling on all the charming play, the intimate, whimsical teasing, so affectionate, that is now habitual between them.

Various incidents of the last séances lead Reine to suppose that Vettellini is much higher than he allows us to understand. She is sure he must be a white Spirit. But to stay in regular and constant communication with us, he has assumed the heavier, more material substance of the blue,—through devotion to the cause which he has at heart.

---

[45] These details are exact.

FORTY-FIFTH SÉANCE

April 9, 1913

(Monsieur A. is with us)

This séance, at which my friend A. assisted, was of no special interest, through no fault of the medium, however, but merely because the elements were rather colorless.

A. brought a letter from a friend, now dead, whose Spirit he wished to evoke. This letter, however, was addressed, not to him, but to a third person who had kept it for five years, hence a mixture of fluids. More than this, the author of the letter died in Switzerland. This was a new experience for the medium. Nevertheless, in spite of these complications, the experiment was, if not entirely, at least sufficiently successful.

Reine manages to reach Geneva, find the Spirit and bring her here to us. But this Spirit (who, says A., was unusually brilliant in her life time) is still plunged in coma and offers no special interest; though the general sense of her replies concerning her family and the circumstances of her life are, with two exceptions, recognized by A. to be exact. In short, nothing of value is obtained. The only point worthy of attention is Reine's analysis of the two fluids impregnating the letter. She establishes a perfectly clear distinction between them, affirming at the same time that different, as they are, they must come from two people of blood relation, for she finds in them a fundamental element common to both. (After the séance A. tells us that this is exact. The ladies are first cousins.)

Next, without comment, I place in Reine's hands a ring habitually worn by A., supposed to be one of Montezuma's jewels, but in any case known to be of Mexican origin. Reine gives a psychometrical analysis, describing the environment in which the ring existed and the dramatic incidents which occurred in connection with it; all of which is interesting because of the picturesque and foreign character of her descriptions, but of no weight otherwise, since it cannot be verified.

Then I try the experiment of vision in a closed box. Complete failure. She says that she would succeed better in this if she were to try it at the beginning of a séance, for it takes a lot of force, and after an excursion she is too tired to see clearly.

So then we turn to conversation. I ask Vettellini if Spirits of high evolution can escape from the terrestrial atmosphere and go to visit other planets and stars. He says that there is absolutely no limit to their passage through space. If inferior Spirits are, by their density, subject to terrestrial attraction, and, by their ignorance, retained in our ambiance, the superior ones are, on the contrary, completely liberated, can travel throughout all space, attain other solar systems and visit the nebula at an incalculable distance, etc., etc. He reminds me that he took Reine once to observe the sun.

Referring to the unusually prompt reincarnation of my friend C. (Forty-first Séance) I ask Vettellini how C. was able to accomplish this, since, having been cremated, there was nothing left to call him back to earth. Vettellini replies that he was aided by the superior Spirits who directed him, and who modified his condition so that he might fall under the influence of the incarnating currents.

A. poses the question of artistic inspiration. In what we call inspiration is there an influence from the Au-Delà? Vettellini affirms that in every noble and uplifted work of human achievement there is aid and influence from the Astral. Even a moderately gifted artist, if he has an intense aspiration for beauty, and if he opens himself, so to speak, to spiritual influences, may achieve the production of beautiful works.

The talk then touches various other subjects. Vettellini declares that morality is not the only element essential to evolution. "Goodness, loyalty, and devotion are certainly beautiful qualities, but they are eminently social qualities, and, alone, they cannot procure a higher penetration in the Au-Delà. For evolution, a parallel development of intellectuality is absolutely essential." The séance drags, our interest languishes, and I decide to waken Reine. Vettellini warns me that she has caught cold again, and I must tell her to take care of herself tonight.

FORTY-SIXTH SÉANCE

April 11, 1913

Reine is suffering from a bad cold but the séance has not been affected by that. When I ask what she is seeing, or has been seeing, she immediately replies that she is just back from a long flight in the high astral spheres where she has assisted at a sort of consultation held by the blue Spirits:

"I went up all alone, high, high, and all of a sudden I found myself near a great assembly of Spirits. There were only high ones, all of them blue, that beautiful pure blue, you know—like Vettellini. They seemed to be considering a very grave question. They allowed me to come quite near them, and, in some way or other, I understood that they were willing that I should listen to their discussion. Oh, not a discussion as we mean it; not at all. First, you must remember that they use no words. They understand each other immediately without words, and immediately they are of one opinion. At their degree of evolution judgment is one and the same for all of them." (Text: *La raison est même et unique.*)

I ask her to describe their aspect. She says that it was a very great assembly. There were thousands and thousands of them, looking to her like small blue lights. Seeking a comparison, which evidently she finds inadequate, she says, "They are like little scintillating waves of blue air, about the size of a hand," and adds what she has already said in a precedent séance, that this is their normal appearance, when they are amongst themselves and have no need to make themselves known.

She had no trouble in understanding them, and remarks that this indicates great progress in her faculties.

Later on she explains that it was Vettellini who attracted her to this reunion and who made it possible for her to grasp its significance. It was à *propos* of the appalling future events on Earth. They, the high Spirits, are going to try to avert, or at least modify, the catastrophe to the best of their ability. There is a fatal element in destiny over which Spirits have absolutely no control; but upon that part which results from the interplay of human character, and upon those events which are provoked by human decisions, the high Spirits have a possible influence. A large proportion of the great movements, of the big currents which sway human society, are provoked or modified by them. In the present case, the result of free play in human passions would be so overwhelmingly frightful that they are going to try to modify its action. Ah, it will be a heavy task! Heavy, because they will be obliged to leave the high ethereal spaces where they dwell and come down to our atmosphere and mingle in our life. In this assembly they were planning their work. Each one assumed his special role. Some are to act upon those who are directing political events—modify their passions and personal calculations; hold in check, and drive from them, the agitators; demolish their vanity; calm their jealousies, etc. Others are to influence public opinion, reassure it, and restrain false patriotism. And to accomplish this, they must weight themselves with our heavy dense atmosphere, must materialize in a way most painful to them. "Oh, yes," exclaims Reine again, "it is a big work—and a hard one!" They broke up into groups, and each group will act upon a certain country, a certain people. At their high degree, nationality no longer exists, of course. Humanity is all one to them. Their sole aim is to avert a check in its general evolution and, in so far as their power lies, they are going to try to do it.

Reine adds that they will not be able to prevent the war—*the wars.* But undoubtedly they will succeed in modifying them, in curtailing the hideous destruction and upheaval written in the Astral, and in warding off the internal strife and revolution. They will, in short, lessen the cataclysm, and protect the bases of civilization already acquired.

I ask if Vettellini is there. Soon we are talking together about Reine's excursion. He says that he wanted her to be present at this gathering so that we might understand, a little, the occupations of high Spirits in astral life. Gradually he will show us their means of action. He has allowed Reine to act quite alone during this experience, observing her constantly, and ready at any moment to come to her rescue. She has done as well as possible. He is much pleased.

We refer to the aid which Spirits give the incarnated; first, in general, to hasten the great movements of evolution; and then, in particular, to alleviate individual suffering. Reine explains that in the latter case, the protecting Spirit *assumes the suffering himself*—and by this fact his own evolution is advanced.

This is anything but satisfactory. I cannot understand it. Why should not a Spirit proceed as naturally as a physician, who is quite able to relieve pain and effect cures without assuming for himself the angina pectoris or the typhoid fever that he is called in to treat? I discuss the point with Reine and spend considerable time before grasping the situation, as she sees it, which is approximately this: Suppose a Spirit passes along a road where he sees some poor creatures—the incarnate— stumbling painfully under heavy burdens. Some of them are broken with fatigue and ready to fall. The Spirit approaches one amongst them, one who interests him, *seizes his load and carries it himself* for a few miles; and when the poor devil has drawn a long breath and gathered his forces, his burden is handed back to him. The Spirits did not create the situation. They find themselves in face of a certain fact,—that of miserable people struggling to accomplish difficult tasks: they give them a lift, they give them a chance to rest a bit. But it is not in their power to suppress the task itself, *for that would be to suppress evolution*. I understand, finally, and pass to another question.

What does Vettellini think of occultism and the value of esoterics in general? His reply—very vague—brings me to a special point, that of the Atlanta continent, and the civilization attributed by the Occultists to the Atlantes. He says that he is not familiar with the question and adds (Reine says he smiles) that, not wishing to make another such blunder as that about the color of the effluvia, he will inform himself, if I am especially interested in it.

Placing in Reine's hands a letter from my cousin, and indicating the direction she must take, I send her to see how he is and if I may be of use to him. She announces her arrival. "Oh, he is much worse than when I first saw him! He is sleeping ... I can speak to his Spirit and even bring him here." Surprised, I tell her to bring him if she is sure that she can. After a short delay Reine tells me that J. is here. I try to express my affection and sympathy, but he is in a dreaming state, it seems, and cannot even see me; everything is dark and troubled for him. He suffers more now and, little by little, forgets the details of his life. A vague conception of his wife still persists in an obscure sentiment of tenderness for her. He feels me, there,—says that he is happy to have come, it gives him something that is better. I try to think of how I might help him. Has he a wish that I could gratify? "No, my only wish is to die." This is his longest phrase.

I send Reine to take him back. Returning, she says that he will live for months yet. At times he is possessed,—that is to say, in the moments of physical crisis inferior Spirits seize and influence him as they will. There is nothing to do. It is a frightful ordeal, but one that will count in his evolution.

The séance closes by some advice from Vettellini concerning a moral preoccupation that is bothering us, advice that is remarkable for its good sense and moderation. "Useless to break your head trying to make it more perfect. Do the best you can and be as happy as you can in doing it," is the substance of his message.

He finishes the interview by speaking of health. I ask if we could do something really efficacious to ease the burden of the brave little Reine. Vettellini replies that the question is too delicate, he cannot discuss it. He adds that the conditions of her life will change before long. Soon she will not pose any more—or at least very little.

"Oh, Vettellini, is it true? I will not have to be a poor little model?" the child exclaims with emotion.

I begin the passes to waken her; she almost comes back to herself again, when, suddenly, she grows rigid, listens, and with the utmost difficulty articulates: "Vettellini says I must take quinine tonight for my fever."

FORTY-SEVENTH SÉANCE

April 14, 1913

Reine, still in bad condition, but gay and valiant, undertakes the séance with her usual good will. Great precautions are now imposed because of her fragile health, and we must no longer hope to obtain the phenomena which can be produced only when the body is completely cold. But those which can be provoked at the degree of hypnosis already attained, are sufficiently valuable. The facility with which she obeys me, the rapidity of her displacements, the precision of her astral vision,—all this becomes more and more marked.

In reply to my inquiry, she says that she is just back from far away, from the high places,—higher even than the last time! She has talked at length with Spirits whom she saw at that great reunion, but this time they were not holding counsel, and she could ask them about anything she chose. She chose to ask about Death.

She transmits abundantly, but in confusion, what has been told her. She has not quite clearly understood. There is a certain amount of nonsense and contradiction in what she repeats, aggravated by the poverty of her vocabulary. To my remark, "All that is none too clear," she replies quite simply: "You must ask Vettellini about it. You know I often don't understand, and then sometimes I repeat badly.—I haven't the right words." And she adds, picturesquely, "My body tangles me up."

So I cut short her narrative and ask her to make an excursion for my personal gratification. Will she go to find and bring here the Spirit of an old friend who died in B. on the Seine, some five or six years ago? The letter which I present, to guide her in finding the fluid, is of an old date; she says there is almost no fluid left in it. So I give her one that has come to me quite recently from his daughter (and which will allow her to find the house where they have lived together) and start her off to B.

After some moments Reine tells me she has reached the spot. She sees a high and ancient tower. "They have pretty well spoiled it," she remarks. I wonder what she means, but have not the time to make her specify,[46] for at once, thanks to the second letter, she discovers the house, not far from the tower, and is not long in entering into relation with my old friend T. himself.

What is his color? (This is now a capital question with me. "Tell me your color, and I'll tell you what you are.")—"He is gray; bluish-gray; about the color of your father." He seems to make some difficulty, objects to follow my messenger, but finally risks it. "He is there," says Reine, indicating by a nod of the head the space just above me.

He answers my banal questions coherently. Yes, he remembers me; he was very fond of me, is glad to have come, etc. He does not wander far from the banks of the Seine and the country round about this place, where he was born and where he died. He is not unhappy, no, … he does not suffer, … but neither is he happy, for he does not know what to do. He wanders about, … goes down to sit by the riverside, exactly as he did all his life long, … and is bored to death! He remembers his daughter with affection, goes often to her house to see her, but he can do nothing for her. And again he repeats: "I don't know what to do."

Reine explains that he is not at all a bad sort—quite the contrary. He is even rather remarkable in his way, for he has had so few incarnations. He is like a child—ignorant, that is all. Again he says that he is glad he came, and asks Reine to explain carefully how he can find his way here alone, for he means to come back.

Another question provokes a characteristic reply. What did he love the most in his lifetime? Reine transmits: "Most of all I loved to stroll about—and to paint." (This is exact. He neglected the most serious affairs to gratify his passion for painting. He left a house full of pictures—and little else.)

All told, the incident offers no great interest, and Reine, after my thanks and *au revoir*, gallantly escorts him back to the banks of the Seine.

---

[46] I was able later to examine these ruins and recognize that they have been "restored" with little skill.

As soon as she returns the child calls Vettellini, and before I have time to speak she is leaning toward him and listening attentively. Presently she turns to me: "Well, ... Vettellini says that I did not understand the communication of the blue Spirits. I made a perfect mess of it,—said everything wrong! But he is going to straighten it out for you."

Resuming, then, the general question of Death, Vettellini, to simplify the explanation, supposes four degrees in the scale of evolution and defines the characteristics of the passage from earthly life to astral life in each one of them:

At the first degree—the lowest—the incarnated being uses his body to the ultimate limit. His spirit literally grapples itself to his organic body, and even sometimes the intervention of the Spirits is necessary to wrest him away from it. At this degree there is not the slightest consciousness after death. Such a Spirit wanders about heavily in the lower atmosphere of earth, in a sort of coma, so to speak, until the moment arrives for another incarnation.

At the second degree, the soul on leaving his body is received by a group of Spirits who try to awaken his conscience and rouse in him a notion of responsibility. They aid him to acquire, according to his capacity, some notion of the phenomenon of Death. And in his next incarnation such a soul will sustain the reaction of what he has done in his preceding life—whether it be good or bad—and through it he will acquire his first inkling of responsibility.

At the third degree, the soul has developed a certain conscience. *He is responsible.* And even before his death, during his periods of sleep or delirium, he will be able to foresee what awaits him. It is this foreknowledge, whose repercussion creates an obscure presentiment in the waking hours, that explains a given attitude in face of death—terror or serenity. The soul, having left the body, is conducted by a messenger-Spirit before an assembly of white Spirits in whose presence he takes a complete and conscious view of his past life and of his responsibilities in it. At this degree of evolution, a disincarnated Spirit is able to accept with understanding and resignation the ordeal of his future life, for he realizes the necessity of it.

And finally, at the fourth degree, a modification of destiny may be offered just before death, as the blue Spirits explained to Reine today, and which Vettellini elucidates as follows: Sometime before the epoch determined for their death—determined by destiny—Spirits who have reached a high degree of evolution are able to disengage themselves during their sleep, or during a state of unconsciousness, and go to consult with the superior Spirits. Aided by them, they will take complete cognizance of their responsibilities in life and the consequences involved. Then, if the soul, though highly evolved, has still to return to earth for a short period of incarnation, he may choose *not to die at the moment normally determined, but to continue to live for some years, or some months, in the same conditions of suffering that he has been enduring up to that moment, and thus terminate once and for all his evolution on earth, without being obliged to undergo the slow ordeal of incarnation.*

This, it would seem, is a great favor accorded by the white Spirits.

This most interesting communication brings me to the precise question I have been wishing to ask Vettellini. It was said in the last séance that the determinism of the elements is inevitable (sidereal evolution, meteorological phenomena, terrestrial convulsions, etc.), but that events that result from the play of human passions and characters may be modified, in a certain measure, by the superior Spirits. On the other hand, Vettellini has declared that astrology is true in principle; that is to say, that the stars and planets do have an influence on human beings, and that there is correspondence between their different phases and the events in a human life.—"Then, there is, just the same, in individual and historical events, a part that is irresistibly fatal—a part that even the high Spirits cannot modify?" I ask. "For example, in the appalling predictions of the war, and the consequent social upheavals, many events must be enchained with the sidereal movement,—the rise or fall of certain men, for instance."

Vettellini replies that it is true: even the highest Spirits cannot touch certain events in preparation. They are beyond all influence. The law comes from on high—higher than they. They have no possibility of averting wars predestined in the Astral with such intense precision. Beyond any doubt the destiny of a Napoleon is determined and fixed. But if it is not in their power to change the essence of events, they have, in many cases, the possibility of modifying them. The race must be run, and the field is given: this is Destiny. But the high Spirits are able to break down, or pile up, the obstacles; and even, if need be, they create new ones. They can also give fresh speed to the runner, revive his energy, aid him when he falls, etc.

I remark that there are, however, certain cases tending to prove that Spirits may have an influence upon the elements. Is there any measure of truth in the stories where they are said to have dissipated a hailstorm, provoked rain ... etc.? The Guide says that it is not impossible.

Very high Spirits, uniting together, may be able to produce, or cause to be produced, certain meteorological phenomena. Since, by the combination of fluids and vibrations, they can momentarily abstract an object from the influence of gravitation, modify molecular cohesion, etc., there is no valid reason why they might not dissolve a cloud, ward off an accumulation of electricity, provoke a current in the atmosphere, etc.; but their action in this field is so exceptional that it is scarcely more than theoretic.

I ask if their power of penetrating matter is without limit, or if certain substances can oppose their passage. "The power depends upon the evolution. A Spirit of high evolution passes everywhere, penetrates everything."—The centre of the earth? I suggest. But Vettellini says that penetration is not possible there after the stratum of lava in fusion. Spirits of his degree can penetrate terrestrial matter even to the bottom of this liquid sheet, but further than that they cannot go. Why, he does not know. It is a limitation which they do not understand, but which is nonetheless effective. With this exception, nothing can oppose their passage, no metal, no substance; they can fathom the profoundest depths of the sea as they can pierce the most resisting plates of steel.

It is said that inferior Spirits may be arrested by running water. Could they not pass above it?—Vettellini says the fact is correct. Very undeveloped Spirits are like cripples: a man without arms cannot hoist himself over a barrier.

I allude to the recent book of two Dutch savants, who claim to have imprisoned Spirits, in conditions indicated by these Spirits themselves, in order that they might be weighed and measured. Vettellini replies that there are practical jokers even in the Astral, and they find nothing more amusing than the grave and scientific joke prepared expressly for the learned. It helps to pass the time in the Au-Delà.

And this brings me to a point of supreme interest. How is it that in spirit-communications of value, where not only a high morality is expressed, but where a philosophical, or even a scientific interest may be found, there is such an extraordinary facility in the use of the name of God, such a familiar use of His commands and His will? One would infer that the communicating Spirits have personal acquaintance with God; that God has engaged and commissioned them. Can Vettellini explain this state of affairs? Never since he has been communicating with us, never in any of his counsels nor in any of his teachings, not once, has the name or idea of God been introduced. Are, then, the inspirers of the religion called spiritualism of mediocre evolution? And how can this be true when some of their communications are so remarkable?

The Maître replies that many of the inspirers of the religion called spiritualism, are of very high evolution, and for that reason know how to use the best means of reaching their audience, the means adequate to their mentality. Those who make a religion of Spirit-presence and Spirit-intercourse are almost always people who have an intense need of faith in God, in a personal God. A religion without God, who is at once king and father, would have no meaning for them. They cannot grasp an ideal that has no representation. And for this reason the inspiring Spirits, observing and judging from their higher point of view, give them the mental nourishment that is necessary, the only one they can digest—and which, consequently, will sustain them.

FORTY-EIGHTH SÉANCE

April 16, 1913

(Madame G. is present)

In spite of Reine's ill health the séance has been good. As excursionist she was evidently less brilliant; she saw slowly, confusedly, and had only one desire—to get back to her body. On the other hand her transmissions were extremely clear.

She sleeps quickly, despite her fever, but does not grow cold. When I question her she says that she sees nothing, that she is there, disengaged from her physical body, and waiting to know what she is to do.

I give her an object that has belonged to my father, telling her to find him and bring him here. (I would like to get from my father himself an account of his death and passage into the Au-Delà. I doubt if he can give a precise analysis, but wish to make the experiment.)

After a few moments Reine announces his presence. I then explain my wish, begging her to make my father understand the great interest that an exact description of his experience would have for me, and for the work in which we are engaged.

Reine listens long to what he has to say, and when I, impatient, urge her to transmit his words, she tells me not to interrupt, for he is in the midst of describing what he can remember. Finally, I gather from what she afterwards reported that he had no sensation of death. He was conscious of nothing, felt no shock. He merely found himself suddenly, as in a dream, surrounded by Spirits who led him off, far and high, very high, to an assembly of other Spirits who, he realized later on, were superior. They tried to make him speak of his past life and to help him understand the good and the bad in it. But it was in vain. He understood nothing. All was confused and unreal for him. In face of his irresponsibility, the messenger-Spirits then led him back to the lower terrestrial atmosphere where they had found him, and left him there sleeping, stagnating in complete unconsciousness, ignorant even of his passage into death. It was only a long time after that the situation became clearer to him; and it is only recently—since he came here to see us, in fact—that he could seize the significance of the different phases through which he had passed. Now light is penetrating; his memories grow more definite; he begins really to understand. (What he says of his condition corresponds, in short, to what Vettellini ascribes to the second category. Forty-seventh séance). After some further talk, I thank my father for his effort ... and ask Reine to make an excursion.

In the hope of interesting Madame G., who is with us today, I send the child to see what is going on in a certain apartment (Madame G.'s apartment), giving her merely the address and directions for reaching it. She obeys—limply; she sees—vaguely; and it is only little by little, that she gives a rather colorless description of the place. She does not see the lady who lives there: she must have gone out. But she perceives the presence of a child and, after some hunting about, discovers the room where the child is at that moment. "A little girl. She is reading near a window." She also sees another person—"Not a servant, ... but she is not a lady either. Well ... after all, she is a kind of servant just the same ... you know? She is sewing. There is a bed in the room. It is the bedroom of this young girl. It is her place—she is at home there." (This was verified later. Madame G.'s little daughter was at that hour in her room, reading at the window, and her English nurse was sewing near her.) I suggest that Reine play a joke on the child, pull her hair, for instance. "Oh, no, Monsieur," she protests, "just think; if I succeeded it would frighten her!" Reine sees blonde hair, the child's hair is dark.

In directing the medium to Madame G.'s apartment, I had asked the latter for some small object which she was wearing that I might know from Reine if the fluid in the apartment was quite surely the same as that contained in the object—a shell comb—which I then handed to her. She compared the fluids and affirmed that she was surely there in the place where I had sent her. But on entering the child's room she quickly picked up the comb again, felt it more attentively and said: "This

163

child, who is here ... h'm ... it's the same fluid as the comb. She must be a daughter,—or at least there is a very close relationship."

I send Reine to find the salon, and, when she is there, ask what she sees on the walls. She smiles: "Oh well, I feel it at once, you know. It's a portrait of yours. Oh, I can't be mistaken in that fluid! There's no possibility of error." Here she appears to be examining something and finally says: "No, it is not a portrait, it's a picture. I cannot see it very clearly, but certainly it is not exactly a portrait of a person—it's more of a picture." (This is exact. It is a picture in which there is a woman's figure.) She sees exactly the arrangement of the room, the position of the window, the piano, etc. It is a pretty place,—sympathetic, she would like very well to live there ... but, after all, she would prefer to come back. And for the second time she insists upon my calling her home.

It is evident that she is very tired.

We learn afterwards that, during her excursion, Vettellini has been obliged to stand guard over her physical body and chase back her astral body which had returned twice, wishing to enter. Finally, however, she is allowed to reintegrate her domicile!

After a short respite, I ask our friend Vettellini to be good enough to answer a few questions.

Is an uncompromising materialist of necessity a spirit of mediocre evolution? The disinterestedness and abnegation of many great savants—materialists—has been admirable. All religions—including Spiritualism and the doctrines having reincarnation for basis—promise, after all, a recompense for effort, a compensation for suffering. Materialism alone is disinterested. What is Vettellini's opinion?—He answers:

"The greater number of materialists persist in their opinion simply because they have not the slightest intuition of anterior existences. Absolutely nothing rises in them, obscurely, to combat the arguments of gross evidence and extreme simplification which, in good faith, they accept. Before their reincarnation, while they were wandering in the Astral, their state was not unlike that of your father before you called him: that is to say, they were in a sleep. Reincarnated, they have not the faintest echo of the past, not the least intuition; and they naturally go straight to the belief that is the most materially logical. This applies to materialists of mediocre value.

"The brilliant ones, even those who have great intellectuality, are often no more advanced in evolution. They have had the luck to incarnate in an organism so perfect, so supple, that it is the organism which does all the work:—a well-trained mount gives an air of skill to the most ignorant horseman.

"But there are savants of the highest value, of admirable disinterestedness, who work for the welfare of Humanity, and with no hope whatever of recompense. Ah, these! They are making a glorious evolution. Their lives of abnegation and research, by which they do not dream of benefitting themselves, will carry them high. But these are rare. And then, you do not know whether even they, at that moment which precedes death, do not say: 'Who knows? I have spent the best that was in me for what I believe to be truth, and so it is well. But ... who knows?'"

I turn to another question: Art. Is there in astral life anything corresponding to the joy procured to us here by music, painting, sculpture, and poetry?

"But it is in the Astral that *all Art* is generated!" exclaims Vettellini. Its essential substance is created in the Astral, and your earthy manifestations are only the poorest copies! Understand me. When a work is of high and noble aspiration *it is the spirit* which has conceived it, and it is *by the spirit* that its beauty will be perceived. When, then, a Spirit is disengaged from his material envelope, it is easier for him to understand and penetrate the very essence of art-creation; he is no longer embarrassed and limited by material conditions. Obviously, Spirits have no musical instruments to play upon, but they can create and combine innumerable vibrations giving the most marvelous sensations of music and poetry. You, the incarnated, have but the mere suggestion, the faintest echo of what it really is!

I then speak of Nature, the exquisite and profound delight we have in contemplating it, and here again Vettellini applies the same reasoning: "When you are in contemplation before a scene of nature, it is your spirit which enjoys, your spirit which is exalted, but, once liberated, your capacity of emotion will be infinitely greater, and you will understand the very essence of what causes the emotion."

At Madame G.'s request, I inquire if the joy of affection persists, if the happiness which we have in our friendships and associations here on earth has its analogy in the Astral. "But certainly. It is always the same principle. All that proceeds from and pertains to spirit is considerably intensified in the Au-Delà. In the groups that are formed—and which themselves are always based upon affinities—certain Spirits are happier together than with the others, they attract each other, and their evolution continues together.

Reine is very tired. I consult the Guide about her health. He can do nothing. The poor child must suffer, she is destined to suffer.

I close the séance by asking the explanation of a strange incident that Reine related when she came today ... Last night, her husband, as usual, wound their two watches. Each one indicated exactly five minutes before nine. This morning, when he wakened, Armand glanced mechanically at the watches and saw that each indicated five minutes before nine. Terrified at the thought of arriving late at his desk, he gave a big groan; but Reine, listening to the noises in the street and in the house, assured him that it could not possibly be so running to a neighbor's door for verification, found that it was only twenty-five minutes after six. The two watches were ticking regularly and were still wound completely. It would seem, then, that some malicious genius had stopped the movements at five minutes before nine last evening and had set them going again this morning at twenty-five minutes past six? Vettellini knows nothing about it; he will investigate; he sees only Jeanik—our old friend Jeanik—who might have wished to recall himself to our attention!

April 18. It seems that it was, in fact, Jeanik, who felt that we were neglecting him too long. It was he who stopped both watches the moment that Armand had wound them. "But," says Vettellini, "his action was limited to that. The two watches were not going when Armand looked at them the next morning. He did not verify this at the moment. It was only when he took them up to set the hands at the proper hour, that the two instantly began their tic-tac."

This rectification is more interesting than the fact itself.

FORTY-NINTH SÉANCE

April 18, 1913

How can one explain this child's incredible devotion to the cause of psychical research (of which she knows nothing) if one rejects the reason given by her in hypnotic sleep, namely, that her role in Vettellini's work was voluntarily accepted by her, in advance?

Reine ought to be in bed: congestion, high temperature, no sleep for three nights. She is pitiful to see. However, as I am persuaded that she would have been informed if the séance held any danger for her, I tranquilly set to work. She is long in sleeping. (Later on she tells me that it has required all Vettellini's influence to affect her. At the début of the séance she saw his eyes fixing hers with great intensity; there was much phosphorescence, and many streaks of light,—a veritable display of fireworks!)

When the moment arrives, I ask what she has been doing during this first phase of sleep. She reports that she is back from those high regions where she has already gone twice to find the blue Spirits. To-day there was no assembly of any kind, simply a few passing here and there, to whom she applied for information. They told her that the great mass of the Spirits whom she has seen in consultation have now descended to the terrestrial atmosphere. Their campaign of modification has begun: all are at work.

At their own suggestion, Reine says that she tried to question them. "But ... I didn't know where to begin. You see ... it's not so easy for me. So

167

then, they said it would be better for you to tell what I must ask them—just as I am falling asleep, you know? In that way the questions will be precise and their answers more satisfactory. Then they advised me to come back here right away, for you were going to send me on a long voyage,—a difficult one, and Vettellini was already waiting to help me."

I had the intention, it is true,—but Reine knew nothing of this—to try to evoke an old friend of my wife's, a remarkable man it would seem, who had been of great importance to her when she was a child, and whom she had adored. He died from the effects of a terrible accident and after long suffering. If the experiment succeeded, it would probably give new and unexpected elements of interest.

As my wife possesses nothing belonging to him, the search is not an easy one. But Vettellini is there; it is he who will guide Reine. Following his indications, we join our hands with the hands of the medium and concentrate our minds on the person whose Spirit we are evoking: at the same time I give Reine the imperious order to go—directing her in thought to the American city where he lived.

After a moment Reine trembles slightly and speaks. She is there: she is in X.

She is beginning to give descriptions when, suddenly, she jumps back in her chair, turns brusquely around to her right, and, with drawn features and frowning brows, examines the space above her. She murmurs words that we cannot seize; finally she leans towards me: "Monsieur Cornillier, he is there,—the one you were calling. He came of himself, all alone, while we were way off there—so far—trying to find him! Ah—ha!" and the poor child sighs long over the voyage so violently interrupted. Later on in the séance she says that she was brought back too brutally, "sucked back in one breath, as it were, by the intense desire of this Spirit."

She listens now to the new arrival, but she is far from comfortable with her head stretched like that to the right and gently asks the Spirit to pass over to her left, which he does, beginning immediately to speak again before I have the chance to place a word!

It is surely he,—the one whom we have called. His very entrance is in itself curiously characteristic, but he gives at once precise elements of identity, *including his name, which Reine pronounces correctly and with the exact intonation.* (In accordance with his wish, however, I will suppress this name for the moment and designate him simply as the old friend.)

As he speaks, Reine transmits. He is happy—very happy. He is of high evolution; sufficiently far from us to have made contact with us impossible unless we had called him. He has never forgotten the child who had interested him so much, and unknown to her, he has always followed her life. He has come here before but could do nothing either to aid or to impress us, until our call, together with the presence of the medium, made an effective force. Now he will come often, we have only to evoke him; or Reine has only to come to find him in the region of the blue Spirits. He suggests that from time to time he might replace Vettellini, whose work is most important. "Ah, you do well to trust that one!" he cries, "he is a very great Spirit. No fear with him! I will try to relieve him sometimes by coming to answer your questions." He speaks of his accident and the last years of his life. "It was bitter suffering, but it was well worth while! It was my evolution ... and the suffering was nothing compared to what I got out of it!"

He bids Reine transmit to my wife (and this with a real solemnity) that he approves of what she did. We know from the phrases that follow that he refers to her marriage with a foreigner, involving a separation from her family, friends and country. (Curious this, coming from the little Reine.) He is pleased with what we are doing (our séances with the medium), "Ah, that is a good thing! That is a good thing!" He will come to help Vettellini in the question of Anne's health; he can, now that contact is established. And as I thank him and insist upon his care of her, it seems that he laughs heartily, and Reine laughs back at him as, leaning towards me, she whispers, "He doesn't think she is so very badly off, Monsieur Cornillier," etc., etc.

We inquire after a sister of his, who had been an important factor in his life and whom my wife calls "Aunt Suzan." His reply is extraordinary. This woman's life, it seems, had been one of devotion and self-sacrifice. And, being very religious, one would have expected her last days to be serene; but on the contrary she was seized with doubt, seemed to foresee something terrifying, and refused to listen to words that always before had sustained her. My wife recalls this incomprehensible attitude to her old friend; and this is his explanation. Sometime before death her spirit, already quite detached, could wander about in the Astral during her organic sleep, and in the course of these migrations take cognizance of the future conditions of her life after death. The high Spirits tried to inform her, to open her eyes; but the force of her religious convictions, her deep-seated faith in the teachings of the "Church" was such that she refused all effort of comprehension. And her spirit, finding only black emptiness there where she had expected seraphs and celestial music and the glory of God, thought she had been rejected,—thrown back amongst the eternally damned. This frightful impression of the spirit had its repercussion in an organism over-sensitive through long illness and gave her, when awake, this vague uneasy doubt and dread. Old Friend explains all this quietly and adds that since her passage into the Au-Delà this Spirit has not made the least progress. He can do nothing for her, they are too far apart, and the intermediaries whom he has sent numberless times—Spirits more material than he, who might have a possible influence—have not succeeded in impressing the first word of their message. She obstinately persists in the faith of her lifetime, in the God of her Church, and wanders about imploring Him and refusing all offer of assistance as coming from the devil.

I ask if we could not help her. After reflection, the Old Friend says that possibly we might, in making her come here, and in doing with her as I have done with my father. *But we must be careful to speak to her in the name of God.* We must place ourselves on her level, assume her convictions and ideas, say nothing, explain nothing, in opposition to her faith. We may try it.

Reine, deeply interested, says: "Do you know, Monsieur Cornillier, I believe your father could help you in that? You know he begins to understand now. He was beginning to open his eyes before we called, and what he saw here has made him reflect. He has taken a big step. He will be glad to do whatever we ask him, for he knows it will help him on. It is through him that we can reach the 'Aunt Susan.'" Old Friend approves. "Without aid she will stay where she is for an infinite time. She is so obstinate!"

After some further talk, he leaves us. Reine follows with closed eyes the blue wake of his passage.

I ask for Vettellini, and after speaking with him of this extraordinary visit, turn to my list of questions. First, what is the origin of special idiosyncrasies, such as an intense and persistent fear of an animal or an element—fire, water, etc.,—which some people have throughout their life? Or, again, the conviction that incessantly tortures one of our friends—that of an imminent accident which will mutilate and cripple her for life? Then, on another plane, the cause of invincible repulsions for a certain odor, taste, or contact? Vettellini replies that the fixed ideas of which I first speak proceed from the spirit and have their origin either in a persistent impression of an accident or of a death determined by the element in question in a preceding life: or in a presentiment, a view of the future, which has been caught by the spirit in one of his accidental sorties, and which makes him shudder intuitively in advance. As to the repulsions or special sensations caused by odors, tastes, or contacts, they are derived from the organism, from the chemical composition of the individual, and have their origin in heredity.

I pass to the second question. Vettellini has explained the composition of the *materialist* and I would like now to have the *spiritualist* analyzed in the same way. The case of my old friend T. (forty-seventh séance) troubles me considerably. This man—very gifted, very intelligent, but of no great cultivation, a dreamer by nature—was intensely spiritualistic. Without the least study or examination of the question, he had a sort of obstinate faith in a future life—faith which I always attributed to a rather high degree of evolution. And now it appears that, on the contrary, this obstinate one is only a poor weak Spirit, comprehending nothing at all of that future life of which he was so sure! This is disconcerting. Vettellini explains the case. This man was surrounded in his lifetime by Spirits of slight evolution, like himself, but who were at the same time good, because he himself was good. These Spirits were happy in his society, enjoyed being near him and observing him, and it is they who gave him his conviction of the persistence of life after death. Unknown to him, they impregnated him with a sense of the reality of their existence and of the continuity of his own life. A dreamer, T. was receptive and open to impressions. If, to amuse themselves, these Spirits had tried to inspire in him the contrary opinion, for example, they would have had equal success. Being a good sort, they had given him a true idea, *but one which was without value for him since he had never taken the trouble to verify it.* And here follows the sharp affirmation: *"What is essential is to understand."*

This carries me straight to a question of high import, and which provokes a most extraordinary statement.—Is it not ignorance which is the cause of all evil?—which is the cause of the very existence of evil? We constantly place evil and good in opposition. Would it not be more exact to say ignorance and comprehension? That is, bad people are merely ignorant people, and good people are the intelligent, the more evolved?

"Not at all," says Vettellini with emphasis.

But, pursuing my idea, I go on to say that only lately have I been able to admit the necessity of punishment and expiation. I understand that the directing Spirits—since directing Spirits there be—find themselves facing a situation which they have not created, in the presence of an established society made up of the good and the bad, and that, necessarily, the direction and administration of this society involves punishment for the instigators of disorder, correction for the parasites who live on the efforts of others, etc., etc. But how is it possible that primitively, originally, the Good and the Bad existed? What is the initial cause of dissimilarity in Spirits? How are good tendencies and bad tendencies generated in Spirits who are equal and placed in conditions identically the same?

Here is the substance of the curious reply which unfortunately could not be stenographed:

Originally Spirits are not very dissimilar, nor have they an essential activity for evil. Left free to follow their natural inclination, they would vegetate in an unprogressive indolence. But (and here Reine speaks with marked authority) you must not forget Fatality. Above the Spirits whom we know, there are others who are higher; and above and beyond these are others still, ... and still others, more and more high. But higher than all, there is Fatality; there is the HAND. And it is in the foreordained order of things that, to provoke the evolution of a race or of a human society, elements of evil are introduced into it. Without that, there would be no evolution. THE HAND, accordingly, places amongst these beings, at the very début of evolution, germs of immeasurable vitality and perversity. They are—or they may be— Spirits of animals who have evolved on another planet and who have acquired there the vibratory forms necessary for incarnation in the human race. The HAND distributes them, sows them for Evil, that they may do only Evil, and thus provoke a force of reaction, a defense, a revolt, in this new race at its very beginning. It is the ferment that is necessary; it is the leaven without which the human soul could not enter into travail and evolve. But these malevolent Spirits are not responsible. They will not be punished for their crimes. Fate conceived them for the role they have enacted, and Fate restores them to the point of development achieved by them when she seized them for her purpose.

FIFTIETH SÉANCE

April 21, 1913

A poor séance, but at the same time, interesting. Reine is in better health but quite upset by the important small events of her daily life (a change of lodgings), and I am so tired that my magnetizing force is undoubtedly affected. She sleeps, however, promptly enough, but without the least change of temperature, and her action is slow and heavy.

I send her on an excursion to Nantes—to the house of a friend. She sees very vaguely. The only point of interest is that she makes no effort whatever to coin information, saying quite simply that nothing is clear to her. She does, however, give an accurate description of one of the members of the household whom she sees there.

I beg her then to find my father and bring him here to me. This she accomplishes with greater ease.

To my father I explain our project in regard to "Aunt Susan" and ask if he will help us. He says that he will do all he can. Our confidence seems to please him, and he proposes to act at once. But, before launching out in this undertaking, I wish to consult the old friend, and tell Reine to go find him.

It seems that he is there—has been observing the séance from the beginning. He gives directions for finding his sister and my father starts out on his strange adventure! After a while he returns to say that he has found her, it is she, there is no mistake about it, but she refuses to follow my father. Reine, who seems deeply interested in this incident, offers to go herself. She will reassure her, will speak to her of her faith, etc. Some moments pass. Finally Reine returns, bringing—so she says— "Aunt Susan" with her. "Here she is!"

Impossible to give the whole scene. I will note only that the moral state manifested by this Spirit is entirely concordant with what Old Friend has told us. She is, in fact, most unhappy, believing herself to be in Purgatory. But she has never doubted God for an instant. It is with greatest difficulty that she recognizes my wife—if it can be called recognizing—though she remarks that she feels something happy and good which she has not known since her death, and says: "It is my first sensation of joy." She speaks of God, and of the Angels, asks us to unite our prayers to hers, and God's goodness will surely manifest itself for her, etc. Reine says that she is not even bluish in color, she is red, but this is because she has had so few lives yet. Her tendencies and instincts are good and elevated, but she is still only a baby-Spirit, so to speak; she is young, and stubborn in her faith, and that is all.

When "Aunt Susan" leaves us, Old Friend declares himself well satisfied with this first step. He will now send intermediary Spirits to aid and influence his sister, and we, on our side, must call her here from time to time: it will help her to understand.

Then he stays on and talks at length with us. Immediately we feel the impact of a buoyant, ardent nature.

From time to time Reine, gazing at the point in space where we infer he is, breaks into laughter and once she explains: "He is laughing, you know ... and when he laughs I have to laugh too—he's so gay!" To a reflection from my wife he answers so sharply that Reine, astonished, breaks off in her transmission, refusing to continue. I insist upon having it, ... insist again and more seriously. After much hesitation and taking precaution to explain that she is not responsible, the child finally whispers: "He said these words, he said, 'Tell her not to be a fool!'" My wife's amusement is not unmixed with emotion. In the frankness of his compliment she recognizes her old friend.

I ask to speak with Vettellini. He is not there, and is long in coming. Reine knows why: the presence of the Spirits who were with us for some time today has vitiated the atmosphere for him. Before he can come to us their vibrations must be spent, for they are like a poison to him.

At last he is here and ready to answer my questions.

I ask first: what influence has a violent death on evolution? Answer: Violent deaths are always predetermined; it is never a matter of chance. They are decided by Fate to hasten the evolution of certain people who are not advancing normally, and who would eternally have to begin over again successive reincarnations. The shock caused by a violent death is such that it produces a strong reaction in the Spirit and causes an immediate forward movement.[47] The Spirit revolts, tries to understand, *"and to try to understand is to evolve."* When the violent death is due to an act of devotion, a rescue of life, for example, all the merit that heroism or self-sacrifice imports is added to the reaction of the mechanical shock, and the Spirit veritably strides up the ladder of evolution.

From what Reine has said in other séances it is evident that there must be a similarity of fluid in members of the same family. And this provokes my second question: Does not each Spirit, then, create his own fluid? And what part has heredity in the question?

To simplify, I will give only the substance of the long reply:

Let us suppose, theoretically, a Spirit who has never been incarnated; his fluidic body is an amorphous substance without special vibrations. Captured in a vortex of incarnation, this fluidic body is, in the course of foetal formation, impregnated and profoundly marked by the vibrations of his progenitors. They give him an organism drawn from themselves, whose indestructible imprint his fluidic body will carry forever. After birth, when personal life begins, it is the reaction of his soul which will come to modify the vibrations of his fluidic body, thus adding other vibrations to those given by his progenitors, but without destroying them.

At death, when this being re-enters astral life, he will possess a fluidic substance influenced, primarily, by the vibrations of his progenitors, and, secondarily, by the reaction of his spirit in the course of his incarnated life—the combination forming an original composition which belongs to himself alone.

When this Spirit reincarnates he will pass through exactly the same process: first, the indelible imprint of his progenitors; second, the modifying reaction of his Spirit on his fluidic substance. These two influences will graft themselves on the precedent vibrations, but always without destroying them, and thus will it be throughout all the successive incarnations of this soul. To sum it all up, the fluidic body of each Spirit is always an original composition; but in this original composition the trace of the vibratory influence of all his past progenitors exists, and may be found.

This leads logically to the question of the evolution of organic substance itself. The incarnated spirit has, by the mediation of his fluidic

---

[47]   Note 3 at the end of the volume gives the reasons for this.

body, a power of reaction against the organic substance. That is, according to the tendencies, aspirations, and will of the soul, the body (his terrestrial instrument) may be made more delicate, more subtle, may, in short, be refined. And this refinement of the organic substance may be transmitted by heredity, and the descendants will thus find better conditions of evolution.

Those who have no descendants will none the less aid a little in the evolution of matter, for the constitutive elements of their physical organism will, after death, serve in the formation of new substances that will benefit by the value acquired.

Here I try to bring order out of a mass of information (transmitted by Reine in a rather disorderly way) concerning evolution in the Astral. I had understood at first that only evolved Spirits could progress in the Au-Delà while the inferior ones remained stagnant, awaiting the moment of reincarnation. But at a certain moment, Vettellini remarking that the Spirit of "Aunt Susan" was always attached to her mortal remains, added: "It is to give her the chance to evolve that she is thus held to her body." I point out the contradiction, and this is the explanation as I have understood it.

It is, indeed, the general law that Spirits of a good evolution continue to advance in the Astral, while inferior ones have need of the life of incarnation for progression. But there are infinite modifications of this law, arising naturally from the infinite diversity of Spirits. In short, *the directing Spirits invariably seek to hasten evolution, and, when they deem it advisable, they do not follow the rule.*

For example, after death the fluidic cord which binds the Spirit to his dead body should, at a given point of organic decomposition, detach itself from the body, thus giving to the Spirit the independence which his evolution commands. But as an undeveloped Spirit is unable to draw any advantage from such independence, and as, on the contrary, the fact of being attached to his body and of being obliged to assist at its slow decomposition is a cause of suffering—and as all suffering contributes to evolution—the directing Spirits sometimes maintain the relation between the Spirit and his body in order to provoke progress.

Another example: An inferior Spirit, detached and independent, wandering about in our lower atmosphere, would inevitably be immediately captured in a vortex of incarnation. But a too speedy reincarnation would in some cases be of no advantage (I will give the reason further on). So here again the Directors maintain the attachment by the fluidic cord to prevent a premature return to earth. It is no longer an ordeal provoking progress, as in the first case, it is merely a mechanical obstacle to reincarnation.

But why this delay in the return to earth of an inferior Spirit?

It would seem that there are periodic waves of incarnation and disincarnation (this periodicity depending upon astral and planetary influences), bringing down or carrying off Spirits who are approximately equal in evolution, and who, for this very reason, have certain solidarity. If then a disincarnate, instead of waiting for the return of the wave to which he belongs, allows himself to be drawn off by another one, he will lose the benefit of this solidarity; he loses his place, he is like a soldier who drops out from the regiment in which he is marching to fall casually into the ranks of another one that follows.

(In view of my hesitation to accept certain statements, Vettellini advises me to admit nothing that I do not understand. I must not be afraid to insist. He is only too glad to explain.)

I was about to forget an interesting point à *propos* of the incomprehensible replies of certain disincarnate Spirits, of supposedly high evolution, to those engaged in psychical research. I say to Vettellini: A highly evolved person passing into astral life disentangles himself promptly from the torpor and obscurity which seem to overwhelm ordinary people after their death. If this is the case—and you seem to say it is—how is it that men of great value who consecrated a part of their lives to research in this question of survival, and who, while still living, planned and promised to manifest themselves after their death, in order to finally give decisive proofs of the reality of survival—how is it that such men have often been quite incoherent in their communications through a medium? In the midst of valuable and convincing statements they suddenly retail such stupidities that doubt is at once created in the minds of even the best intentioned?

Vettellini replies: "Men of great value on earth—conscientious students, authorities in their specialties—are not necessarily Spirits of high evolution. In the case that you cite, for example, these men have possessed a marvelous organism, an instrument so supple, so malleable, that, unsuspected by them, great Spirits may have made a most profitable use of them in the achievement of a special work. All unconsciously, they have become mediums of a superior order, doubly valuable by reason of their culture, their tendency to investigation, and the admirable activity of their organic brain. But, once dead, the Spirit disengaged from this remarkable organism is disconcerted. No longer aided, they are merely themselves, and necessarily less great than they had appeared to be. The worst is that their habit of importance persists—for a time. They are in the dark, they do not understand very clearly, but they go on talking just the same."

This explanation may be correct. It is certainly cruel. My wife hastily protests: "But how is it that the great Spirits, who have made use of them, do not prevent them from spoiling their own work in this way?"—"The Spirits sow the seed; they consider an indication sufficient. Each one must find for himself the elements of his own conviction" is the substance of Vettellini's reply. But the rigor of the communication is attenuated by his remark that the conditions which Spirits are forced to endure in order to communicate with us—the entering into a heavy and material atmosphere, which stifles and oppresses them the more as their evolution is the higher—that these conditions are a great obstacle to lucidity. And, again, in many cases it is the mediums who are responsible for the stupidities and errors. Personal experiences and opinions are frequently tangled up in their transmission; or, tired, they answer without taking the trouble to be exact or to verify.

I know a number of examples myself.

FIFTY-FIRST SÉANCE

April 23, 1913

(Monsieur R. is present)

A bad séance. The presence of my friend R. was quite evidently disturbing. There were points of interest here and there, but obtained after much effort and presented in such great confusion that R.'s influence was, so to speak, materially visible. Never have we had such an impression at any other séance.

As soon as the medium is sleeping I call R. into the room and begin my usual catechism. As she says she has done nothing, seen nothing, I send her to the boulevard Montparnasse, to that house near the cemetery, where she has already been (thirty-eighth séance) and ask what she sees there. Just as at her first visit, she enters the apartment by a window. Immediately, I feel that the experiment will be a failure. She sees everything "black"— nothing is clear; she is heavy and hesitating. It takes ten minutes for her to discover the presence of Madame R. Her descriptions are colorless and without precision. Not only does she see badly, but she makes a false interpretation of what she sees;—and this has never before occurred. (Certain incidents mentioned by Reine were, upon R.'s return home, proved to be false.) On the other hand, she once more gives proof that mindreading and thought-transmission play no part in her method of procedure; for she takes absolutely nothing that exists either in the conscience or sub-conscience of R., nor in my own mind, in spite of the fact that we both place any number of images and thoughts at her disposal.

Exactly as at her first visit, she feels strangely uncomfortable in this apartment, but this time she understands the reason of her trouble. It is because the place is impregnated with heavy vibrations. The proximity of the cemetery turns it into a sort of "happy hunting ground" for the red Spirits whose presence disturbs the atmosphere. The occupants of the house unconsciously suffer from it. "It is one great reason for the depression and uneasiness so frequent with them," says Reine, describing a state of mind that unquestionably exists.

After some talk about this interpretation of the case, I tell Reine to come back and make another effort;—one that will be quite as painful as the first one. She must return to the cemetery Montparnasse and hunt for a Spirit (R.'s father). I give her several objects that have belonged to him. She obeys me; finds the Spirit, and brings him here. But he is so little evolved that he can say nothing at all, not even his name; nor does he even remember whether he was a man or a woman! (This in spite of a big lock of hair—*coming quite evidently from a man's head*—which I had placed in Reine's hands and which she had carefully examined.)

I pass to another evocation which gives no better results, but this time because the Spirit called (R.'s mother) has reincarnated. Vettellini comes to inform Reine of this fact, to avoid a long and useless search. Briefly, nothing of interest is obtained in any of our efforts.

So then I beg Vettellini to come and talk to us. Perhaps finally we may get something that is worthwhile.

And, as a matter of fact, things worthwhile are abundant, but Reine's transmissions come with difficulty and in a confusion and disorder not at all natural to her. Throughout the entire interview the disturbance and irritability of the medium—as well as of her Guide—are quite perceptible. Twice Vettellini abandons us, and Reine has to call him back. This was explained to me later on. "You know it's a big sacrifice for Vettellini to come to us. He leaves his high spheres, and weighs himself down with heavy fluids before he can enter into contact with us. That in itself is painful enough; but if he finds antipathetic vibrations he cannot stay,—it is too much."

Questions:

First: On the theory of the moment, *Idéoplastics*. Vettellini affirms that it is an error: "Ideas and thoughts produce radiations, waves, but never images or forms of three dimensions. *The photograph of an idea is an impossibility."* The phenomenon designated by these words has another origin, which he will explain to me.

Second: On the Spirit-faculty of recognizing the fluid of a person amongst the billions of fluids that must exist.—Vettellini says that it is a fact which he himself is unable to explain: they in the Astral use this faculty without an exact comprehension of its causes.

Third: On the constitution of the Earth.—He says that the centre of the Earth is hard, of density beyond our conception. All the planets composing our system have this same constitution of a hard centre; all except the Sun, whose role in the system is a special one. For the Earth, once the belt of liquid lava, which exists at a certain depth, is passed, matter begins to solidify again, grows hard, and the density becomes more and more intense as the centre is approached.

Fourth: On the position of the Earth in the hierarchy of planets.— The conditions of habitability of a planet and the evolutive degree of its inhabitants are in relation to its distance from the Sun—those farthest away being the least advanced.

Finally, I ask if a Spirit always conserves the same fluidic body (modified, naturally, in the course of his different incarnations) as long as he remains attached to the same planet. Vettellini replies that the manifold reincarnations of a Spirit on the same planet are always made with the same fluidic body, modified gradually in the course of evolution. But after the last passage on earth—or another planet of equal development—the Spirit has attained a degree of evolution that places him beyond the necessity of reincarnation on the physical plane. He is no longer attached to any planet or star. From this moment, a fluidic body—which is merely an intermediary between spirit and organism—is of no further use to him, and he abandons for ever this substance which, in turn, goes to form new combinations on its own proper planet. Completely liberated from all shackles, the Spirit then exists as Spirit only—a state of being inconceivable to our human intelligence.

To terminate, I establish contact between Reine and R. by placing his hand in hers, and ask Vettellini to give advice … An evasive response. R.'s vibrations are evidently antipathetic to the skeptical medium. His skeptical mind irritates and offends Vettellini. I object that R.'s skepticism is not willfully obstinate; he has studied, and still studies, this question very fairly, and asks nothing better than to be convinced; but for that he must have facts and arguments that appeal to his reason.

My remarks are unheeded, I am conscious of an irritation, of a curious antagonism, and do not insist.

My wife and R. leave the room. I am about to waken Reine when, with all her habitual charm and vivacity, she begins speaking again with her Guide. And now Vettellini bids her communicate his impressions of R.:—"He carries with him a painful atmosphere. His aura is impregnated with the influence of the red Spirits who live there in his dwelling near the cemetery. He himself is good, but he is doubly intoxicated, first by these guests whom he involuntarily receives, and then because his own Spirit has sad and somber tendencies, carrying as it does the weight of many anterior existences without great progress. His soul needs a thorough washing out, so to speak, needs to create a new atmosphere for himself. Then he would make a beautiful evolution. But ... will he do it? Doubt reigns in him,—authoritative, imperious doubt. Vettellini speaks at length of this strange case, and of the impression which Reine will retain even after waking.[48]

Thursday, April 24, 9 a.m.

Last night, some moments after I had put out the light, my attention was drawn to the most obscure corner of the room by the scintillation of a beautiful blue star. It was about eight feet from the floor and persisted an appreciable time,—perhaps two seconds. It was not the light, or the phosphorescent nucleus, that I have seen several times. It was a star,—*a scintillating star.*

Friday evening, April 25

At the séance today Vettellini communicates that it was he who produced this star, to compensate for the bad Séance of the afternoon with R. He said that he made it again last night, but at the precise moment, I turned my head in another direction and did not see it. He could not begin over again as this production involves an enormous expenditure of force.

---

[48] Reine was curiously uncomfortable after waking, almost ill, and this condition lasted for some time.

FIFTY-SECOND SÉANCE

April 25, 1913

Not a thrilling séance from the point of view of incident, but the communications were admirably clear, and, even, their verbal form was remarkable considering the character of the subjects. Reine's tendency grows more and more pronounced. It is obviously useless to count upon her for material phenomena; her spirit rebels.

When Reine is sleeping I send her to the realm of the blue Spirits to ask them this:—Is there, from the very beginning, inequality in Spirits? And, if so, what is the cause of this inequality?

She goes at once to the high regions and speaks there with a great blue Spirit, who gives a sufficiently clear exposition of this subject, which Reine transmits to me. But as Vettellini afterwards voluntarily resumes it in greater detail, I give here only what came to me from this latter source.

The report of this first excursion terminated, I tell the child that I am obliged to scold her very seriously for what happened in the last séance, when I sent her to the boulevard Montparnasse. Seeing nothing, or seeing very obscurely, she has nevertheless talked,—tried to make up some kind of a story for us. I show her the harm in such proceedings, point out the opprobrium that would fall upon our investigations, whereas the simple avowal of seeing nothing is no disgrace whatever.

Reine replies: Never, never, does she invent, nor does she pretend to see when she does not see. As to her visit of Wednesday in the boulevard

Montparnasse, she supposes that if she reported an incident that did not occur—it was undoubtedly due to the miserable little red Spirits who infect that place, and who, seeing her disturbance and discomfort, took advantage of it, possibly, to create a false image and amuse themselves at her expense. She explains that in spite of her determination and desire, she cannot interest herself in these material experiments. It would be well for me to speak with Vettellini about it,—ask his advice. Not only does she wish to please me, but, more than this, she herself understands perfectly the necessity of getting positive proofs; for only positive proofs count with the skeptics. And she confesses that so ardent is her wish to succeed, that, all alone by herself, at home, she tries for hours together to provoke some small material phenomenon. Never once has she succeeded. She only falls asleep, and immediately her spirit flies off.

(Later on, I ask Vettellini if it is the most essentially pure part of her spirit which thus liberates itself, or if it is rather the vitality of her fluidic body which drags her into this sort of vagrancy,—like a schoolboy playing truant. He says it is the soul itself, the pure spirit, and this is why he, Vettellini, is helpless in the matter. He tries to hold her back, to keep her attention fixed on a material point in question, but the spirit of Reine has its own autonomy and once completely disengaged becomes perfectly indifferent to the contingencies of terrestrial life.)

My scolding administered, I ask for Vettellini.

He has been there all the time, listening to our discussion. We begin at once to talk about the inequality in Spirits and the dissimilarity existing between them from their very origin. Are they not, then, equal at the moment of their sortie from the Absolute?

The reply comes in measured and precise terms, and without the least confusion. First the Maître observes that it is just such problems as these that occupy high Spirits in the Astral. And alas! Despite their enormous superiority over the incarnated, despite their unnumbered possibilities of investigation, they succeed in only extending the frontiers of human comprehension. *For them also there is always an Au-Delà.*

They can, however, follow the evolution of matter and of consciousness throughout an immense extension. They can go back over the entire road covered by the spirit and observe the different phases of development. They can trace back to the original cell. And that is all. The *"Beyond"* is as great a mystery for them as it is for us.

But Vettellini absolutely affirms this: *There is no such thing as blind chance in the play of cosmic Forces.*

The power (which those of his evolution have) to foresee the fate of beings and things, the permission which is sometimes accorded them to modify a written fatality, proves a Plan,—a Direction. What is this Direction? The immense knowledge of the highest Spirits is but relative to our ignorance. The ultimate Mystery remains impenetrable.

Evolution is the Law. Everything that exists evolves. But the modalities of evolution are infinite. Certain stars and planets evolve only inorganic matter; on others, vegetable life develops; and, finally, there are stars that push evolution to the point of animal life. And thenceforward, consciousness, as we understand it, exists.

At the evolutive moment determined by the physicochemical conditions of the ambiance, interplanetary emigration takes place. The Spirit which has acquired the supreme degree of evolution afforded by the constitution of a planet, leaves that planet and goes to continue evolution on another. And when he has reached the point where all that matter can give has been gained, he is no longer under necessity of incarnation on the physical plane. He continues his evolution on the ethereal plane.

And here, for us—the incarnate—the limit of comprehension is reached. But Spirits have a longer view. Vettellini can follow a spiritual evolution inconceivable for our intelligence; but only up to a certain point ... beyond which, for him also, there is unfathomed mystery.

But we have wandered far from my question. So then I come back to it once more: Is there original inequality in the different "seeds of life"?

Yes. From the very origin there is a virtual capacity for dissimilar reactions: each life-seed holds a mysterious germ of individuality.[49] Why? What is the cause? Vettellini does not know.

I ask if, in his present judgment, this does not seem an injustice.

He replies that this inequality at the origin of life is a subject of profound meditation. But, on the other hand, he knows that the responsibilities of each being are established in accordance with his original force of reaction. He knows, too, that Fate—which Reine calls "the Hand"—places, all along the path of evolution, a ferment of evil to stimulate the reaction of the Spirit. These ferments exist in the lower animal kingdom as well as in the human races of highest consciousness.

---

[49] This passage seems in contradiction with what has been said on the subject in the Forty-ninth Séance, but it is rather the fault of my wording. "Inequality" is too strong a term, "mysterious germ of individuality" is better.

Those to whom fatality has given the role of ferments are not responsible: when their task is finished they resume the degree of evolution which they have acquired.

It is to the study of such problems that the high Spirits consecrate a part of their activity. And the impenetrability of the great Mystery is often no less a sorrow for them than for us. Certainly they are, or they may be, profoundly happy; their capacity for enjoyment is increased a hundred-fold by their disengagement from matter, but their capacity for spiritual anguish is correspondingly increased. They, too, must suffer ... to evolve.

After this grave question (resolved as well as it can be, no doubt), I return again to the idéoplastic theory—the mental fad of the moment.

Once more the Maître affirms that an idea or thought has never a representative form. The so-called photographs of ideas are produced by another cause altogether. It is not the ideas or thoughts that are photographed, it is the *images*, which are created either by the medium—consciously or unconsciously—or by a Spirit assisting the medium. Vettellini, for example, often imposes an image on Reine's brain. It is generally a subjective perception, but occasionally, if he has a reason for so doing, he gives it an objective reality—by means of fluidic combinations, if the image is simple; by the instantaneous addition of matter, if the image is complex.[50]2 In such a case the image may be photographed, and even, sometimes, it may be perceived by those assisting at the experiment.

I refer to the photographs of flat images obtained with the medium Linda, and the experiments of Doctor Ochorowicz, and others.[51]3 Vettellini says that his explanation holds for these different cases. The medium Linda is probably very strong. She may be able to obtain this phenomenon of materialized images by her sole force, or, it may be, she is aided in her task by Spirits. But once again it is asserted that the phenomenon has no connection with ideas or thoughts existing in a brain. It is an operation analogous, if you will, to that of a drawing instantaneously executed by an artist.

I take advantage of the turn of the talk to ask the significance of certain ridiculous but authentic materializations: for example, that

---

[50] If a strong materialization is needed, he calls upon less evolved Spirits to work for him.

[51] See *les Annales des Sciences Psychiques* of the last few years.

phantom of Bien-Boà, photographed by Professor Richet—a phantom provided with a helmet, a gorget, and various other masquerading accessories. Vettellini once more explains that occasionally inferior Spirits try to amuse themselves. Some of them, though inferior, know how to make use of the forces of a medium. They have learned by watching and listening to the more evolved ones; and when there is a reunion with a good medium of rather low order, they seize their chance for fun. Sometimes even it is with the best intention. They do what they can, according to their grade of intelligence.

I ask if the great Spirits could not prevent such manifestations which provoke ridicule.—"No, except in extreme cases, we cannot. Spirits are, in a certain measure, free. It is for the living to distinguish. It is study, it is the effort to understand, that makes evolution. *If all the Verities were handed over to the incarnated, there would, be no more struggle to conquer them, and, consequently no more evolution."*

In their talk at the end of the séance, Vettellini teases Reine a little about her weakness for mirrors, and she, in a fury, sharply retorts that it must be a weakness shared by him, for every time she would look at herself his face comes up to spoil her view!

FIFTY-THIRD SÉANCE

April 28, 1913

(*Monsieur V. is present*)

The usual preparation.

Reine announces that she has made her excursion to the blue Spirits to whom she communicated the questions with which I charged her in the beginning of her sleep. The reply which she brings me, clearly expressed, gives rise later on to an incident which I note at once, because of its great significance. When, at my request, Vettellini comes to talk with us, in the latter part of the séance, *he spontaneously informs the medium that she has made a big error in the reply she has transmitted from the blue Spirits. And he rectifies it.* (For simplification, I will give here the communication as it was corrected by Vettellini.)

The account of her voyage terminated, I send Reine to get news of my poor cousin. She obeys,—finds him easily.—"He is gradually growing worse:—much weaker than at my last visit. Just at this moment he is calm.[52] Although he is not sleeping his astral body is entirely outside: it is a bad sign. He is seated,—stupefied, prostrated: his astral body is just above him."

At my request, Reine enters into contact with him. She asks if there is anything she might do for him: has he a wish for something? With difficulty she obtains "I would like to die ... I understand nothing ...

---

[52]   His wife, who was with him at that moment, verified this statement later.

I doubt even the efficacy of death." She reports him as much heavier mentally, more vague, than in her precedent visits, but she is not sure that this does not come from the fact that his physical body is awake. After some attempts at consolation, she leaves him and comes back.

(Later, Vettellini confirms Reine's last observation, but adds that as death approaches J.'s comprehension will become more and more obscure by reason of his evolution. He will regain consciousness slowly after his passage into the Astral.)

Next I ask to speak with the old Friend, to know if I may call "Aunt Susan" today and try to help her a little. "Better wait till we are alone for that," is his reply. So then we talk of other things. I ask if, at his degree of evolution, he can look back over all his past incarnations and follow inversely the different stages of his progress. After an interesting misunderstanding (he thought I had asked if he *did look back* and promptly answered, "certainly not!")—after this misunderstanding, he replies that he has only to wish it, only to fix his mind on the past, and he could re-live all over again his successive lives. But there is no further interest for him in all that, he has thrown it aside. No need to hark back to it. *He has something better to do!*

I ask if amongst themselves the high Spirits can mutually see into each other's past, or if that would be considered an attack upon individual independence. Before I can finish my question the answer is flung back, with a brevity and spontaneity wholly characteristic of the man in his life time: "At our degree of evolution,—all being equal, and having gone through about the same kind of trouble—nobody wants to conceal anything, nobody is ashamed in face of the others. If it pleases us, we can see the different phases in the evolution of our equals or of our inferiors. But our inferiors may not take that liberty with us."

My wife asks if his last life would give the impression of the high evolution which he has reached. He replies that his evolution had been much more active in other previous incarnations. In the last one it was, above all, the long suffering after his accident which made him progress. He adds that in the course of his last life, however, he has given proof of remarkable intuitions—"and that is always a sign of evolution; it is an evidence of the soul's acquisition." We thank him, and I ask for Vettellini.

As soon as he comes I beg him to complete the information gleaned by Reine in her visit to the blue Spirits today (it is here that he sharply reproves an error in her transmission), concerning what I have termed "the waves of incarnation" and the "waves of disincarnation." Vettellini communicates: "there are periods during which Spirits inevitably re-incarnate. These periods are determined by the influence of the stars. The passage of certain planets, or the approach of certain stars, pro-duce fluidic currents that beat down the disincarnated souls and throw them back toward the earth—thus exposing them to capitation. Even those of fairly high evolution cannot always escape this influence; they are forced by it to approach the terrestrial atmosphere. The passage of these stars is irregular; or, rather, the intervals between their epochs of passing are not equal. There is never a solution of continuity in the influence of incarnation, but there is a rising, a maximum point, and a decline in it. Astrologists could verify exactly the effects of this law by establishing statistics of births in relation to planetary movements."

In the same way, and from analogous causes, disincarnation is de-termined. But the disincarnating planets pass regularly, and at equal intervals. Their approach provokes fluidic currents which, on the con-trary, call and attract the incarnated Spirits, and hasten the detach-ment of those on the point of rupture, etc., etc.

I bring the séance to an end rather brusquely, having noticed a pe-culiar agitation both in the medium and her Guide. When I am alone, Vettellini tells me that the fluidic atmosphere was not harmonious today.

FIFTY-FOURTH SÉANCE

April 30, 1913

Ⅰt is difficult to give, in a summary account, an exact impression of this séance which, while not especially impressive, has nonetheless been remarkably interesting. As usual we alone were present, and undoubtedly this very fact was an element in the success; for the medium was calm and confident, and we ourselves had not the preoccupation which the presence of a stranger inevitably provokes.

In hypnotizing Reine today I give her no order.

To my inquiry she replies that—for her own pleasure, out of curiosity, she went to look at the sea. She supposes, at least, that she succeeded, and that what she saw was really the sea,—at any rate it was like the pictures she has seen, and like the descriptions she has read. First she went to Tours; passed on to Nantes, which she remembered perfectly, and where she saw again those foolish little bonnets that the women wear; and then the idea came to follow the Loire down to the sea. She describes a city, which evidently is St. Nazaire, and gives characteristic details of the north side of the Loire.

Her story told, I send her to find the old Friend. He agrees that we should try to talk with "Aunt Susan." I send Reine to find my father who must serve as messenger. It is stipulated by the old Friend that I am not to take part in the interview. It is he who will do the talking and will try gently to help his sister to understand a little.

My father starts out on his mission. But he comes back empty-handed. The person does not wish to come, and my father cannot compel her. Reine then returns with him, and evidently knows how to inspire confidence, for this time the Spirit comes to us.

Old Friend speaks with her, and Reine says that my father stays near them, finding the interview profitable for himself. The child sees them all three in a corner of the room, and describes with great interest the beautiful blue flame of the old friend—so intense and so pure—the reddish light of the stranger and the grayish tone of my "papa." Strange adventure! It is really difficult to keep serious.

While they are thus engaged, I propose an experiment with a view to discovering how Reine sees on the physical plane now. It seems to me that her faculty of clairvoyance grows less, and I would like to have an exact idea of her condition. So I begin by some persuasive remarks about the purpose of this experiment and its value in our work. She assures me that she understands and will do her utmost to satisfy me. I put my wife in contact with Reine, telling her to consider Madame Cornillier as myself. I then order her to follow me (in fluidic body) and observe my acts, to describe them to my wife and to remember what she sees, that she may again describe them to me when I return. I pass into the studio and go through a number of unusual gestures and attitudes; from there I go into a room still further off, where canvases, etc., are stored. Coming back, I learn that Reine has *seen* nothing whatever; she has perceived my presence and my moving about by means of *fluidic contact*, and that is all.

I resume control and ask my wife to go out of the room, making Reine follow and observe her. The child makes evident efforts, works hard, but she cannot see. She perceives the presence of my wife and her moving from one place to another,—nothing more. Once again Reine's sincerity is demonstrated, for I myself could understand certain of my wife's movements from the different noises that accompanied them,—such as opening the doors of a cabinet, stepping up on a chair, closing a window, etc.

The fact is then established: Reine, today, has been able to see nothing. And yet her sleep is excellent; her fluidic body quite disengaged, alert, and ready.

I report the result to her.—"Well,—you will have to ask Vettellini why it is ... As for me, I wish and intend to obey you. I understand why such experiments are useful. But ... there's something strange about it: *My spirit doesn't want to bother with it.* When my spirit is entirely disengaged—and that is often now—it seems to become entirely independent. I don't know why. You remember ... I used to see better? Ask Vettellini."

(And the old friend, his sister and my father are still over there in the corner—talking!)

I ask for Vettellini. He comes at once and immediately enters into an excited conversation with the medium. From words that Reine lets fall I gather that it concerns the failure of the experiment. After a few moments she transmits from him the following explanation:

The kind of hypnotic sleep to which we have constrained Reine has, above all else, developed her faculties of vision in the Astral. Because of her evolution she has been able to acquire rapidly the very highest mediumistic power: that is, the vision of Spirits in the ether and the faculty of entering into relation with them and of receiving from them the highest teaching. As this was, after all, the final purpose of the work which we have undertaken, I have allowed her to skip over the lower degrees of mediumistic development. In this way, we have gained much time. But her spirit, because of this training, has lost the possibility of working well on the material plane. You yourself must have remarked that mediums who see very well in the physical world,—certain somnambulists for example,—do not in the least perceive the Spirits who, nevertheless, surround you on all sides. For Reine the exact contrary is true: one leap, and she was over and beyond that class of mediumicity.

Now, understanding this, you ask if it would not be possible for us to help her in her excursions in the material world, in order to give the skeptics positive proofs—the only ones which they admit. At the début of these séances Reine was aided, and several times she gave exact information. But you saw how they were turning? Such aid can be given only by inferior Spirits—intermediaries far from reliable. You must remember that the majority of ordinary Spirits are either in a dull state of coma that unfits them for any precise work, or they are full of a vitality which is rarely employed except to do harm or to set up jokes for their own amusement. Doubtless a good Spirit might be found, sufficiently evolved, who would consent to serve as aid,—but once, or perhaps twice,—and when it pleased him: we could not count upon him.

Here Reine interrupts her transmission to say eagerly: "It's hard for us to understand that, but Spirits of good evolution are mighty busy. They have their work to do: each one belongs to some group, united for a special purpose, and they cannot come, like that, just to please us,—to help in experiments which, oftener than not, they consider futile. Then, too, you mustn't forget that Spirits keep their characters in the Astral: they are not always so obliging and devoted! As to the great ones, they rarely come down to us, and when they do come, they always suffer; they are poisoned by our heavy atmosphere. In coming as he does Vettellini is carrying out a high and admirable work; but those like your grandfather and 'Old Friend,' come only to aid someone whom they love, by reason of real affinity, and it can be for only a short time, *and never for material experiments.*"

"So then," resumes Vettellini, "it is better that Reine should act alone if you really consider this kind of experiment absolutely necessary. And, in that case, we must go backwards a little and consecrate several séances to this special sort of training. The methods that you now employ for hypnotizing are of no use if you want vision on the physical plane; for their effect is to liberate only the purest and highest part of the spirit. I will give you another method, and, after a few séances of training, Reine will recover the condition necessary for precise vision in the material world."

As I express regret for the loss of time involved in this change of direction, and fear lest this special training may diminish the capacity for seeing in the Astral which Reine now possesses, and which seems to me infinitely more important, Vettellini observes:—"It is certainly a pity to change the character of the séances which are going very well now. This is what Reine might do: she might work by herself all alone outside of the séances here. I will give you a method of auto-hypnotization which she will use to put herself to sleep. She should practice it every day at a fixed hour. She must be installed for writing; and for this she must fasten a pencil to her hand by means of a slight cord, so that she may not lose it while she sleeps. Once asleep, we will take care that she occupies herself with the physical world only. First, she will come here and observe all your acts. This will be easy because of her constant relations with you. Then, little by little, she will go elsewhere; and each time she will write what she sees and bring the writing to you that you may verify it. In this way, gradually, without changing our séances, and without stultifying her faculty of penetration into the Astral, she will develop a faculty of vision on the material plane."

My account gives only the sense of Vettellini's communication, and in no way expresses its vivacity and spontaneity. He insists that if there are seeming contradictions in his teaching, they must be examined and explained. I must not fear to bother him. There is no mystery in what he tells us about life in the Astral, it is clear and logical: my report must be the same.

Reine again speaks on her own authority to explain the difficulties in transmission created by her body: "My spirit understands everything that Vettellini says, but I haven't the words—I don't know them. Sometimes he gives me the words himself, but then I repeat without understanding and so, of course, I may mix them up."

Poor child! She valiantly accepts the new task which her Guide imposes. When I protest on account of the fatigue, she exclaims, "But everything is fatiguing! It would tire me to pose quite as much as to do this. No, I'll eat a little more and sleep a little longer. *I want to do it!*"

I ask further information concerning the incarnating waves, and Vettellini clears up the question as follows. Amongst the Spirits belonging to a wave of incarnation some are highly evolved. These may die young (infants or children) and the gain acquired by this new swift passage in terrestrial life renders them independent; they are no longer obliged to follow the wave, they will henceforth incarnate voluntarily. Some amongst them may never even return to earth again, they will continue their evolution in the Astral. The other average Spirits—the mass—hold together. The fact of having been conceived and born under the same astral influences gives them, approximately, the same longevity. They all return to astral life at about the same period, and all come back to earth again together:—like a regiment, where soldiers, non-commissioned officers, officers and commanders make a campaign together, they come back to their country together and, together, start off again on a new expedition. But some are promoted to superior grades and leave their regiment, to go to more important posts; while others are liberated entirely.

Before closing the séance, we have our usual personal talk. Reine tells me that she came here (in astral body) on Monday evening, but found no one. She wandered through the apartment, then came back to the studio, much disappointed, but suddenly she saw Vettellini, standing near his portrait, and laughing at her surprise. He told her that we should be very late in coming home. They stayed talking together for some time, then Vettellini escorted her back to her own place. (It is correct that we spent Monday evening with friends, and it is certain that Reine could have known nothing about it.)

I ask the explanation of a sudden and violent shock of damp air that struck my face at a moment in the night. Vettellini says that it was not he, then, after an instant, adds, "It was 'old Friend' who came to make you feel his presence."

He certainly scored a success. What a gale!

FIFTY-FIFTH SÉANCE

May 2, 1913

(Monsieur A. is present)

For the first time the presence of a stranger has had no bad effect. On the contrary, the investigations which his questions provoke add a new element of interest to the mass of evidence we already possess.

When Reine is sleeping I call my wife and A. and begin my usual questions. She has seen nothing, done nothing; she has stayed there beside her physical body—waiting. I send her to an apartment in the rue Ampère, giving the number and the floor. (It is A.'s house.) She wanders about some time before reaching the place. She has never been in this quarter, and I myself, not knowing the best way to direct her, hesitate in indicating the itinerary. Finally she announces that she has found the apartment and is in it. She is sure of it because she discovers the same fluid as that of the letter which I have given her—(a letter from A.) I ask her to look around the place and report what she sees. From the vestibule she passes into a room which she thinks is "a kind of drawing room." She is struck by the portraits and "images" on the wall. There are two windows. There is a piano—a big one—which is placed at the end of the room on the right of the windows. She says the piano is closed. (After the séance A. declares that this description is exact,—I do not know the apartment myself.)

But there was someone in the salon whom the child did not see. It is curious, for she noticed such details as the piano being closed (verified by A. when he returned home) and in spite of my repeated question: "is there any person in the room?" she has seen no one. A. knew that somebody was there, and it was of far greater importance in his mind than any detail given by Reine. (Another proof that her information is not drawn from the minds of the people present.)

As I have more interesting projects than the inventory of furniture, I cut short Reine's description. Can she find trace of a spiritual presence in this atmosphere? She must try to discover if any Spirits frequent this house.

The child works valiantly. She sniffs about, she inhales the fluids, trying to get at their origin. First, there is that of the letter which she is holding; that, without any doubt, is the fluid of the master of the house. But there are others ... yes, there are several others ... But one grows more definite than the rest, ... asserts itself ... imposes itself. It is not material, that one. It is the fluid of a Spirit—of a very high Spirit. He must come often ... Yes, he seems to dominate here. Reine who up to this moment, has evidently been feeling her way, now starts off frankly: "The man who lives here must himself be of a good evolution. He must be occupied with—high things,—with Art! It is not painting—I'm sure of that—but it is Art ... Music perhaps ... Yes, oh yes, it is music! At least the fluid which is all around everywhere, which impregnates the whole place, seems to condense especially around the piano. It is good; it is high."

I tell Reine to follow the spiritual fluid and discover its generator. She must go out and rise above the house. She obeys, but in vain: she loses trace of the fluid in rising, and her call to the Spirit (made at my suggestion) remains without effect. Coming back, she emphasizes her analysis: "This Spirit is a sort of Vettellini for the man who lives here. He pushes him on, inspires him. And you know, he's a high one!" I interrupt here to make her rest a while before passing to another experiment.

Without any warning, I place in her hand a gold ring which A. has just passed to me. At its contact Reine jumps as though she had been galvanized. She sits up, rigid, and seems both frightened and attracted by the object. She examines it most carefully (her eyes closed), then suddenly speaks: "I say, Monsieur Cornillier, ... this ring! H'm. It doesn't come from around here.—Oh, no! ... It doesn't belong to you. And it doesn't belong to the person who has it now. It comes from far away ... and from long ago. It comes from a country that is hot, where the skies are blue, and the cities white; from a country where the sun is burning.

It is a ring that has known many influences. The person who wore it did not die as we die. Oh, many things ... many ugly things are mixed with it! This ring comes from a strange place, a tomb,—yes, yes,—that's it, a tomb! Wait a minute ... I must feel it better."

Reine throws herself back in her chair, pressing the ring against her forehead. Soon she resumes with emphasis: "This ring has been stolen—oh, not an ordinary theft, no! ... It was stolen from the hand of a dead man—in a tomb—an embalmed body. It was stolen from the dead hand of its owner ... Ah! ... He curses them. It is not good to do a thing like that. He was important in his country, oh, long ago!—Back, far back ... a barbarian. He did many villainous deeds, that one! ... And now I am absolutely sure: *This ring was stolen from the hand of an embalmed body, stolen from his tomb, and sold.* It must never be worn. It has a bad influence. The person who wears it will fail in all he undertakes. There are people who laugh at that,— but it is the truth!"

She gives details of the country from which the ring came, of the people and their costumes.

After the séance A. tells me that the ring had been found (bought) by one of his relations in an Aztec tomb, during an exploration in Mexico.

I relieve Reine of the ring, whose contact seems to make her suffer, and after a few moments of rest, ask for Vettellini's presence.

"Come, my Vettellini. That's it. Here ... I will make a little place for you." And the child leans back into the depths of the chair, leaving a clear space on left.

A. has charged me to ask if certain lights and phosphorescences which he often sees about him, in the dark, come from disincarnate beings, or if they are merely the result of fatigue of the optic nerve. Reine, after transmitting the question, listens; then begins to laugh.— "Tell me, ... is it true what Vettellini says? ... The gentleman for whom you ask that, is he here? And I went to his house a few minutes ago? Oh, of course, I can't doubt Vettellini ... But it's so droll, all that! I don't remember it at all, you see.—Yes? Ha! Well then you're right after all, Vettellini! Monsieur Cornillier, you may tell your friend that it is not because his eyes are tired. He has a guide, a Spirit guide, who is constantly in his home. He's a musician, your friend? It is Vettellini who says so—I don't know myself. But, anyway, the Spirit who protects him has been a great musician—whom we all know, it seems—and now he goes to this gentleman's house to inspire him, to urge him on to create a beautiful work. He wants him to succeed; and to influence him more easily, he stays there almost all the time and often manifests his presence by those lights. And for that matter there are several who go there, but he is the Guide."

To A.'s question, "May I know who this Spirit is?" Vettellini replies that he will bring him here, at another séance; but that the Spirit will probably not reveal his identity to A., as it might be detrimental to his work. Vettellini will tell me his name, but I must not communicate it to A. until the work is finished. A. should invoke him,—open himself to the inspiration, that the task may be less difficult for the Spirit. He is under good influence, certainly, and has— ... Here Reine turns swiftly to the right, glaring into space with frowning brows. One would say she had been hit. She mutters to herself, then smiles, "Ha—ha! Mr. Old-Friend!" We turn our attention to our brusque visitor; but he tells Reine not to interrupt the séance. He comes in just to see how we are getting on; he will go over there by his friend Anne, we must not bother about him.

So I address myself to Vettellini again and ask if our social morality, considered broadly and in its best sense, is, from the point of view of the high Spirits, the most effective code of morality for a society constituted as ours is. He considers that no better one could exist for us. For those of his evolution there is no code of morality. There is no further need of one. But for us it is necessary; and the principles of our morality are those required by the conditions of our society.

Another question:—Since the great Spirits sometimes provoke a modification in social and political movements (to hasten evolution), do they, then, attribute a sensible superiority to any given form of government?—"It has nothing whatever to do with evolution whether there be a king, an emperor, or a republic," is the reply. "All that has no importance. Men must be directed and governed since, actually, they are not capable of living free. But the form of government has no importance, nor has it any influence upon the evolution of a people. Equality is impossible. Hierarchy is necessary. But evolution does not depend upon political forms." Vettellini treats with solid good sense my rather insidious question,—for I had half suspected him of scorning a republic.

Before closing the séance, has the Guide anything to tell me about the Atlanteans and their continent?—Yes, he has talked a little with other Spirits who are informed on the question, and now he can affirm this: The continent has really been inhabited by a human race. This race was black. They had attained a high degree of evolution. They were a pastoral people, profound students of cosmic law and sidereal phenomena. They were past masters in astrology. Their industrial development was nil. Their continent gave way and sank—the result of geological convulsions, such as will soon destroy the European coasts. And now the Atlantic Ocean serves as its shroud.

And the actual fate of the Atlanteans? I ask. Vettellini says that he cannot know that. Undoubtedly they continue their evolution ... and on a very high plane. They are infinitely above him, for their disappearance dates ages back. He remarks that the physical aspect of a race, considered as an expression of evolution, may easily not accord with our prejudices. The Atlanteans were black.

The séance closes with a scene between Reine and her Guide, who begs me to scold the child when she wakens. She has been imprudent again—and from coquetry. She has put aside her woolen underclothes and has consequently caught cold. Reine refuses to transmit the message: follows a scene of wrath, humiliation and revolt. However, she ends, as always, by capitulating, but not without making him pay dearly for his excessive care of her. What mockery and derision! It is matchless.

FIFTY-SIXTH SÉANCE

May 5, 1913

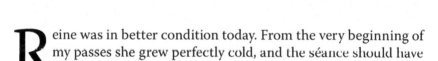

Reine was in better condition today. From the very beginning of my passes she grew perfectly cold, and the séance should have been excellent. Unfortunately, the chief part of my program could not be realized and, taken by surprise, I had not even an interesting question prepared for Vettellini.

To my usual question, Reine replies that she has been to see the great blue Spirits, who carried her off into the high regions of space. She asked no questions (I had charged her with none), and she has nothing special to relate of this excursion except that, several times, she felt strange fluidic currents, which she believes have something to do with the different works undertaken by these Spirits, and are undoubtedly connected with their efforts to modify human destinies. She did not dare to ask them. It is for me to find out about it at another séance.

When she has finished her report, I tell her that I wish to see my grandfather and she must go to find him. But scarcely have I expressed my desire and placed in her hands the little apron of the *Rose-Croix* when she cries out in astonishment: "But—there's no need to go, he is here! Yes, yes, it is he. He says he knew you would call him because you have been thinking of him all these days, and this morning you held this object in your hands and decided that you would call him this afternoon." ... (This is exact. This morning, while alone, I took the apron from the drawer of a desk and, as I examined it, decided the questions that I would put to my grandfather at the séance today.)

After a word of welcome, I ask him if he has kept in contact with his second son.—No, not at all. He vaguely recalls that his second son died before he did; and that is all. He does not even remember his name—nor anything else concerning him.[53] This astonishes me and I ask if, at his evolution, the mere fixing of his thoughts on an incident is not sufficient to re-establish it exactly. He says that this is true, as a matter of fact he could do that; but he is so far, so detached from everything not connected with plans for general evolution (and his own), and "all that" seems so futile to him, that he does not consider it worth the effort he would have to exert to accomplish it. He is too far away from it all.

As I continue to express regret, Reine tries to explain the situation: "Of course, it is hard for us to realize, but you must remember this: relationship, kinship, does not exist in the Astral. *One tie only persists—the affinity of spirit.* Your grandfather had not the least affinity with his son. So then, dead, both of them, and stripped of the organism which, on earth, held them in relation, they are absolutely strangers and separated. And your grandfather, continuing to evolve higher and higher in the Astral as he has done, has even lost all recollection of

---

[53] This, once again, proves that mind-reading is not the source of Reine's transmission. If, in truth, she could find in my consciousness or subconsciousness the elements of her information, why, always and always, should she disdain the facts and incidents that do exist in my memory? For example, I have in mind incidents, both vague and precise, relating to my grandfather's second son, who was drowned in most dramatic circumstances, and a hundred small details concerning my cousin—of whom I speak further on. And Reine does not read one of them, but gives me a psychological analysis of the moral traits of these two people...? It is at least strange! The psychological elements of her "creations" are surely more difficult to gather up and form into a real character, corresponding to a real existence, than would be the reading of more or less important images or memories existing in my mind.

And on the other hand, it is easy to understand that these same details become totally indifferent to Spirits who have disengaged themselves from terrestrial conditions. We can admit that they forget them, since even we ourselves forget. There are many episodes in the lives of different members of my family that I cannot recall, and I have even quite lost the names of some of my relatives who live in another part of the country and with whom I have had no contact for years past. And how many of the circumstances of our youth—even important ones—fade from our memory completely as we grow older!

this momentary tie. It no longer exists for him. And the effort to recover consciousness of such details would be better employed in another cause. He comes back to you, yes—but because he has affinities with you; and though it is painful for him to come down to our atmosphere, he keeps coming because he can help you. No,—it's not easy to understand, Monsieur Cornillier, but that is the way it is ... What do you want of him? He asks how he can be of use to you."

I explain that I would like to speak with my cousin (son of his second son) and, having nothing in my possession which belonged to him, I wish that he would find him and bring him here. He says he will try, but it may take time for he does not know what modifications the fluid of this grandson may have undergone. Having no object containing the fluidic vibrations of this person, he will be obliged to hunt for a fluid possessing the vibrations of our family fluid, and modified by two generations. It is extremely complex, but he will try.

"You see it is different for Vettellini," explains Reine. "He could give you details of his past life because, in order to work with us, he had to plunge back into the terrestrial substance again. He is here constantly now, he lives with us, he knows all our interests. But it is not the same with your grandfather. He comes suddenly, from far and high, and just for a moment's contact." We wait for my grandfather's return, but as his quest is prolonged, I turn to another experiment. Without saying any words, I place a small stone in Reine's hands. She seems to have pleasure in touching it ... "Curious: I feel as though I had found a little thing I cared for—something I had lost." (This is interesting taken in connection with what Vettellini said to us, sometime ago, about one of Reine's precedent lives on earth—the one before the last—which was passed in Egypt: for this little stone comes from an Egyptian necklace.) "I can't tell you the strange feeling I have in just touching it. It comes from ... h'm ... It comes from ... Oh, from Egypt! Yes, yes, *surely* ... It was in a bracelet ... or a necklace. It has so little fluid that I can't see any more than that, but I know it comes from Egypt. Oh, the joy of it! ... I wish I could wear it on my neck?" Here she turns about swiftly in her chair, looking on all sides: "It's Vettellini,—I feel him; he must be very near ... Ah, yes, here he is! Come, my Vettellini." She listens. "Monsieur Cornillier, he says he came because your grandfather will not be back for a long time yet: he does not find the trace. It is better not to wait for him."

I speak of the manifest difference in the way of feeling and being amongst the less evolved Spirits: some seem endowed with an extreme vitality, while others are plunged in torpor. Vettellini explains that at an equal degree of evolution, Spirits may be quite differently affected by their transition to the Astral. In fact, their reaction is determined by their individual character,—just as it was in their life of incarnation. For some, incomprehension is suffering, for others it is a matter of complete indifference. These are the "jolly dogs" who waste no time on trying to understand. They have a certain vitality and they use it. It is they who make the tables dance and who answer in language not always polite when one asks who they are.—They "get on" in death as they "got on" in life.

I pass to another question: Artists of talent, even of great talent, are often aided and inspired by Spirits,—well and good. But the rare exceptions, those whom we on earth call men of genius—are they also aided? ... A Michael-Angelo, for example? The answer is long, my summary must be brief. In general, all those who produce are aided, are inspired. But one has the inspiration and the inspirer that one merits, and in accordance to one's degree of evolution. The Spirits give the grain, and the artist is the gardener—good or bad—who must make it germinate and bloom. Sometimes, however, the mechanism is inverted: the artist produces the grain and the Spirits aid him in bringing it to flower. (For example: It was I who had the idea of Vettellini's portrait, and I was aided and directed in the execution.)

I speak of the suffragette movement, and ask Vettellini what he thinks of it. He approves the claims of women in so far as they pretend to rights equal to those of men; but he absolutely disapproves that they should claim the same social role as men. Woman has her own proper line of evolution, parallel to that of man, but not to be confounded with it. This rather banal appreciation is followed by a most unexpected remark: "Maternity is one of the most efficient factors in woman's evolution. It refines the most vulgar, raises her; and, from this point of view, accidental maternity, the imposition of a child, has a great value." I protest in indignation. But Vettellini insists: "Socially it may be shameful, but for individual progress it is a violent stimulant. Sterility, however, is not an inferiority. The women who do not bear children have other lines of progression; and, for that matter, sterility and fecundity are both determined by Fate, by "the Hand," and even the high Spirits do not understand the reasons that decide it."

The séance drags. I ask the Maître if I may make a recapitulation of the teaching transmitted, so that contradiction or errors arising either through a fault of the medium, or my own interpretation, may be eliminated. He approves.

FIFTY-SEVENTH SÉANCE

May 7, 1913

Reine is suffering from a bad cold, but sleeps well in spite of this. As soon as she is sleeping, I charge her to ask the high Spirits for an explanation of those currents which she perceived during her last promenade in their regions, on Monday. When the moment arrives, she gives her interpretation of their reply; for she finds it impossible to translate exactly into words conditions absolutely nonexistent to our senses. She tries first to describe the sensations produced on her by these currents:—"A sort of straight rush of fluid ... and then a whirling around." Not particularly clear, this! Then she explains their significance for the Spirits:—It is by these currents that they take cognizance of human destinies,—general and individual: and it seems that, in a certain measure, they have possibility of modifying these currents by a fluidic force which they themselves generate ... etc.

I neglect for the moment this account of phenomena which are inconceivable for us, and begin to ask Reine if any trace has been found of my cousin, when I see that she is busy, talking with the invisible. The few words she lets fall persuade me that it is with my grandfather, and, in fact, she very soon says that he is there, waiting to speak with me. He explains that he did not come back (at the last séance) because, in spite of his efforts, he had not succeeded. The Spirit in question must be of slight evolution, and to find trace of him my grandfather would be obliged to descend too low. If I am really anxious to come into relation with this cousin, I must procure a letter, or any other object containing his fluid, and Reine will be able to reach him readily. My grandfather adds that he will not come again to see me for sometime. It is Vettellini's work here, and no one else is needed for the moment. He himself belongs to a group working on quite another task—that of modifying political and social movements; and all his efforts are spent in this direction.

When he has left us, I propose to Reine a visit to the Egyptian museum in the Louvre,—of whose existence, even, she knows nothing—and indicate the itinerary. Very soon she tells me she is there.

Her first impressions are rather indifferent. She sees stones, statues, tombs; thinks that she must have seen them before, for she seems to recognize them, and sees the country from which they came: the sky, the atmosphere, the inhabitants are described with some particular detail, but, on the whole, nothing of special interest is given as long as she stays on the ground floor. It is only after she has gone upstairs and reached the third room that she has a really precise perception. Here, suddenly, she is conscious of a fluid that attracts her: and she finds and describes the mummy in its exact place. This mummy gives her an intense sensation. She has much to say about it: perceives a persistent vitality in this preserved body and thinks it probable that the Spirit is still attached to it. But the crowd of visitors in the museum, and the heavy vibrations emanating from them, trouble her, and prevent her seeing clearly. So then, I suggest that she should go back there one of these nights with Vettellini, it might be interesting. I recall her. Immediately Vettellini manifests his presence and approves my plan.

We begin, as was agreed, with a recapitulation of what has been already given on the subject of Death. I verify my notes with extreme care, obtaining in the end a clear description of the process of passing into the Astral at different degrees of evolution. As what I have already given on this question is sufficiently correct, I will note here only a few slight emendations:

The life of a human being is determined by Fate—"The Hand." Given conception and birth under the influence of certain stars or planets, the date of death is normally determined. But this determination is subject to modification. It is here that the Spirit-judges may intervene. If the evolution of the individual would be aided by it, they have the possibility of hastening or retarding the moment that has normally been determined by planetary influences. (Example: Reine's paternal grandmother has recently died. Vettellini told us that, according to her astral influences, her death should have come later, but the protecting-Spirits, judging her suffering sufficient, had delivered her at once. The contrary will occur for her maternal grandmother who, normally, should have died in April.)

The "Messengers of Death" are not a special category in themselves, devoted to this work alone: they form part of the assembly whose duty it is to take charge of the newly released soul; there may be several messengers, or only one.

The soul who is capable of understanding his responsibilities will be faced with all the acts of his life as soon as he has passed into the Astral, and the regret and remorse that this scrutiny provokes will stimulate him to an effort that will prepare his progress in the following reincarnation. But it sometimes happens that, even though incapable of recognizing his responsibilities, he is nevertheless conducted before the great Assembly; for this may produce an impression, vague but persistent, which, at some future moment, will provoke him to reflect and investigate.

He who is sufficiently developed will have the privilege of choosing his new fate. He is no longer subject to the influence of the incarnating wave. He may, if he wishes, remain in the Astral, continuing his evolution there; or he may deliberately reincarnate in order to stimulate the evolution of his fellow men, gaining thereby a great increase in his own. Evolution in the Astral is the more profitable but it is also the more difficult; and many prefer to advance more slowly but less painfully. We, on earth, are not qualified to understand in what this astral evolution consists. The only point we can grasp is that the one who chooses it must first cut himself free from all earthly ties and interests. Little by little he will reach the evolution where he may have a modifying influence on the lines of a given fate, himself thus approaching Fatality—without, however, comprehending it any the better ... A part of the activity of the high Spirits is spent in efforts to penetrate this mystery of Fate. They know that, implacably, it imposes itself on the life of each being. Certain events, happy as well as unhappy, are inevitable: "The Hand," the mysterious, enigmatic hand has pre-arranged them.

Vettellini estimates that about one-half of the various circumstances in any given life are determined by the law of Fate. Of the remainder, one half is under the control of the individual and the other is subject to the modification of the high Spirits. This division of the influences which govern the life of each being is clear, formal, and transmitted with marked authority: *One-half of life is dominated by Fate; one quarter belongs to the free will of the individual; one quarter is subject to the influence of the great Spirits.*

It is evident that the modifying influence of Spirits is necessary; otherwise, Fate would be absolute, Humanity would be overwhelmed, and evolution retarded.

I ask the significance of suicide.

Response: The eventuality of suicide is placed before a being by Fate, but his one-quarter of free will can refuse it; he can struggle against circumstances, react against hereditary tendencies, and, according to the case, and according to his merits, his Spirit-protectors will help him, or not.

Another point of interest: It has been said that evolved Spirits may, if they choose, stagnate in the Astral, egotistically enjoying the superiority which, it is true, they have gained at the price of great effort. But this *dolce farniente* may not continue indefinitely. It seems that at certain periods powerful magnetic currents pass in the cosmos, which violently beat these Spirits down towards earth, and thus force the idle ones to abandon their state of inaction.

The séance closes with some personal advice. We are urged to realize a plan we have been cherishing—a short trip. Vettellini says he will keep Reine at work during our absence, that she may lose nothing of her faculty. As usual, the question of health comes up. He gives a minute prescription for Reine's husband, who is ill.

FIFTY-EIGHTH SÉANCE

May 9, 1913

During her first sleep, Reine went again to see the blue Spirits, and this time she assisted at one of their moments of repose and delectation. She tells me that in her actual fluidic state she surely would not have been able to discern these extraordinary astral delights, but she was aided; her perceptions were rendered more sensitive and she became spiritualized to the point of being conscious of harmonies so marvelous that no language can express them. She is obliged to use the term "music"; it is the word which, for us, corresponds the most closely to the cause of the enchantment which still holds her in strong emotion. But what a poor, thin, little word it is! ... How toneless! ... How inadequate to convey the intensity of that thrilling harmonious vibration!

She says that all very high Spirits are able to generate enchanting melodies, but, when they unite to combine these waves of harmony, their beauty is prodigiously exalted and glorified. And so it is that often, after grave meditations or periods of great activity employed in helping the human race, they assemble together to produce—or to perceive—these extraordinary vibrations, the very essence of what we on earth consider our most sublime art, but which in reality is only a poor cracked echo of the divine original emission.

Since the hour is musical I attempt a visit to A.'s apartment, in the hope of discovering his Inspirer; but Reine, who goes to his place, says that A. is not at home—(verified)—nor is his Spirit-Guide present, though she clearly perceives the fluid of the latter. (Detained up there at the concert, no doubt!)

Suddenly Reine jumps back, frowning—then laughs. "Old Friend" is here, gay and vigorous as always, and announcing his arrival with his usual impetuosity. He is pleased when we ask him to come to see us occasionally on our trip, and tells us to notice how, without any apparent reason, his friend Anne will suddenly feel all alive and alert—it will be because he is there with us. He will come often; every day. I ask him to make occasionally that puff of cold air which startled me so one night. Instead of transmitting his reply, Reine gives a confused little laugh; but I insist. "He says won't; that sort of thing bores him!" I pocket the snub, but—does he read my thoughts? One would say so, for he adds: "Oh, well, I'm not a Vettellini!" He scolds his friend Anne. She is getting discouraged again; there's no sense in it: "Come along! Brace up!" etc.

But here is Vettellini.

He begins by giving some details concerning the musical assemblies of the blue Spirits ... Then we talk of our trip. Methodically he arranges the order of the séances that Reine must have alone during our absence; noting the smallest points, even the cushion for her head, the elastic around her fingers to maintain the pencil, etc., etc. He forbids me this time to try to magnetize her from a distance. I must get all the rest the trip can give me. He will look out for us, will come every morning to follow us a while. In case of accident or anxiety I must evoke him: he will be there. He urges me to be happy—to be gay; it is almost a duty.

He allows a few questions, reminding me, however, that I must not fatigue myself by too long a séance, for the first days in the open air will be hard for me.

I ask if Spirits who are not very evolved retain their terrestrial habit of thinking in the words of their former language.—Certainly; it could not be otherwise. When they begin to come out from their state of coma, they try to define their astral sensations, and it is necessarily in words of their former language that they think. Little by little they acquire the mode of thought without words, so incomprehensible to us; but this comes only with evolution.

I ask if Vettellini could carry Reine to another planet—Mars, for example—so that she could observe the physical world there and its inhabitants (alluding at the same time to the alleged voyages of Mlle.

Helene Smith[54] and the criticism it has provoked). He replies that when the medium attains the cataleptic stage of hypnosis, it will be easy enough—as will be all the other phenomena that have been promised. It depends upon her health alone; everything is retarded by her physical fragility.

I speak of the role of the organism in the life of the incarnate, and express astonishment that it is sometimes so disproportionately important. A person seems intelligent, cultivated, brilliant, he has moral qualities, is energetic, etc., and at his death, stripped of his organism, nothing remains but a poor, feeble, bewildered soul? How can this be?

The reply is long and somewhat confused:—The Spirit in many cases has not as much influence as many spiritualists think. On Earth, the body is often the dominating element, against which the spirit must react, of course, but which, nonetheless, possesses a real autonomy. It is a mechanism that may be mediocre or excellent; and, in the latter case, even a dolt obtains a good result with it. The example already given of the horseman and his mount is recalled. I remark that this point of view— were it accepted—would singularly modify our mutual judgments of each other here on earth, and add that, all the same, destiny must sometimes seem bitterly cruel to the Spirit suddenly plundered like that—stripped of what he had every right to consider his own! ... But Reine asserts that, on the contrary, it is a benefit in any case, as there is always the reaction of the soul; and the soul retains the advantage accruing from the use of a superior instrument to which, in reality, it had no claim.

My wife asks if the actual complexity of social life is not a decadence. Was not the "good old time" healthier and better? Is there any real progress? Is it not rather a different distribution of the same elements? Vettellini laughs:—"No, what we say of the past our grandfathers also said, as did their fathers before them. Yes, there is progress: a development of intelligence, of goodness, of spiritual qualities. In Art, it is true, there has been no progress in this actual period of our civilization. This is due to the fact that the great artists of former epochs have not reincarnated, and that, in general, the actual 'practitioners of art' are young Spirits who have not always been judged worthy of aid. But if there is a crisis in art (in plastic art) it is only a crisis. There is a change ahead," ... etc., etc.

Amusing scenes follow, Reine and her Guide tease each other as usual, and the séance closes with laughter and a gay *"Au revoir."*

---

[54] *Des Indes* à *La Planète Mars*, Prof. Th. Flournoy, Paris and Geneva, 1900.

FIFTY-NINTH SÉANCE

May 19, 1913

We resume the séance today in the usual conditions.

During our absence of ten days, Reine says she has obtained nothing of any interest. She has carefully followed the instructions given, has installed herself every afternoon exactly as has been directed, but nothing has come of it all. She has merely fallen into a stupid kind of somnolence which did not, however, destroy consciousness of outside happenings; and when after an hour, or an hour and a half, she came back to her normal state, she was broken with fatigue?

On the Tuesday after our departure Vettellini appeared as she was preparing to sleep. She saw his head distinctly. His lips moved as though he were trying to speak; but she could neither hear nor divine his words.

We begin at half past three. Immediately Reine falls into a deep sleep. When I finally question her, she announces that she has been to see the blue Spirits with Vettellini. She went straight up to them, at the very beginning of her sleep, without effort or difficulty. Her Guide is pleased. He tells me that Reine has not lost ground in these last ten days, and explains why her efforts in our absence have met with no success.—"The method of auto-hypnotization which I indicated was efficient, but the hypnotizer which you selected was worthless." (I had chosen a brilliant ball suspended by a twisted string which, in untwisting, made the ball whirl around.) He says that the ball, having no scintillation, could provoke only a painful torpor in the medium. Consequently he had tried in the very beginning to arrest the séances on that Tuesday when he appeared and spoke to her; but she was already drowsy and did not understand. Quite the contrary, in fact, for in spite of her great fatigue she persisted, fearing to be scolded if she stopped. Notwithstanding the failure, her efforts have kept her malleable and supple: but I must find another object of more effective action. The next séance must be one of long magnetization without special experiments—for training simply. I see that Vettellini expects to realize the two forms of research—physical and astral—which will complete each other. But Reine's health seems to preoccupy him seriously.

After the usual play between them, Vettellini suddenly remarks: "Madame Cornillier is burning to see 'Old Friend,' but she does not dare to ask for him."—"Why, it is true!" cries my wife. "I was just wishing he would come." But he cannot come down to us today, he has a mission; he will come at the next séance. He had said that he would join us every day during our trip, but he could come only once—the first day—for he was obliged to bend all his energy on this mission, which was certainly more important etc., etc.

Various points of personal interest are discussed. Reine is happy in her new lodgings. She installed herself the day we started off, and on Sunday, for the first time in her life, slept in *her own home*. Vettellini says that he passed the night from Friday to Saturday there, in order to observe the different fluidic influences, to chase out the inferior Spirits who had wandered in, etc.—in short, he had policed the premises, and now Reine will be happy there, for there are only good vibrations left. Vettellini, moreover, spends much time there. (Reine when awake, says she is constantly aware of his presence.)

Before leaving us, Vettellini says that all is going well with my father: he is trying to make it out, trying to understand and is really progressing. I may be happy, my efforts have not been in vain.

SIXTIETH SÉANCE

May 21, 1913

This séance, though nothing super-normal occurred, is never-theless one of the most remarkable, by reason of the prodigious reality of the dialogue. Certainly the information and ideas have their interest, but the spontaneity and individuality in the form of the communication were amazing and, alas, impossible to convey.

At the last séance Vettellini ordered only a good training exercise for Reine today, and, in consequence, I magnetize for about an hour and a half, attempting no experiment, and waiting for her to come of her own accord to the phase of transmission. She reaches out her hands, verifies me, so to speak, and begins her report. There was another concert today, up there, where the blue Spirits live, and she could again rejoice in those harmonies which had so enchanted her once before. When she came back down here, she wandered about the neighborhood a little and was joined by my father who was waiting for a chance to communicate.—"He wants very much to see you, so I brought him back with me. He is here."

We talk together, and my father confirms the fact that he is more contented. He is working,—follows after the Spirits superior to him, and begins to understand the reasons of his own condition. He says that he has gone several times to see the Spirit whom he once brought here to us, ("Aunt Susan") but he has no great success,—is not even well received! She continues to cherish her fixed idea, and my father has not the slightest influence upon her, etc.

This communication finished, I ask for the old Friend, who has promised to come today. Vettellini answers: "He will come later, and while we wait we will just talk together ourselves." He begins by saying that the revolving mirror which I bought for Reine to use in her auto-hypnotizing will be all right; needless to hunt for something better. She may begin tomorrow; but it will certainly require several days before she will be able to write what she does during her sleep; and it would be well for me to encourage her and enjoin great patience, for she is in despair over her failure, and is convinced that I am displeased by it. We continue to talk of these séances and of the efficacy of the mirror, when Reine suddenly bounds up, exclaiming: "Well, that's a little too much!" She turns to me in indignation: "You don't know what he says! He says that mirror is just what is needed to catch a linnet like me!" At this moment someone rings the bell vigorously and insistently, and as Reine, hypnotized, hears nothing, and as in her vehement retort to her Guide's sarcasm she raises her voice, my wife—fearing that the person at the door may hear her—tells me in a low voice to stop her talking. But, amused by the scene, I do nothing of the kind, ... and my wife gets worried. But right there Reine stops short, frowns angrily, and, suddenly flinging herself around in her chair, squarely turns her back on Vettellini. Sulking? We learn, later on, that Vettellini has sharply imposed silence, and Reine, not understanding the reason, is offended. It is a curious scene and quite inimitable: *Vettellini has heard the bell ring, remarked my wife's uneasiness, and acted in my place.*—We sit there quietly, thinking to exhaust the patience of the visitor, but it is he who exhausts ours and finally, exasperated, my wife jumps up to open the door, and I hear her conducting someone to the fifth floor.

My attention comes back to Reine, who has not budged and who sullenly maintains her ugly expression. But when I explain the cause of the interruption and the reason of her Guide's sharp order for silence, she immediately resumes her good humor.

I ask Vettellini if chastity should not be the law for a medium. To my surprise he flatly says no. "This natural function of the organism has, on the contrary, a favorable influence on mediumicity, developing the impressionability of the organic matter." And passing to the general question of celibacy, he says it is one that should be discussed at length, and later he will return to it.

We speak of the terrible events—wars and revolutions—that have been predicted, and I am led to ask how the book which I am to publish from the notes of our séances can possibly create any interest if, as has been said, the country is to be wracked by war and all hearts crushed with anguish. Who could give thought to any other consideration at an epoch of such disaster and confusion? Vettellini says that, on the contrary, so far as he can see, the work will fall just at the right moment. I must get my documents in order before the terrible hour arrives. The publication may be made at the end of the hideous nightmare when everyone will be in such a state of prostration and doubt that their need of hope will be as imperious as hunger or thirst. "So far as I can read destiny—a part of which remains veiled even for us, Spirits—our work will be realized. Political and social events may separate us; you may be driven away, may undergo various tribulations; but, so far as I am able to see, you will survive, and the work will exist—in time. The crisis may be deferred, perhaps? But in any case when it comes, I will give directions for the security of the work. It is meant to be, and it will be."

At this moment my wife returns to say that some friends who are passing through Paris wish to see me. She does not know what to do. It is not possible to send them away! Quite true; but, on my side, I certainly cannot dismiss Vettellini! A small discussion ... and a great perplexity. It is Vettellini himself who intervenes, telling me not to be so nervous: I can very well go away for a few moments; he will look after Reine and prevent her coming back to consciousness. I can go without anxiety; she will be safe and in good shape on my return.

A quarter of an hour later, when we come back, I find Reine sleeping tranquilly; and we resume our conversation at its point of interruption:

The material actually amassed in my notes is valuable.

We must now review the question of Birth, which is the more difficult in that a portion of the physiological phenomena affirmed by Vettellini is in opposition to present scientific theories. Consequently I must not hesitate to question him, to pursue to the very end this subject of the different phases of incarnation. "All must be clear and logical, must hold together solidly and in such a way that, if we cannot convince the physiologists, we shall at least have planted a doubt in their minds."

Reine gives a startled laugh: "Oh, there's no mistaking you now, Old Friend. It could not be anyone else. Well, at least you can tell us what you've been doing, that you have to come so late?" ... (Evidently they are more familiar now, since they "thee" and "thou" each other.)

Old Friend says he is happy to see us all together again, and then in his brusque and jovial way, so characteristic, corrects a statement made by Vettellini concerning him: "Vettellini told you that I went only once to accompany you during your trip—the first day. It is true that I *accompanied* you the first day only, but every day, and often several times a day, I went to pass a few minutes with you, to see that everything was going all right, only I could not stay long. My own work keeps me busy."

I ask what this work is. "Busy in modifying international events," is the reply. Every day he goes to see people of political importance—to influence them, to help them come to certain decisions, to dissuade them from adopting others, etc., and all this requires an enormous effort.

Reine, of her own impulse, asks what he does outside of this mission, as relaxation and repose. The answer suffocates her: "Oh, no ... not really? Ah, no, Old Friend! It's not possible! ... But do you know what he says, Monsieur Cornillier? He says that after this hard work he goes to the ... the" ... (she makes him repeat exactly the words) ... "Chamber of Commerce. What's that, Chamber of Commerce? ... to the Stock Exchange! And he looks into every thing going on ... and even sometimes gives it a push along!" The child bursts out laughing; this is too much for her, she cannot recover from it; nor we either, for that matter. We look at each other—stupefied. The trait is so characteristic, so illuminative of the identity of this man about whom Reine, naturally, knows nothing whatever.

But Vettellini claims our attention by gently remarking that such distraction as that would have no great charm for him; to which the other promptly retorts that this is his pleasure only when he has nothing better to do. It is an old souvenir of his last incarnation, and that is all. But changing his tone, which has become a little sharp, he adds with deference: "And then ... there are not many Vettellinis; I certainly am not one of them."

Reine, hearing me remark the extreme dissimilarity of our two protectors, gives her own views on this subject: "Old Friend is a high Spirit, certainly, but he is not like Vettellini. Business, politics, were his interests on earth, and it is since his death that he has gone so high, but Vettellini was a thinker—a savant—even when he was living here; and he loved the arts. Oh, our old friend is very high, but Vettellini has gone farther; he is finer, he is purer. As soon as his work is finished he will pass into another sphere, and earthly questions will no longer interest him." Here Reine realizes that this implies the departure of Vettellini, his disappearance for us, and she is deeply affected. Turning towards him, she cries with emotion: "But is it possible, my Vettellini? *How could you abandon us now?* But you will come back often to see us ...Tell me, my Vettellini?" and the tears roll down her poor little face. He consoles her, tells her that in any case he will be able to aid and direct us from afar.

"And at our death?" I ask. "Oh, when we are Spirits we can communicate with him, and he will help us to evolve towards his sphere," says Reine; then hastily: "Oh, talk of something else. It's too sad, all that!"

The talk leads Old Friend to define his affinities with my wife; and he says that he is attached to me by, and because of, her, just as Vettellini is attached to her by, and because of, me. My wife admits that she is afraid of Vettellini—does he know it? He replies that he knows everything she thinks and feels. He knows, for example, that the eyes of his portrait seem to her always the eyes of judgment. (Exclamations. I learn later that this is true.)

"Madame Cornillier is quite wrong to be afraid. Vettellini is so good!" interrupts Reine. And she goes on to say that she knows now that he and she have been friends in a former life—in Egypt. It was in the life before his last one. In his last and recent incarnation he was the savant, the thinker, of whom she sometimes has a vision; who is in a laboratory surrounded by alembics and retorts; or who again, bareheaded and meditating, paces up and down the long alleys of a beautifully wooded park. "He was not French," says Reine, "probably Italian; but he himself will tell you all about that later on. He travelled a great deal, and it was during one of his trips in Brittany that he saw you, a child, Monsieur Cornillier. He says it was at—(she listens,—makes him repeat) at Nantes? Yes, Nantes.[55] He was deeply attracted by this child, and when—after his death—he conceived this work and looked about for the people on earth who could realize it, he came to stay near you and decided that the ground was good. Then he followed you through your life, and, little by little, prepared the circumstances. After this, he found me again and influenced events so that we should meet. I kept coming here in spite of all obstacles—do you remember? And now we are together and the work is being accomplished."

The recital of this strange romance is cut short by Old Friend, who, with his usual vigor, begins to plague Reine. She retorts tartly and to the point. "The child's tongue is hung in the middle!" is his only comment.

My wife asks why he does not materialize for Reine as Vettellini has done. "Because I don't choose to! I will when I see fit. If, for example, Vettellini should leave you, I would take his place, and then, to enter into closer relations, I would materialize like Vettellini, who almost

---

[55] My childhood was passed at Nantes,—it is exact.

lives with you now—for he is either here or with Reine the greater part of the time."

This leads me to ask the Guide why he so often produces, or causes to be produced, those creaking noises in Reine's home, while here we never have them at all. What is the reason of these noises? He says that Reine is frequently a prey to an intense sadness, due to the hyper-sensitiveness developed by her training, and that these noises, which he produces by means of two inferior Spirits, serve to make her conscious that he is there watching over her, protecting her. It cheers her up a bit, encourages her.

I ask if we have not, all of us, our Protectors. "Yes, generally speaking, each person living has one or more Spirit-friends; but not everyone is able to keep his friends. Often they are rebuffed and discouraged by your incomprehension, or your bad instincts, which attract lower Spirits around you. Each one creates his own astral society; he has around him the friends whom he merits. As a rule, if a Spirit is to remain the constant protector of an incarnated being, that being must be in the same current of evolution and not too inferior to his Guide; otherwise he could not fall under the influence of the latter nor comprehend his inspiration."

Various small incidents follow. Reine reminds me that when we were talking together this morning, she spoke on questions quite beyond her personal comprehension. "It was Vettellini who whispered them to me," she says. "When I am just myself I know nothing at all about such, things; but he made me answer you like that." (This morning, when the sitting was over, we spoke together for a few moments on serious matters, and I noticed that her speech was automatic and conveyed a judgment quite unusually profound for her.)

Vettellini cuts us short: "Reine has been sleeping a long time now. You must waken her." Just as she is coming back to consciousness she arrests my passes, listens, and with great effort mumbles: "Vettellini wishes me to take *tilleul* tonight. Fever still. Don't forget."

It is quite true. The poor child is burning.

SIXTY-FIRST SÉANCE

May 23, 1913

After the usual proceedings and questionings—to which Reine replies nothing at all—I ask her to go to a certain house, in X. street, and try to perceive and analyze the moral atmosphere of the place.[56] My wife has a great affection for the lady who lives there—remarkably interesting for her combined qualities of intellect and heart—and she is anxious to know if she may not speak to her of our investigations and open her mind to conceptions that might help.

I indicate the itinerary, and after some hesitation Reine finds the house and enters by a window of the first floor, which gives (apparently) directly into the bedroom of Madame T. First she discovers the bed, then rapidly a person who is lying down—"a lady; an old lady. She is sick—oh, yes, she is even very sick!" Then, after a few words, pronounced slowly and as though she were studying the situation, she begins to speak with vivacity and conviction. "She has been ill a long time, and she will not go much further now. I see that because her spirit is quite detached from her body—it is all around her, and above her. You remember ... I have already described this condition to you once before? Ah, but this one is not a red spirit, no!—She is already quite evolved; better than gray, you know, ... bluish,—in a good state of evolution. I will try to enter into communication." ... A moment, then Reine exclaims:

---

[56] The house is the place of reunion of a certain religious sect, and I am interested to see if Reine has any impression of this fact.

220

"But why is she so frightened? It is odd, you know, her spirit is terribly frightened and runs away, and—how curious!—instead of entering her body, moves further away and turns all around it! Ah, that shows that the end is not far, you know; the spirit has already the habit of doing without the body." I tell Reine not to persist in her effort but, rather, to study the room, to try to understand the atmosphere of the house and discover if there is anything of special interest there.

After a few moments: "Monsieur Cornillier, there is another Spirit in the room, and bluish too, like that one. Wait, I will go nearer to see ... But ... how strange! It's the same fluid as the old lady! Wait a minute, I'll see if I can enter into relation with this one." Reine's lips move, she appears to be speaking to some one. Presently she leans towards me: "This one too seems ... not at all pleased to see me. It is the Spirit of a woman who died some time ago. She says that it is for her to watch over this lady—and for no one else; that it is her role, her mission, and that I have no need to come interfering and disturbing."

Immediately my thought reverts to a daughter of Madame T., who died some years ago, and I tell Reine to ask the Spirit's name. She obeys, but her expression grows hard and frowning. I gather that she is meeting with a rather cool reception.—"She says that there is no necessity for me to be so busy about her! She is there waiting for a chance to help this lady who has already often repulsed her—from fear ... It's curious that she should be so frightened.—Not red, she ought to understand better than that! ... The Spirit refuses to tell me her name; ... she is not going to be bothered in this way; ... she means to watch there alone. She has been waiting a long, long time for the moment when finally this lady will lose her fear and allow her to come in contact with her. She will not say another word! ... She wants to be let alone!"

Then I give this order: "Reine, you will transmit this word to the Spirit: *Mildred*. Say it distinctly. Pronounce this word *Mildred* as though it were a name and you were calling someone. Now!" We see the child preparing for an effort. Then in a strong voice, imperatively, she shouts: "Mildred!" A commotion, a cry of terror, and Reine is back in the depths of the big chair, her arms folded across her breast, in an attitude of fear and defense. Her expression is acutely anxious. She is expecting an attack. Surprised at this unexpected consequence, I try first to reassure her: "What is the matter Reine? You must not be afraid. This Spirit can do you no harm, you are above her. What's the trouble?" The child is all trembling. She answers without looking at me, gazing into space, terrified:— "Monsieur Cornillier, she wanted to hurt me, ... I'm afraid ... When I said that word Mildred, she sprang out towards me like a fury—and she meant to hurt me!" Then, little by little, growing calmer, but still not withdrawing her gaze from that point in space, she asks: "But that is her name, then? Because she cried out, 'How do you know me?'" I beg Reine to explain to the Spirit our aim in sending her to this house, my wife's affection, etc.

Gradually she becomes more natural.

She announces that this Spirit is the daughter of the old lady. "She is there because she wishes to help her mother. It is a mission which she has chosen, she wants to accomplish it, she must accomplish it. Her mother would not have suffered so much if only she had allowed her, Mildred, to approach her. But you know," (Reine lowers her voice) "she is jealous. She wants to succeed all alone."

I tell the medium to transmit to Mildred that we understand and respect her wish in this matter and that we will not annoy her. She must not be offended. Madame Cornillier had merely hoped to help Madame T. in speaking of our experiments here. Mildred grows gentle at once. "Then tell her to come quickly—come and speak to her: I, on my side, will do all I can to aid her." And at the moment when I call Reine back to us, she adds: "Thank you."

The child draws a long breath: "Ah well,—that was a fright!—Ah, ... that *was* an adventure!" Vettellini who announces his presence just at this moment, laughs at her a little. He was with her all the time, but he did not let her know it. He wanted to see how she would manage alone. In case of conflict he would have intervened. He confirms Reine's statements and says that Anne must go to see Madame T, and try to help her.

(In the course of several visits, Madame T., led to speak of psychical phenomena, etc., frankly declared that she did not wish to examine the question. With extreme good sense she said that she was subject to the universal law, which could not be other than just. But—and the point is interesting—she confided to my wife that for some time after the death of her daughter, she had heard raps and strange cracking noises all around her room which disturbed and troubled her, and that she had put an end to them by saying aloud very firmly: "If that is you, Mildred, *go away!*" The noises ceased.)

As has been agreed with Vettellini, I begin the recapitulation on the subject of Birth, proceeding methodically in my questions and obtaining exact statements, the essential of which are as follows:

The first point to be remarked is that in the primitive, living sub-stance it is not, as I had supposed, the introduction of a vital principle, of an animating soul, which causes the division of the cell. The cause of the division is in the chemical constitution of the cell; it is the reaction of the substance which provokes the transformation. At this point there is not yet an intervention of spirit.

Human Reproduction: Sexual union is, so to speak, the provocation of incarnation, whose express material condition is the penetration of the ovule by the spermatozoon.[57] It is in the matrix, at the moment of coition, that this penetration should normally occur,[58]but there is great irregularity in these phenomena arising from individual temperament, health conditions, etc.

The disincarnated Spirit, whether he comes consciously or unconsciously to incarnate, is attracted and caught in the vibration determined by the conjunction of the spermatozoon and the ovule. After contact with the ovule the Spirit is free to leave it again, but from that moment on he is attached to it by a fluidic line.

Contrary to what I supposed, two or more Spirits cannot be captured at the same moment. One single coition can give birth to only one child. This is absolute. It is only by a repetition—the period of receptivity may extend over several days—that a second Spirit may be captured by a new penetration of a spermatozoon into the ovule,[59] and

[57] The fact that in certain inferior orders of the animal class natural fecundation has been replaced by an artificially introduced chemical agent, is of no value in the higher order of animals. The eggs of these animalcules can develop parthenogetically, and the irritating agent that is introduced simply determines the means of development. It in no way creates the evolutive force of the egg, it merely provides the occasion for its manifestation.

[58] According to certain specialists, fecundation is not always instantaneous. The penetration may occur several hours and even several days later on. A reply to this objection may be found in Note 1 at the end of this book.

[59] Doctor. G. reading this text tells me that he has lately observed a curious case that would find its explanation in this teaching: A woman, wife of a workman whom he had treated for a recent syphilis, became enceinte and gave birth to twins, one of whom, after two or three days, was covered with syphilitic ulcers and in spite of drastic treatment died on the eighth day. The other child was entirely exempt from any symptom of the disease and developed in to a superb baby. Doctor G. supposes that the last child might be the result of union with a healthy man preceding or following that with the infected husband.

into the same ovule, for only one fecundated ovule can exist at a time. Several spermatozoons may have entered but only one will determine the fecundation; the others pass out naturally and disappear. There is, then, only one spermatozoon by fecundation, and it is the quality of its vibration, more or less intense, which determines sex at the conception. This vibratory quality depends upon the special condition of the progenitor.

A Spirit of high evolution, reincarnating voluntarily, is able to choose his sex either by taking advantage of a favorable condition of the progenitor, or by modifying this condition in advance.

During a period of eight or ten days there is possibility of modification in the phenomenon. Vettellini affirms that the ovule—whether by reason of a renewed union, or whether by another kind of shock (but this rare),—may contract and then open, thus letting escape the substance that has been received; or, on the contrary, it may be penetrated anew by one or more spermatozoa.[60] But it is absolutely essential that there should be a definite beginning of foetal formation, an independent cellular division in the ovule, before a new fecundation can take place. If the interval of time were not sufficient to allow this independent cellular division before a second reception, the result would be the birth of a monster, ... a child with two heads, for example.

I ask what epoch gives the maximum of vitality to an incarnation. Vettellini replies that one or two days after menstruation, when the ovule is well down in the matrix and the spermatozoon can reach it at once. It can, it is true, go up into the *trompes de Fallope* and even, exceptionally, into the ovary, but it loses force in proportion to the distance, and the maternity will be affected in consequence.

There may be foetal formation unaccompanied by the capitation of a Spirit, but in this circumstance the phenomenon will terminate in miscarriage. (Reine remarks that such a case is almost always imposed by Fatality as a burden, a task, to hasten evolution.) Fecundation would be possible during menstruation in spite of the fact that, normally, the ovule descends only afterwards, but coition in this case produces such intense vibration that the ovule falls suddenly and may be impregnated. But the penetration of spermatozoa at this moment

---

[60] This is in exact opposition to the opinion of specialists who esteem that immediately after the penetration of a spermatozoon there forms on the surface of the ovule a coagulation which prevents either an exit or a new penetration.

incurs the risk of introducing into the ovule the impure elements inherent to the general condition.

Vettellini is perfectly aware that his teaching on this subject is in many points in disaccord with scientific opinion. To my objections he replies simply that scientific opinion will gradually correct itself on this question as on many others. No need to worry about it. The explanation which he gives here may even enable certain savants to reach a solution of their problems.

To change the subject, I now ask the Guide to give a few more details on the subject of the last séance.

He tells me that he died about twenty years ago. Reine was just born; I was about thirty when he came to watch and examine me again. In his last incarnation he was a savant, a philosopher, living quite alone and absorbed in the study of the great problems of life. Even then, his sensibility was so subtle that he perceived the fluidic vibrations thrown out by people, and unconsciously preserved them in his memory. "This is how," says Reine, "having seen you as a child, he retained the impression of deep affinities existing between you, and why, after his death, when he planned this work, he came back to find you."

Vettellini gives directions for the séances which Reine continues at home. Henceforth she must take one day of rest during the week, in addition to Sunday. Otherwise she will suffer. He is evidently familiar with all that concerns her life, and this gives rise to scenes of mingled wrath and mirth, amusing,—and indescribable.

When she came in today the child told of a violent ringing of her bell yesterday. She jumped precipitately to open the door: no-one! Vettellini explains now that it was our old friend Jeanik who wished to recall himself to her attention. "Be good enough to send him somewhere else another time—here, to Monsieur Cornillier;—he can stand it. It's not good for me!"[61]

Vettellini announces that the musician—the Guide of our friend A.—will come on Monday to inform us about himself and his work.

---

[61] Saturday, May 24, four o'clock. I was working in my atelier when the bell rang. I went to the door immediately. No-one ... neither on the landing nor in the staircase.

May 29. During the séance Vettellini informs me that my visitor was Jeanik, ever anxious to display his talents.

We will see.

I begin to waken Reine, when the scene of the last séance recurs. Her Guide returns to say that she must take aspirin tonight. Tomorrow, before beginning the auto-hypnotization, she must consult the table. Vettellini will tell her whether she may have the séance, or whether she must rest. He adds that he is not at all easy about her ... He is, in fact, anxious.

May 29, 1913

May 30. Once again the séances are interrupted, and the training for a certain class of phenomena must be indefinitely postponed. Reine is quite ill. After numerous reports from my wife, who has gone every day to see her, I went myself yesterday, and finding her better, proposed to try the table so as to obtain some word of advice from Vettellini. She told me that she had already made the experiment the day before and that the table had tapped: "Forbid sleep (by means of mirror): wait Cornillier."

Scarcely had we placed our hands on the table when this message came: "Mesmerize Reine. Yes, at once. No danger."

She sleeps rapidly, and begins a mute conversation; her lips move, she gesticulates. Several moments pass thus, then, reaching out her hands to find me, she communicates the message from her Guide:

First of all, I am not to worry; Reine is better now,—so much better that we may resume our regular séances next week, but she must abandon those at home. She has not strength enough to carry on both at the same time. Her present indisposition was inevitable; it was written that she must endure great suffering at this moment. Vettellini had no control over it; all he could do was to prevent it from affecting her mediumistic sensibility. He has worked over her in the night, and during her periods of somnolence in the daytime, and there will be no setback. We will resume the séances exactly where we left them. There follows advice for her daily life and care, and then Vettellini proposes that we talk a while, if I have any questions, for she is sleeping well and it will not hurt her.

I accept with pleasure, for there is a point that bothers me in the account of the visit made to our friend Madame T.

Reine found in the room the Spirit of Madame T.'s daughter, Mildred, who seemed to be installed there, patiently awaiting a call, an appeal, from her mother which would give her the possibility, the right, to aid her.

Now my wife, going to see the old lady, learned that Mildred's body had been cremated; and, according to Vettellini's teaching, the fact of cremation cuts off the possibility of the Spirit's return and of any relation with the elements that constitute the material and sentimental life on earth. How then does Vettellini explain the presence of Mildred's Spirit in her mother's room?

A moment's delay. It seems that he has gone to verify the facts which I have given. Then comes this reply:—There are two reasons that permitted her return and explain her presence near her mother. The first is that she died some time ago, (verified: about eighteen years) and the other is that she accepted a mission—this mission—as a means to her own advancement. At her death she was not very evolved, sufficiently so, however, to be able to choose the ordeals she must undergo in the Astral; and, having passed through these, she deliberately chose to support this one because of her affinity and her enduring love for her mother. It is hard bondage which she has accepted, for she may not leave her post until the end comes; she is chained there by her mission. For a Spirit this is veritable imprisonment ... In such circumstances the law concerning the consequences of cremation may, with the help of the directing-Spirits, be modified. Vettellini adds that Reine has probably been too absolute in her transmission on this subject. If a Spirit whose body has been cremated is sufficiently evolved, he can, by undergoing the necessary ordeals, resume contact with the earth in a comparatively short time, always on condition that this contact is in the cause of a good work and for the purpose of evolution. The law has a thousand modes of application.

I ask Reine if she was conscious of any abnormal impression on Tuesday evening. She reflects and recalls that on Tuesday evening, about eleven o'clock, she fell into hypnotic sleep and came here, attracted by my thoughts. She found my astral body completely disengaged, floating about the room and vainly trying to get out. We (our spirits) talked together, and from this moment the idea which had been pursuing her—the idea that she must die soon—had completely vanished, and she had regained her accustomed gaiety.

This is interesting. For on Tuesday evening, towards eleven o'clock I made a violent effort to disengage myself, and go to find Reine. Concentrating my mind intensely on the successive phases of an astral sortie,

I willed with all my might to go to Reine with a view to encouraging her. What she tells me now, proves that I partially succeeded. Feeling my thought concentrated on her, Reine came here.

She transmits, from Vettellini, that the prostration I have felt during the past three days comes from this alone. I expended a large amount of nervous force, excessive for me, and am paying for it. Such experiments are not for me, I have not the strength for them.

Various incidents, the usual play—not to lose a good habit—and I waken Reine.

SIXTY-SECOND SÉANCE

June 2, 1913

Reine's sleep was rapid and profound today, but her transmissions were rather confused—quite as though we had a guest with us! She is still far from strong, and this may be one reason. Then too, following my instructions from her Guide, I have magnetized her only twenty minutes instead of the usual hour,—and this may be another reason.

She begins by announcing that Vettellini has accompanied her in her habitual excursion to the realms of the blue Spirits, whom she found few in number, this time, and exceedingly busy: "They seemed to be occupied with ... with ..." (she cannot find the words to express what she has seen) ... "It was like threads ... like fluids ... currents, on which they were coming and going, back and forth. Perhaps, even, they themselves produced these threads,—these currents? They went up, they came down, they passed and repassed. It was exactly as though they were playing on a gigantic chessboard." Vettellini, to whom she turns for help, says that it is impossible to make me understand what they were doing; there is nothing in our experience to correspond to it. She may simply say that they were engaged in the work of modifying terrestrial events.

I propose another subject.—Is there a constant and indefinite creation of Spirits throughout all time, or has the same number of Spirits existed from all eternity, their dissimilarity and variety resulting merely from the diverse and multitudinous conditions of evolution? The reply—or at least the transmission of the reply—is very confused. As a matter of fact, in view of Reine's condition, I should have chosen another subject. Of it all, I retain only one affirmation, but that one is precise, namely: *the creation of spirit-germs is continuous throughout all time.* And for the moment I neglect the rest.

I do the same in regard to my next question—concerning the constitution of matter and the precise moment when the spirit-germ separates from the Absolute and comes to animate matter—noting however, one curious statement: "The Spirit finds the conditions propitious for an entrance into matter when matter breathes." This is the language of occultism, but the point is to know just what it represents in the mind of its author. I will take up the question at another moment, when the medium is more lucid.

Abandoning the transcendental, I ask for news of the Spirit-Guide of our friend A., who was to have come to talk with us, if Reine's illness had not interfered. Vettellini thinks he will be able to come on Wednesday; he will ask him. Our old Friend, too, will come on Wednesday, he is occupied today.

What is the import of the two new visions of war that Reine had yesterday when in a state of somnolence? Vettellini says that it is he who produced these premonitory images of scenes which, later, she will see in reality. I must make a note of them.

These images were, first, the passing of regiments through the streets of Paris, at the moment of their starting off to war, arousing intense enthusiasm; and second, the return of these troops after action, almost extinguished, lamentably sad, the uniforms ragged and stiff with mud ... Reine, à *propos* of these scenes, makes two remarks that should be retained: First, she distinctly saw *foreign soldiers*. She is not familiar with the uniforms and can affirm nothing—"They might be English ... I cannot say surely, but I know they are not of our nation." Second, the scene of the last vision is placed in winter. This, too, is sure.

I try to obtain an exact date, but receive only an affirmation of the tragic destiny: "*Neither the war, nor the interior troubles can be averted. The Spirits are doing all in their power to mitigate this most appalling catastrophe, but the storm is there; it is almost upon us; it is bound to burst. It will be delayed; but it is inevitable. 1913 was the date ... By dint of infinite precautions and compromises, time will be gained. But to what avail? A simple gesture, and the evil will be let loose.*" This is asserted with such intensity that we sit stunned as under a blow.

Different incidents follow, but nothing especially noteworthy, none of the gay, familiar trifling.

I had finished writing my notes on this séance, and was about to go out, when I stopped a moment near the portrait of Vettellini, for it seemed to me I heard a slight cracking in the frame—an abnormal working in the wood ... I placed my right hand flat on the surface of the canvas saying aloud, "If you are here, Vettellini, strike two clear blows under my hand." Instantly two hard, strong, distinct raps replied. There was no possible error in the objectivity of my sensation.

SIXTY-THIRD SÉANCE

June 4, 1913

A séance difficult to note, so abundant and varied is it. "Maître," Vettellini undoubtedly is; but he is also an amusing companion, a doctor, and a friend. His role of hierophant accomplished, he does not disdain the most meticulous details of daily life, gives little recipes and malicious prods, is broadminded, kind, human.—In short, he both amazes and amuses us.

Today, for the first time, we have the possibility of verifying the information given, a convincing proof for us, who know the psychological and moral qualities of the medium, but of no value for strangers, evidently. In any case it is a good beginning.

When Reine has lost consciousness, I charge her with a mission to the high blue Spirits, and, when she seems to have understood my message, I renew the passes and continue to magnetize her a long time, convinced that she is going to execute my errand, and that I shall receive a satisfactory reply. But when I question her, later on, she very calmly says that she did not go up into the higher spheres today; she has done nothing, seen nothing. I do not insist, but tell her to ask Vettellini to come at once. He is here. I remind him that he gave us hope of seeing the Spirit-Guide of my friend A. today ... Reine informs us that Vettellini has gone to find him.

A moment later she starts: "Here they are, both of them,—Vettellini and the other one." She remarks that the new Spirit is blue,—very blue. I bid her to first thank him for coming and then to explain that we would be glad of any precise information about himself—information that may be verified. It would be most useful in the work we hope to accomplish.

He says that he will give his name, the date of his birth and death, and the name of the place where he lived,—all of which may be easily verified. He became a guide, an inspirer, for A. because of the affinities between them. He had not known him, nor had he even met him in the past; but he had been looking amongst living musicians for one well-gifted and sensitive, whom he might aid in producing works having the character and qualities which, now, he most esteems. For the music which he himself composed, when living, and which sometimes had such great success, now seems to him utterly mediocre;—he cannot endure to think of it! Chance carried him to A. with whom he had found affinities that made it possible for him to exercise an influence. Collaboration is firmly established between them. We shall see later on: there will be a beautiful work. He rarely leaves A. now; in fact he lives with him, etc.

A rather long moment of silence. Reine appears to undergo a curious impression. Then her speech, which, up to this time, has been fluent and facile, changes completely. She articulates like an automaton, in detached syllables, her voice is harsh.—"He—died in—eighteen—hundred and—eight (1808): forty ... three years old. He was born ... at ... M-a-l-t-e—Malte! But ... he travelled a great deal. He came to Paris towards 1800. His name is Ni—o—" (a big effort then finally she jerks out, spelling each syllable as under dictation)—"Ni-co-lo, Nicolo! He was born in ... seventeen hundred ... and ... seventy ... five (1775). He was between twenty and twenty-five years old when he came to Paris. He had a turbulent life. Oh! He had great success in Paris, but ... his life was crammed with all kinds of adventures!" etc., etc.

I ask for the name of the place where he died and the titles of some of his works. He replies that he does not know the first, and the second have no longer the slightest interest for him—no longer exist for him. At my request he again repeats the dates and statements given, and then announces that he is going now to rejoin A. The name of Nicolo, composer, was—I admit it with shame—totally unknown to me, and it was with some anxiety that I made investigations. But all was exact,—facts and dates; and the biographers informed me that Nicolo was indeed a musician of reputation, whose success has been brilliant in its day and time. I must add that to my proposal to conceal his identity from A., he answers that the work is now so well established that there is no objection to giving his name. I may inform A., and even advise him to invoke his Guide, by name, in his moments of uncertainty or anxiety. The call will reach him more easily in this way.

A silence; then Reine spontaneously transmits from Vettellini that she could not go to the blue Spirits today, but that he will himself answer the questions that interest me.

He begins by correcting a transmission given so confusedly in the last séance that I did not even make note of it; a fact which makes the rectification doubly interesting.

"It was of the Earth and the solar system that I wished to speak when I said their evolution would come to an end, *and not of the Cosmos*. Reine was very tired and could not give the transmission. No, certainly not; even for the highest Spirits the conception of an end or of an interruption in cosmic evolution is impossible. Transformation, yes; and Eternity—eternal Eternity."

After this rectification (which shows that the Guide has no intention of allowing an error to remain) I ask a number of questions which provoke a series of remarkable replies, bearing in mind what the little Reine really is. The gist of her transmission is as follows:

The centre of every star or planet of the heavens is hard. This comes from the more intense integration at the centre of the primitive condensation—an integration caused by molecular attraction, rotation, extreme pressure, etc. Around this hard centre the accreted substances grow less and less integrated, are even almost liquid up to the limiting periphery, upon which is formed a hardening crust, of complex composition, from which the first forms of vegetable matter spring. (The matter that breathes.) *It is at this period, of the star's evolution that the first descent of the spirit-germ takes place.* (Grain of life, germ of a future consciousness, coming out from the Absolute.) Its arrival provokes centralization, limitation of form, hierarchy in the proto-plasmic substance: *A differentiated entity is in course of evolution. Each differentiated entity has, then, its spirit-centre, progressing under the action and reaction between its substance and the surrounding ambiance.* Each tree, each plant has a spirit-centre enveloped in a fluidic body—the medium of relation between spirit and organism. When the tree dies, its spirit is disengaged, and wanders about until it meets with the conditions necessary for a new descent into matter. Plant a peachstone, and it is at the moment when chemical and physical combinations determine germination[62] that the liberated Spirit finds the conditions essential to its capture. The modalities of capitation are infinite, but the principle is the same as for the superior orders.

Vettellini says that Spirits very clearly perceive the fluidic bodies of vegetables floating about, just as they see those of animals: the former are of an extreme tenuity, mere nothings, but nevertheless perfectly perceptible to them.

In my haste to record these statements I have omitted an incident, trifling it is true, but worth noting because it tends to confirm the reality of the pretended presence of Spirits, as well as the psychological identity of one of them. We were in the very midst of Nicolo's communication, all three excited, and with attention strained, when Reine swiftly swings around and looks angrily to her left, then pouting, she disdainfully shrugs her shoulders and without a word becomes again absorbed in the transmission of the musician's statement. The scene could not possibly escape us, but it had entirely passed from my mind until, immediately after the departure of Nicolo, Reine again seemed sharply pulled towards her left, and this time she chortles gaily: "I suppose you know who is here, Monsieur Cornillier?" and, without waiting for an answer: "Oh, you! You are always in a hurry. What business had you to pull me like that when we were so busy? Can't you wait a single minute? But, no—of course not! *He wants to talk, and he's going to talk!* ... Well, then—out with it! What have you to say that's so important?"

Old Friend was merely feeling happy, and his vigorous exuberance had to have expression. He wants to say to his protégée that he knows we are off for the country and that he will accompany us as often as possible on the road and will come frequently to see us when we shall be settled. She must pay attention, when she is alone, or talking with me, she will feel a sudden breath on her face, a caress on her forehead, her hair ... It will be he. He will come often,—and ironically he adds, "Oh, it will not interfere with the Stock Exchange!" He will come often, but, on the other hand, he wants his friend to brace up a little; one must take life gallantly, and: "Goodbye till Friday," all in the same breath.

---

[62] From this it would appear that matter has its own autonomy ... I allude to the speculations of different schools that consider matter a mere illusion, a subjective sensation, etc. ... Vettellini absolutely rejects this conception, and affirms that even for them, Spirits, *matter is a reality.*

This incident occurs immediately after Nicolo's departure, and it is only the *"Au revoir"* of our impetuous friend that allows Vettellini to enter upon the scene. "Ah, it is you who come last, my Vettellini!" murmurs Reine; to which the Maître replies simply: "It should be so—since I am the host." He talks at length of our approaching absence: then tells me to cut a lock of Reine's hair very close to the temple; it will aid me to reach her fluidically. On Friday he will give, by writing, all his instructions, but today there is one at least which is formal: "Vettellini forbids you to attempt the smallest experiment for the first ten days. You need rest. You must think of nothing connected with our séances. Get all you can out of the trip. Have a good time. When you begin your séances in the country, be careful, for this magnetizing at a distance eats up one's force. Here, there is, of course, an immense expenditure of fluid, but you recover it quickly; almost all of it returns to you. But what you may send to me at such a distance will be practically lost, and you will feel the effects unless you take every precaution. After each séance you must eat—and drink something strong and reviving. But for that matter Vettellini will look after you."

My wife asks if she really saw a blue star today, at a moment when she was alone with Reine. (It is the first demonstration of the kind that she has ever seen.) Yes. Vettellini says that he made it to give her pleasure. This reminds me of the two raps under my hand when I placed it on Vettellini's portrait. Was it really he who answered? The reply is sharp and prompt: *"No Spirit would dare to touch that portrait!* Certainly it was I!—In answer to your request."

I refer to the projected visit to the Egyptian Museum. He says that Reine is so feeble, so fragile just now, that he is obliged to move very cautiously: a mere nothing, and she would collapse. It is discouraging! All the successive projects that might be so interesting have to be abandoned. But, as soon as it is practical, he will take her to the museum; and if it is after our departure, he will make her write her impressions of the visit.

I am finally on the point of waking Reine. The Guide retires, my wife leaves the room. And suddenly here is Vettellini again, to say that *he knows* that we are wondering what may be the impression of these séances on our servant; and that already we are anticipating the complications that will arise when Reine comes to join us in the country. How will Julia accept the situation? The question worries my wife especially. I am bound to recognize the truth of this. Vettellini has read our thoughts or overheard our talk on the subject! He comes back to reassure us. No need to worry. It will go all right.

SIXTY-FOURTH SÉANCE

June 6, 1913

Reine had been sleeping about three quarters of an hour, and I was still continuing the passes, when I perceived that she was in conversation with an invisible somebody who certainly was not Vettellini. I could not catch a word of what she was saying but noticed her great respect, and even a kind of fear, which evidently bespoke the presence of a stranger. And, in fact, after some moments of silence following this conversation (I had heard her say *au revoir* to the unknown visitor), she reached out her hands to find me and give a report of the conversation.

First, she had gone as usual into the regions of the blue Spirits where, for the first time, she had found Vettellini, Old Friend, and my grandfather, all three together, all happy, and speaking with great satisfaction about our work. Then a white Spirit, barely perceptible to her, came to join them, and wanted to carry her off towards another sphere. But Reine, frightened, flatly refused to go with him. Whereupon, the three friends—who she believes were united there for this very purpose—encouraged her to go, and finally, in view of her persisting fear and defiance, *ordered her* to accompany this great Spirit, holding themselves guarantees of her security in the adventure. Then Reine consented.

Up, up she went, so far that she no longer perceived anything of our worlds. The Great Spirit talked to her, explaining what she would have to do to advance the work. In that sphere where she found herself, she experienced sensations wholly new to her—impossible to translate into words. She perceived, confusedly, a condition of matter quite unlike anything she had ever known before, ... a sort of spirit-life,—inexplicable. And the Great Spirit told her that she must penetrate into these superior conditions; and try to carry back impressions so precise that she would be able—by images and analogies—to make me understand something about it. Then he explained what she must do in order to come and find him again in this region (in her séances of auto-hypnotization during our absence). Finally he brought her back here and before leaving her, so as to be sure that she has fully understood, he made her repeat the purpose of his intervention. (It was at this moment, evidently, that we saw Reine speaking so respectfully to someone invisible.)

A shock, a jump backwards, and a smile,—we know our "Old Friend" by this time ... I ask him why his coming provokes such a commotion in the medium. Reine transmits: "He says that, first, in his lifetime he was always rather brusque; it was the natural expression of his vigorous nature, and he has conserved this characteristic in the Astral. Then, too,—and doubtless because of this intense vitality—amongst the works which Spirits undertake for influencing those on earth, he has assumed those that exact an unusual force; so he retains this characteristic vibration: he hits hard." But abruptly he changes the subject. He has come so quickly because Reine has forgotten to transmit an important injunction from the white Spirit,—a detail, it is true, but the disregard of it might prevent her flight in the ether: When she has her solitary séances, *she must install herself in such fashion that it will not be possible for her feet to cross each other, nor for her hands to join together*; for this would prevent her fluidic body from disengaging completely. This point is of such importance that not only must I insist upon it when, after the séance, I give Reine her instructions, but even before waking her today, I must make the imperious suggestion that she shall pay strict attention to this order.

He refers again to our life at St. Lunaire: "When Anne feels depressed, she must call me. I'll give her a shaking!" He calls attention to the fact that she is much more alert and gay these past days (exact). It is he who has caused it. No, it does not bore him in the least: There is great affinity between them. He repeats: "We are all satisfied with the work that is going on here." Then abruptly—as he came—he leaves us.

Serenely, gently, Vettellini takes his place, and begins at once the instructions for Reine's solitary séances, which will continue three times a week, the same days, the same hours, as those we have had here together. He assigns her duties (which I must repeat to her when she wakens) and then tells me how I must proceed, to magnetize her at a distance. His instructions are precise and most prudent. I must stop at the first sign of fatigue; my normal life must not be affected by this expenditure of nervous force; I must be in good health and spirits for the work to have its full value and significance. (Unnecessary to give here the details which are carefully noted elsewhere).

This leads me to ask Vettellini if his work—as it is being realized by us—is not a rare, or even unique experiment. In all my reading on psychical phenomena, in all the fairly complete literature of the subject which I possess, I find nothing similar to this series of séances … He replies that there are a few examples of analogous work, but that, as a matter of fact, exceptional conditions and circumstances are necessary for their full realization. The first essential is harmony, a vibratory synchronism between people of different categories. We do not all belong to exactly the same evolution, and each one of us has a strong individuality; we are very dissimilar, but nevertheless in fluidic unison. It is this that allows him to live amongst us without too great suffering.

Here Reine speaks on her own authority and gives a remarkable analysis of our temperaments and the existing conditions. I will note only one curious point: the affirmation that her ignorance is ignorance designed and voluntary. *Her role in the work required this ignorance, in momentary co-existence with a highly evolved spirit incarnated in an organism of extreme sensibility.* Otherwise she could not have been passive and submissive to my direction, for one of her evolution may not, normally, be employed as medium. Her humble situation, her absolute lack of instruction, the miserable conditions of her present life, have all been determined in advance, and voluntarily accepted by her Spirit.

I ask the Maître to confirm a capital point in his teaching which I personally find difficult to accept, namely *the duality of Spirit and matter co-existing in a sort of independence.*—"Matter," he replies, "is merely a support for the evolution of Spirit. But I, Vettellini, in common with the disincarnate of my evolution, believe that matter and spirit have each their own essential character: at least, after our observations, we infer this to be the truth—but without pretending to fathom the mystery of the Absolute."

We speak again of Nicolo. Reine frankly finds him charming.—"You would not have found him so charming in his last life," exclaims Vettellini, "He was not exactly a model of behavior." Reine, sniffing gossip, is keen at once to know something more definite.—"Oh, it's just as well not to go into details ... Nicolo could very well have given more information about himself and the people he knew, the places where he lived, etc., but he does not care much to recall that life on earth." ... Reine insists, and gradually wrests from the grave Vettellini bits of unexpected revelation: "singers," "actresses," ... "perpetual spree," fall excitedly from her lips. She is in a fever of curiosity. But she observes with surprise, in which I share, that Nicolo is none the less a blue Spirit now!—"It is in the Astral that his great evolution has been made," explains Vettellini, "and he has chosen to aid the musician A. precisely because he esteems his life, and still regrets not having lived that way himself."

We pass to other subjects. Once again Vettellini demonstrates that he is aware of all that concerns us, that he knows our very thoughts, and amazes my wife by revealing one of hers which she had supposed quite secret. Again he reassures us as to the attitude of our servant at St. Lunaire. Then Reine's health comes under discussion. But it is time to separate. *Au revoir*, till the next reunion at St. Lunaire.

ST. LUNAIRE (BRITTANY)

Saturday Morning, July 5, 1913

We left Paris on the 10th of June, reaching St. Lunaire on the 28th. All this time I attempted no experiment with Reine. But she, during this period, was to continue her three séances a week of auto-hypnosis by means of the mirror. In addition to these three séances she had, in the intervening days, to spend hours in her armchair doing nothing, and, as far as possible, thinking nothing—in a state of inertia.

It was agreed that she must keep a journal in which she was to note any incident of her daily life which might have a bearing on my investigations, and send it to me from time to time. I have not yet received these notes, but she has sent me three automatic writings produced in hypnotic sleep[63]—two of which are brief and confused statements of what she was in the act of doing. (She speaks in the present "I am

---

[63] Writings which she has not examined. As soon as she wakens, she folds and places them in an envelope. My faith in her loyalty is absolute, but naturally I do not pretend to impose my confidence on others.

going up," "I see," "I understand," etc.) The third, written under her Guide's dictation, informs me of the progress of her séances and gives me instructions. These documents are certainly interesting, but valuable only because of my confidence in their source. I am waiting impatiently for the notes of her journal; judging from an allusion in one of her letters they may be of interest.

Yesterday I began the experiment of magnetizing from a distance, starting, as was agreed, at nine o'clock in the evening, and following the method given by Vettellini in Paris. Needless to say that this extraordinary experiment—as I am now attempting it—will have no weight with others. I have no means of verifying anything that Reine may choose to tell me. But if the actual attempt seems to succeed, it will be easy enough to repeat it under conditions that admit of verification.

Saturday Evening, July 5

Having received no letters from Reine for some days now, and a little anxious—for, as a rule, she writes regularly—I propose to my wife that we try to obtain some information by means of the table. We place our hands on a small table which after about ten minutes begins to tap feebly and inconsequently. In a moment or two we abandon it.

Sunday, July 6

Nothing from Reine. Again we try the table. This time there is not the slightest movement.

Monday, July 7

Still no letters. We begin to be really anxious. The child must be ill.

In the evening I decide to make a last effort with the table. After a short interval it rises and begins to tap regularly. "Is this Vettellini?" I ask. "Yes." And to my successive questions the reply comes that Reine has not written because she is ill! "Very ill. Pneumonia."

I interrupt by a question irrelevant to the situation, but one which I consider important; the table, instead of replying, taps "Purulent; purulent pneumonia," and goes on to say that tomorrow morning we shall have a letter from Armand (Reine's husband). Neither he nor Reine realizes the gravity of her condition. I ask what we can do for her. "Magnetize her." The usual method? "Yes." But there is a particular point to be observed: "Before the glalmp ... glmapp." Impossible to understand. I try another way, only to have the same result: the table that has rapped with regularity for the other words cannot produce this one, but coherently it spells out: "Reine not properly cared for. Am doing all in my power to save her." Is Vettellini alarmed? "Yes." Does Reine need money? "No; doctor." Shall I send my friend Dr. B.? "Yes." Another incoherence follows, so I propose to begin magnetizing at once. "Yes."

Vettellini will come about four o'clock tomorrow to give us a report.

Tuesday, July 8

No letter this morning. At four o'clock we resume the table. Vettellini's presence is announced by the words: "It looks bad."—What can I do? "Magnetize her," taps the table. Then all movement stops for some time, when finally it begins again, more slowly, and with less precision. I ask if my magnetism had influence on Reine last evening. "No."—Why? "You should have continued longer." Then incoherence again. Impatient, I insist upon knowing if it is Vettellini who is communicating. "No."—Then who is it? "Old Friend. Vettellini's gone back to Reine."

Instructions follow. I must magnetize her at once, and again this evening. She is in a very bad state. I say that I did not inform Dr. B., as was advised, because the letter from Armand, announced for this morning, did not turn up, and I do not care to trouble my friend without a real necessity. The table then taps twice over, clearly and with decision: "Telegraph doctor immediately. He must go this evening."

And still I hesitate, skeptical in spite of all. I will telegraph tomorrow if I receive a letter from Armand. But the table insists vigorously: "No, not tomorrow; *tonight* ." I am perplexed. My wife is for acting at once. But no, decidedly, I prefer to wait at least for the evening post. And we discuss the point together, forgetting entirely the table which suddenly intervenes and taps the word "Hope," *in English.* This persuades me. While I prepare to magnetize Reine, my wife starts off to send a telegram to the doctor, begging him to go quickly to see a little model in whom I am interested and who, we hear, is very ill.

The table taps that old Friend will return this evening about ten o'clock to give us news.

Wednesday, July 9

What is going on is extraordinary. But what is it? A marvelous proof of transcendental influence? A strange prank of our subconscious? A practical joke of some inferior Spirits, out for fun? However one explains it, the incident is curiously interesting.

Last evening, at seven o'clock, after the communication of the old friend and after the telegram had been sent, I was perfectly convinced of Reine's illness. But at seven-thirty the postman brought a letter from Reine, written on Monday afternoon, a few hours before the table announced to us her purulent pneumonia. In this letter no real fear for her health is expressed, simply this: "I have another cold but am taking good care of myself." She gives sufficient reasons for not having written lately, and speaks gaily of her approaching arrival here. A separate envelope contains several sheets of automatic writing produced during her séances of Saturday, the fifth, and Sunday, the sixth of July.

This letter, with no reference to the pneumonia, is somewhat disconcerting. I should not be surprised if my friend B., an important and exceedingly occupied man, found the joke rather lacking in savor.

Impatiently we wait for ten o'clock—the hour fixed by the old friend for his return to the table. Promptly to the moment he manifests his presence. I demand an explanation. He says that in the afternoon, when Reine wrote, she did not suspect that she was ill. It was eleven o'clock in the evening when she suddenly realized her condition. (It was about nine o'clock that we had the announcement of her illness.)—"Reine is very ill. It was necessary to send the doctor. He has just left. He considers her condition grave. He will write tomorrow."

We discuss the situation, my wife and I, when the table spontaneously taps: "Your doctor will cure her"; then confused phrases, impossible to understand. We withdraw our hands a few moments. Replacing them, I ask the cause of this scattered incoherence—"The Spirit employed is ignorant," is the reply. I ask Old Friend to come back tomorrow at the same hour—10 p.m.—"No: will come at 5."

I ask if they—Vettellini and Old Friend—foreseeing this illness, have arranged events in this way, that the disease might be attacked from the very beginning.—"Yes." More incoherence. We abandon the table.

On the whole, this explanation is acceptable, and is even an interesting proof of the transcendental foresight of the Guide.

But just as the situation is becoming clear to us, in this light, a telegram from Reine is handed to me. Sent from Paris last evening, at nine o'clock, it reads as follows: *"No occasion for anxiety."* And once more we are at sea! We must wait till tomorrow, when the doctor's letter will give us our bearings. He may have found grave symptoms requiring observation, in which case our first interpretation will be the correct one: or, he found nothing alarming, and in that case, what is the meaning of all this comedy? *Tricks of subconscious?* That is not an explanation; merely a label stuck on to a bottle,—"Contents Unknown." Why, and to what end, for what incomprehensible reasons, would our separate and individual subconscious take the trouble to bother us like that?

The hypothesis of a farce played by ordinary Spirits seems, perhaps, the most probable ... It has at least the merit of conforming to information given us ... But, on the other hand, how would inferior and malicious Spirits dare to make use of Vettellini's name or assume the role of the vigorous Old Friend?

We will see what the table gives at five o'clock.

Wednesday Evening

Another communication, and more despairing than ever:—"The doctor can do nothing for Reine. She realizes now the gravity of her condition. Tomorrow you will have a letter from the doctor, and another from her. The case is about desperate. The end, however, is not immediate."

Thursday, July 10

Today we are absolutely sure of at least one fact: *Reine is in perfectly normal health.*

But the riddle has yet to be solved.

This morning we received a letter from the doctor and a good long one from his patient. The doctor—charmingly and without malice—expresses his surprise at finding a moribund in such excellent health. Reine weeps tears of despair over our anguish, and tears of gratitude for our care. She easily explains why she has not written for the past eight or ten days. But this does not clear up the mystery. We can only wait for her arrival and hear the solution in a séance of hypnosis.

Tonight I will resume the magnetizing at a distance.

July 20

I did not resume the experiments of magnetizing at a distance, for the day after this fantastic episode we left for a few days' trip. Then Reine fell ill, and veritably, but with nothing purulent this time,—just plain rheumatism. I decided to wait for her presence here to understand the situation. She should arrive in a day or two now—always supposing that she is able to travel.

Tuesday, July 22

Reine arrived yesterday, shockingly pale and feeble. The poor child has passed eight or ten hideous days of intense pain and fever. The day before her departure—Sunday—she was not able to move. But Vettellini had assured her that she would start Monday and, joy aiding her, she decided to chance it. She arrived exhausted, but without having suffered during the trip.

Today she declares that she is almost well—fair sleep and a little appetite. Her delight at being here will do the rest.

She at once handed over her journal and gave me a message from Vettellini enjoining a séance the day after her arrival, to map out a plan of work.

Naturally we have spoken of the grotesque performance of the table. Reine understands no more than we. But, to my surprise, she says that several times she herself had incoherent, alarming, and coarse communications by the table. In answer to her complaints, Vettellini had said that he could not prevent this, and that he would give the reason at the first séance of hypnosis at St. Lunaire.

What gives interest to this statement *is the verification by Reine's journal that these vulgar and offensive communications were made to her on the very days that the mystifying messages were given to us.*

I wait with curiosity for Vettellini's explanation.

SIXTY-FIFTH SÉANCE

July 22, 1913

At the prescribed hour, and in the room designated by Vettellini, I begin to magnetize my little model for the sixty-fifth time! Without taking the trouble to darken the room completely, I merely close the blinds and install the child in a deck chair. Scarcely have I begun the passes when she is sleeping. At a certain moment she sits upright and, with a contemptuous expression and brusque gesture, pushes aside an invisible something ... then again lies back, retaining for some time her irritated and indignant aspect ... I resume the magnetizing.

Suddenly, all smiles, and fluttering and babbling with delight, she turns eagerly to the left and reaches out in a passion of joy. I stand bewildered.

It can be only Vettellini ... Reine's voice grows more distinct and we assist at a charming renewal of the familiar scene. First it is an exchange of exclamations and compliments spiced with the inevitable affectionate jibes. Then comes the general tendency of my efforts here. Reine, who has entirely forgotten my existence, is invited to let me into her *tête-à-tête*. She holds out a hand in my direction ... and I am admitted to take part in the conference.

Six séances a week, if you please!—Three on our regular afternoons and three short ones in the intervening evenings, after dinner. If I feel the least fatigue, Reine must work alone.

In the first séances I must make her review all the incidents that have occurred during our separation. By following her journal methodically I shall be able to find an explanation of all of them.

Then, spontaneously, the Maître speaks of the false communications by the table. He explains that our house and the neighborhood are occupied by Spirits—inferior but strong—who have lived in this very spot, and who, after all, *are at home here.* They are not vicious nor malevolent, but they consider themselves the proprietors, the masters,—"and in fact they are," adds Vettellini. They regard strangers as intruders and lose no occasion to plague them. It is evident that the fact of sitting at a table, in expectation of a message, implies a receptivity open to any influence. Such has been our attitude, intensified by anxiety: they maliciously took advantage of it.

Not once did Vettellini or Old Friend come to communicate by the table. They even were unconscious of what was going on; but had they known about it, the probability is that they could not have prevented it. As I express astonishment at this statement, the Guide explains that these Spirits are so material that it would be impossible to influence them without descending almost to their level, and the circumstances were really not grave enough to warrant that. They have a real force, in that they are at home, that they are legitimate proprietors of the place. (Curious this. Here is the right of property established even in the Astral. Shades of Proudhon!) They have no power to reach us if we do not lay ourselves open to their influence by attempting to enter into communication. As a consequence of my magnetic relations with Reine a fluidic line exists between us; and, by it, they were even able to go to her and combine their tricks in which, here and there, a certain amount of truth was mingled—just enough to perplex and disquiet us. Oh! ... one must laugh now and then, it is sometimes such a bore to be dead!

The Guide seems to think that Fernando Kerloz—who has never ceased to prowl around Reine ever since his eviction from the séances—has also played an important role in the comedy.

It seems unfortunate that inferior Spirits should be able to use the name of Vettellini, to impersonate the old friend. Can nothing be done to prevent it? Is it not possible to punish them?—"No more than you could prevent a practical joker from assuming your name," is the reply. To punish these Spirits we should have to become as material as they are. It is simpler not to lay one's self open to their influence, never to attempt to use the table or any other material means of communication here.

And here we have the explanation of Reine's furious gesture at the beginning of her sleep. She says that one of the Spirits of the place—a red one—stationed himself near her for an instant saying: "Don't sleep.—Above all things, you shouldn't sleep." She drove him away, and he did not insist ... There are none around us now. My room was chosen by Vettellini because it would seem that my personal atmosphere, the sortie of my astral body during my sleep, chases away the ordinary Spirits (?): in another room our séances might be disturbed."[64]

I express astonishment that our desire, our appeal to Vettellini when we used the table, did not inform them of the situation.—"But sometimes our calls do not reach them," says Reine, "they may be too far; or, even feeling the call, they may be unable to respond if they are on a mission. Like a friend you send for, if he is absent or busy he cannot come."

The ridiculous episode of the table is, in short, explained *by the mere application of theories already given us.*

Vettellini informs us that Old Friend is coming in a moment. He speaks of Reine's health and discloses a few facts which she, from delicacy, had concealed from us. Mutiny, mockery, cajolery—the whole gamut of their familiar play is touched on to delight us.—A brusque movement, a shock, and Reine nervously exclaims, "Can't you find any other way than that to come?" Then, smiling affectionately, and as though to excuse her words: "You know, you're not always exactly ... *gentle*, Old Friend!"

A few moments of intimate talk and the séance is closed.

---

[64] I had decided to hold the séances in a small room near the attic, which could easily be darkened and where we would be isolated. Vettellini's choice had annoyed me, but I could not persuade him to change it.

SIXTY-SIXTH SÉANCE

ST. LUNAIRE. July 23, 1913

L ast evening at nine o'clock we had a second séance.

Almost at once Reine reached the point where she could see and hear her Guide and transmit his communications. But it was in reality she herself who, surveyed and aided by him, explained to us her impressions during a new visit to the celestial spheres.[65] She talked at length and, although Vettellini seems to attach great importance to the information given, I will make no note of it for the moment. It is too vague. I will wait for an explanation.

The Maître advises no séance for tomorrow (today). The child must rest.

---

[65] Similar to that which she made at the beginning of the Sixty-fourth séance.

SIXTY-SEVENTH SÉANCE

July 24, 1913

(*Thursday Evening*)

As the evening séances must be short, I spend this one in the examination of different incidents noted in Reine's journal, first reading to her the passage that interests me, then asking her to explain it,—with Vettellini's aid, if need be.

Résumé of her journal: Thursday, June 19. Reine during her séance of rest, in an armchair near an open window, sees sparkling lights in the air, followed by cloudy forms that move about and jostle each other. At the same time she perceived a confused sound of voices. Frightened, she rises to close the window, resumes her seat, and loses consciousness.

Explanation now given by Reine in hypnosis:

"All that is exactly true. I was not mistaken when I was awake, for as soon as I became unconscious I saw and instantly recognized the Spirits who had entered my room. I saw them first in the Egyptian museum, when Vettellini carried me there." (I have not yet had a report of this visit to the Museum, but note the incident as it was given.) "They came to return my visit; and, to show their satisfaction, they sang some of their songs to me—oh, such strange songs!—Slow, sad, and very ... very ... (Vettellini gives her the word '*scandés*') ... rhythmic. It was ... h'm? ... (She leans close to catch the words of her Guide). Yes, it was Egyptian music. Oh, it pursued me, that music! Long after I wakened I heard it still, that *strange* music—like nothing I have ever heard before.

The journal: Monday, June twenty-third, Reine, looking in the crystal ball, sees an elderly person lying in a reclining chair and seeming to suffer. Near the lady, whom she seems to vaguely recollect, was Madame Cornillier, looking very sad.

Explanation: "That is nothing at all. I saw that, but in my memory. You know you sent me once to see a very sick lady whom Madame Cornillier loved—the Spirit of her daughter was in the room, don't you remember? Well, this was a jumbled reminiscence of that visit. I put Madame Cornillier in because she loves that lady so much. *But it was all imagination*, nothing else."

The journal: Thursday, June twenty-sixth, in the night, Reine wakens and perceives a tall white form regarding the portrait of Vettellini—(a small copy of the portrait, which is placed on the mantelpiece in her room.) After remaining in the room a moment the cloudy shape disappeared.

Explanation: "Monsieur Cornillier, it was you! I was perfectly sure of it myself, but Vettellini has just confirmed it. You were anxious about me, you wanted to have news, and during your sleep you disengaged yourself and came. You went to the portrait and stood there near the fireplace because a number of things there contain your fluid, you know ... the drawing, the portrait, a number of little things.—To be near all that gave you more force."

The journal: Sunday, July sixth, in the night, but when she is wide awake, Reine sees a vaporous form that grows gradually more precise and becomes the phantom of a woman wrapped in veils. After walking about the room a little, the phantom stops before the long mirror of the wardrobe to arrange her veils, then disappears. Reine, contrary to her habit, is not in the least frightened.

Explanation (given with Vettellini's aid): "Yes, I saw that! It was a woman—a tall woman; but that's all I know ... (She listens to her Guide.) Vettellini does not know her, but he knows that she died only a short time before and that she was hunting for you,—for you and Madame Cornillier. She went to your house but, not finding you, she wandered about the apartment, discovered my fluid and followed it, because she felt it was mixed up with yours ... She was attracted to my room because there are a lot of things there belonging to Madame Cornillier and you—clothes, bits of stuffs, things you have used, etc. She went straight to the things that contain your fluids, then she stopped before the long mirror to arrange her veils. Vettellini says that undoubtedly she has something to ask you. She was a friend of both. He says that it is about twenty days ago, in our time, that she died.[66] You will certainly hear from her again. Madame Cornillier must not be afraid. Her fluid is good. She is already of fair evolution."

Since the séance has to be brief, I am forced to interrupt it ... But though the Guide has himself warned me to waken Reine, they go on talking together, he and she, as though neither time, nor we, existed. Silent and captivated, we assist at the pretty scene which, though familiar, is never the same. Instead of the half hour prescribed it is an hour and a half that passes before I bring Reine back to her normal condition. Old Friend was to have come, but could not manage it: "Too busy."

---

[66] Some days after this séance, as I reflected on this incident, I suddenly thought of an old friend of ours—and she was tall, to note a detail—whose death had been announced to us by our servant on the 10th of July. She had heard of it through a friend of hers, a concierge. Since ten years our relations with this lady, which had been intimate, had ceased. Our servant did not know the date of her death, but we requested her to inform herself on this subject, and she received the reply that the funeral service had taken place on the 2nd of July. This would correspond with what Vettelini has said. I will investigate the question when we are back in Paris.

SIXTY-EIGHTH SÉANCE

July 25, 1913

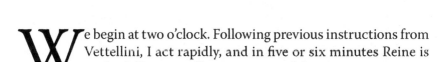

We begin at two o'clock. Following previous instructions from Vettellini, I act rapidly, and in five or six minutes Reine is in the full swing of her mysterious life again.

Almost immediately she pulls back sharply but, after a quick frown, her habitual expression returns and she breathes regularly without interruption. I surmise that it is the Old Friend ... And, sure enough, after a few moments of calm, she begins to mutter and grumble, then makes a sign to the invisible, to pass over to her left, flinging out shortly: *"No, it is not a fad*! It is more convenient for me, that's all. I'm more comfortable on this side. Besides, what difference can it make to you? ... I don't see that you can say much, any way ... Just look at you! ... Always so abrupt! ... Yes, yes, I love you just the same, of course,—but not like my Vettellini—no! Well, what of that? My Vettellini comes for me, and you ... you come for Madame Cornillier!"

Old Friend is here to say that Vettellini will be late today—he has a mission elsewhere. Then, amongst other things, he tells us that he came in the night, when Madame Cornillier was so enervated with sleeplessness, and chased away two red Spirits who were in her room and who, though she was unconscious of it, were exasperating her.[67] "He says they were vagrant Spirits," adds Reine; *"Had they belonged to*

---

[67] My wife confirms that she did not sleep the greater part of the night—tormented by nervousness.

the place, he could not have chased them away." (This coincides with what has already been given by the Guide.) After a few more words, Old Friend repeats that we must wait for Vettellini, and then—abruptly—he leaves us.

We wait.

Reine, who has been lying back in her chair, now seems to become uneasy. She leans forward, looks fixedly at a given point, and finally says: "Magnetize me more. There is something there that I feel, but, I can't see it yet,—a Spirit, perhaps? I'm not sleeping deeply enough to see."

I renew the passes and, when I cease, Reine is sitting upright—alive with interest.

Softly she whispers: "Monsieur Cornillier, I know him. He came once in Paris ... You know, it's that one who sang those lovely things to me at a séance ... I put it down in one of those writings I made while I was asleep ... Didn't you read it?" (It is true that in one of the mediumnic writings Reine sent me, dated June 14, she mentions the apparition of a new Spirit who was singing to her—operatic airs—and who announced that he would come to see us when we should all be together again.) "He is a musician. I'll ask his name." She listens, then repeats: "Mé—? Méhul? He says Mé-hul."

Then I question "Méhul," who declares that he is the composer himself and that he will give me proof of it in Paris; he has not force enough here. It is with difficulty that Reine can even see him, ... and then, too, we are in the midst of work which he would regret to interrupt. But next winter, in Paris, he will come back and give diverse incidents of his life which I will be able to verify. He will have Reine write fragments of his works. He produced a quantity,—but he had still so much to give! He has been hunting a long time for a living musician whom he could inspire, who could serve as medium to him; but he has not found one as yet. Through Reine he will communicate some unpublished melodies. He says that the melody that Reine remembers—whose words "*Je pars au loin*," etc., may be found, he says, slightly modified, in two of his works. He will see us again in Paris ... and, in a way, it will be helpful to our work. He leaves us.

And still Vettellini does not come. Reine becomes impatient.

To engage her attention I speak of an incident noted in her journal—a visit which she and Armand made to the cemetery *Père Lachaise*, and in course of which she had such acute impressions. It was on Sunday, July 6, when Reine, wandering through the cemetery, felt herself impelled toward the crematorium. Her husband refused to accompany her; *but Reine, irresistibly attracted, entered, and, despite her horror, was forced to assist at a cremation.*

Now that she is in hypnosis, I speak of her impressions, and ask her to explain the causes. She begins to reply volubly, but suddenly breaks off with a gay laugh.—"It's Vettellini—he has been listening!"

After the usual friendly informalities between them, I come back to my point, and again ask the child why she has such horror of cremation—an operation which I have always considered very decent, to say the least. She repeats that she is still overcome by the memory of the shocking spectacle. But this impression, she explains, is in reality only a physical repercussion of the certainty which her spirit has acquired: that cremation is a wrong to one's self, and to others as well. We have already been warned of its unfavorable influence on personal evolution, cutting off, as it does, all contact with earth and thus rendering incarnation more difficult; but Reine now gives a quite new and unexpected view of the question:—

"All living creatures must evolve and must find their ways and means of evolution; the most humble creatures, the lowest,—the worms that live on dead bodies, as well as any others—must evolve. Well, don't you see, the incarnation of such creatures in a human substance is of immense advantage, of enormous benefit to them, ... and it is not just to deprive them of it. Not only is the decomposition of a dead body a cause of evolution in the Spirit that animated it, but more than that, it is the source of evolution to millions of spirits barely escaped from unconsciousness, and to whom our human matter offers a marvelous field of progress. It is wrong to deprive any creatures, no matter how low and mean, of this benefit. It is spoliation. It retards their march towards conscience. It should not be." And with great energy Reine insists: "Cut that out of your will, Monsieur Cornillier; Vettellini orders it."

I inquire what may be the result of excess in the other direction, that is to say the quasi-eternal preservation of the body by embalming. Reply: Embalming is a misfortune for the Spirit in that as long as the body persists and endures, the Spirit must remain attached to it; he can neither liberate himself nor reincarnate.[68] But he alone suffers from this, and generally has no regret, for he died with the intense desire of being embalmed. It was his pride, his glory,—and he knows no better.

I protest that amongst the Egyptians there were many of high evolution—the priests, the "Grands Initiés,"—who should have known

---

[68] A later communication slightly modifies this absolute statement.

better.[69] Reine replies that even a high evolution does not always prevent a fixed opinion, a prejudice. She adds,—and how astonishing it is, coming from this uninstructed child!—"In spite of their great science the Egyptian priests were mistaken on this point. They obstinately stuck to this idea that embalming was important, was valuable—*Mon Dieu*, just as we ourselves undoubtedly cling to other errors! It is perfectly possible that those who come after us and who examine our theories and doctrines will be amazed that we could attach such importance to certain points." Later she says, "The Spirits of the Egyptian mummies, for example, suffer terribly when the curiosity of scientists, or chance circumstances, destroy their mummified bodies and liberate them."

As to the second aspect of the question—the evolution of animalcule—Reine says that nevertheless the embalmed body serves in their production; and that, moreover, the viscera and a large part of the elements available for the incarnation of animal Spirits are cast aside, and consequently also serve.

I would like, if possible, to get a rational idea of Reine's impressions during her flights to the high realms of Space, and to this effect ask her to describe, first, what she felt; and after that, what she was able to comprehend in her ethereal visits. She replies at length, and, in the main, clearly. I see that she has made her own experiments and, so to speak, verified the information Vettellini has given concerning the modifying influence of the great Spirits on human destinies. Here is what I have retained of her communication:

Each star in the heavens is surrounded by its own atmosphere, which is an extension of its conditions of habitability for its disincarnated Spirits. And just as, in flying away from the surface of the earth, one passes from a thick and heavy atmosphere to a lighter air and, finally, to the subtle ether, so one passes from the obtuse unconsciousness of undeveloped Spirits to the conscious state of high Spirits, always more and more lucid and, correspondingly, ever increasing in the power of directing and modifying earthly destinies.

From the surface of the earth to the regions of the clouds, red Spirits are encountered. Beyond these are the gray ones,—who become less and less gray the farther one goes. Above the clouds is the region

---

[69] According to certain occultists, embalming was practised in Egypt to maintain the Spirits of the dead in a certain dependance, thus rendering more easy their avocation and their aid in the practice of magic.

where blue Spirits may be found, and still beyond in the rarefied ether, in the interstellar space, is the sphere of the white Spirits.

In this sphere are generated the fluidic currents destined to modify the events established by that mysterious fatality, *The Hand*. These fluidic currents would seem to be an adaptation of magnetic and electric forces existing in our solar system and in cosmic matter, and the aim in using them is to guide and hasten evolution.

We have already been informed of this in precedent communications, but what is new is that Reine, conducted by a great white Spirit, *has herself felt and perceived* these currents and the intense life of the Spirits who were generating them.

She was also able to understand that this work is not of sure result. These modifying fluidic currents may be diverted from their course, diminished or absorbed by various physical phenomena, cosmic forces that are antagonistic, etc.

I ask if this experience that has been offered Reine is not an extraordinary favor—almost unique.   Vettellini answers that the favor is not exactly for Reine, but for our work.—Then I confess that if I, personally, appreciate the admirable adventure at its value, I fear it will leave my contemporaries—and even the elite amongst them—absolutely indifferent; the smallest millet seed would have more weight! The Guide does not discuss my opinion, he merely says: "That has no importance. The immediate judgment of the work is not the only one that will be rendered. The book will be completed and produced: time will pass: other people will come who will seize its meaning. It will hold indications for future students. It will open the way to new fields of investigation. Evolution will be more advanced, then people will understand better. And, for the moment, it is perhaps not in France that it will rouse the greatest interest."

Vettellini asks me to give paper and pencil to Reine who transmits this curious request in writing: "Monsieur Cornillier, I will ask you to waken Reine (in future) when the half hour is finished. I myself do not calculate the time, so much do I love talking with this child."

SIXTY-NINTH SÉANCE

July 26, 1913

(*Evening*)

As the séance must be short I limit myself to two questions. First I would like to know if the magnetization at a distance (which I attempted five or six times only, and not consecutively, for various reasons—health, false communications of the table, our absence, etc.) had any influence on Reine.

It is she who replies: "Yes, without the least doubt, each time you magnetized me it helped me. I am perfectly sure of it, because at all my other séances it took me a long time to go to sleep, and I always felt a great fatigue; whereas on the evenings that you sent me your fluid, I fell into hypnosis at once, and woke feeling rested."

I observe that it is impossible to be certain of the efficacy of my action because Reine used the mirror just the same and, also, she knew the hour when I was to make the experiment. Nothing proves that it was not auto-suggestion that came to add its strength to the effect of the mirror?

But Reine maintains that this is not the case, stating, in support of her opinion, that on one of the evenings when I operated she was feeling so miserable that she decided she would not have her séance. Her indisposition had delayed their dinner hour, and they were at table when, all of a sudden, she sank back in her chair, overpowered by sleep. Seeing this, Armand removed the lamp from the table and arranged cushions around her so that she would not hurt herself. It was after nine o'clock.

At the end of half an hour, she came out of the sleep which she declares *hypnotic*. "It's a very different thing, you know; I cannot confound it with my natural sleep; and certainly I was not thinking of you at that moment, and the mirror was nowhere near me. I had fully decided not to have the séance, I was too miserable!"

Then I ask about the magnetizations made by the treacherous advice of the table, when that famous purulent pneumonia was at its very height. Reine does not know about that. She leans over to consult Vettellini and transmits: "No,—Vettellini says that they did not reach me. You know those inferior Spirits gave you false communications."—"Yes, I know that," I replied. "But if their communications were false, my magnetizing was none the less true—and even more intense than usual because of my desire to relieve you. But you were not informed and you felt nothing. So then, I am forced to conclude that it is auto-suggestion and not my fluid which influences your sleep."

Vettellini insists that though my fluid did not reach Reine in this given case, he is quite sure that I am able to magnetize her from a distance without having prepared her for it. Naturally, I must be in good form, the conditions must be favorable; but as they are now, I could do it. I should try the experiment; it will succeed.

I now ask Reine for an account of her visits to the Egyptian Museum in the Louvre.

(She gave a brief report of it in one of her mediumnic writings, stating amongst other things that she had found there *traces of my fluid*. Now, before leaving Paris, *and without a word to anyone*, I went to visit the Egyptian Museum. In the course of my stroll there, I placed my hands on a statuette which stands in a corner near a window, with the express intention of impregnating it with my fluid. After this I went up into the room of the two mummies and, placing my hand on the glass, hoped to leave there also a trace of my passage. Impossible for Reine to divine this dark plot.)

Now, in hypnosis, she tells me that twice, in the night, during her natural sleep, she has gone to the Louvre. It was Vettellini who took her there, but for some reason or other, he left her to make her visits alone. Her impressions are somewhat vague. As soon as she entered she felt confused, surrounded by hidden, indefinable forces, not knowing where to turn ... when, suddenly, *near a window she found my fluid*. This reassured her a little, and helped her. She followed this fluid and *finished by arriving at a glass case containing two mummies.* She describes them, observing that one is the mummy of a child. She describes, too, the cover of a coffin that lies on the upper shelf of the case. (All is correct.) Beyond this she has no definite impressions. She had a sensation of being pursued by heavy fluids that wanted to retain her there. She wandered about anxiously, came back to the sculpture on the ground floor, where she saw phantom forms more clearly and where she felt more sympathy. But she realized that she was being mislead intentionally, just to keep her; and she was uneasy, not knowing how to get out. It was only later on that the idea came to her to pass through one of the big windows.

In short, the only interesting point is the discovery of my fluid and the description of the mummies.

Since her life before the last was lived in Egypt, I ask if she had the impression of something familiar, something known before, either in the things which the museum contains or in the Spirits that infest it.—"No, no,—nothing. All that seemed quite foreign to me. I did not feel at all familiar with it. Those objects and those people must belong to a time much more barbarous than the one I knew. They belong to a quite different race and to another evolution." After a moment she exclaims: "you know it was certainly Spirits from the room down stairs who came to sing those strange songs to me. They were pleased with my visit and came to thank me. They reached me by following my fluidic trace."

Since we are on the question of fluids, I ask if a pictorial or sculptural representation of a person possesses, by the fact of its resemblance, any fluidic property of that person.

"Not the slightest," replies Vettellini. "There is no relation between a being and a representation of him, unless it be that, intensely captivated by the work which reproduces his features, he should come to contemplate it long and often, and thus project upon it his own vibrations. He could also come unconsciously in the night, in the astral body, to impregnate it; otherwise there is no possibility. On the other hand, the work is unalterably saturated with the fluid of its author."

We talk at random. Old Friend could not come this evening. "But," says Vettellini, "he stayed a long time with Madame Cornillier last evening while she was alone, and after Monsieur Cornillier came in he went upstairs to her room where he also stayed long."—"What was he doing," demands Reine,—"all alone in that room?" Here ensues a dialogue of which we naturally hear only one side. "Looking at his portrait? What portrait, Vettellini?" Reine is ignorant of the existence of a small photograph of the old friend which is, in fact, in my wife's room. Vettellini explains this fact, adding that it is better for her not to see it, for when, at a given moment, it pleases Old Friend to materialize for her, it must not be argued that she describes him from a recollection of the photograph. Reine admits the good sense of the precaution, but curiosity is roused and pushes her to a question—"Sly boots," retorts Vettellini, "would like to pump me without my knowing it!" Reine's disconcerted face is her only protest. Vettellini says that she is feeling the effects of fatigue, that she must stay in bed till 9 or 10 o'clock tomorrow, and lie down again for two hours after lunch. To console the child, who is anything but pleased at this prospect of long rest, he promises to carry her to Paris during her nap, to see her husband. She will see what he is doing and I must verify her observations. Reine is enchanted.

Sunday, July 27

Reine slept two hours in the afternoon. When she came downstairs she said that she had dreamed of Armand. She saw him just starting off for a walk with her mother and a young girl whom she detests,— Mademoiselle Marguerite. I note the description carefully in order to verify it by writing to Armand.

Monday, July 28

In hypnosis today Reine—questioned about her visit to her husband yesterday—says that it was not a sortie of her fluidic body, merely a dream of no importance. Vettellini confirms her statement. Reine was too tired; he had not thought best to take her. Useless for me to write for a verification of the vision which was only a combination of her dominant thoughts at the moment when she fell asleep.

SEVENTIETH SÉANCE

July 28, 1913

Vettellini is there, waiting to be questioned.

Once more I revert to *the currents generated by the white Spirits*, hoping to reach a clearer comprehension of the question. First, I make Reine state again with extreme precision that she has not only felt and perceived the presence of the Spirits and their activity, but, more than this, that she has directly observed the different elements of the phenomenon. She speaks with great vivacity, stopping occasionally to catch and transmit the exact words of her Guide, and ends by giving me what I wanted: a relatively clear notion, verbally comprehensible at least, of the mechanism of the work of these Spirits.

What bothered me was the statement that the Spirits employed natural forces—magnetic and electric—to act upon human intelligence. How is it possible? We observe on our physical plane the phenomenon of *telepathy*. We know—though certainly we do not understand how it is accomplished—that an idea or thought, emanating from one brain, may be received by another brain, whose thought will be modified thereby. We know also what may be produced by certain magnetic or electric currents, phenomena of attraction and repulsion; but these are of a physical order and, so far as we are conscious, have no influence on our mentality. How, then, can the white Spirits modify human will, hasten evolution—which, in this case, is only a transformation of mentality—by means of currents of physical derivation? In all the telepathic phenomena a thought is carried from the emitting brain to the receiving brain by waves, fluids, that are generated by the organic and the astral body. But the white Spirits have neither a physical organism, nor an astral body, nor any attributes whatever perceptible to our senses. Then how do they operate?

This is what the child replies: "If the Spirits tried to act upon us by the sole projection of their thought, we would feel absolutely nothing; for their thought is of too subtle a quality, too unlike our own for us to perceive it directly. Consequently, in order that their thought may reach us, *they are obliged to materialize it*, and this they do by incorporating it in certain magnetic or electric currents. These fluidic currents, quitting the ethereal regions and directed towards the earth, are employed as vehicles; they materialize, they reduce to the conditions of terrestrial telepathy the thought impulsions of the high Spirits with which they are charged."

Reine remarks that she uses the terms "magnetic and electric" only because they come the nearest to expressing what she means, but in reality the forces employed by the Spirits have not the same origin as those familiar to us under these names in our daily life. They are forces still unsuspected by us and whose discovery reserved for the future—will be a new source of prodigious activities! She adds that it is precisely the physical quality of these telepathic currents that renders them so susceptible to disturbance by natural phenomena—meteorological and others, etc., etc.

Considering this question of the astral currents as clear as it can be for us, I pass to another subject.

It has seemed to me that the relation between Vettellini and Reine disengaged in natural sleep, is different from that between Vettellini and Reine disengaged in hypnotic sleep, and I ask if my observation is just.

The Maître replies that it is a fact, and explains it as follows: "When Reine is sleeping naturally, and her Spirit disengages itself, there is no need to maintain relations with her organism, for it is not serving as a medium; and it is really with a *Spirit liberated from matter* that I communicate. But when you hypnotize Reine, it is in order that she may serve as an intermediary between you and the astral world; and her spirit must maintain relations with her organism, so that the latter may transmit the messages communicated to her. In this condition her spirit not only retains the characteristic tone of her actual personality, but even finds again a faint accent of other organisms, in former incarnations,—whose essential vibrations are forever conserved by the fluidic body." And Vettellini adds that every once in a while he catches a note expressive of the person Reine was in her last incarnation, when they were together, and knew each other so intimately.

Reine, interrupting, says that she has an inherent affinity with whatever is small, delicate, or even weak in organization; she does not know why. In this present life she voluntarily chose to be "a little thing," but in that other life, too, she was a fragile creature, whom Vettellini watched over and guarded as one guards a child.

The Maître confirms this, adding that it is precisely in talking with Reine *hypnotized*, that he discovers traces of that old-time friend, so delicate, so fastidious, a little over refined, whom he loved to follow and protect. This glancing back to a former life, this stirring up of sentiments normally effaced, but quickened by contact with the medium, has so real a charm for the grave Vettellini that he often loses our idea of time. ("I, myself, do not calculate the time, so much do I love talking with this child." These words given at the end of the sixty-eighth séance are thus explained.)

Recalling a note in Reine's journal, I ask what value the unconscious disengagement of my spirit during sleep may have for me—for my evolution. For example, what is the consequence of the visits to Reine? Is it any advantage to me, or is it a purely mechanical act?—"First," replies the medium, "you often go out like that,—almost every night, in fact. In Paris, you frequently go to your atelier. Several times last winter your spirit conversed with Vettellini. He gave you indications, ... directions for our séances. This possibility of freeing oneself bears a relation with one's evolution, and you certainly gain much in this way, since you learn to comprehend many things which, when you are awake—in normal life—become intuitions. But when you came to my place ... Ah ... that was something! It was a *big* effort ... and you did it quite alone, nobody helped you at all! And that time Vettellini talked a long while with you; you stayed out of your body for more than an hour.

Old Friend will not come today,—too busy; but this evening he will be here. For that matter, whenever he is free now, he comes and stays near us; or, if not near us, he goes up to our rooms.

I ask Reine what on earth he can find to do in our rooms, and my curiosity is satisfied:—"But you know that Vettellini and he have to materialize in a certain measure, in order to communicate with us. They could do this easily by taking directly from our substance the necessary fluids, but that would fatigue us; it would be too great and too sudden a loss, and we would feel the effects of it. So then, since the fact of our living in a place, moving about there, sleeping there, impregnates that place with a deposit of our fluids, they go to collect what has been left there. The clothes we have just discarded, towels, gloves, the chair in which we were sitting, all these things retain a portion of our fluid. They gather all this carefully and, by means of it, they can materialize without our having to suffer. It forms a veritable fluidic envelope for them,—a body, so to speak, which allows them to enter into relations with us."

Spontaneously, Vettellini speaks of the conditions between Reine and our servant. Julia, delighted at first by the presence of the child, soon began to suffer because of our manifest affection, and now treats her very curtly. Reine, though trying in every way to please her, only succeeds in aggravating the situation.

Vettellini seems perfectly informed of this and says that he will take the matter in hand. We are not to worry.

SEVENTY-FIRST SÉANCE

July 29, 1913

(Evening)

A short séance, only two points in which I will note. All day yesterday the good Julia (our servant) continued to be rudely disagreeable to Reine, but towards evening there came a complete and sudden change. She was all at once amiable, kind, and—most curious of all—happy. This agreeable transformation has persisted today and seems established.

This evening Vettellini proffers the information that it is he who has influenced her. Seeing Madame Cornillier annoyed, and in view of the general discomfort which threatened to upset the tranquility of our atmosphere, he had attempted to modify Julia's sentiments—"I expected more resistance on her part; but no,—she responded immediately."

Reine explains that Vettellini had combined her fluid with Julia's, mixing them together etc. Here is good domestic chemistry! We are all highly pleased with the mixture.

The second point is an incident which shows the logical coherence of Reine's sensations. In the course of the séance, she announces that the old friend is there. I silently reflect that Reine has not jumped as she habitually does, but I do not say a word about it, preferring to observe her; and we go on talking with Vettellini. After a while, as Old Friend does not intervene, I ask to speak with him. Reine replies that he does not come near us. He is there, she sees him, but he does not come down to us. I ask why. She turns to Vettellini, who explains that it is because he has shortly to go on a mission to the white Spirits and that, consequently, he does not want to charge himself with the material fluids necessary for communicating with us, for they would make him heavy and he could not accomplish this mission. He came just to see us; but he cannot come nearer, and cannot speak with us.

And now I understand why Reine did not jump.

Vettellini insists that I am tired, and the order of proceedings must be changed. On Monday, Wednesday and Friday we will have a séance in the afternoon for serious questions. On Tuesday evening a short chat together. On Thursday, Saturday and Sunday a complete rest for me; for Reine a short séance by herself in the evening. More than this, he forbids my writing up my notes immediately after the séance, or even on the same day. It is too much for me. He will see to it that my impressions are as clear and keen the day after.

SEVENTY-SECOND SÉANCE

July 30, 1913

Reine appears to be sleeping well; but when the moment of entering into relation with Vettellini arrives, she hears with difficulty and sees as through a fog. After some hesitation and uncertainty she understands: he is telling her that I must magnetize her more profoundly. This I do for six or eight minutes and, finally, the communication is clearly established between us.

I am interested to know how the great Spirits see the microscopic world,—the world of microbes, and so on, down to the atom. This prodigious life that is revealed to us only by the aid of refined instruments,—what is it for them? Can they observe it? And how far down in the scale of the "infinitely small" can their observation go?

Vettellini says that they have a perfectly precise vision of the various manifestations of the microscopic world, they could analyze all the elements contained in a drop of water, in a molecule of air, see all the different germs, etc. But it is not only as we see them with the microscope, no it is chiefly by their chemical and atomic constitution that the great Spirits take cognizance of this infinitesimal world. They penetrate deeper than we, it is true, but for them also there is a limit. They suppose that they can perceive life at about the point of its sortie from the Absolute, but the creative source remains an enigma ... In their march of evolution they leave behind them Cause—a mystery unexplained—to advance toward Finality—a mystery inexplicable.

Here Vettellini, as in an outburst of high confidence, gives us a glimpse of the real life of Spirits of his quality. *"Out from what is the Au-Delà for us*, comes, occasionally, a Spirit with the mission of instructing us, of revealing to us the higher truths—in short, of doing for us exactly what I am doing for you. It is in this way we have been told that the ultimate work of Spirits is to direct the cosmic forces. The formation of worlds, the order of the different systems, and their disappearance, are determined by Intelligences, of which cosmic forces and universal laws are only manifestations."

Vettellini says that in the communications which they—he and others of his evolution—receive from these higher Spirits, it is extremely rare that anything could be even fugitively grasped by our earthly intelligence, but when such a case presents itself he will tell us what he is permitted to say.

This leads me to ask him for details about themselves. We know that they are extremely occupied and that, either in groups or individually, they are engaged in important works whose purpose in general is to hasten human evolution. But, outside of this, what is their life?

Vettellini replies that, in the first place, they have various modes of life that are inherent to a condition of matter unknown to us; their concepts do not exist on our plane: of these, then, he cannot speak. But, in the order of comprehensible experience, he can say that the essential source of our Art is in the astral life, as is also the essential cause of our emotion in contemplating the manifestations of Nature. They, the Spirits, can travel throughout all space, observe the revolution of worlds and assist at their manifold phenomena. Musical harmonies are a source of never-ending pleasure for them. They have no instruments, evidently,—they have no need of them. It is in combining vibrations that they create what is the very essence of the harmonies of sound that we call music, and often they meet together for this purpose. And they also have an interest and even, sometimes, high pleasure in following our earthly manifestations of Art, and in inspiring them. It is indeed rare that Spirits are not present when we unite for an expression of elevated art. Their capacity for affection and emotion is intense. The tender interests of their earthly life continue, and our good actions, our efforts toward high ideals, have a repercussion of happiness for them: for example, Vettellini and Old Friend have profound joy in this work we are doing. Their approach to us, their descent into our ambiance is painful, but it is also a keen delight for them that their aid is understood, that their efforts are bearing fruit.

And here Vettellini makes a new and rather curious confidence: "Spirits though we be, we have need of a certain renewal of force to stimulate our spiritual life: without it we should grow stagnant. To render our life more intense we must have fluidic sustenance, and we have to work to find the fluids. There are lazy Spirits who prefer to stagnate." (But, as has been previously said, these fall at a given moment under the domination of cosmic currents, which oblige them to struggle against their line of evolution.)—"In short," says Vettellini, "Astral life has its joys and its sorrows just as earthly life has. But it is infinitely happier, infinitely more extended, more intense and more luminous."

I ask the Maître to explain what sleep is,—its physiological reasons and its significance. Would not an exact exposition of this subject give an indirect demonstration of the independence of the spirit and the organism? He says that he will gladly do this, but the question is of extreme importance, more so than I imagine, and several séances will be required to elucidate it. Reine's total ignorance of scientific terms makes the transmission of his thoughts on such questions particularly difficult.

Old Friend—having given Reine his usual shock—has been waiting for some time. He is not pleased with his friend Anne and has come to tell her so. He told her to walk regularly, for the sake of her health and spirits "She walks, yes, but she goes at it as though it were 'hard labor,' and that is exactly what it must not be. She must be glad, walk tranquilly, happily,—enjoy it!"

My wife wants to make an English translation of my notes. Old Friend approves the idea and says he will help her. She must work on it only when it pleases her, without regularity. She should begin it on a Friday, preferably the first Friday of the month, and after three o'clock. To my "why?" he says it is because of her planetary influences. Any work begun under favorable influences has the best chances of success. In my work, to follow my own good pleasure would, on the contrary, be a prejudice. I have innate need of regularity and discipline. But—and the injunction is serious—I should cease work the instant I feel fatigue.

A few words from Vettellini close the séance.

SEVENTY-THIRD SÉANCE

August 12, 1913

I resume these notes after an interval of thirteen days.

In his communication of July 29. Vettellini forbade my writing my report on the days of the séances, because of my great fatigue. I obeyed for the séance of the thirtieth, writing only on the next day. But, being interrupted, I could not finish my notes that day and, to get rid of the task, I set to work on them again on Friday morning, August 1—day of a séance—knowing perfectly well that I was disobeying orders, but attaching not the slightest importance to this fact:—very tired, it is true, violent headache, etc.

For the séance, the usual procedure. Reine sleeps. But when I begin to question her, she looks around vainly; her Guide is not there. We wait ... He does not come, ... nor does any other Spirit come. She begins to worry. I reassure her, saying that we have plenty of time; he must be occupied elsewhere, he will come surely in a few moments, etc. But time passes, and there is not the smallest manifestation. I, too, am surprised, for when Vettellini cannot come he informs us of it. Never yet has an absence like this occurred.

To divert Reine I ask her to give a psychometric analysis of two letters. But she is enervated, distressed, cannot sit quiet an instant. My words of consolation grow less and less assured. Then I have an idea. Since Vettellini does not come to Reine, Reine must go to Vettellini. Immediately the child is happy again:—"Why of course! Quick, quick,—send me to him. I'll find him all right, only I'm not magnetized enough to free myself entirely; magnetize me deeply and send me ... Oh, I'll find him!"

I use all my force and all my will to put her into a profound sleep, and must confess that I am feeling all but exhausted when Reine, violently thrusting aside my hands, sits up and cries: "Ah! At last you are here! Well it's about time! What were you doing?"

She listens, and her expression of joyous surprise rapidly transforms into one of anxiety. From the disconnected words that fall, it is evident that I am the subject of discussion:—"quite unreasonable,"—"formally forbidden," etc. We see her reaching out both hands that seem to grasp and hold on to something:—"Oh, no, my Vettellini, no, no! Don't leave me. Yes, I will ... yes. I'm going to tell him; ... only stay, my Vettellini, ... stay!"

The child decides to communicate the reprimand, but it must be a very difficult thing to do: she hesitates, ... postpones, ... does not dare. The fear of losing Vettellini must be acute before she yields.—"H'm ... Monsieur Cornillier ... Vettellini is very angry with you. He cannot allow you to disregard a formal order from him. He would not have come today if he had not seen that we were both of us making ourselves sick to reach him. He says that in overtaxing yourself you do me harm as well as yourself, *because you magnetize me with bad fluids*. Instead of getting ahead with the work, you are only retarding it."

I receive the douche with mingled emotions—not pleased with myself for having disobeyed, and a little vexed at being scolded so curtly, but the ridiculous and comic side of the situation is so evident that my contrition is mixed with a malicious and irreverent hilarity. May Vettellini forgive me! ... I laugh ... I laugh, ... but never again will I transgress his commandments!

The séance then continues, but there is a slight chill on each side, a little embarrassment. Vettellini specifies that that for the moment I must not magnetize Reine; I absolutely must rest. She will have her solitary séances, auto-hypnotizing herself by means of the crystal ball; and, if Vettellini has any communication to make she will write it.

Reine wrote at length during her solitary séances of August 4, 7 and 8.

In the writing of August 4, the Guide informs me that he has asked a doctor—a friend of his, if Reine may take the sea baths. The doctor allows and even encourages it: sea baths will be good for her. (The child has not wished to take them.)

In the writing of August 7 comes an ironical word for me: "I was under the impression, Monsieur Cornillier, that I had told you to rest?" (This because I had tired myself in cleaning my car.) Then news of my cousin, of whose condition Vettellini keeps informed in order to advise me.

In the writing of the 8th, Vettellini's sympathy returns to me ... a little. As I have taken two whole days of absolute rest, I may begin to magnetize again Monday, August 11.

During this period I have observed several small incidents, but note only one of them. It was six o'clock in the afternoon: I was with my little model on the terrace, looking at the sea, when she had a vision—a vision of oriental scenes (people and architecture) which from time to time vanished to give place to draped figures moving about, etc. Reine was quite evidently in a semi-hypnotic state—but perfectly conscious, nevertheless—and described in detail the scenes she was observing. Later Vettellini tells me that he took advantage of a special physiological condition of the medium,—*which gave her the possibility of disengaging herself without apparent sleep*—to carry her off to the Orient. They were not subjective images, but real scenes which she was in the act of observing.

SEVENTY-FOURTH SÉANCE

August 11, 1913

After an exchange of civilities, Vettellini informs me that, as events are now shaping, I will do well to prepare for the publication of my notes.—"The great Spirits have succeeded in holding the war in check for a time,—oh, it is merely adjourned. It has to be. It is fatal. But at least there is no immediate fear of trouble, and in any case, it would be well to have the manuscript ready for the end of the year." And he indicates the best use of our time, with this end in view.—I observe that we already have more than enough matter for a book, but that, on the other hand, we still lack a few precise and indisputable facts to prove the spirit-origin of our communications. A case such as that of Nicolo has value only for us who have followed the development of Reine, but skeptics will not hesitate to accuse her of having merely opened a dictionary to find the information she has transmitted to me. If Vettellini means that the book shall have a veritable import, and be considered other than a curious romance, he must give us some absolutely conclusive facts. Predictions seem especially to exasperate him. Well and good; there are other means. And then, after all—if we want to reach the public interest, we must do what is necessary for that purpose. Does he understand my point of view?

Assuredly he understands my point of view, and he will give me satisfaction. Material phenomena are no longer of his sphere, but he will provide the means of establishing proofs of Spirit identities. He cannot disclose his own before his work is terminated, it would be an obstacle to its accomplishment, but he will bring Spirits, perfectly unknown to us, who will give verifiable information about themselves. He realizes that this is needed to give weight to the book, etc., etc.

The séance closes with advice for Reine. Vettellini says that as long as she is here at St. Lunaire he is responsible for her, and we are to have no fear in leaving her alone on the beach or on the rocks. He watches over her. (We are in fact always anxious when Reine is alone on the rocks, fearing that she may slip and break something, or that she will be heedless of the tide; for she is like a child of ten—imprudent, unconscious of time, jumping into pools waist-deep to reach a shell that attracts her.)

SEVENTY-FIFTH SÉANCE

August 13, 1913

Astormy and oppressive atmosphere. Our medium sleeps bad-ly. When I think the passes are finished, the Guide intervenes. Articulating painfully, Reine transmits that I must magnet-ize the very top of her head. During all the first part of the séance she communicates with greatest effort; it is only after three-quarters of an hour that her habitual vivacity is recovered.

We speak of the future book. The Guide asks me to read the intro-duction to him. Following his directions, I cover the eyes of the medi-um,—that the light which I need for reading may not reach them,—and I take her left hand in my left hand. Thus installed, I begin reading to my invisible auditor!

The preface is approved. I am advised merely to enlarge a little my criticism of the scientific fetishism so prevalent.

We speak of personal matters. Vettellini wants me to procure some objects containing the recent fluid of my cousin.[70] He cannot go con-stantly to see him, he has other occupations, but he wishes to keep me informed of his condition. When Reine will have taken contact with these fluids, he will be advised of any interesting changes without be-ing obliged to go himself to examine him on the spot. *He fears that a final crisis is approaching.*

---

[70] Being at St. Lunaire, I could not get hold of any object belonging to my cousin, and so was unable to give anything to Reine when she left us.

Yesterday we took Reine with us in the car. At a certain moment she declared that our two friends were with us. Today I ask Vettellini, "How do you make your presence felt when the medium is awake and in a normal state?"—"By entering into contact with her aura (fluidic body) which always lies outside her organic body. I have only to graze it, so to speak, and Reine is immediately conscious of my presence."—"When it is Vettellini," says Reine, "it is light and caressing, but when it is Old Friend, oh là là,—it's a good pinch!"

SEVENTH-SIXTH SÉANCE

August 15, 1913

Hardly asleep Reine jumps excitedly and with frowning brows and ugly expression sits up straight in her chair: some mumbled and unintelligible phrases, some indignant gestures, and she falls back again. I resume my passes, thus interrupted, and in a few moments she is calm again and talking with the invisible. Of course it is Old Friend, but this time he has been more violent than usual. He comes only for a moment to say that Vettellini will be a little late today, and that I must continue to magnetize Reine on the top of her head. The atmosphere is bad: adverse fluids, heavy and material, are surrounding us, attracted here by the habitual occupants of the place. The medium is susceptible to all these influences and her sleep is painful. Vettellini, too, suffers from these conditions and we ourselves are unconsciously affected by them. Reine adds: "Old Friend is so strong that I understand him easily. If it were Vettellini speaking, I probably could not even hear him." Old Friend speaks with his protégé a moment, then, seeming to regret the violence of his arrival, says to Reine: "You mustn't be angry with me, you know ... *Au revoir*." No time for a reply.

I continue to magnetize Reine's head. After eight or ten minutes, she gently lifts her face to the left and, with a gay laugh, falls at once into a happy babbling and chirping, which she breaks off just long enough to say to me: "I suppose you know who it is? It is my Vettellini!" I had even suspected it and, calmly, I await the end of their effusions.

At last the Guide, turning to more serious affairs, tells me to begin the reading of my first notes (recopied) as has been agreed.

I install myself according to his renewed directions (Reine's eyes bandaged; her left hand in my left hand; the light centered on my manuscript.) I read four chapters. The child seems exhausted. To my inquiry, she says it is infinitely more fatiguing than the usual transmissions. I ask if Vettellini understands me easily and am told that, by reason of the conditions established, he understands exactly as though he were there in life beside me. Reine, on the other hand, understands nothing whatever: she is a mere inert duct of transmission. It is Vettellini who makes use of her organism.

After some criticisms, uninteresting to others, I change the subject. How is it that certain people who are probably of rather inferior mentality—ordinary somnambulists, fortune tellers, palmists, etc.,— are sometimes able to make important predictions, proved in time to be exact, when high Spirits like Vettellini seem to foresee rather obscurely the events that are interesting for us? The Maître replies that these different inferior mediums are generally aided and inspired by Spirits belonging to their own evolution: that is to say, by Spirits who are living around us, in our atmosphere, and who are consequently informed of all the influences that govern our terrestrial relations. They can thus easily foresee small future events. For example, Fernand Kerloz, had we followed him, could often have given us phenomena that would strike public attention. But Spirits of high evolution live in another part of space. Their task is to modify human tendencies, to stimulate the currents that will impel us in given directions; and, as a rule, it is only the great determining causes which they foresee, or the general consequences of an ensemble of events, etc. I accept the explanation, not without remarking, however, that the formidable storm that was to shake all Europe to the roots, the tragic vision which Vettellini has given Reine could hardly be considered a trifling terrestrial event? Vettellini announced it *as a great crisis in modern civilization* and— most happily indeed!—his forecast seems to have been mistaken. Why? Were these terrifying visions mere images created by him to illustrate his opinion, dramatized, moreover, by the emotion of Reine?—"No," returns Vettellini, "those were not pictures such as I sometimes make to inform Reine of certain facts, no! They were exact views brought by the fluidic currents which announce future events. My sole intervention was to make Reine capable of receiving and understanding them. It was true at the time, and it is still true now."

"The great Spirits have united their efforts to retard the catastrophe and mitigate its horror. Their influence on Fate has been effective, but you must bear well in mind that it is always restricted. WHAT REINE SAW, WILL BE. Let these visions stand as they were written in your notes, FOR THEY WILL BE REALISED—though at what moment I cannot say. For us, Spirits, there is no division of time, we do not feel it passing, and it is difficult for us to put ourselves in the conditions necessary to understand it as you do."

SEVENTY-SEVENTH SÉANCE

August 18, 1913

I have barely begun to mesmerize Reine when she stiffens and in an angry and imperious voice cries: "No,—no. I will not have it! Don't you touch it!—Go!" Her face is as expressive as her words: frowning, and with ugly, menacing lips, she has the air of defending herself against an invisible enemy. A moment, and I resume the passes silently, thinking that possibly some wandering and undesirable Spirit has ventured in our midst. Sleep, and the arrival of her Guide, calm her. They talk together and give an explanation of the incident: "Ah, Monsieur Cornillier, you don't know, but I have just had a bad fright,—and I was furious! Only think,—I had just fallen asleep when I went off to the studio.—Yes ... I wanted to look about there a little.—And what do you suppose I found? A lot of dirty little red Spirits all around your portrait!" (A portrait of myself, painted by me, which stands there on an easel.) "And who even touched it and wanted to carry it off! You can imagine;—I was furious! Vettellini says that they were only trying to tease me ... They would not have dared to touch his, but they put their dirty little paws on yours. H'm! ... I stopped them." Vettellini laughs at her susceptibility, then tells me to begin my reading.

I read four chapters (which provoke certain interesting rectifications that are noted in their place), when the Maître stops me to make an important and evidently painful communication, for he puts on gloves to soften the blow.

Reine must go back to Paris at once. That is the brutal fact, but how skillfully he has announced it! Armand, sensitive and fragile by nature, suffers from her absence. He makes no complaint, but he does not eat, does not sleep, and is gradually falling into an extremely nervous state. Vettellini fears that he may become really ill if Reine does not go to take care of him and bring some gaiety back into his life.[71] Armand sick, evidently everything would be disorganized in the life of Reine. But she has been touched exactly as she should be. There is a lump in her throat at the thought of leaving us, but not an instant of hesitation: Armand needs her, and she goes. Resolutely she asks, "When, Vettellini?"—"Saturday."—A choked sigh from the child ... "Ah? ... so soon!"

We talk at length of this disappointment, and the little Reine shows such signs of affection that we are really touched, my wife and I. Certainly we shall regret this charming child and, quite apart from the séances, we shall sincerely miss her.

Given the short time that remains, a séance is ordered for every morning at 9 o'clock from now on. In this way I can still obtain a quantity of information or rectifications if need be.

So then—certain in advance of his reply—I ask Vettellini his opinion of the famous fourth dimension. Not understanding a word of it, Reine has difficulty in transmitting my question. Finally she makes a concession: "Well—I don't know what you are trying to say, but I will repeat your words to Vettellini." And the Maître replies that the notion of a fourth dimension is a true one. "The fourth dimension exists, and even others beyond that; but you cannot conceive them, for they have no utility on earth."

I am sufficiently crestfallen, for I confess that I have always considered the fourth dimension as a sort of mathematical freak![72]

After this, we speak of the transfer of physical suffering from an incarnate being to one disincarnate. Vettellini often relieves Reine of an attack of acute pain *by assuming it himself.* What is the mechanism of this operation and how can a Spirit be conscious of a physical sensation? He explains that a part of the suffering comes from bad fluids and vibratory disturbances. A Spirit can release a sick person from

---

[71] The séance began at three o'clock. At eight that evening Reine received a letter from her mother saying that she was much worried about Armand, afraid that he was seriously ill.

[72] See in the Appendix Note 7, which modifies this answer.

these prostrating fluids by attracting them towards himself and taking the brunt of them. These fluids cannot be destroyed immediately, they must wear themselves out and gradually disperse.

SEVENTY-EIGHTH SÉANCE

August 19, 1913

Vettellini comes at once. Reine announces it gaily, adding that the séance will be excellent today as her sleep is much better than usual. For the first time, here, she is in deep hypnosis, feels perfectly lucid, and sees me as she does in Paris: that is to say, she sees my physical body in its normal aspect, and, just above it, a portion of my fluidic body, disengaged. Even, as I closed her eyes, she already noticed blue flames coming from my fingers, and, at different stages of the magnetizing, she saw me surrounded by a vaporous substance.

It is thanks to Old Friend that the ambiance is good. He came before the séance, bringing with him a whole troop of Spirits who, says Reine, often serve as escort to him, and they have in a way purified the atmosphere.—"He is still here, but he stays in Madame Cornillier's room. I will go to find him. Open the door." (Door of communication between the two rooms.) "Open the door, Monsieur Cornillier," she repeats with insistence; for I hesitate, supposing that she means to really go, in person, and fearing that the bright daylight in the adjoining room may waken her. But perceiving my mistake, I rise and open the door. Reine changes position, turns her head in the direction of the room and in an instant laughs: "Yes, here he is! I'll bring him in.—When the door is opened, you know, I pass more easily," she explains to me.[73]

---

[73] Colonel de Rochas has already remarked this curious impression of mediums who, without an instant's hesitation, will pass through a wall but who

284

Our old friend is happy and expansive as usual. He chats with his friend Anne, speaks of his gifts as an orator during his life on earth, even recalling it with some satisfaction.—"But," exclaims Reine, "it is just the same now! If you could only hear the ease with which he speaks! Oh, yes, he is eloquent!"

I install myself and read four chapters which Vettellini comments upon in most interesting fashion. Some points are explained while others, due to the bad influence of Fernand Kerloz, who undertook to guide Reine at the debut, are declared false. Vettellini tells me, at first, to suppress these, but upon my objection, he recognizes that it is only just to retain the contradictions and errors as they exist in my notes.

I pass over the commentary, save certain details concerning the astral body, or double, of living beings:—The liberation of the double, in normal life, is in accordance with the degree of evolution. In the greater number of cases it projects from one-quarter to three-quarters of an inch over the whole surface of the body; in some instances the projection is greater; and, occasionally, it is even seen almost completely disengaged, standing above the head of the physical body or, oftener still, at its left. Its role is exactly what has already been specified in the tenth séance. It must, however, be noted that in the case of highly developed mediums, or in that of people having the chemico-physical organism of mediumnity, the facility of liberating the double is no longer in relation to the evolution of the spirit. It is merely a faculty resulting from a certain organic constitution—one permitting an easy filtration of the fluidic substance—and is, indeed, the characteristic faculty of mediumship in general. Reine observes that she herself, for instance, is not a very good medium, that her organic constitution is far from being adapted to her actual role, and this is why she has such insignificant results in material phenomena.

Her remark brings back to mind a statement in one of the early séances—"Later it will require an enormous force to magnetize me, but for the moment you are what is needed,"—and I ask if this judgment still holds good.—"No," she replies. "No one but you can ever hypnotize me now,—not even that strong one you spoke about.[74] At first you

---

will suddenly stop short for a moment in face of a closed door. Durville, I believe, has also noted the fact. It is doubtless an unconscious souvenir of normal habits.

[74] The case of a friend who feels to an extreme point the fascinating influence of the magnetizer Pickmann.

were rather feeble in fluidic force, and it was difficult to know just how it would turn out; but now it is quite another thing,—you have developed what is necessary. It is by your patience and perseverance that the work will be put through, and when it is once accomplished, I will no longer be a medium. I will never serve in other experiments. Never shall it be said that I accept payment for the transmission of communications. In this, our common work, all has been disinterested. The relation will always be maintained between us, but no other than you will ever be able to employ me: my spirit would refuse. But even if it did not, *I should be stopped just the same.*" Vettellini then speaks of my role in the work. Evidently I am risking my reputation as a man of sane mind. But the risk is not so enormous after all, for having neither honors nor office, I have little to lose, and can sustain the shock—without great merit!

Here Old Friend interrupts to say that he would have been greatly astonished if anyone had undertaken to talk to him about all this in his lifetime.—"Not only were such questions of no interest to me, but I held them in contempt ... Oh, I would have been the first to ridicule you then! But now I know it's a grand thing you are doing!"

Reverting to the subject of reproduction in the lowest form of animal life, I ask for an elucidation. Take for example the polypus—where a reproduction, a new individual, is formed by a simple division of the mass, or by the tearing off of a part which reforms or completes itself according to the original type. Are there already little spirits in the original substance awaiting a possible individuation? Or does a Spirit come, after the division, to introduce itself into the fragment liberated? Vettellini answers that in each individualized mass there is but one spirit-centre. For some moments, or for some time after the division, the fragment is mere stagnant matter; and it is only when a germ of life, a wandering Spirit of the required degree, takes possession of this stagnant matter, that it once more becomes active.

SEVENTY-NINTH SÉANCE

August 20, 1913

I begin with the reading which provokes several corrections. The incidents of the early séances—such as the history of the needle woman, my precedent lives, and various other communications which I have not troubled to report—were mere fantasies of Fernand Kerloz or the jokes of Spirits brought by him. Exception is made, however, for the amazing incident of the fourth séance, which Vettellini says is true; and he therefore advises me to give only the initials of the names, for as the fact cannot be proved, I might expose myself to legal action.

Our friend, Mademoiselle S., being with us for a few days, I ask if she may be present at tomorrow's séance. Reine in transmitting my request adds that she feels greatly attracted toward this lady, but her words end suddenly in a choked and confused laugh, for Vettellini lays bare a secret vice by saying: "And her tobacco, as well, has great attraction for you!"

Then Reine confesses that, finding herself alone in the salon last evening, she had sniffed with rapture a package of the English tobacco that Mademoiselle S. affects.

EIGHTIETH SÉANCE

August 21, 19I3

Hardly have I begun the magnetizing which, in view of Mademoiselle S.'s presence, I had intended to prolong, when Reine sits up to say that her Guide allows the young lady to come in at once. She will not interfere in the least. Vettellini has been to see her, her fluid is good, he can even make use of it for the séance, and we shall be relieved thereby.

So I summon the ladies, and, after they are seated, begin the reading. Various small criticisms.

Then I refer to the curious state in which Mademoiselle S. sometimes finds herself—the complete impossibility of expressing in words, thoughts which she nevertheless insists are perfectly precise, and not necessarily complicated conceptions, but sometimes even quite simple ones. Her acute consciousness of this limitation amounts to suffering, and she would like at least to know the reason of it. Vettellini's explanation conforms to his teaching. It is the case of a Spirit already evolved incarnated in an organism not only inadequate but untrained. All the difficulty of expression proceeds from this fact.

I now ask Vettellini if he will not help the medium to remember one of those strange songs that the Egyptian Spirits from the Louvre sang to her. Can he not help her to give us an idea of the character of the music? This would be of special interest to our friend who is a musician.

Reine listens to Vettellini. Leaning towards him slightly, she emits a few notes, seeming to take the key ... Then stops, ... listens again, and

288

makes another start. One would say she is repeating, trying to reproduce what she hears. Finally, after some hesitation, she risks it. The song comes out clear, distinct, and well timed. It is most impressive, for the melody is of real beauty. She stops, to resume in graver key and with different modulations the same air, which seems to be a sort of march, strongly rhythmic and somber, even tragic. Later she tells us that in singing it she has the vision of a procession passing through the midst of a crowd, who are seated on the ground, and who repeat certain parts of the song.

Vettellini proposes to have a séance in Paris, this winter, consecrated to Egyptian music. He will make her sing other melodies, older than this, which were sung in various circumstances of their social life. "For it is a part of us,—that. Those songs are our songs," says the child, alluding to lives that Vettellini and she have had in Egypt.

Old Friend interrupts us. My wife is waiting to ask him certain questions, but he is cross-grained and not disposed to be amiable today. After all, what interests him most is the world of business, and as soon as he can, he goes where it is doing, and we may consider ourselves in luck when he takes the trouble to come to see us. Sentiment be hanged! Goodbye!

And the séance is closed.

This point however should be noted: I remarked today that Reine, listening to Vettellini, leaned forward, instead of to the left as is her habit. Abruptly I ask her the reason of this. She says simply that during the entire séance Vettellini has stood there in front of her. Why? She does not know, but she will ask him. Suddenly she breaks out with "Oh, well, my Vettellini, you mustn't consider me in the least.—Did you ever hear of such a thing! I can be jealous, you know ?" Turning to me she explains that the Guide has placed himself quite near "the young lady," that he might more easily avail himself of her fluid. He has taken almost nothing from us today, and, certainly, this time we shall not be tired.

EIGHTY-FIRST SÉANCE

August 22, 1913

For our last séance at St. Lunaire Reine has been of remarkable lucidity.

Vettellini begins by giving instructions relative to our separation indicating the exact disposition of our time. Poor Reine will have more than enough to do. She will reach Paris tomorrow evening, will rest on Sunday, and on Monday will begin her séances. Every day at two o'clock she will install herself comfortably in her armchair. If at three o'clock she feels quite awake, she may get up and go about her own affairs. If, on the contrary, she is somnolent, she must hasten the hypnosis by means of the mirror—previously arranged in such fashion that she has only to reach out her hand to set it in motion. Vettellini thinks of everything: each detail is scrupulously specified.

A fluidic excursion that Reine made in the night leads to certain moving descriptions and explanations. The day before yesterday, in the course of the séance, she had expressed the wish to go in the night (in fluidic body) to see Cape Fréhel, which she visited with us once in the day time and which had greatly impressed her. Vettellini promised that he would carry her there if she would take her tonic faithfully,[75]

---

[75] Another detail to note. I had brought from Paris a bottle of a creosote preparation ordered by Vettellini. Not having needed it during our trip, I had left the bottle in the trunk, wrapped up in paper as it came to me. I

upon which I declared that if taking a tonic was all that was needed to be carried to Cape Fréhel in the night, I inscribed myself at once. This morning when she came downstairs, Reine told us that she had had an absurd dream, but so intense that it seemed like a reality. She saw herself in my room: I was sleeping. Vettellini, who was with her, told her to kiss me. Indignantly she refused, but Vettellini insisted. Was it idiotic enough? Then she saw thousands of seagulls flying around her: even yet she could hear their strange plaintive cry. And it was terribly sad! Without any reason she was feeling tired and depressed, etc., etc. I thought to myself that this dream was possibly a repercussion of a real experience.

And, sure enough, during the séance Reine says that she went to Cape Fréhel with Vettellini in the night. They both came first to my room to take me with them: "You were about half disengaged, Monsieur Cornillier, and you stood just above your bed, while your body was in heavy sleep. Vettellini told me that to liberate you entirely I must place my lips on your left temple. I hesitated to do that, but at his injunction I obeyed, in order to provoke your complete sortie. Once disengaged, however, you refused to come with us, saying that it would tire you too much for the séance today, and that was true; and Vettellini agreed with you. Then we started off without you. But all of a sudden, *en route*, I thought that possibly Madame Cornillier might come with us; so I came back to find her. She too was disengaged, but when I wanted to speak to her, although she recognized me, she was afraid; and after a few moments I gave up trying to get near her, it disturbed her too much."

So then, Reine returned alone to her companion, whom the old friend had meanwhile joined, and off they went, all three, for a last look at her favorite haunts round about here,—the little valley, the villa Revaud, the neighboring beaches, etc. It was in the recital of this strange promenade that little Reine revealed herself a marvelous and most dramatic raconteur. Her impressions, exquisite and poetic, when she is passing through these different places, become oppressive and tragic when, having reached Cape Fréhel, she flies over the formidable cliffs

---

was the only one who knew this, and, moreover, I had entirely forgotten it. Reine's voice growing hoarse in the course of the séance, Vettellini spontaneously remarks: "That syrup in your trunk would be good for her; she should take it for several days." The trunk in question had been stored away with the others in a closed room in the attic.

down towards the sinister rocks which, for her, are so many fantastic chateaux, haunted by thousands of creatures weeping and groaning. The bitter cries of the numberless birds—sea gulls, cormorants, scoters, etc.,—that, dwell in the gigantic flanks of Cape Fréhel, are for her the lamentations of souls in pain. The painful impression pursues her still, and is the cause of her sadness when awake.

I ask if her astral vision of these scenes is different from what she perceives in her normal state. She finds no difference. She had exactly the sensation that she might have had in an airship that was moving slowly, and obedient to her will.

The usual familiar play between them, teasing and tenderness, close the last séance at St. Lunaire.

ST. LUNAIRE

September 8, 1913

On Monday, September 1, on the receipt of a telegram announcing the death of my cousin (of which Vettellini had not informed me), I left for Paris, and the following day went to Reine's house to surprise her. Surprise is not quite the word, for she was in a state of extreme anxiety, almost expecting me, she said, because of the dreams she had had in the preceding nights. After telling me these dreams, she showed me the notes of her journal which established their authenticity. (Naturally, I have this journal on file.)

In the night of August 26, she sees me taking the train: then I appear to her in evening clothes, looking very sad, etc. The night of the 28th, the same dream. The night of the 30th, she sees me preparing a valise; profoundly sad; then, again, I appear in black,—in evening clothes. She becomes alarmed believing that some danger menaced me. (I arrived September 1, and, as a matter of fact, assisted at the burial of my cousin in evening clothes.)

I propose to Reine that we try the table.

Immediately we are told to have a séance the next day in my studio.

The account which follows is taken from the notes which I set down in the course of the séance.

EIGHTY-SECOND SÉANCE

September 3, 1913

Paris

The usual preparation. Reine sleeps easily and manifests by joyous exclamations that she is at St. Lunaire, where she has gone to see Madame Cornillier. She is enchanted to find herself there again and to discover my wife in the salon, writing near the window.—"It is not a letter she is writing—no. *It is about our affairs* ... you know? She looks into a notebook, then she writes. Oh, but she is serious! She stops now and again, ... looks off in the distance, ... she speaks aloud," ... etc. The child whispers that she would like to kiss her? I encourage her to do so, and with a gay laugh she exclaims: "I did! ... But she did not feel it!"

Then she thinks she would like to see the servant, whom she finds in her room making her toilet after her work. "Oh, just the same, she is clean, that Julia!" Suddenly she is all a-giggle ... "And now, if you please, she's powdering her nose!"[76]

I tell Reine to come back, for Vettellini must be here. He was waiting and immediately began speaking of the preface of our book, which I had brought with me expressly to have his opinion. He tells me that he has examined it during the night, as it lay there on the table, the

---

[76] Verified. My wife at that hour was busy translating the notes, and the servant was in her room.

leaves scattered, just as I had thrown them down from my valise. He approves it, then puts this question: "What is your title for the book?—for I found no title." This is interesting: for, in the haste of my packing, the sheet which enveloped the preface, and upon which the title was written, had been overlooked—left behind. I tell him what I had almost decided and he tells me not to seek further, that one will do.

Spontaneously he remarks that I am worrying too much because I am not painting, and that I am wrong. The work I wish to do will surely be realized, in time.

I speak of a book I have recently read—*Glimpses of the Next State*, by Admiral Moore: a huge volume reporting the research made by that patient and clever investigator of mediumistic phenomena during a period of more than ten years. Side by side with communications corroborative of certain teachings of Vettellini, flat denials of reincarnation may be found, and incredible details concerning the fate of children in the Astral,—such as their training in a sort of kindergarten where they are educated by Spirit professors ... etc. Why these absurdities? And what may be the explanation of this divergence of opinion about astral life?

Vettellini says that first we must take into consideration the enormous difficulty of communicating and the consequent frequency of errors, and the ignorance of the greater number of the Spirits who communicate. "They continue to give information on subjects in which they have no proper knowledge, just as they did in their lifetime.[77] You must remember that it is extremely rare for high Spirits to communicate ... However, it may happen that even an evolved Spirit denies reincarnation. *Entering astral life with the firm conviction that this theory is an error, having himself no further need to reincarnate, and finding himself in the high spheres where questions of this order are no longer discussed,* he may easily persist in his conviction ... for a while."

I planned an experiment with a view to discovering if the phantom seen by Reine in her room the night of July 6th (recounted in her journal), might not be the Spirit of Madame L.—an old friend with whom our relations had ceased, and whose death had been announced to us, about the tenth of that month, by our servant, at St. Lunaire. The epoch of her death would coincide with the information given by Vettellini.

---

[77] See at the end of this volume subsequent communications elucidating this much vexed question.

I took a letter written by Madame L. and two written by other people, placed them in similar envelopes and shuffled them together so that I no longer knew myself which was which. I now give these three envelopes to Reine telling her to analyze their respective fluids, and see if she finds in any of them that of the phantom whom she saw on the night of July 6th, and who, very exceptionally, had not frightened her. One of the envelopes she eliminates immediately: "Not that one." Between the two others she hesitates, holds one indefinitely a moment, only to discard it, and, handing me the third, says that she thinks this one recalls the fluid which she felt that night. I open the envelope and find the letter from Madame L. But the test has really no value, for Reine has only a vague souvenir of the fluidic impression given by the phantom.

I propose another séance tomorrow before leaving Paris.—"No, you are too tired." And Vettellini formally orders me to rest an entire day on my arrival at St. Lunaire: "Neither writing nor auto: absolute repose."

October 29, 1913

Paris

Returning to Paris on Saturday, October 18th, I saw Reine on the following Monday. She handed me her journal relating the different incidents that had occurred during our separation and said that that very morning she had had an order from Vettellini for a séance the next day, Tuesday, at three o'clock.

This surprised me, for at St. Lunaire he had especially recommended me to wait a week before taking up our work again. Reine could only repeat that the order given by the table was clear; we could not possibly be mistaken.

Accordingly, we had a séance Tuesday, October 21st, in which Vettellini gave certain directions of immediate utility and renewed, not the advice, but the injunction that we must now rest the entire week; not even am I allowed to look over my notes:—"Put them all aside in a drawer and lock it. Don't touch them, and don't think of them." Reine, too, must dismiss all preoccupations about the séances: a week from Wednesday we will take them up again.

Before speaking in detail of the eighty-third séance I must note some incidents that have occurred since September 8th,—date of my last writing. After Reine left St. Lunaire, I observed diverse phenomena:

first, whiffs of cold air on my face, generally after I had gone to bed, but sometimes, too, in the salon when I was at work on my notes. (Useless to insist that in either case this sensation is not to be confounded with a draught of air of normal origin.) Secondly, phosphorescent effects, sparks, and streaks of light, which I perceived either after retiring, or during my evening walk. Once, as I stepped into the garden, I distinctly saw two zigzagging, phosphorescent lights on the ground at my feet. On Thursday, September 18th, after dinner, I tried magnetizing Reine at a distance (naturally unknown to her), operating according to my instructions, and persisting for about three-quarters of an hour. On September 24th a letter from Reine informed me of the various incidents of the past few days, saying amongst other things that at about nine o'clock in the evening of the eighteenth, Thursday, she was suddenly seized with a violent fit of crying, without any reason whatever. In the eighty-third séance Vettellini, whom I questioned on this circumstance, affirmed that Reine's impression and her crisis of tears on this Thursday evening were caused by my fluidic vibrations, which were not strong enough to determine hypnosis, but sufficiently "attacking" nevertheless to provoke a modification in her nervous state. He adds that I have only to continue my efforts.

During this same period nothing of special interest has occurred on Reine's side. The visions of Vettellini, in her normal waking hours, become more and more precise. The cloudy and vague aspect of the first apparitions is transformed. He now shows himself with every appearance of a living being. It is also to be noted that "Monsieur Cornillier" is abandoned: he now calls me "Pierre" in his communications. Different incidents related in Reine's journal are curious enough, but certainly the most valuable revelation of these daily chronicles is that of her sincerity. The circumstances would so easily have allowed her to invent a little ... But no, on the contrary, nothing happens. She deplores the fact, it worries her, for she is afraid my interest will wane. She is desolate, redoubles her efforts and obtains just nothing at all,—neither mediumistic writings nor dreams of portent.

And then she is sick again. I am sorry enough, not only for the poor devoted child, but for the work, as there will be another inevitable delay in the positive manifestations which are so much desired.

EIGHTY-THIRD SÉANCE

October 21, 1913

After a long magnetization, Vettellini manifests himself, and explains the reason of this unexpected séance. It was the simplest way to give the instructions necessary for resuming our work. Before beginning the magnetizing, we must remain seated in obscurity for about ten minutes, in a state of complete relaxation, mental and physical. My wife must assist at this preparation, the purpose of which is to provoke gently and without nervousness, the liberation of our fluidic force. The amalgam will thus be better.

Various information follows. Vettellini allows us to understand that in a few months, Reine will be obliged to take a complete rest and abandon mediumship: otherwise life would become intolerable to her. Her Spirit has now so great a habit of wandering off that soon it will neglect to observe the required conditions of union with her body. She will want to pass her life in the Astral, the consequence of which would be a pernicious disturbance in her physical life. Vettellini says that he is watching over her carefully—"*for, incarnated, you must live the life of the incarnated.*" And also, for the end in view, Reine must preserve her poise and must in no way run the risk of being considered unbalanced.

I ask why Reine sees certain Spirits with the physical aspect they had on earth, while others appear to her as tiny flames of light. Vettellini says that this depends not only upon their degree of evolution but, even more, on their personal tendencies and preoccupations. If their constant wish is to approach the earth and the incarnate, they learn how to employ the vibrations necessary for materialization and thus—relatively—to participate in our lives. If, on the contrary, their idea is to mount higher in the ethereal spheres, their efforts carry them further and further from terrestrial conditions. Certain Spirits could easily materialize if they wished to. It is a question of mood. Old Friend, for example, can do it when it pleases him.

Reine recalls that in the course of her excursions in the Astral, during these last few weeks, she saw a group of Spirits working to influence several savants that they may discover a new and mysterious force, analogous to electricity, but even more marvelous: a discovery that will lead to many extraordinary inventions. These savants are absolutely unconscious of working under influence. They will merely thank their lucky stars when, in hunting for pebbles, they unearth a treasure.

EIGHTY-FOURTH SÉANCE

October 29, 1913

Sick again—this time with a sort of grippe—bronchitis, Reine has been obliged to stay in bed the last few days. This morning she thought she would not be able to come, but, on consulting the table, she was told she would feel better at two o'clock, and that we might have a short séance. She coughs, has fever; I hesitate. But she insists that she is all right and that Vettellini is helping her at that very moment so that she may sleep.

We begin by the prescribed ten minutes of repose (in the course of which I see a cloudy and floating substance condensing between Reine and me.) Then I magnetize her. Her Guide manifests his presence at once and speaks of her health. Alas! The poor child has not finished with physical suffering. Vettellini says it is her destiny; he can only slightly alleviate her ills. After this present crisis she will have another and more serious attack: he will warn me in time, that precautions may be taken to keep it in hand. Today she should not have left her room, but she was in such despair at the idea of not coming that he took a portion of her suffering himself. The séance will not harm her, but she must nurse herself most carefully during the next few days. He gives me detailed instructions as to what must be done from now on till Sunday and warns me to carefully conceal from Reine, when she wakens, that another illness is in store for her.

I must even allow her to think that she may begin again to pose this winter. Let her accept the proposition of Mademoiselle H. for December.

On the other hand, she must refuse all other engagements that will be proposed to her in a few days from now, by a photographer, a manager of cinema, etc.[78]

We continue to talk, sadly enough—for it is painful to think that the child must always suffer in this way—when in the midst of these somber prognostics a comic note is struck. I had just had a visit from the artist X., who, last winter, behaved rather odiously with Reine, and as I now incidentally mention this visit, she suddenly has an inspiration:

Since Vettellini is able to take away her pain by assuming it himself, he could quite as well take it from her and give it to another, could he not? That should be mere child's play for a great Spirit like him. Well, here is X.—just the ideal person!—"Give it to him, Vettellini,—my bronchitis, my fever, my pain, and my insomnia; in this way all things will work together for the good, and our séances will not be interrupted."

Reine's seriousness reaches such a point of drollery that the séance ends in a shout of laughter.

Poor X. had a narrow escape!

---

[78] The propositions referred to were, in fact, made a few days later, and though extremely advantageous, she refused them, on my advice, without the least murmur.

EIGHTY-FIFTH SÉANCE

October 31, 1913

As Reine is too ill to come to us, we go to her house where, upon order, we have a short séance. Vettellini gives hope that she may be able to go out on Monday.

EIGHTY-SIXTH SÉANCE

November 3, 1913

Reine arrives, but she is still miserable and sleep is long in coming. Vettellini appears promptly, only to say that it would be prudent to abandon the work this week. On Wednesday Reine may come, and we will try the table to know when she will be in condition to resume the séances of hypnosis.

November 5, 1913

Reine arrives: we try the table. After twenty long minutes, various crackings and movements give us hope. From a few words, obtained with great difficulty, we learn that atmospheric conditions are such that communication cannot be established today. (Odious weather—warm and damp.)

November 7, 1913

Reine comes again today. We try the table, which immediately taps: "Everything all right. I am pleased. Séance Monday."

EIGHTY-SEVENTH SÉANCE

November 10, 1913

I n spite of the medium's condition—which has scarcely changed in the past ten or twelve days—we have a most interesting séance, of which I will note only trifling incidents, the important ones being of too intimate a character for present publication

And now, we speak of health. Reine, beside herself with suffering, shows signs of temper. She frankly tells Vettellini that she has quite enough of his advice about care and food. She has been nagged all she intends to be! ... The good Vettellini seems little afflicted by her irony and, as he has noticed that it is principally during her sleep that she catches cold, he gravely orders her to immediately provide herself with high-necked and long-sleeved nightgowns, buttoned at the throat and wrists. The child is in a fury of rage. "Never!" she screams. "Never would I wear such a horror! ... Never. Who ever heard of such a thing! ... No—it's useless. Don't talk about it ... *Never!*"

In the séance at her house October 31st, Reine announced that the Egyptian Spirits from the museum had come again to serenade her. I now ask if she cannot recall one of the melodies. She tries, and ill and hoarse as she is, succeeds nevertheless in giving fragments of two very curious songs. She says that next Wednesday, if I wish it, she will do better, for meanwhile she will ask Vettellini to give her a rehearsal ... Then she transmits that Vettellini sees that—(abrupt pause)—that

Madame Cornillier would like to have a good talk with her old friend. My wife admits the impeachment. Wednesday, then, may be used for this talk and the Egyptian songs. The program is accepted with pleasure, but I try to know why Reine hesitated in speaking of my wife. She is silent ... seems embarrassed, ... but finally, encouraged, she leans towards me and whispers: "Vettellini called Madame Cornillier 'Anne' ... but I didn't dare to say it."

Several days ago, on arriving, she told a dream of the precedent night: She had assisted at a gala performance in a theatre, with beautiful music and great luxury—a magnificent display. I first thought that it was probably a sortie of her astral body during her sleep, but when she specified that this vision had come to her between two and three o'clock in the morning, I concluded that it was a simple dream. Now, in hypnosis, she again alludes to this dream, which she had been unable to explain in her normal state, saying, "You remember my dream, Monsieur Cornillier? Well, it was *Méhul* who gave me an image of one of the representations of his time" ... Here she is interrupted by Vettellini, who bids her transmit to me these words: "The judgment of Paris." Reine asks if I know what he means by that. I confess to understanding what the judgment of Paris means, but I do not see the present application ... unless it be the title of one of Méhul's operas—the one performed in her vision? After a short consultation she turns back to me: "Vettellini says 'Yes ... and no.' What I saw at a certain moment of my vision was called *The Judgment of Paris*, but it is not one of Méhul's operas, though they played his music." I ask the key to this enigma and am told that Méhul himself will explain it; he will come soon now to see us—probably on Friday.

When I asked her to sing the Egyptian songs, the child answered drolly: "My mind has them completely, but my mouth doesn't know them!"

EIGHTY-EIGHTH SÉANCE

November 12, 19|3

Reine—always in the same state of health—seems especially tired on her arrival today.

She sleeps long without giving sign of activity. At last she mutters a little and reaches for my hand.

I ask Vettellini if he is willing to help elucidate the mystery of the phantom seen by Reine in her bedroom on the night of July 6. I suppose it might be Madame L., but would like to be sure of it. He says that I must give Reine something which has belonged to this lady, that she may compare the fluids. I place a package of letters in the hands of the medium, who holds them for some time: "I know this fluid. Haven't I already had these letters?" I tell her that once before she did touch one of them. (Séance, September 3, when I was called back to Paris by the death of my cousin.) She seems to reflect ... "Yes ... but it is not only that. I know this fluid in another way. It brings me another impression." Here, quite evidently, she is afraid to go further, and in a low voice consults Vettellini, who encourages her to speak. Finally, she risks it: "this is the fluid of that phantom woman whom I saw one night in my room when I was awake,—do you remember?" Again she leans towards her Guide, who confirms her statement and himself declares: "I affirm that the person who wrote these letters is the person who went to Reine's room in the night of July 6. She was a friend of yours. At her death she was seized with remorse on account of her attitude towards you, and before dying she desired, ardently desired, to see you both. In consequence of this intense wish she went to your house immediately after her death. But you were absent. And then, trying to find you, she followed the trace of your fluids straight to Reine's apartment. Alive, she certainly would never have gone to you, but now she will come back without any hesitation." I ask Vettellini if he will not aid Reine in bringing her here.

"Willingly ... but not on Friday, for Méhul is coming.—On Monday perhaps."

Communication is difficult today. I am obliged to re-magnetize the medium several times, due, says Vettellini, to her great fatigue and also to the fluidic currents of the atmosphere.

Old Friend arrives. To show his good intentions, he has tried to come gently, so as not to shock Reine, who notices his thoughtfulness and thanks him. He knows that his friend Anne wishes to have a long talk with him and he is pleased. My wife comes nearer and, following instructions, joins her hands to mine while mine are placed on those of the medium; in this way the communication is established for her. I transmit the questions which she has prepared, but which were unknown to me. As these questions concerned only intimate sentiments, it is unnecessary to report them here, but I can affirm that the replies of the old friend were prodigious: my wife was profoundly impressed. He certainly has a caustic tongue, and the schematic portraits which he gives are drawn with cruel precision. In transmitting his abrupt and vigorous communications Reine seems several times to suffer from it. And once she cannot refrain from saying, gently, "But—it must hurt you, Old Friend, to think that of your brother!"

Asked what were the happiest events of his life, he answers: "my marriages—*and both of them.*—" (I did not know that he had married twice, but my wife confirms the fact.)

We ask if during his last incarnation he had been aided from the Au-Delà. Had he a protector?—"*I, a protector*? I would have sent him to the devil!" Turning to the medium—à *propos* of the publication of the book,— he tells her in plain language that she will be considered *an intriguante and a liar.* Reine jumps. For an instant I am afraid she is going to lose control of herself, but no, she falls back to her usual attitude and calmly says ... "After all, that doesn't matter, ... since I am not one."

Reine is extremely tired. I think it prudent not to ask for the Egyptian songs.

EIGHTY-NINTH SÉANCE

November 14, 1913

(My friend A. is present)

Though evidently enervated, the child sleeps at once, and begins to show signs of agitation before I have finished my passes. She hears Vettellini calling her, but cannot see him. She is visibly disturbed and her anxiety becomes rapidly acute. She sits upright, searching minutely around her big chair ... above ... below,—frightened now, and all in tears, for she is sure that this is an expression of her Guide's displeasure. I bend all my force to reassure her, but not for an instant does she heed me, seeking only to find him. She gives the impression of listening for a voice that is faint, and far away. Suddenly she grows calmer. At last she has understood that the physical conditions are such that Vettellini cannot come to us in his usual way. He tried to inform her of this the night before, by means of a dream (related further on) whose significance she did not grasp. In view of her despair, he is making an effort to reach us for a moment, using Reine's substance and force for this purpose. But he warns her that her fatigue will be extreme as he must take an excessive dose of fluid—energy from her. Does she still wish it?—"Oh, anything ... and all you need;—only speak to us!" murmurs the poor child.

He then makes her write the following:

"Pierre, you must waken Reine at once. Impossible for us to communicate with you; the elements are opposed. Only a séance postponed. Must not worry. All is well. It is we who cannot act; Reine would be ill. Will explain why in Monday's séance. Am taking all my force from Reine to say this. Must stop now."

The child has infinite difficulty in writing this communication. Her efforts to hear and to understand are painful to see.

307

Vettellini gone, she is inconsolable, and I have all I can do to persuade her that it is through no fault of hers, and that he is not displeased with her, etc.

This is the story of the dream to which allusion has been made:

When she arrived today Reine said that she had dreamed of a certain gentleman who was here at a séance last spring,—a tall man, with a beard. She was sure it was he. In her dream he was seated at a piano, playing most beautiful music; and I, too, was there—looking anything but pleased. She did not know why, but certainly I was annoyed.

Evidently she has dreamed of my friend A. The fact is curious, as it happens that I had invited him to come today, believing that the Spirit Méhul might make us a visit. But now Reine, in hypnosis, explains that it was not a dream; that Vettellini had tried, by this vision of my friend A. and my discontented attitude, to warn her that the séance would not take place, but she had not understood. She does not know whether Vettellini carried her (in astral body) to the house of this gentleman or whether he simply created an image for her; but she is inclined to think that she really went there, for she so clearly saw the salon and A. seated at the piano. "He was composing, and behind him was his Spirit-Guide—the one who came here to see us. He was working with him, exciting and inspiring him." And she adds that, watching this process of "pushing and goading," she had not been able to suppress a laugh, and that the Spirit-Guide had turned on her roundly, and told her she was lacking in manners. This offended her, and she left at once without ceremony.

I have great trouble in waking the medium, who is in a state of prostration for a long time after the séance.

NINETIETH SÉANCE

November 17, 1913

(My friend A. is present)

Viewing these phenomena with but a skeptical eye, one must nevertheless marvel at the prodigious faculty of invention of our little medium who, at the ninetieth séance, still finds means of varying her effects,—of producing with the same elements, as it were, a quite new representation. Who is the dramatic author who would not envy this precious gift of renewing himself?

Reine is in better health; no headache for two days, at which she is surprised, and quite cheered.

We begin at two o'clock: but before I can finish the customary routine of passes, she suddenly, in a feeble and trembling voice, begins to sing a sort of operatic air. From this I gather that we are to have today the program which we were expecting at the last séance, and hasten to call my wife and A., who has come back again.

The song continues ... without great interest, for Reine is not equal to the task: the air abounds in trills and vocalizations far beyond her modest means. Several times she breaks off to protest at the demands made on her:—"I cannot! ... Oh, yes,—I hear you perfectly well, but my voice can't do it,—it doesn't know how!" Again she begins with a slightly firmer accent, trying all she can to show her good will in the matter, but I have had enough and cut the song short by a question.—"What are you doing, Reine? Who is there with you?" She starts violently at my interruption, grasps my hand to make sure it is I, then sighs: "Ah! ... You know, it is Méhul. He came of his own accord. I didn't have to go for him. He wants to make me sing his music,—you know, his own,— that he made himself. But I can't do it, my voice doesn't obey me."

I beg her thank the great musician for coming, then frankly and immediately begin the investigation of his identity, hoping by banal questions to lead up to significant disclosures.[79]

First of all, where was he born?—"Givet," is replied after a moment, with difficulty but firmly, then repeated: "Gi—vet. Ar—dennes. He was born in 1763; died in 1817." The syllables are detached, automatically enunciated, and this characteristic persists throughout the entire communication. Reine makes an enormous effort to understand, sitting stiff and straight to listen, lifting herself in her chair, her neck stretched tensely, and all the while protesting that she cannot hear. As I express surprise at this, she turns to say: "Méhul is a very high Spirit, and as he comes for only a moment he doesn't take the trouble to put himself into the physical conditions in my range, as Vettellini does. I shall get used to it—perhaps—but just now it is very difficult for me."

I ask for details concerning his works and himself. He replies that he composed many works, and had still many more to follow. Before his death he burned one that was already far advanced and which had cost him infinite labor. It was entitled—or rather, the projected title was: *L'Exil.*—"What was the subject?"—"*Napoléon one*" repeats Reine.[80] I ask if he knew Napoleon personally.—"Yes, and the *Austrian* as well,— Marie-Louise." He went to court, he had friends there: and amongst them a marshal—Masséna—who died the same year as he did, in 1817. As notable people of his epoch, he cites Lavoisier, whom he knew intimately in the latter years of his life. I ask him if he liked Napoléon, and Reine transmits: "Too much bloodshed."—What does he think of modern music? Answer: "It has no power,—it has no soul. *Nobody believes*

---

[79] It must be noted that I knew absolutely nothing about Méhul other than that he was the author of *Joseph and the Chant du Départ*. A. knew hardly more, though after the séance he says that he should have remembered, as titles of his works: *L'Irato* and *Stratonice*. He supposed, too, that Méhul was a pupil of Glück.

[80] This is possibly an example of the translation of thought vibration into terms of language, and of the deformation that such translation may create. *Napoléon the First* becomes *Napoléon One.*

anything enough. There is no passion in any belief now, no real faith ... *no patriotic faith.*" Will he give the name of a modern composer whom he admires? With infinite trouble poor Reine transmits, Bet ... bet ... tou ... vene. (Beethoven).—Who was his master? Here there is a long struggle. Reine seems to no longer seize the vibrations sent by Méhul. She is exasperated to such a degree that I am about to renounce all further effort when, at last, she pronounces the beginning of a name: "Cret ... Crent ... Gret ?"—Grétry? I suggest.—"No, it's not like that," she replies. In a low voice A. proposes "Kreutzer," which I tell Reine to transmit to Méhul.—"Ah, it is that! He says 'Yes: Kreutzer.'"—I ask his opinion of Glück.—"He had great qualities but I have reservations."—Who was the musician of your time whom you most admired?—"Kreutzer."—Which of your works is your favorite?—*"Joseph."* And he remarks that this work gave rise to a lawsuit because he had an engagement with the Opéra, and it had been produced at the Théâtre Feydeau. Amongst other favorites he cites *L'Irato, Stratonice*, and then what is evidently intended for *Ariodan.* All this is Greek to Reine, who transmits the sounds as well as she can, and, little by little, I make sense of them. He says that he wrote any number of songs and hymns, and mentions as most famous amongst them *"Le Chant du Départ,"* but adds that he wrote another quite as beautiful on the legend of Roland.

What he had tried to make Reine sing, at the opening of the séance, was a fragment of the work he had burned,—*"L'Exil."* He will try it again another day; it will go better.

Le Jugement de Paris is indeed of his composition. It is a ballet for which he wrote the music. But it is not that which Reine saw eight or ten days ago, it was a representation of Joseph at the Théâtre Feydeau, pictures of which he had projected upon her brain while she was sleeping. She hesitates to pronounce the title "Joseph," she is sure, poor child, that she has misunderstood: "That cannot be right. It's no kind of a title for a play; it's the name of a man!" Then, to convince her, Méhul says "But don't you remember, Reine, there was *Benjamin*? And the *Bon Dieu*, too,—they talked about him?"—A shout of joy: "Oh, yes, Benjamin! yes, I remember him ... And all those people who were wearing those great cloaks caught up on their shoulders," etc., etc. Her souvenirs come crowding back now, but, noticing her extreme fatigue, I hasten to ask one last question.—Were you married? Had you any children?—"Oh,—all that bores me!" And he is off, taking time, however, to say that to please us he will come back again, and bring Kreutzer with him, who also will give proofs of identity.

Poor Reine falls back exhausted, but her prostration lasts only a moment. She seems to recover her normal condition by contact with Vettellini, with whom she is soon talking as easily as usual.

The Guide thinks that I ought to be pleased, for Méhul has certainly given all the information I could have hoped for. He explains that last Friday's séance was impossible because of the interposition of certain fluidic currents between the Spirits and the incarnated. At given epochs the Earth throws off special radiations that come into violent collision with the currents of the interplanetary spaces: and when this happens, Spirits of Vettellini's composition are, so to speak, pushed back. In order to descend to our plane, and stay there any length of time, they would be forced to draw upon a very considerable quantity of our own fluid, and in this case it would have involved a useless fatigue for us, which he consequently had avoided.

A-propos of last Friday's séance I try to get some elucidation of Reine's dream, in which she saw A. at his piano, composing. Vettellini says that it was an image which he had created, but not a subjective image. *He reconstituted for Reine*, whom he had taken to A.'s apartment, in the night, *an objective representation of the scene.*—"A., while working in his salon during the afternoon preceding this visit, left in the ambiance atoms emanating from his substance; and I used these emanations to create an image, not exactly material, but sufficiently existing to be perceived *objectively by Reine's astral senses.*"

(It must be noted that this explanation conforms in all points to the theory of subjective and objective creations and materializations, given by Vettellini exactly ten months ago in the sixteenth séance.)

A. asks what Vettellini thinks of lycanthropy. Reply: Sorcerers, magicians, etc., who are supposed to have the power of changing themselves into animals, are mediums who, by certain proceedings, succeed in sending their disengaged fluidic bodies to startle a person whom, previous to their disengagement, they have selected as victim. Vettellini asserts emphatically: "It is absolutely impossible that the incarnated spirit of man should transform itself into an animal or assume the aspect of a monster. But the medium-sorcerer who wishes to give this impression, provokes in the brain of the person whom he seeks to influence a picture-idea that completes and defines the sensation received from his astral body."[81]

---

[81] In a subsequent séance I cite the experiments of Colonel de Rochas (*Les Vies Successives*) and certain passages in the book of H. Durville (*Le Fantôme*

In such a case there is an association of two phenomena: telepathic suggestion, provoking a subjective image in the brain of the percipient; and an objective sensation from the astral body capable, in a measure, of materialization. Finally, the magical effect of the sorcerer may be augmented by the aid of very inferior Spirits (even sometimes those of animals) whom he has subjugated, or who may come voluntarily to associate themselves with such maleficent work.

Vettellini tells Reine that he has relieved her of headache for the past two days so that she might be more cheerful and have a good séance, but that now he is obliged to hand it over to her again. It will come back this evening. Reine promptly declines: "Oh, no,—no, I don't care for it. Give it to someone else—or keep it yourself—I've no use for it!" Vettellini has to remind her that he cannot keep it for ever. The better way is to accept the inevitable ... since she is destined to suffer.

He seizes the occasion to tell me that her health will never admit of pushing hypnosis to the point of catalepsy. She is too frail; she might slip out entirely. Her spirit has now such a habit of disengaging that it keeps but slight hold on her body; a mere nothing might detach it: hence, of course, all those phenomena that are possible only in a state of catalepsy must be cut out.

Here Reine and Vettellini talk together for a few moments, but I understand nothing, as the child's head is turned towards her Guide and she speaks in a whisper. Trying to insinuate myself into the conversation I say: "What is it all about, Reine?" She turns back haughtily, and drily says, "But ... I am talking with my friend."

My wife and A. leave the room. I begin the process of awaking my medium, when she arrests my hand and begins again her conversation with her "friend." This time I hear. He scolds her because she has not been kind to her mother. It is true, they had a dispute this morning. Reine argues, protests and weeps; but, in spite of Vettellini's insistence, she refuses to take me into her confidence. Useless for him to say that *she must, for she will not.*

The end is unexpected. All in tears, the child leans towards him, sobbing; "You are going away? ... Well, then ... kiss me, my Vettellini ..." and she lifts her brow. It is done with incomparable grace and simplicity. It is charming.

---

des Vivants) concerning the transformations of the fluidic body influenced by the will of the medium. Vettellini confirms the above statement; adding that *only a disincarnated Spirit* has the power of transforming his fluidic body, but that, as a matter of fact, not one of the evolved would abuse himself by representing an animal or a monster.

NINETY-FIRST SÉANCE

November 21, 1913

As I myself have been suffering with grippe for the past few days, I thought that Reine would certainly have received notice not to have a séance today. But upon her arrival she says that she has had no warning whatever, though she now recalls that her table did make a strange and strong cracking to which she gave no attention, feeling too ill to care. The frightful headache came back two hours after the séance on Monday. She is beside herself with pain.

The brave little thing is nonetheless ready to begin again, and at three o'clock I proceed to mesmerize her. Barely asleep, she is whispering and muttering. I catch finally the words,—"Didn't understand, ... never occurred to me. All right. I'll tell him." She seeks my hand and says that I must waken her, for we are both ill; the séance would be bad for us. Vettellini tried to inform her this morning but she had not understood. He hoped, by that loud cracking in the table, to make her come to it for a communication; but, absorbed by her pain, she had not heeded. He adds that there is no cause for anxiety. Monday the séance will be good; Méhul will come back.

Just here Old Friend manifests his presence. He merely wishes to say that he is pleased: his friend Anne must have perceived that although she was well started on an illness, her condition was suddenly modified in a few moments. (The fact is exact; we had both remarked it with astonishment.) He says it is he who brought about the change; but she must be very careful, for he has been able only to hold back the bad influence, he could not destroy it. He would like to go on talking but Vettellini intervenes, saying that he thought it was understood that we were not to have a séance today,—then?

Till Monday, then.

Before waking, Reine marvels that the arrival of Old Friend had not disturbed her today. It is the second time.—"He must be trying to be careful now,—or is it that I am growing accustomed to his vibrations?"

NINETY-SECOND SÉANCE

November 24, 1913

(My friend A. is present)

O n her arrival, Reine tells me of a dream she had the night be-fore,—a strange dream. I must ask Reine, hypnotized, to give an explanation of it.

When she has been sleeping for only a few moments I realize that Méhul is present. He tells me to ask for any information needed as proof of his identity.

I begin by remarking that, in spite of its great interest for us,—who know Reine—any statement that may be found in dictionaries or biographies of celebrated men has no value whatever for the skeptical mind. The medium may always be accused of having cribbed her communication in advance, or of having dragged it out of the unknown depths of that famous subconsciousness which plays the same role for our savants today that the Devil played for the theologians in the past. What we need, then, is an unpublished fact; something unknown to the biographers, but which, nevertheless, may be verified by us.[82] From this point of view, what he has said of his process with the Opéra concerning his work *Joseph*, and of *L'Exil*, the work which he burned, is very valuable, if we are able to find any trace of these facts. Where, and how, are we to verify them?

---

[82] The problem cannot be solved. Recorded, the information may always have been read or reported; unrecorded, it is not susceptible of verification.

Méhul replies that the lawsuit came up in 1808 and that proofs of it must exist in the archives of the Opéra. That should not be difficult to establish. As to *L'Exil*, he will give me any complementary details that I may wish. So then, I ask him to confirm the subject of the composition, and to name the author of the poem. Reply: "Yes, the subject of the work was Napoléon. But it was not after a poem that I composed the music. It was from a work in prose that I drew my inspiration—a work written by a woman: Madame de ... de ... (transmission very difficult, Reine not understanding) ... de St ... a ... ël,—de Staël." He goes on to say that he had been presented to Madame de Staël by Ta. . Tal . . ley ... rand, and it is through Talleyrand that he was able to procure the pages which served as theme for his *L'Exil*. Suddenly Reine stops short in her communication; but, recovering herself, begins again ... and again hesitates to transmit. She is sure she has misunderstood. But upon Méhul's affirmation that he means what he says, she burst out laughing: "He tells me that he knew her *husbands*. You understand what I say, Monsieur Cornillier?—and I'm making no mistake—*he knew her husbands*. The idea! You can have only one husband ... isn't it so? ... But no, he says *her husbands* ... just as easily as that! Ah, well, ... my compliments!" The child chokes with laughter,—and we, too, for that matter.

Méhul continues. He knew personally many of the celebrities of his epoch, amongst others Mademoiselle Lenormand, whom he had consulted the year before she was arrested, and who enchanted him,—"a woman of astonishing intelligence." He says that he has found her again in the Astral and that, if I wish, he will bring her to us.

Here I call attention to the fact that he has come alone today, though he had proposed to bring us his professor.—"Ah ... Glück," he says. Surprised, I ask: Who was your professor?—"Glück."   I beg him to remember that at the last séance his professor had been Kreutzer, and that he had seemed to have certain reservations concerning Glück. What does he mean? He reiterates that it is Glück who was his real *Maître*.—"It is Glück who took me in hand, who developed me. From Kreutzer I did, indeed, receive counsel and criticism—but in the quality of friend."

Trying to discover the cause of this error I provoke an indescribable scene. Méhul evidently accuses Reine of having transmitted carelessly, for she defends herself like a little fury. Clutching the arms of her chair and shaking with indignation, she angrily retorts: "It is your own fault! Yes ... yes, you certainly told me that!" But he answers sharply, and Reine, offended, fiercely calls in Vettellini as witness. Vettellini, apparently, finds her in fault. Upon which she promptly flings herself around in her chair, turning her back on her enemies. She sulks.

A long silence ... Then she sits up again to discuss with them. Oh! Well ... all right, then, she will say the fault is hers. And leaning towards me she confesses: "Well ... it seems that I transmitted badly. But," (here her wrath leaps up again) "I'd like to know how I could help it! *He doesn't even give himself the trouble to speak*! I can only half understand him ... and, anyway, it's much too difficult!"

Tranquility is restored ... and the point is settled: Glück was the master. Méhul's reservations concerned the man and not his works, for which he has great admiration. But they did not get on well together; Glück always wished to impose his own opinions. On the other hand, he had unmitigated admiration and friendship for Kreutzer,—"an admirable violinist and a composer whose works will endure."

I ask for something more definite about the song on the legend of Roland, of which he spoke in his first visit, but which I do not find mentioned in a list of his works. Possibly it was merely a fragment detached from a work and published as a hymn or an independent song? For example, a fragment of the opera *Ariodan*, which was drawn from L'Orlando Furioso, I think ?—"Not at all," replies Méhul. "It has nothing whatever to do with *Ariodan*. It is a song complete in itself, like *Le Chant du Départ*. Not an important thing, but one of my favorites."

Here I try to get certain details of his private life. Did he die in Paris? Does the house still exist? But this kind of question irritates him and, in spite of Reine's insistence, he invites me to find a more interesting topic.

A. would like to know the name of his favorite interpreter—as singer. He replies that his interpreters were so numerous, and so many of them satisfied him, that he does not know how to recall a special favorite. Reine insists, thus provoking a new passage of arms between them.

Spontaneously he proffers the information that he adored the ballet and that the dancers of his time were far superior to those of today.— Will he cite a name? ... After waiting vainly, I ask if he knew Vestris.—"It is precisely he whom I most admired" is the reply. I then try to make him mention a famous danseuse of his epoch ... "Madame ... Madame?"—hoping to provoke him to speak of Madame Sacchi—but he tells Reine that I seem to be guying him. Protesting my good faith, I seek a better footing.

Where was he at the time of Lavoisier's death? "I was in Paris."— Was it a great grief for him?—"No, not grief exactly."—Had he personal anxieties during the Revolution?—"No, but many of my friends had ... " (here the transmission grows confused) ... "I passed quite easily through those terrible days; but others, who had been able to pass, died in '70." I ask what he can possibly mean by such a statement. Once more it is poor Reine's fault. She has misunderstood his communication which is finally given again in this way: "Friends of mine, who perished in great numbers at the time of the Revolution, reincarnated rapidly, only to become again new victims of violence during the war of 1870 with Germany."

By this time Reine is so enervated that she declares she will transmit no longer unless Vettellini helps her to understand Méhul better. It is too exasperating!

Again I try to get the name of a singer but succeed only in raising a tempest which provokes an exchange of most uncivil compliments. The child is furious; Méhul, evidently, offended.

With a view to establishing peace I bid Reine to say politely, that, in any case, we are grateful to Méhul for the information he has given and exceedingly obliged for the trouble he has taken.—"You say it, but you don't believe a word of it!" is his sharp retort. This is so unexpected—and so true—that we all burst out laughing: upon which I do thank him—and this time more sincerely—expressing the hope that he will bear no grudge against us. He must surely understand that it is in the cause of the work that I thus insist? It may seem stupid to him, but, if we are to convince people, we must have many undeniable proofs. He seems somewhat mollified and goes off ... calmer, I hope. Reine, spent, falls back in her chair.—"Ah, no! I prefer my Vettellini."

And then we take up our ordinary relations. Vettellini and Reine make an interesting commentary upon the difficulty of communication between the great Spirits and ourselves. She compares their efforts to those we would be obliged to make were we trying to converse with animals.

I give our valiant little medium a moment of respite, then send her to find the composer Nicolo (for my friend A.), but Vettellini interposes to say that she is too tired, the séance has been difficult. Naturally I acquiesce, but Reine protests. No, she wants to go; if I will only be good enough to magnetize her a little more, that will help her.

Scarcely have I made a few passes when she checks me.—"Here he is—Nicolo! He was just outside in the street. He says he knew that we would call him and he was waiting." I ask why he did not come in.—"Because I was not invited," is his swift reply. (These gentlemen of the Astral are truly punctilious!)

I put a series of questions on A.'s behalf, to all of which Nicolo gives satisfactory answers. One of them is rather curious, in that only Nicolo and A. were capable of understanding it. A. had been baffled and completely held up, last summer, by a bit of orchestration on the composition upon which he was working. After innumerable fruitless attempts, he decided to momentarily abandon the passage in question, promising himself to come back to his orchestration later on. Now he asks Nicolo's advice on this point. How may the difficulty be conjured?

Reine, listening to the Spirit's reply, mutters: "What on earth do you mean? I don't understand ... Say it better than that, Nicolo ... Not necessary? ... He will understand? Ah ... Well, if that is so, I'll repeat it, but it means nothing to me." Leaning then towards me she says: "Tell your friend to turn it over—to turn it upside down, and it will go of itself. See if he knows what that signifies,—for I don't. It is Nicolo who says that—'turn it upside down.'" I glance at A., who declares that it is perfectly clear to him and he sees at once the advantage of this inversion.[83]

The talk continues for A.'s benefit. Receiving some definite advice, he asks the reason of it. Nicolo replies that he is sure of the practical value of his counsel, but he is unable to explain the reason of it. If A. wishes to sift the question to the bottom, Monsieur Cornillier has only to ask Vettellini: he will know. This was done; the Maître's explanation was perfectly clear. Nicolo leaves us.

I would like the visit of another Spirit, but this time Vettellini's refusal is final. Reine would suffer. All he allows is a brief talk together before she is wakened.

I start to speak of certain sparks of light that I saw last night just after retiring, but barely have I begun when Reine, turning to Vettellini, exclaims: "Twelve? He saw ten.—You made twelve? Well, he lost only two, then!" It is exact, I counted ten. Vettellini says that he has often made as many for me, but that I did not see them. I become more sensitive. Then he informs me that I was wrong to go out this morning,—not strong enough yet—and forbids my leaving the house before

---

[83] The advice was good as the following lines testify: "My dear friend, I was able day before yesterday to prove the value of Nicolo's suggestion. I followed his advice strictly, and immediately, as by enchantment, everything fell into its proper place. Yours, A."

he gives permission. Possibly I remember that he is capable of getting angry? (Ouf! I grow very small.) Goodbye, and off he goes.

The séance is finished; my wife and A. have left the room when suddenly Vettellini is back again.

"There are certain things I could not say before a stranger," he explains, and with no further ceremony he begins to scold poor Reine. She washed her linen this morning, and she must not do it. It hurts her. And she must not eat too many lentils,—nor pork either,—it is bad for her ... etc., etc. Impossible to describe the scene between them.

It must be noted that when I asked her the significance of her dream of the precedent night she said, "Oh, it was nothing at all,—just an ordinary dream, wasn't it Vettellini?"—"Yes,—only a dream."

THE VERIFICATION OF MÉHUL'S STATEMENTS

It has been easy to verify all that is relatively unimportant in the communication of the great musician, that is: place and date of his birth, date of his death, titles of his principal works, name of his master, etc. I had only to open a dictionary and glance through a biography to see that all was absolutely correct.

But when I wished to assure myself of the authenticity of unpublished information, it was quite another matter. Logically, since the facts were unknown, nobody could be found who knew them. Having exhausted my relations in the musical world, having addressed myself to several specialists and musicographers, having consulted the library of the Opéra, etc., etc., I have managed to verify two of the statements. This is something, and I do not despair of establishing the truth of the others, for all resources are not yet spent. But the importance of the effort, and the time involved in the research, has for the moment arrested me.

In any case, the trouble which I have been obliged to take—I, who have certain relations and various means of investigation—prove how impossible it would have been for my little model to obtain, by any ordinary procedure, the facts in question—all coherent, as they are, and all bound up with the personality of Méhul and the history of his time.

Here is the report of my investigations:

The proofs of Méhul's admiration for Kreutzer, and of their friendly relations, is to be found in a pamphlet written in 1859 by a devoted disciple of the Maître—P.A. Vieillard (*Méhul, Sa Vie*, etc.: Library of the Opéra). I could also, by means of a *Notice sur Méhul*, by Maurice Thierry (Library of the Opéra), verify Méhul's statement concerning his *Chant du Roland*, which is, in fact, an independent work, complete in itself. According to Méhul I should have found in the archives of the Opéra proofs of the process in 1808 concerning his work *Joseph*. Unhappily there is a big gap in these archives, extending from 1785 to 1814. All the documents of this period have been either burned or destroyed. The accomplished biographer of Méhul, Arthur Pougin, whom I consulted, told me that he recalled no trace of a process in all the many documents he had examined. But, like several other biographers, he called attention to the fact that the relations between Méhul and the imperial Academy of Music were quite strained. (Méhul, for that matter, had no part himself in this lawsuit, which was entirely between the Opéra and the Théâtre Feydeau.)

I found no trace of anything concerning *L'Exil*.

To reach complete satisfaction, I should have to read the long correspondence of the last years of Méhul's life and to consult innumerable documents. And for this I have not the time.

It may be that chance will serve me, an erudite reader, or someone possessing a document?

NINETY-THIRD SÉANCE

November 26, 1913

A séance of profound interest for us but, unfortunately, for us alone. First, because many of the transmissions are too personal to make public; and then, because we alone are able to recognize their value, both as to the characteristic expression of the Spirit who communicates, and as to the circumstances referred to.

Reine sleeps normally. When I think the hypnosis is complete, I place in her lap a package of Madame L.'s letters,[84] and, without commentary, order her to find the Spirit who, in her earthly life, had written them. Reine carefully examines them with her hands, seems a little disturbed, then becomes immobile. Some moments pass. She whispers and mutters under her breath, but finally raising her voice, says: "Monsieur Cornillier, I find no trace of this Spirit in Paris. Send me where her body was buried." This in itself is interesting, for as a matter of fact Madame L. did not die in her house in Paris. She was buried in Giverny where she had a little place that she adored.

I wish to send Reine to this place, but she does not know how to find it, and I am puzzled as to how I may best direct her. After much effort and waste of time, she finishes by reaching Giverny and rapidly, then, discovers the house in question. But she does not find the Spirit. She is positive that this is her home, however, for the whole place is

---

[84] See in the Eighty-eighth Séance the passage concerning Madame L.

pervaded by the special fluid contained in the letters: but it is her detailed description of the garden and the house that convinces me that she has found the spot. She says that Vettellini has helped her to reach it and that he seems surprised by the difficulty they encounter in their search for the Spirit. He is puzzled by an unexpected situation ... But suddenly Reine breaks off talking, to look piercingly above her head and to the left.—"She is here, the person you want to see. Yes,—here! She was helped to come,—directed to us. She is speaking," Reine listens and repeats:

"She says that she has felt our call for a long time now, but she could not come; she is not free to act. She is kept at a distance, because she is to reincarnate in special conditions. She is guarded, because she might easily be caught in a vortex of incarnation. She is expressly held back and separated so that, later on, she may be placed in a particular environment. This is why we could not find her."

This unexpected explanation upsets the order of my questions, so I leave Reine free to transmit the communication as she receives it, begging her only to thank the Spirit for coming and to say that I would be glad if I could be of use to her. She replies that nothing can be done for her. She is not happy ... She has been here before. She came immediately after her death, but without an exact consciousness, pushed by a sort of instinct. She wished to be forgiven ... yes, *forgiven*. But now she is no longer her own mistress. Already her return to earth is being prepared, and we can do nothing for her ... except to pardon her.

Surprised, and even moved,—for certain painful scenes had, it is true, interrupted our relations—I assure her, through Reine, that I have not the slightest ill will against her, cherishing in memory only the happy moments of our friendship ... If she would like to help us, will she describe what she felt at the moment of her death and after her passage into the *Au-Delà*?

Reine transmits her reply: "As the end approached she was seized with fear—great fear. She believed in the survival of the soul but she had no conception as to what form that survival would take. Just before her death she saw Spirits surrounding her, who came to help her: then all became obscure. She knows now that they carried her far away. They led her before an assembly of superior Spirits, blue ("White," interrupts Vettellini. "*She is mistaken.*"), before a tribunal,—but not a tribunal as we conceive it. It was to make her understand, make her conscious; and she was able to look back upon her past life and understand—oh, but very obscurely."

Here the medium speaks on her own responsibility: "You know she is well started, but not yet able to choose her means of evolution. The high Spirits, seeing that she would gain nothing in the Astral, have decided that a prompt reincarnation will be her best means of progress. They will lead her to incarnate in the most propitious environment. It must be humble; *she must be insignificant* in her next existence. It will come soon now, and you will know it, for just before her capture she will come to tell you of it. This will be accorded for the sake of the work."

I ask Madame L. to tell me an important fact, a significant incident in her past life which will really be a proof of identity.

Reine listens for some time, hesitating to transmit, but upon evident confirmation from the Spirit she murmurs: "Very well, then; I will repeat it exactly." Leaning towards me she pronounces two words evoking a moment of great importance in my own life, as well. These two words are followed by the avowal of the unhappy influence which she had tried to exercise over this event,—influence which *I did not suspect at the time, but whose probability I can readily admit.*—"And that is why she wished so much to see you before she died. She wanted to be forgiven. It is this persistent desire that brought her here after her death and made her follow your fluid to my house, without an exact comprehension of what she was doing. But at that moment I could not have seen her, if the Spirits who direct her had not made her visible to me; they did this so that I might keep the souvenir of her visit and tell you about it."

I give Reine an affectionate message to transmit to the Spirit from me. And this provokes a reply that gives so profound a revelation of the conscience of each one of us—Madame L., my wife and myself—and that only she, Madame L., could disclose, that for us there is no further possible doubt as to the identity of the Spirit who pretends to be our old friend.

I try to get more details of her past life, citing various names and circumstances that would lead her to recall others. She feels obscurely that "all that" has been in her life, but it has become so vague ...Yes, she remembers, ... but as one remembers a dream. She will come back to announce her reincarnation ... and, then, oblivion for her.

I ask to see my father. Reine finds him quickly and brings him back with her.

He begins by saying it is a long time since I have asked for him. He is happier now, certainly he is; but, on the whole, he does not care for astral life. Oh, earth is much more agreeable!—There are more pleasures of all kinds! It is too difficult to understand, astral life,—at his degree of evolution, at least.

I slip into Reine's hands a meerschaum pipe.

"That's mine, that pipe!"—"No," protests Reine, "it is Monsieur Cornillier's!"—"Yes,—*now*!" is the caustic retort. (Correct.)

I ask Reine how she sees him. She sees him as a grayish-red light, rather pale.

Then I ask my father to try to materialize,—to make an effort to assume the form that was his in earthly life and to show at least his face to my medium, so that she may describe it to me. (Reine knows absolutely nothing about my father.) He says he will try: he will take substance from us for this materialization.

Reine describes the different phases of the process. First there is a grayish-blue cloud, a sort of smoke that slowly condenses into a mass. Then the volume of the head takes shape and, little by little, she sees the face defining. She describes the features: "A long face,—thin; a long, big nose,—Oh, you couldn't mistake it!" she exclaims. "A heavy moustache." (The lower part of the face is vaporous for a long time, but finally takes form.)—"Ah ... he has a beard! Oh, yes, a fine beard, full, heavy, much longer than yours. He looks about seventy, I should say.[85] He is quite gray. But what hair—what a lot of hair! He's certainly not a bald old man, anyway. And his eyes! Ha! They laugh, his eyes,—they are deep and brilliant. Oh, you know, just his eyes alone, and you'd know he was laughing! Cheekbones are marked. H'm ... do you look like him? (She examines carefully.) Yes ... there is something: when you laugh a certain way you look like him. But ... it's quite different just the same: your face is ... cut another way"... etc., etc.

We speak of his impressions. He is bored. He regrets the Earth, and his only distraction is to come to take part as much as possible in the life here. He likes to roam about and observe everything that is going on in our world, it is his pleasure. No, he sees no friends in the Au-Delà. Oh! he might easily find some, but he prefers to be alone, etc.

Since he so deeply regrets terrestrial life, I ask what interested him most, what he liked the best, in his last existence here. Reply: Smoking,

---

[85] I must explain that when I begged my father to materialize he inquired, "But at what age do you wish me to show myself?" *Without giving any figures,* I said "Show yourself as you were at the time of your death." Reine gave to the materialization the approximate age of my father when he died. He was seventy-four years old.

... talking with his friends. And then, the theatre, oh, that was a great pleasure for him! Cards, too, ... he liked cards. In his youth what he had preferred above all else was the sea. Ah, he adored the sea! ... And ships! And when he was not on the water, he still loved to contemplate it hours at a time, musing and dreaming. (All that Reine has described or transmitted—from the physical portrait to the tastes and tendencies—all is characteristic of my father; this passion for the sea, and the joy he found in its mere contemplation is absolutely exact.)

Wishing to obtain certain statements from him, I refer to an event in our past life together, but an excited colloquy between my father and Reine cuts me short. The child is scolding him roundly—as though she had caught him with his fingers in the jam pot.—"But what are you shoving in for? Did you ever! I can't believe it! What nerve! You don't even know that he's higher than you? ... But, certainly he is! Ha! ... You drove him away, did you? Well it's a pretty mess! ... Don't try to jump in like that again, please. He obeyed you? Of course he did—he isn't awake yet; he has been dead only a little while ... But before long he'll show you whether he obeys you or not!"

This is bewildering. But in the end we understand that, coming into the atelier recently, my father perceived a Spirit who seemed to have established himself there, and assuming that his past paternity implied the right of police, he forthwith chased out the intruder, who offered no resistance to his authority. It was Paul, who often comes to be near us, but of whom I have not spoken, simply because up to this moment he has given nothing of special interest. Reine with an almost cruel precision explains to my father their respective positions. Henceforth Paul will be allowed to stay.

Our visitor is about to leave when a new conversation begins between him and Reine who, this time, has another tone.—"Ah, that is good! But why didn't you say so? You should tell me everything. Ah, that is really good; it is kind, you know."

Turning to me, she explains that my father has voluntarily returned several times to see "Aunt Susan." He always speaks to her of the *Bon Dieu*, but it does not work very well: she has no confidence, she is too obstinate. And it is far, far away! My father does not even know where it is. He has only to wish to find this Spirit—and he reaches her; but he could not explain how.

Is he often in Nantes?—"It is my native town. I go to see the ships, for I still love them."—Does he go out with them sometimes, cruising or fishing? He says that he often accompanies for hours the big ships that are going far; but he keeps above them—looking out, observing the atmospheric conditions, etc. He meets many of these big ships when he goes to see "Aunt Susan," for he has to pass over an immense expanse of water to reach her.

Here we say *au revoir*, for I want to have a few words with Vettellini.

Was Méhul really angry when he left us the other day? "No," says Vettellini. Once more I explain why I insist so much upon material details that may be verified. It is my opinion that they would give weight to the book, but if Vettellini thinks I am wrong, I will yield the point.

He replies that, as regards certain questions, we are just like children: our "why?" cannot always be answered because many things are incomprehensible to us. For example, the difficulty of communication,— *difficulty which increases in proportion to the evolution of the Spirits*; and, also, the reasons why, in coming to speak with us, they lose the memory of many facts and details of the past. It is inexplicable to us, in our conditions, but it is a fact.—"In certain manifestations which you have obtained, the very limit of possibilities in communication with the Astral has been reached. One can go no further. The great Spirits, so essentially different by their very substance, can bring themselves no nearer to your level, ... and this is why distrust offends them so. After their painful efforts to approach you, doubt insults them. Oh, the lower ones communicate easily enough! They are not obliged to change their condition, they have not to plunge into a dense and suffocating atmosphere which, for the high Spirits, is exactly what sinking in a mud bath would be for you. They can speak abundantly, and abundantly they can blunder and lie ... Nevertheless, I do not oppose your insistence. Be tactful with them, be shrewd; get all you can out of it if you believe that through such testimony the book will have more weight."

I ask what provoked the visit of Méhul. He says it was the fluid of our friend the musician which first attracted him; that he followed it to our house, and then became interested in our work.

I again point out the advantage we should gain from the visit of a Spirit of moderate evolution, but lucid, and who could give us precise material details, to which a high one could not lower himself. It should be *someone unknown to us all*, who would give proofs of identity which I might afterwards verify. Vettellini approves and promises to give me satisfaction.

NINETY-FOURTH SÉANCE

November 28, 1913

A rather gray séance, but satisfactory by reason of the clearness and precision of the statements.

We have no stranger to interview today: Vettellini prefers to discuss the points that preoccupy me.

And it is true, I continue to be a bit troubled by certain communications—exclusively Anglo-Saxon in origin—in which entities, seemingly conscious and lucid, deny reincarnation[86] and I am anxious to clear up this subject. How is it possible that a superior Spirit may be ignorant to this degree? Vettellini has affirmed that a highly evolved conscience, looking back after death, can take cognizance of the different phases of his evolution. Consequently, then, given a certain level, one has necessarily the proof of successive lives. On the other hand, it is inconceivable that an advanced Spirit should not have reflected on the question of individual consciousness and its origin, and should not have tried to comprehend its development. If incarnated beings of mediocre evolution have—thanks to the magnetic passes[87] of Colonel de Rochas—been able to see their anterior lives, it is incomprehensible that high Spirits should be totally ignorant of this crucial condition of progress.

---

[86] ecently, however, several curious and interesting books have been published in England and in America—alleged communications from Spirits who definitely affirm reincarnation.

[87] See *Les Vies Successives*, by Colonel de Rochas.

I abstract the main points of Vettellini's reply, which was long and given with great precision: First of all, very evolved Spirits communicate rarely. The immense majority of those who communicate are mediocre entities, who, as a rule, retain in the Astral the opinions which they held on earth. This may be difficult erroneous opinions: for example, how many there are amongst the so-called "intellectual elite" of the world, who entirely deny all psychical phenomena! It is the same in the life after death.

Secondly, in many cases, the negation arises from a mistaken interpretation of the medium or a confusion in the communication. As has been said, the higher the evolution of the Spirit, the more difficult is the communication of his thought, and the more susceptible it is to distortion ... "You had a very good example of this when Méhul came to speak with you; yet, with Reine, the conditions are infinitely above the average. Let a word be badly transmitted, a thought-vibration misinterpreted by the medium, and immediately an error is affirmed ... And the error will be propagated."

Incidentally Vettellini remarks that experiments such as those of Colonel de Rochas are deeply interesting, but very dangerous for the medium, who might easily stay definitely in the Astral: for, in order to obtain the view of anterior lives, the magnetizer must succeed in gradually disengaging from its various fluidic envelopes that part which is essential spirit. It is a big risk. He adds that moreover it is quite probable that in the experiments cited, the spirit of the medium did not see by its own means alone. Undoubtedly, unknown to her, she was aided by protecting Spirits who, to avoid the danger, created for her the images of her past lives.

I ask for Vettellini's view of the case of W. Stead, who went down with the Titanic, and whose identity has since been established by convincing testimony obtained through different English and American mediums.[88] First, is he informed of this formidable catastrophe? His answer makes Reine jump.—"Why, what are you saying? ... What do you mean? You knew it in advance, it was prepared in the Astral, and you never said a word about it? Ah, that is too much, Vettellini! Why, what are you thinking of? It is just such a prediction that would count for us. And you knew it beforehand! ... And you did not speak! Well, I call it ... incredible!" and she turns to me in indignant astonishment. (Reine and I—too—in the blank surprise of the

---

[88] See *Has W. Stead Returned* (James Coates, London).

moment—forgot only one point: the disaster of the Titanic occurred before our séances began.)

I come back to the case of Stead, giving details of his life—such a generous life—and of his death. According to the communications, he was perfectly conscious immediately after his death. His joy seems profound, he constantly insists upon his ineffable happiness, etc., etc.—Vettellini knows nothing about Stead, but says that to have immediately experienced such felicity, he must have been a very high Spirit,—"and for that matter, what you tell me of his life proves a great evolution," he adds.

I ask what may be the explanation of the fantastic details communicated by him. (He speaks of astral palaces, of walls decorated with scenes depicting the good deeds of his life, of marvelous places of repose prepared for him, etc.) Vettellini says that these are *interpretations for our human intelligence* of astral sensations and perceptions that are incomprehensible for us.

Here Reine, speaking on her own authority, reproves my astonishment that a Spirit such as Stead should speak like a pastor in his Sunday sermon: "You seem surprised that he attributes to God the sublime beauty and emotions he finds in the Astral,—and that he constantly uses that name in his communications. We, of course, would say Fate ... the mysterious Force ... 'The Hand.' But one might just as well say God, Monsieur Cornillier." The child is not wrong, and possibly the sermonizing character of Stead's communications has an influence on the Anglo-Saxon temperament that the sober and precise language of our Vettellini could not obtain.

I observe that Stead seems sublimely happy in his new life. It is, then, more and more confirmed that Death is "a marvelous and big adventure" for people of high evolution. But the inferior, or even the average, person seems rather to regret terrestrial life? "It is not so," replies Vettellini. "Amongst the average Spirits many are happy. In death, as in life, there are the anxious, and the happy-go-lucky. To sum it up: when lucidity is once recovered, the soul capable of spiritual interests and joys is happy; the soul whose happiness depends upon material pleasures, regrets the earth. It is logical."

A sudden commotion, a startled laugh:—"Ah, it is he, there's no mistaking him! What are you so busy about that you're never here any more?"—"Well, I'm here now!" is the brief retort of our old friend. And the talk begins.

He is so gay, so charming today, that one dares even to ask personal questions:—"Do you remember Colonel P.?"—"I should say I did! I thought little enough of him on earth,—and less here!" My wife mentions an incident in their relations and Reine says that it makes him laugh: "Yes, I was never more pleased in my life! He was furious!" (Correct appreciation of the fact.)

On the other hand, he has no recollection whatever of a friend who was especially dear to him in his lifetime. He announces that he went back to his old home the other day, and Reine, in transmitting, *gives the name of the city with the exact American pronunciation.*

I beg him to make a distinction, for us, between his duties and his distractions in the Astral. He declares that one and the other are joys for him. Ah, no! He certainly would not care to return to Earth; he is only too happy to be disincarnated! His distractions carry him to the Stock Exchange, the Courts, the Banks, but his duties also attach him to the question of affairs. He has to establish the proper influences in cases where general evolution would gain by a given situation. He is occupied with international interests and relations.

And abruptly, without the slightest ceremony, he goes off, leaving an impression of intense vitality and gaiety behind him.

The séance closes with a few words about health. Vettellini tells Reine that I should order another "glass" of the tonic I have been taking.—"Another glass? What do you mean by that?" says Reine.—"Yes, yes,—another glass, another bottle, it's the same thing, and you understand perfectly well," replies the Maître. *"Call a bottle a glass?* Oh, Vettellini, you, a Spirit!" shrieks the child with mocking laughter. It is true that in certain cases the words "verre" (glass) and "bouteille" (bottle) are synonymous.

NINETY-FIFTH SÉANCE

December 1, 1913

P oor Reine is suffering again—this time with neuralgia. During the séance she says that Vettellini has helped her to sleep; my magnetism alone would not have sufficed, the pain was too acute. Immediately the Guide informs me that he has brought two Spirits, absolutely unknown to us, who are ready to give proofs of their identity, proofs that may be verified. But Reine is in no condition to receive these communications: we would better postpone them till Wednesday. Just now all that can be asked of the child is a short talk between ourselves. "However," adds Vettellini, "your grandfather told me he was coming this afternoon, and you must have a few moments with him."

Unsolicited as it is, the remark is interesting. For this very morning I was thinking of my grandfather, as I examined a pen-drawing of his, *and mentally I decided to call him* and, if possible, get him to describe his sensations when he passed into the Au-Delà.

Vettellini suggests that we use this séance to speak of sleep. Agreed. But before attacking this serious question, I would like to know if I was mistaken on Saturday when, at A.'s house, I repeatedly felt on my face the light fresh breath by which for some time past Vettellini has announced his presence. Reine listens, then transmits: "On Saturday, Vettellini stayed with you during your entire visit. And someone else was there, too. Guess? Why! Old Friend. He went to be near Madame Cornillier. Oh, you may be sure he did not stay long—that one!"—"And who else was there?" interrupts Vettellini, "for we were three." Reine does not know, nor can I imagine who, of the world invisible, made the third.—"Isouard," says Vettellini very simply. And, indifferently, he repeats, "Yes, ... Isouard was there, too."—"Issoire ... Isard—who's he? Don't know Isoir, objects Reine." (No more do I.)—"But yes, yes, you know him! Isouard ... Nicolo," confirms the Maître placidly. I smell fire.—"Nicolo is Nicolo," cries Reine irritably, "What's this Issoire?"

In spite of his gravity Vettellini is amusing himself hugely. A few words make us understand that Nicolo's real name was *Isouard*, and that *Nicolo detests to be called Isouard*.[89] It is just one of those jokes that a good friend never resists on earth—nor in the Au-Delà, apparently!

"And now," says Vettellini, "let us talk about sleep." It is extremely rare that he proposes a subject, waiting generally to be questioned, but today he spontaneously proffers the following information.

Reine is tense with attention, but she does not understand: it is most interesting to observe her. I hear her refuse to transmit because she can make no sense in the communication.—"Begin again, Vettellini. Find another way ... Put it differently. You know I cannot repeat it well if I do not understand."—Finally, however, she has grasped the idea and begins her transmission, which may be summed up in this way: Sleep is not a repose in the function of the different organs. All of them, including the brain, retain their physiological activity during sleep. What causes sleep is *a disunion between the astral (fluidic) body and the physical body*. The purpose of this disunion is to liberate sufficiently the astral body, so that it may go to gather from the ambiance the vital force contained in the magnetic and cosmic currents, whose emission or passage is intensified and facilitated by the night. In this way the stock of force that is spent in daily activity is constantly renewed. The amount supplied by the physical body—by means of food, respiration, etc.,—would not suffice to sustain life if the breath of the vital, cosmic force did not come to fortify it. And this is universal law,—governing all living creatures.

This sortie of the astral body for the purpose of gathering the nourishment necessary to organic life, is not to be confounded with the disengagement of highly evolved beings in quest of information or influences that may develop their consciousness. The first is common to all animals, to everything that lives; the second is the privilege of a Spirit that has already attained a high degree of evolution.

---

[89] I verified this statement. It is history.

I ask if the orientation of the body, in sleep, is of any importance. To my surprise Vettellini seems not to attach much weight to this point; but he especially insists that the body should always lie in the axis of a window, or other opening communicating with outside space,—feet towards the opening, to facilitate the absorption of the fluids. "This is a general rule and good for everyone, whereas the orientation must vary according to individual constitution," (planetary influences.) A-propos of this, Vettellini remarks to Reine (who had been astonished) that, in spite of her own desire, and not understanding why, she had been obliged to change the position of her bed, and to place it perpendicular to the wall, the footboard towards the window. It was he who influenced her to make this change.

In the midst of this important communication occurs one of the many incidents that give such confirmation of Vettellini's presence. Reine, concentrated and attentive to his words, that she may understand and transmit them without error, has tensely clasped her hands together. This is contrary to the regulations given at the beginning of our séances.[90] All at once, I see her jerking her head and shrugging her shoulders, then, precipitately, she unlocks her hands, angrily sputtering at the same instant: *But they're not crossed,* I tell you! What a bother you are!"

But here is my grandfather. Reine suddenly announces him.

I hold up the drawing of the ship. Does he recognize it?—"Oh! I was always making them … I loved it … I loved everything connected with the sea!" He says he does not often come to see us because he knows we have no need of him, but he passes by occasionally without my knowing it. And neither does he need us. We can do nothing for him, he is happy,—oh, yes, profoundly happy! (Reine says he seems proud of it.) His chief occupation is to modify the fluidic currents influencing human destinies. His recreations are difficult to define in our language. They are in their very essence superior to ours, and yet there are certain analogies at times; for instance, there are the joys of affection, of emotion, but infinitely more exquisite than ours on earth. (Decidedly the good old days of life on earth do not unduly torment him.)

Is he willing to tell me what happened at his passage from life to death? He replies that he foresaw his death very clearly; he had visions during his last moments; Spirits surrounded him—waiting for him.

---

[90] The crossing of hands or feet checks the sortie of the fluidic body.

After his death he fell into a sort of sleep, and it took about six months of our time for him to come to a clear consciousness of his condition. He had been helped by protecting Spirits, and as he was sufficiently advanced to choose his own way of evolution, he had, without any hesitation, preferred to stay in the Astral.

All this is somewhat vague. I ask if, to help me in this work, he will not try to recall one or two characteristic facts of his earthly life, facts that will definitely identify him.—Yes, he will think it over and will give them. Whereupon he leaves us.

December 3, 1913

If I needed proof of Reine's sincerity, I had it today. There was an easy and rather tempting occasion to trick, if such were her habit.

She arrives almost distracted: the neuralgic pain has not ceased for four or five days now. She does not sleep, eats nothing, and does not know what to do. But here she is for the séance just the same.

It is a great bore, for it happens that I have invited Miss S. and A. this afternoon, and it is more than possible that nothing of interest will repay them.

However, I begin magnetizing at three o'clock, forcing the dose. Reine not having stirred for more than ten minutes, I suppose I have succeeded in making her sleep. But when I cease the passes, she opens her eyes and says: "I'm not sleeping,—only torpid, that's all." So I begin again, proceeding methodically, and more and more intensifying the magnetization. This time I am sure she is in hypnosis and in a low voice ask: "Reine, are you sleeping?"—"No,—not sleeping. I hear all the noises. I'm dull, but the least shock rouses me," and in despair she exclaims: "To think it had to happen today—Ha!" I console her, saying that we will try something else.

Calling in my wife and our friends, we form the chain, hoping in this way to obtain some kind of a manifestation. But when after ten minutes nothing at all has happened, we abandon the effort and go into the atelier, where I suggest that we try the table.

The table, which generally taps at once, stands motionless. I send Reine away. A few movements result, but no communication. Then I send our friends away, and we three—my wife, Reine and I—resume our places; but the table does not budge. Finally, after seven or eight minutes, there is a wild balancing to and fro, then these words: "You must stop."—We obey.

The only interesting point in all this is the clear sincerity of the medium.

NINETY-SIXTH SÉANCE

December 5, 1913

Reine, following my instructions, consulted the table this morning to know if we should have a séance today. The answer came: "Yes,—at two o'clock. Even if there is no result it will at least keep you in condition." It is pitiful to see her suffering; so much the more that she tries to smile, and pretends to be happy here.

As we begin the séance, she exclaims that she has no pain at all,—it has stopped all at once. And as a matter of fact she sleeps promptly.

I wait long before speaking, hoping that this tranquil sleep may rest her. Suddenly she trembles, turns her head to the right and laughs. With a gesture, she sends the invisible person over to her left, leans towards that side, and begins to talk gaily,—too gaily, I think, to be receiving Vettellini. And at that instant she announces the old friend. He arrives first today because Vettellini could not come at once. The fluidic and atmospheric conditions have been so bad for several days past, that he has great trouble to reach us. Old Friend, vigorous, less ethereal, penetrates more easily the dense currents that surround us. It appears, moreover, that we are in bad form. The planetary influences are execrable just now; we suffer from this, and they, the Spirits, sustain the reaction of this suffering when they try to approach us. The trouble last Wednesday came from that alone. Vettellini could not even get here. It was he, Old Friend, who had tried to communicate by the table.—"Oh!" interrupts Reine mockingly, "that's why it was so prettily done! Yes, yes,—I know, tables bore you. No use asking you to make them talk!—certainly not!"—He goes on to say that it is a little setback, of course, but nothing can be done about it. If they were not looking out for us, we would be even more depressed than we are. He, for example, is doing all he can to shield Madame Cornillier from painful discomfort.

Then off he goes, as brusquely as he came, without waiting for Vettellini's arrival.

Reine begins to show signs of uneasiness.—"I do wish he'd come, just the same! Why is he so long?" But the words are hardly spoken when a blissful smile announces the presence of her Guide.

The Maître explains at length the bad influences that we are undergoing just now. They will be at their worst from the 12th to the 15th, after which period things will go better. It is almost universal. Actually the entire earth is as though under a spell. Our work will be retarded, but we must not worry about that: it cannot be helped.

I speak of political events.—"The high Spirits have indeed modified the written destiny," says Vettellini, "otherwise the situation would be much uglier than it is. But it is only held in check. *All will happen as I have revealed it to you*—or at least approximately. Certain events are beyond any modification ... A great and neighboring kingdom is entering upon its fate. *The most mighty monarch will fall. It is inevitable. They wish the Republic* ... Much blood will be shed ... The movement is already started. A few months more ... and you will see! France will be caught in the whirlpool in another way. She will engage in it to stand by a friendly nation ... and she will live to rue it. Once in full battle, her colonies will revolt and assert their independence. Political intrigues are already on foot ... All signs point to a complete upheaval."

I allude to the Poincaré administration, which Vettellini had affirmed would not outlive November.—"His political life has been prolonged to relieve the tension of the situation. But it is only postponed."

Prophecies already given are renewed. I note two precise predictions: railroad catastrophes, provoked at the moment of mobilization by spies or revolutionists,[91] and appalling surprises as to the condition of our naval forces, nothing being in accordance with the preparation affirmed by the politicians.

---

[91] January, 1915. Although no catastrophe was announced during the tragic days of mobilization, I have been informed that a terrible accident occurred on the line of Cherbourg and another in the region of Blois.

Vettellini thinks that we may have the two unknown Spirits on Monday or Wednesday. The earth is enveloped in a kind of sooty fluid, and, even the Spirits themselves suffer from it. It was with the greatest difficulty that he could reach us.

The question of health comes up once more, and poor Reine has plenty to hear. She is peremptorily forbidden to have a tooth extracted—as is her secret intention—and the menace is heavy, in case of disobedience. Vettellini has taken her pain during the séance, but he will hand it over to her again when she wakens. He cannot keep it. Reine strongly engages him to hold on to it. Why, *he is a Spirit*, and his teeth can't ache—he hasn't any! And as for her, she does not know what to do with that pain any longer. She is worn out with it!—And she implores him, the poor child, crying and laughing at the same time. The scene is both lamentable and comic. Vettellini comforts her like a mother, but at the end of the séance she must take up life again with the neuralgia.[92] "Well, then,—wait at least till I get back home," she whispers, "I can be as bad as I please there—Armand will know something about it!"

---

[92] The pain came back a few moments after she wakened.

NINETY-SEVENTH SÉANCE

December 8, 1913

Reine is still in torture. Not having slept at all these past nights, she is now dead with sleep; and falling into a chair, waiting to begin the séance, she dozes fitfully.

We begin at three o'clock. She seems to sleep profoundly. Vettellini comes at once, they talk together and I catch the following words:—"But he will be angry. No, I will not tell him; he won't like it ... Ah, no,—I don't want him to be sick! But since I am sleeping just now, we might as well get something out of it? No? ... Ah, well, I'll tell him that first!—That will please him!—And then ... I'll tell the rest afterwards." I have no idea what it is all about.

Reaching out for me, Reine now says: "You're going to be pleased,—yes! Vettellini thinks that you may begin to go out now. You must be careful, but you may go out!" (Here comes "the rest.") "You know, Monsieur Cornillier,—it's too stupid, ... but you must waken me. There can be no séance today, we're neither of us up to it. It would tire us too much. Vettellini says that he allowed the hypnotizing only to keep me in training. We shall not be in much better shape on Wednesday, but he hopes that by Friday all will be well again."

She remarks that when she got into her big chair she was afraid she was going to fall asleep naturally,—she was sick with need of it; but that I had scarcely put my hands on her when she was at once completely aroused and, after that, she fell normally under the influence of my passes. "It was Vettellini who made me feel awake like that," she explains.

The child uses all her wiles to retain him, and Vettellini—though protesting—lingers.

NINETY-EIGHTH SÉANCE

December 10, 1913

bout the same in health, our medium is nevertheless in a better mood today, and I hope for a good séance.

She sleeps promptly, and I immediately send her to find my grandfather, who has promised to establish his identity by giving me details of his past life. Shortly she is talking with someone, but I get nothing of the conversation beyond a few expressions—"Don't quite understand," … "I can hardly hear," … "Say it more plainly," etc. Finally she turns to say that Vettellini is there and my grandfather will not come.—"It is not that he *will not*," corrects Vettellini, "but today he cannot; he is busy. Moreover we shall not have a good séance. Communication is next to impossible, the ambient conditions are so unfavorable that it is useless to try for anything. And you, yourselves, are especially run down. It is wiser to content ourselves with a talk together. If you have any questions, I will answer them."

As I am just now copying my notes on the subject of birth, I ask if the laws concerning the capitation of a Spirit of the human race hold good for animals also,—i.e., only one Spirit captured at a time. Reply: the law is different for animals. A single union captures several spirits in that class.

I struggle to find interesting questions, but my head is empty, I feel a great fatigue. Reine, on her side, speaks with difficulty, seems heavy and exhausted. We talk at random.

Question: Is there an anatomical change in the brain during sleep? Answer: Yes, but it is not the anatomical change which causes sleep.

It is the sortie of the spirit, which arrests the interrelation of the nerve cells, and provokes the retraction of their ramifications. Normally, the circulation of the blood should diminish; but often it becomes, on the contrary, more intense—caused sometimes by the position of the head, which should always be on a level with the body—and dreams are provoked thereby. In a good sleep one should not dream.

Question: How does the astral body escape when it goes to find nourishing fluids in the night? Answer: By the mouth. And it enters by the mouth. Whereas, in spontaneous or provoked sorties of the spirit, it escapes in a vapor from all over the body, as has already been said. In a natural death it comes out in a vapor, slowly. But if death is violent, it comes out by the mouth and all at once, instantly. After death the fluidic line remains attached to the mouth,—or, more exactly, to the brain through the mouth passage.

I remark that certain occult doctrines hold that the fluidic line is attached to the plexus? Vettellini maintains that such is not the case. It is always through the mouth that the line is attached.

The reason why he advises that, in sleeping, the feet should always point towards a window, is not that the fluids penetrate by the feet alone; but because, entering the body at that point, they can run along its whole length, surrounding and bathing it like a current of water, and so be more readily and regularly absorbed than if they struck it on the side.

I ask the Maître how it happens that he seems to be neither occupied with, nor interested in, the efforts made by other Spirits in different centers—in America, in England,—to propagate the doctrine of survival. People have been working on this question for fifteen or twenty years. Both on our side, and on the side of the Au-Delà, enormous efforts have been made to come into contact and establish proofs of the persistence of consciousness after death. Certain mediums, such as Mrs. Piper for example, have unquestionable merit, and Vettellini does not seem to even know of them.

He replies that he knows perfectly well that there are groups of Spirits engaged in special tasks. But there are also works undertaken by solitary Spirits. His is one of them. He is alone; he has preferred to be alone. His first conception of this work came during his lifetime. It is he alone who has arranged, and directed, the conditions which have permitted us to obtain in one year results which in other circumstances would have required ten years of effort and experiment. What has already been realized is extraordinary. One may not penetrate the Au-Delà further than we, in certain cases, have penetrated it. It is our health, the health of each of us, which unhappily has arrested the experiments in other directions. Neither Reine nor I have the necessary strength. Actually, we have about reached the limit of our possibilities. To go further would be disastrous for our health, and this must not be. Soon, the work he has wished to accomplish will be terminated, and we must take up again the normal life of the incarnate.

No, he will not abandon us. He will perhaps have even more facility in manifesting himself when we regain our normal health. Reine will probably be able to hear him. Then, too, if there is a serious reason for communicating, he will provoke her sleep. Even when he has passed into another sphere, he will come back to see us and watch over us.

Replying to another of my questions, he says that he knows three of our anterior lives. He was obliged to know them à *fond*, in order to be sure of the characters which he had chosen for the accomplishment of his work. Will he tell us something of these former lives?—"No, it would only trouble you."

There is a possibility of the visit of Doctor G., whom I have invited to come and examine the notes of my experiments. Vettellini says that I should also ask him to assist at a séance, and leave him free to examine the medium or make any test or verification he may deem useful. Before his visit the Maître hopes to give us new proofs of Spirit identity. But we are about spent,—he is obliged to go slowly, to be extremely prudent. Méhul was to have come back today to give new details; Vettellini prevented him. We shall feel the effects of the little we have done today. Perhaps on Friday the séance will be better—though the distressing fluidic influences will be at their maximum.

He warns me that I caught cold again when I went out this morning. As a matter of fact I am so exhausted with fatigue that, for the first time, I long for the séance to close.

NINETY-NINTH SÉANCE

December 12, 1913

(A. is present)

On arriving, Reine says that she was informed by the table yesterday that the séance of today would not be good—and for reasons already explained. She speaks of a strange dream she has had and which still impresses her. I will ask about it during the séance.

Sleep comes quickly, but she is motionless for so long a time that I finally take her hand and question her. She says she has been up high—very high. She has been with Vettellini in the region of the blue Spirits, where she has not gone for a long time now: and then higher than that,—and much higher still! They reached the sphere of the white Spirits, but there she could not maintain herself because of the currents. She was forced to go down a little. She did nothing, saw nothing special; it was merely an excursion with her Guide.

Vettellini informs me that, once again, he cannot give me what I wish, for the adverse fluidic influence is still strong. But he thinks that by Monday communication may be resumed under good conditions; and, in any case, he will bring a Spirit, unknown to us, and capable of giving proofs of identity.

Again I hark back to the question of the fluidic line which, after death, attaches a Spirit to his body. Vettellini has stated that it is attached to, or through, the mouth. Well and good. But when the person has been decapitated, for example, or when his head has been crushed in an accident, to what part of the body is the fluidic line then attached?—Reply: The fluidic line remains attached to the head of the decapitated body, with infiltrations into the body if this has been readjusted to the head: if the body remains separated, the fluidic line rests attached to the head alone; and in this latter case, the body is only a mass of organic substance, having no relation with the disincarnated Spirit. When the head has been destroyed, when it no longer exists, the Spirit resumes complete liberty and abandons all relations with physical and terrestrial conditions. The consequence is the same as in cremation.

A-propos of a disincarnated Spirit whom I recently evoked, I inquire: How is it that he has no recollection of the facts of his past life—neither of people, nor conditions, nor sentiments—and that he yet possesses a sufficiently complete language? In our earthly conditions, when a person falls into a state of paralysis or idiocy, he generally loses a certain series—or even the complete series—of cerebral faculties: his language is always affected, and, often, it is the first faculty to be affected.—Vettellini's reply is precise and clear: "The case is not at all the same. You are quite wrong to establish an analogy between a pathological condition of the organic brain (lesion, hemorrhage, etc.) and that of a Spirit in a state of torpor, precisely because he has abandoned his physical organism. The coma in which the Spirit is plunged after death would be of no value whatever to his evolution, if he did not retain his power of reflecting and, consequently, of developing his consciousness. He must be able to investigate, to inform himself, and language is for him an indispensable tool in this work. That is why it is left to him."

This torpor, then, into which the majority of Spirits fall after their passage into the Astral, would seem to be not only a natural reaction from the shock of death, but also a condition imposed by the higher Spirits, to force the soul to a mysterious personal travail in this birth of consciousness.

I remark that it must be prodigiously interesting to penetrate and comprehend the essence of other individualities by such examination as Vettellini has mentioned, with reference to our preceding lives. Is it not a marvelous study, even for a high Spirit? He very soberly answers that those of high evolution can, it is true, make such researches, but as a rule they respect the legitimate right of each soul to the mystery of his own individuality. Rarely, indeed, do they exercise this power. The examination in our case was permitted him because of his high purpose. He was obliged to know à *fond* the material he was using. It was not curiosity.

We speak of the book. I must get it into shape now. We are reaching the end of our possibilities. And again he says, "Your time is limited now."

I try to express the great loss we shall sustain when the séances are ended, and he gravely answers: *"It is not I who will leave first."* Then, assuming his habitual tone, he adds that he will continue to see us, aid us, and watch over us.

I think of the dream that Reine told me when she came in today, and ask the significance of the scene that had so painfully impressed her. The rather evasive answer is given that Reine is now able to read, of herself and unaided, the currents and fluids containing the projection of future events. Often now, in the night, her astral body goes into the high regions where these currents exist; and, when she wakens, the souvenir of her readings is confounded with the dreams of her organic body.

My wife and A. leave the room to allow me to waken Reine, but immediately after their departure Vettellini returns to speak to me concerning my future.

ONE-HUNDREDTH SÉANCE

December 15, 1913

One hundred! And our interest only increases.

Before the séance my little model makes the customary report of her various happenings:—impressive dreams again, premonitory certainly, but whose significance I alone can divine. Then visions of Vettellini; one of which, this morning, in Mademoiselle H.'s atelier,[93] was accompanied by the apparition of a smoky substance, about twenty inches high, which formed in a somber alcove at the back of the studio, just after two significant noises had drawn Reine's attention there.[94]

She confides to me that she grows more and more nervous, depressed and irritable. She deplores it but says she cannot control herself and it is her poor Armand, gentle and good as possible, who has to bear the unhappy consequences of her condition.

At three o'clock I magnetize her. Vettellini arrives immediately. Unprovoked, he gives additional information which must be added to his remarks on sleep: "During a natural sortie of the fluidic body, an accidental change may occur in the organism, which closes the door, so to speak, and prevents the re-entrance of the fluidic body. The organism, thus deprived of its spirit, will continue to live in sleep; and

---

[93] She has begun to pose a little these past few weeks.

[94] These cracking noises were unquestionably real, for Mademoiselle H. heard and remarked on them.

this may last a long time ... weeks ... months. It is generally a shock, a brutal intervention, which opens the door again, and allows the fluidic body to enter.

"If meanwhile, the person, considered as dead, has been buried, he will die more or less quickly, according to the conditions of his burial."

I ask what are the normal relations of a Spirit to his dead body. Reply: "The Spirit is attracted to his body after death in the measure of his subjugation to it while living. If the body was the important and dominant element in his life, he is inclined to return to it constantly and suffer from its decomposition. If the Spirit is of greater force, or indifferent, this condition affects him very little. And, finally, if he is of high evolution, he is on the contrary almost happy to see that his body is useful, serving in the development of other creatures."—Here Reine is really eloquent, speaking with curious ease on this strange question—the evolution of the infinitely small. She describes the joy of a great Spirit when he sees the activity of these animalcule ardently taking advantage of the good substance of evolution, which his own dead body offers them, and his satisfaction that the matter through which he himself has progressed, is still of use and profit to others.

She specifies too the best conditions of burial:—"Oh, above all, nothing in lead or hard wood! A simple pine coffin is the best. No paving of stone or marble; no covering of cement. Just earth,—a deep hole in the good earth. And the best would be to lay the body there quite simply, without wrappings. But, in any case, let no rich casket check the disintegration, ... no antiseptics, ... no embalming."

When the body is in complete decomposition, the soul is free. For the average person, it is the essential condition for reincarnation: for the advanced, it is liberty to rise higher, and attain a superior sphere.

Vettellini says that the planetary influences continue to be bad and that it is still difficult to communicate. Nevertheless, the unknown Spirit, whose presence he has promised, will come. There will be little of interest today, but Reine will at least make acquaintance with this new vibration so that she may understand it better Wednesday.

The Spirit is here. Reine announces the presence, seeming already to suffer from its approach. She breathes with difficulty and transmits painfully the first words:—"I died five or six months ago."—Here I thank her for coming (Reine has said that the stranger is a woman), and say how glad we shall be if she can aid in our work by giving proofs of identity. She replies that she is here because this white Spirit brought her. The words have not fallen on deaf ears. Reine leaps to the occasion: "This white Spirit? ... Ah! ... Ha—ha! my Vettellini,—caught! ... *White* Spirit! And of course it never occurred to you to tell us—Oh, no! ... Well, you needn't think it is such great news for us ... And, anyway, tell me, why are we not to know that you are white?" The scene is diverting, but I drag Reine back to duty by inviting the unknown guest to tell who she is.

She says she was Madame B. She was forty-seven years old when she died. She lived in D. street. She was a milliner. No, she did not have a shop; she did business in her apartment. She is much disturbed by the conditions in which she has to communicate and cannot recall the number of her house, nor the quarter of the city in which her street is found; but it is in Paris. She had a son, etc., etc.

The medium sees her slightly materialized and begins to describe her appearance, but evidently suffers so much from contact with this presence, that it seems prudent to cut the interview short. So then I invite Madame B. to come back on Wednesday, but, before saying *au revoir*, I ask if there is anything we can do for her. She replies that what we are doing now helps her a little. To bring her here, our Guide had wrapped her in a special fluid which lifts her up, in a way, and does her good. She leaves us.

Vettellini forbids our going further today. Reine would have suffered much from a prolonged contact with these new vibrations,—though he had tried to accustom her to them a little, this morning, by taking Madame B. near her when she was posing in Mademoiselle H.'s studio. It was this Spirit who had appeared in the alcove,—a long, vertical, smoky apparition.

On Wednesday, Madame B. will complete what information she may have to give about herself, and in such a way that it may be verifiable.

And then we speak of Reine's curious dreams. Vettellini says that she is now strong enough to be entirely independent. He cannot prevent her from running about to investigate for herself and read the future events that are held in the astral currents. It is in this way that she saw that big house with its beautiful terraced garden overlooking the sea, and that sky, so blue. It is not in France. She will live there, later on, and she will be happy, though there will, indeed, be something missing. She turns to me, "Vettellini says that you will understand, Monsieur Cornillier? But I—I don't know what that means." I understand.

Reine, speaking for herself, confesses that her sensitiveness, developed now to an extreme degree, troubles her even when she is awake. She reads clearly the thoughts of people with whom she comes in contact, and it greatly embarrasses and disturbs her for she sees so much ... duplicity.

We are warned of a railroad accident which will soon occur in France—by the end of January or the beginning of February. It will be terrible.[95]

This incites me to again ask confirmation of the power possessed by the great Spirits, of modifying a destiny, when they deem such modification advantageous to evolution. The Maître repeats and emphasizes what has already been given on this subject: *"The great Spirits can modify a written fatality when they judge it advisable,—even the fatality of death."*

In view of the expected visit of Doctor G., I ask if I may affirm that Reine will never be hypnotized by another than I. Vettellini says that not only may I affirm it but, if need be, I may allow anyone the liberty of experimenting: "Reine is too strong to be hypnotized by the will of another, except when her own spirit allows it. And that will never be. Try it ... if you care to. Oh, naturally, certain people, vexed by failure, will pretend that she never has slept, that all has been simulation and fraud in these séances. But what of that? In spite of their scoffing, many will be troubled, and will even believe, without having courage to avow it."

A-propos of the milliner, I remark that certain Spirits seem not only to remember very precise details of their earthly life, but also to see, hear and understand exactly what is done, said, or purposed at the very moment of its occurrence on the physical plane. (As shown, for example, in the remarkable experiments made with Mrs. Piper, Mrs. Wriest, etc.) Vettellini says that this is perfectly exact; there are Spirits who see, hear, deduct and foresee with extreme precision. *But this is not at all a sign of evolution.* It is a faculty which proceeds solely from the persistent interest of the disincarnate in this domain. The higher the Spirit, the more will he be interested in the sublime mysteries of astral life, the less will he concern himself with the puerilities of life on earth. And by reason of this very fact, he will become more and more incapable of giving details whose value has ceased to exist for him.

---

[95] This catastrophe did not take place.

One more question: When they have recovered from the shock of death, how do average Spirits perceive physical nature, people and things? Vettellini affirms that they discover in nature infinitely more beauty than we can conceive. As to people and things, they see both their external form and their essential constitution, of which they may have a profound and searching knowledge, unimaginable to us. This individual capacity develops in accordance with their interest in it.

Reine is exhausted. I close the séance.

ONE-HUNDRED AND FIRST SÉANCE

December 17, 1913

(A. is present)

It is written that no séance shall repeat itself. The one-hundred-and-first is strangely different from the hundred that preceded it.—Indeed, it is not a séance at all; and from this very fact brings unexpected elements of interest.

Reine is in better health, and gayer than of late, but something pre-occupies her. This morning, as she was posing for Mademoiselle H., she saw—in the alcove already mentioned—a slight materialization of Vettellini. To her amazement, instead of seeing him as she usual-ly does,—that is, the head firm and well formed, the torso vaporish,—she saw him full length, and wrapped in a big cloak, a sort of Italian cape,—"like someone starting off on a voyage," she explains. She is sure that the cloak (which she has never seen before) has some significance which she should have grasped, but she cannot imagine what it meant. The vision was brief, for Mademoiselle H. suddenly rose from her chair just at that moment, and Reine's attention was brought back to her.

We begin at three o'clock. Reine sleeps heavily. After a few moments I call her and ask for Vettellini. No answer. I wait a while, then repeat my demand. She does not stir. Another pause, a fresh effort; but this time I insist. Whereupon she straightens up and whiningly protests: "I have started, I am hunting," ... then falls back in her chair.

I remagnetize her and repeat my call, this time touching her hand. Twice I ask her where she is, but there is no evidence that she has heard me. Finally, at a third and more imperious summons, she answers with marked excitement: "But I am hunting for Vettellini, I'm hunting ... And I can't find a trace of him!" She has no idea what it means. She will start again. Old Friend seems not to be there either.

I tell her to ask information from a blue Spirit; but she is off and does not even hear me. Some time passes. Now she sits up to examine the room, searching high and low, and all around her. Then she reaches for me and anxiously says: "I find neither Vettellini nor Old Friend ... But it is strange, you know, ... *not one single Spirit do I see!*"

She has gone through all the regions where, habitually, they are; she has gone up higher still, very high. She has not encountered a Spirit ... not one. I insist that she must find a blue Spirit and ask him; but on her side she repeats, and with irritability, that there are none. What can it mean? Oh, she sees plenty of the red and gray ones of our atmosphere, but they know nothing, that kind!—They could not inform her. She will go back again ... She is frightfully worried ... What can have happened? ... Why isn't Vettellini there? ... Is he angry? ... She begs me to remagnetize her, and send her off to hunt once more. She starts out again.

In five or six minutes she is back,—literally terrified.—"All space is empty. There is—*nothing!*" ... In those high regions where Spirits are always passing, always in greatest activity,—NOTHING: It is like death ... "But ... what can it possibly mean?" And the stupefaction caused by this mystery attenuates her anxiety about Vettellini.

I send her then to A.'s house, to try to find Nicolo. He is not there. Not the smallest trace of a Spirit of high evolution anywhere. But the others? They may know at least more than we do. She will look for my father. She finds and brings him to us soon; but he seems ignorant of the situation, says that he feels nothing special himself and yet ... he had remarked groups of Spirits—who he thought were high ones—passing rapidly through the atmosphere and all going in the same direction. But this is all he knows.

Hoping to tranquillize Reine, who by this time is distracted, I speak to my father on subjects touching our researches. How does he see nature and people? Will he define his actual sensations and compare them with those he had on earth?—He sees about the same as he saw when living, though always a little indefinitely in the house. Out in the air he is more at ease and distinguishes with precision. Generally, when he enters a room, he feels a bit confused. He believes this depends upon the fluids that are there, ... but he does not understand why. He distinguishes clearly between day and night, and sees better at night: for instance, he cannot judge my pictures in the daytime, but at night he sees them perfectly well.

I ask other questions but, quite contrary to his habit and nature, he seems irritable. Reine remarks: "He's not as nice as usual, ... seems cross for nothing." So I do not try to keep him.

I propose another experiment, but Reine is nervous and demoralized, says that she cannot see clearly now. I tell her then to come back and rest a while.

But despair seizes her once more. The mystery becomes anguish. "If only he isn't lost!" she moans. "Will he never come back? Is he angry with me, do you think?"

I try to console her; nothing avails. She must go straight back again to hunt for him. But she no longer has the force to disengage herself; she cannot get free.

Then, plaintively, she calls: "Vettellini ?" She implores him: "Vettellini, oh my Vettellini!" But to no effect. Then she appeals to the old friend—softly at first, and choking with tears. Still no response. In the end she loses her temper and summons him irritably: "Come, Old Friend, come! Come!" ... Then one final vibrating call, imperative, dramatic: "*Old Friend!*" And, extenuated, she falls back in her chair ... only to leap forward again with a shout of joy: "Ah! ... it is you!" Her hands reach out eagerly towards him, her little body is shaking with sighs: "At last!—Now you will tell us. Speak!—Speak!"

Her desperate cry has reached him. He has come. It was not easy, but her torment had to cease at any cost.

Vettellini had tried this morning to warn her of what was happening, but she had not understood. They themselves (the great Spirits) have been suddenly surprised by an extraordinary condition in the cosmic currents. The interplanetary spaces, where they habitually dwell, have been literally swept by the passage of vibrations against which they have no possibility of struggling. They were all obliged to retreat, to move off out of reach. It is absolutely impossible for Vettellini to come down to us at this moment. He, Old Friend, has been able to accomplish it because he has more resistance, he is heavier. This condition began yesterday and will continue throughout tomorrow. He seems to consider it the passage of great subversive disorders on earth. But we must not be alarmed. This extraordinary influence will soon cease, and we shall resume our research with no other loss than that of time. Even tonight Vettellini will try to approach us; it may be possible towards eight o'clock.

He continues to speak a few moments longer, especially addressing my wife. Then he leaves us.

I discuss these strange happenings with Reine, still under the influence of her great emotion—"Well, you see, I'm not worth much without my Vettellini!" and once more the fear of his displeasure seizes her, "Oh, if only he is not angry with me!"

She had asked Old Friend, "He isn't going to get lost, is he?"—"Oh, no fear! ... We don't lose ourselves," was the jovial reply.

My wife and A. leave the room., I am on the point of waking Reine when I see that she is sobbing and weeping like a Madeline, "But ... I love him, my Vettellini, ... and I'm afraid of losing him!"

ONE-HUNDRED AND SECOND SÉANCE

December 19, 1913

Vettellini manifests his presence as soon as the child is sleeping. After a most delicious scene, where she expresses all her joy at finding him again, he explains the cause of his absence Wednesday. Reine has not quite accurately interpreted the communication of the old friend. The cosmic currents in question existed just as she reported them—vibrations sweeping everything aside, a precursory omen of terrible upheavals. *But it was precisely with a view to combat their fatal influence* that the great Spirits had withdrawn from the terrestrial atmosphere, all to unite in an immense effort to extricate France, and protect her yet a while from the imminent catastrophes.

To my enquiry: "Why this special protection for our country?" Vettellini replies that it is not a sentimental favor accorded to the French. It is a measure of utility for general evolution. It is better that France should not be swept into the tempest at this moment: it is better for all nations.

But the storm is only held in check; nonetheless inevitably will it break. It may be in February … it may be later, … but it is near. The hour will strike. *A great monarch will fall.*

The Maître observes that my fluid is extremely feeble. Reine and I are reaching the limit of our force … And for this reason he allows only one visit today, that of the Spirit of the woman who came last Monday. We will finish her case now.

I ask him, then, to let her come at once.

She arrives. This time she is quite materialized. Reine sees her distinctly and gives this description: Tall, rather thin, very dark, with fine black eyes and a long nose,—a beautiful Jewish type. The Spirit repeats her name and, at my request, spells it. There is no mistake, it is B. Her Christian name is Jeanne. She was forty-seven years old at the time of her death. She lived in D. street, number 3, second floor. But it was not there that she died. She had been carried to a hospital for an operation: appendicitis—infectious appendicitis. After her death her body had been carried directly to B., her native town. It was her son who accompanied her there.

I inquire about her husband. Was she a widow? Or, if her husband was living, why did he not escort her body himself? She answers that her husband was, and still is, living, but she had been separated from him for a long while. "Divorced?" I ask.—"No, not divorced: separated." She explains that her family is very religious, as she herself had been for that matter—and that her mother had threatened to disinherit her if she divorced. For her son's sake she had obeyed.

I ask the name of this son, his age and situation: "My son is twenty-five years old. His name is Marcel. He is a soldier at B., in the cavalry, but I cannot remember the regiment." To my remark that at twenty-five he should be liberated, she replies that he is studying to become an officer. She adds that he is a fine boy. They were devoted to each other.

I try to get more precise information about her husband. Her tone sharpens a bit. "He is a miserable creature, who made me most unhappy!" He was a bailiff. She has also lived in F. street number 15.

Thanking her for this information, valuable even as it stands, I ask if she will not give me some intimate detail of her life,—a characteristic fact, unknown to others, but of which I might nevertheless find trace. She must understand what weight such a fact would give to her testimony. Will she, for the sake of the work, confide in me?

She replies that if I will keep her secret,—that is, if I will promise on my honor not to give her real name in my book,—she will disclose the most intimate and the most important fact of her life.

I give my promise.

Then she says: "A priest was my lover. It is he who helped me to bring up and educate my son. After my separation from my husband I was obliged to learn a trade—millinery. I was twenty-four years old. He (the priest) helped me, and I managed at last to succeed."

I ask if this priest, this friend, still held a place in her life during the latter years—"Oh, yes!" was the swift reply ... "and my death was the greatest grief for him."

What was her impression after death? Was she surprised by the astral life—so different surely, from what she had expected, if she was, as she says, a good Catholic? She answers that it was indeed a great surprise; that at first she had suffered, not finding God—the God in whom she had believed. But this had not lasted long, because she had understood comparatively quickly that there was something else. Now she is happy,—"Oh, yes, *happier than on earth*! No more worries. I feel tranquil." She says that she has found some old friends, etc.

To my inquiry, she replies that her vision of our physical world is the same as when she was living here, only a trifle less distinct. She stays about Paris almost always. She loves Paris. And often she visits the churches; it continues to be a pleasure for her. She no longer believes, but she "honors the cult," etc.

Again I ask if we can do anything for her. But no, she wants nothing, she is happy. So then I thank her and she leaves us.

I will place right here our verification of the information given by this Spirit.

December 22, 1915

I have been able to verify the statements made by Madame B.
All, absolutely all, are correct in every detail.
By a curious chance, Madame Cornillier obtained the proof—quite unhoped for—of the existence of a priest in the intimate life of this woman. And it came about in this way: Madame B., milliner, had a faithful client, a certain American lady. When Madame Cornillier, an American, presented herself at the house indicated by the Spirit, the concierge—misled by her accent—mistook her, in the dim light of the lodge, for this client, and began with great volubility to give all the details of the illness and death of Madame B. It was only sometime after that the concierge, asking my wife if she still lived in the *rue Alphonse de Neuville*, discovered her error,—a most happy one from our point of view. By a judicious question here and there *absolutely every detail was corroborated*—illness, operation in hospital, death, burial at B., husband, son, priest, each statement made by the Spirit was reiterated by the concierge.

To return to the séance.

I ask Vettellini to clear up a point that has always been obscure to me. When, in the thirty-ninth séance, I evoked C. L., he, because of his very high evolution, had great difficulty in communicating. Reine could neither see nor understand him. This is in accordance with what has been told us about the constitution of Spirits belonging to a superior sphere. But, as I recall the scene, the Spirit C. L. was not much more successful with Vettellini, who was present. How, then, is it possible that Vettellini—a white Spirit, as we know—could not understand another white Spirit, even admitting that the latter be of higher evolution?

The Maître answers simply that, in order to come down to us and have the possibility of staying in our atmosphere three or four hours, he is obliged to place himself in special conditions, to surround himself with dense fluids, a heavy substance, and by this mere fact he is completely separated from his own class. It is a veritable cuirass that protects him, and momentarily deprives him of his normal relations. Reine compares the situation to that of a diver in his diving-bell.

This explanation is the more satisfactory in that certain incidents at St. Lunaire would tend to establish the same principle. I recall perfectly that on two different occasions, Reine announced that Old Friend was present, but that he could neither come very near us, nor communicate with us, because later on, he had to go to confer with the white Spirits, and he must not put himself in the conditions necessary for contact with us: it would render him too material and handicap him in his mission.

Harking back to the question of suicide, I remind Vettellini that he has definitely stated that those who commit suicide—all, without exception—place themselves in a bad situation. How then could Reine have seemed to say, incidentally, that this act sometimes helped in an evolution? Reine listens to her Guide, then turns to me: "Well, it's my fault again! I transmitted badly. Suicide always blocks evolution,—and painfully. A person who commits suicide is like one who has lost his way; who wanders about in space without comprehension,—and it may be for an endless time."

But what about the suicide committed as an act of supreme self-sacrifice, with the high aim of serving others?—"In any case evolution is arrested," affirms Vettellini; "but when the act has been accomplished from a high motive, the great Spirits recognize the fact and it counts to the good, when the normal course of evolution is resumed."

We talk book. Vettellini leaves the details to me. I, living, should know the best way of presenting our work. However, it seems to him that too huge a volume might be discouraging. Why not make two? He uses the word *tome*. Reine interrupts her transmission to say "Two ... what? Tome? ... *Deux Tomes*? What does that mean, Vettellini? Ah, I see ... that's not my business! Monsieur Cornillier understands. Hmm!" And vexed, she mutters to herself: "*Tome ... Tome*? It's the name of a dog!"

A-propos of Reine's dreams, to which she now refers, I express astonishment at the extraordinary power the great Spirits have of modifying individual destiny. What! They can decide suddenly, like that,—according to the stagnation, or the rapidity, of an evolution—to shorten or prolong a human life? This seems to me so tragically grave, and of such formidable consequence, that I am astounded that the personal decision of one, or any number of Spirits, no matter how high their evolution, should have weight in the question.

The Maître declares that the Spirit-Judges are incapable of error. The modifications made by them in a destiny, are always profitable to the evolution of the incarnated Spirit, and of his environment. For example, the normal destiny of Reine (according to planetary influences) has already been modified twice in the course of our association. She was destined to die very young. But her life was prolonged, the first time, on account of her role in this work. And now, because of her absolute devotion, and also as a legitimate reaction of the advantages that others will gain from this devotion, she will live to be happy herself. She wishes it, and this satisfaction will be given her. Moreover, the prolongation of her life will stimulate the evolution of those around her.

December 22, 1913

Reine announces that a message from Vettellini this morning warned her not to have a séance today.

I decide to consult the table, which immediately taps: "I forbid the séances for this entire week. You are too tired."

ONE-HUNDRED AND THIRD SÉANCE

December 29, 1913

I have realized the wisdom of Vettellini's injunction. I certainly could not have magnetized during the past week.

Today we begin as usual at three o'clock. Reine is sleeping profoundly. Her Guide comes at once to say that we are not in condition to receive the second unknown Spirit who has promised to give proofs of identity. Contact with new vibrations is the cause of great fatigue, not only for the medium, but for me as well, since she is obliged to take more of my force in order to resist. Today, again, we must be satisfied to merely talk together.

I wish to speak of my friend N., who came recently to read my notes and who begged me to transmit certain questions from him to Vettellini,—two of which I will record, as they are of general interest.

First: What is the significance of a souvenir which has obsessed him ever since his earliest consciousness—a scene of whose reality he has an intuitive conviction, which his reason cannot destroy:

He sees himself—and he comprehends that it is before his birth—surrounded by a group of white and luminous figures who are accompanying and leading him to a certain point in space. There these luminous phantoms encourage him, and say goodbye. Then he has the sensation of being caught in a sort of whirlwind and falling into an abyss, ... and it is over; he loses consciousness. From infancy, as far back as he is conscious of anything, he has been conscious of this vision; and from the moment that he began to express himself he spoke of it and asked *when and where it had happened.* His parents, naturally, considered it pure nonsense and set him down to toys, to dissipate such foolish dreams. But the child's obsession persisted, and throughout his entire life he has been pursued by it. Even today he sees that strange scene and, despite all his reasoning, it has the full force of reality for him.

(My friend is a doctor and a savant of high authority.)

Vettellini, who had taken contact with N. during his visit here, says that it is the persistent recollection of what veritably happened at the moment of his reincarnation. This reincarnation was voluntary, and decided by common accord between the great Spirits and himself, in order that he might gain in this new life that in which he was lacking. His preceding life had been particularly valuable and had brought him to a very good degree of evolution. He had remained only a short time in the Astral, preferring, of his own free will, to finish quickly; and having, moreover, but little to acquire. His present life is, relatively, one of repose. And it will suffice. He will not reincarnate.

Second question for my friend: Can Vettellini foresee the future of Islam?

Reply: There will be in the future a prodigious development in the Islamic peoples. But we shall not see it, at least not from this side. What we are going to see is, on the contrary, a diminishing of their power, both political and martial. But they can wait; all time is theirs. *The moment will come when the peoples of Islam, united, will rise and cast out all foreign elements and influences.*

Vettellini remarks that the revolt of the Mahomedans subject to the French or British rule in the colonies, revolt which may give them back certain conquered territories and a relative independence, must not be confounded with this formidable expansion of the Islamic races. I ask if the Slavonic race also is not destined to a considerable development. *"It is destined to be sorely tried. The Slaves will drown themselves in blood,"* replies Vettellini, *"but unlike the Latin and Gallic races, they will resist by their number. Nevertheless, the future centre of world power lies in Asia, not Europe."*

I want to be sure that I have made no mistake in writing that all stillborn children are of high evolution. Is it absolute? Are there no exceptions?—"It is absolute. All children dead in confinement—whether it be premature or retarded, by accident or by surgical operation,—all without exception, are Spirits of high evolution lacking only one small point, one jewel in their crown, which they gain in this way. For this imprisonment in matter is most painful for a Spirit who is conscious. If the child lives a few weeks, a few months, or a few years, it is because his degree is less high, and he has something more to gain. Each individual case is predetermined,—premature confinement, mortal accident, idiocy, etc. *Chance has no part in any of them."*

And this rouses again my old obsession: the formidable power of the great Spirits to interfere in the life of a human being. Can they, then, never make a mistake?—"No. They cannot make a mistake." And Vettellini adds: "Do not try to understand what is so far beyond your actual means of comprehension. This power of the great Spirits astonishes and terrifies you, and yet it is nothing—or, in any case, little—in comparison with what is. Already, in what I have disclosed to you, there are points that will make people doubt your sanity. But you have, so far, been able to grasp my teachings—or at least to have a presentiment of their value. And what I have said is just nothing compared with what I might say. But it is enough. First, because it is about the limit of your comprehension, and then, too, because more might destroy the value of what may be considered rational in my communications. It would only provoke doubt ... And you yourself would lose your footing."

I had decided to evoke again the Spirit who came with such pitiful results at the fifty-first séance, thinking that the failure may have been due to the presence of my friend R. (son of the Spirit), whose fluid is always more or less disturbing to my medium. I had asked R. to confide the lock of hair to me for this purpose. Curious to see if, after seven months, the evocation has the same result, I now place the little package of hair in Reine's hands.

She says that she knows this fluid, ... she has felt it before, and she does not like it,—not that it is bad ... no, but it is young. And, anyway, she does not like it! Vettellini intervenes to say that it is useless to send Reine to seek this Spirit. We could get no more from him today, nor at the end of a year, than we had the first time. He is, and he still will be, in a state of unconsciousness.

I explain that I wish to repeat the experiment because I have reason to believe that on earth he was a man of superior cultivation, and it seems impossible that he should still be in a state of coma thirty years after his death—not even knowing whether he had been a man or a woman in his last incarnation! But Vettellini asserts that the case is not so abnormal as I seem to think. Time does not exist in the Astral—not, at least, in our sense. Thirty years is an important period for us: for a Spirit it is neither much nor little. The reason why this soul does not waken from his torpor is simply that he is just beginning, that he is young. He will reincarnate blindly, swept along by the wave of incarnation to which he belongs. He has had only a few human lives as yet, but the last organism in which he was incarnated was of such perfect constitution that, with just a little start, it ran along of itself. He understands nothing of the Astral and needs terrestrial life for his evolution. "Every one has to begin," says Reine. "We have all been like that. Each one his turn."

I remark that our social order would be pretty well upset if individuals were to be considered from this point of view. After all, is there any criterion for estimating an evolution? Any signs revealing the level of an incarnated Spirit?—"Beyond intuitive recognition,—i.e., the recognition of soul by soul—there are a number of exterior signs," replies Vettellini; "one or two of them I will give. First, *bonté*. But the *bonté* that understands: that is to say, an indulgence for others proceeding from a deep knowledge of the human soul. This *bonté* is intelligent and recognizes the necessity of sanction and severity. *Bonté-sévérité* (a benevolent severity) is, then, one sign to remember. Second: interest in the humble, the unimportant, the weak,—an interest which is necessarily accompanied by an indifference to social success, honors and position. And, finally, all inclination for philosophical speculations, all preoccupation in the mystery of the Au-Delà, and all effort to penetrate that mystery,—this is evolution itself!"

I ask if the relations which we just now have with the Au-Delà, are not, in a way, abnormal and contrary to the natural law.—"Yes, certainly they are!" exclaims Vettellini. "All communications and teachings, all open and direct influence, will cease on the day when the majority of people regain the simple sure faith in survival after death. Materialism, should it prevail, would end in not only provoking a suspension of evolution, but in a return to barbarism and animality. It is to check this retrogression that the Spirits have decided to manifest themselves from time to time, to here and there light a torch, so to speak, as a guide to humanity."

"But," interrupts Reine, turning to us, "you notice that they do not mean to help much, either. People often say that if they really exist and can manifest themselves, very well, they have only to do it openly, and all the world would believe! *But that is just what they cannot do! Unveiling the mystery would not advance the spirituality of people. Each one has to work for himself and conquer his own evolution."*

A-propos of destinies, and the prescience that great Spirits may have of them, I say that it has seemed to me, from certain words and incidents in the course of the communications, that Vettellini, in spite of his high evolution, has not been able to foresee with absolute certainty just how his work would turn out; that, great Spirit though he be, he was obliged to reckon with the unexpected. And he tells me that *at no moment in the construction of his plan has he been sure of the result.* It was not permitted that he should know the future of his own work: he could only study the field of operation, and prepare his tactics. He began by analyzing our fluids. That was one of the essential bases. Despite their dissimilarity, they had to be able to combine and work together without friction. Then came our various degrees of evolution—another primordial element. After that followed the, not intrinsic, but very important questions of situation, environment, independence, etc. The careful study of all this brought him a conviction, but not a certainty. The unforeseen, the unexpected, was still considerable, and had to be reckoned with: our health, the accidents of circumstance, *our own free wills*, etc., etc.

We have seen how the medium's health, as well as my own, has completely arrested all experiments in material phenomena, whereas her extraordinary devotion, and my perseverance, have permitted an unexpected development on another plane,—communication with superior Spirits. Vettellini was so far from foreseeing this, at the debut, that it had been his plan and intention to have Reine give in automatic writing, all the communications which I have received directly at each séance. He, too, had hoped for materializations, but to pursue this direction would have been to risk the child's life.

ONE-HUNDRED AND FOURTH SÉANCE

December 31, 1913

Reine comes late and in bad condition, worn out with the neuralgia that had not ceased to torment her for days. Yesterday she was impelled to try the table, but though it responded immediately to contact with her hands, she could not follow it for even two minutes, so exasperated was she with pain. She is sure that the communication was important, but she could not sit long enough to receive it; she suffered too much.

I hypnotize her without difficulty, giving, however, a little more time than usual. Vettellini comes at once and tries to communicate, but Reine only half hears and does not understand. Undoubtedly, then, in face of the difficulty, her Guide changes his method, for after a short delay, the child's usual delivery is modified. Quite evidently it is no longer she who transmits what she hears; it is he who speaks directly through her organism. The voice is deep and hoarse, and the words fall peremptorily from her lips. "Pierre," says the voice, "I forbid the séances during the whole month of January. You are both too ill. Listen to me. You will have the proofs you want just the same; I promised them; they are ready. I hoped to finish in a few days now, but Reine has reached the pitcher's limit: one drop more, and it might overflow! At this moment rest will restore her, whereas if I taxed her ever so little, her health might be permanently affected. Meanwhile, you will work on your notes; I will be with you. In case of doubt or difficulty use the table."

After a short rest for the medium, he resumes: "When I began to employ Reine, I knew that she would suffer from it; but I concealed this from you, for you would have refused to go on with the work, and it was necessary to go on with it. *It had to be.* Moreover, it is evolution for you both. But we must not risk the irreparable. The week's rest she has just taken, brought no change in her condition, and this shows it is time to stop. A month will be none too long. But I will not leave you, I will be there helping you, stimulating you. If you need to consult me, question me aloud at the table,—as though Reine were not there: she will remember nothing."

The direct transmission is finished. Reine seems to escape from her torpor and speaks for herself, showing that the chief point of the message has impressed her: "But why do you stop the séances Vettellini? No, no, I'm not ill!" She discusses the question with her Guide and, from words that fall, we learn that yesterday when she was suffering beyond endurance, she had appealed to him as to the *Bon Dieu*, beseeching him to help her, *to take away her pain.* Vettellini evidently reminds her of this, to make her understand why she absolutely must stop and rest. Turning to me, she says with emotion: "You know another,—even a high Spirit—would not have hesitated to break me to get the result. In one year we have had what should have taken at least three. And of course my health had to suffer— but just see the care he takes of me! How he has watched over me!"

Here again Vettellini seems to borrow Reine's vocal chords to enunciate with a deep and noble gravity, difficult to imagine when one has not heard it: "*I must not do otherwise than well,*" ... And after a moment's silence he adds with tenderness: "Nor you either, for that matter."

One incident follows another; impossible to note them all. Reine tells us the sentiment she has for her Guide, how she fears his displeasure when she is in her normal state, awake; but how she sometimes tries to trick herself into believing that he will not see her when she does something which she knows she should not do. A certain window-washing scene is matchless. Vettellini had expressly forbidden her to do any scrubbing—of linen or apartment—and after the séance, when she was awake, I had transmitted the order to her. So then, she knew perfectly well that she was wrong to wash the windows. "But," she now explains to me, "they were dirty! So then ... h'm ... what else could I do? And anyway, *tant pis!*—He can't always be there watching me!" But as soon as she began washing them on the outside, she felt the breath of Vettellini on her face and understood, perfectly well, what it meant; but determined to have a clean house, she resolutely muttered: "Oh, that ? That's only the air!" and continued ... A new and more imperious warning made her jump down precipitately and close the window. Still rebellious, however, she said aloud: "Well, any way, I can wash them on the inside—that couldn't hurt anyone!" And again she set to work. Another blast in her face and Reine, hurrying on all the faster, cried: "Oh, that's nothing!—It's just wind from the door! But at that very instant she sprang from her perch, hastily gathered up cloths and basin, flew to stow them away and, her back bent, her knees trembling, threw herself into an armchair, *frightened to death*. Outside, against the window pane, with stern eyes and frowning brow, the head of Vettellini had appeared!

Now, in hypnosis, she laughs at the scene, and slyly confesses: "I knew quite well that it wasn't the wind!"

We speak of the following day—January 1, 1914. Reine is coming with Armand to wish us a happy new year, and half-laughingly, I say that we would all like to wish it to Vettellini, but probably the end or the beginning of a year are equally indifferent to him?

Immediately he protests. It is not at all indifferent to him to receive expressions of affection; sympathy is most precious to him. He will be here tomorrow to receive our good wishes. And, after a moment, as we were all reflecting, he gravely says: "Am I not living in your midst?"

Impossible to convey the tenderness of the words. We are silent with emotion, when he adds: "My greatest satisfaction is your confidence. Yes, *I know* that you have faith!"

Old Friend arrives. Knowing that this is our last séance for some time he came to talk with his friend Anne.

Vettellini interrupts to give various recommendations for Reine's health. Again he alludes ambiguously to our destinies.—"You will finish the book and see it published ... You will have to defend it."—"You see, it has to be you," remarks Reine, "what could I do? I am too little!"

Vettellini says that, before waking her, I must imperiously suggest that when she makes her astral sorties in the night, she must not try to discover our destinies by reading the signs of the cosmic currents. It seems that she revels in this kind of investigation, and what she discovers becomes mixed up with her organic dreams, so that when she wakens, she is profoundly troubled. This does her no good. I must order her to keep quiet for this month.[96]

---

[96] I made the suggestion as imperiously as possible. The 12th and 16th of January she spontaneously expressed astonishment that she, whose head was always upside down with dreams, dreamed no more.

I speak of the various phenomena which I see or feel almost every night now, as soon as my light is extinguished: sparks and phosphorescence; or a slightly luminous cloudy substance which condenses around a brilliant centre; and, occasionally, what looks like waves of light. Often, too—and this even in the day time and generally while I am working—I feel a cool and moist whiff of air on my face, the left side usually; sometimes a light touch on my face and hands; and—rarely this—raps on my pillow or the wall. Reine says that perhaps, in the end, I shall see a materialization of Vettellini's head, for it is in this way that her own visions began. In explaining her experience she makes use of the word "condensed," but stops short in confusion. It is Vettellini who cuts off her phrase with a laugh: "'Condensed,' forsooth! You don't even know what that means." Reine is vexed. First of all she can use the word that pleases her! And, after that, "condensed" means "put together" ... Anyone knows that much!

January 16, 1914

Reine came to see us this afternoon. We tried to have a communication by the table. After a few moments of contact it tapped: "I authorize a séance Monday."

January 19, 1914

No séance today. A new communication forbade it. We are not yet in condition, it is more prudent to wait till Wednesday.

ONE-HUNDRED AND FIFTH SÉANCE

January 21, 1914

W̲e begin at two o'clock. Reine sleeps well and gives at first different communications of no general interest.

I call Vettellini's attention to the criticism that may legitimately be made of the remarkable case of identity furnished by Madame B., the milliner. She lived in Paris, and in Reine's quarter of the city. The immediate thought of an outsider will be that Reine knew beforehand the circumstances which she transmitted. I ask him, then, to procure us the identification of a Spirit who has lived and died in a distant town that neither Reine nor I have ever visited.[97] Vettellini promises to give me satisfaction.

An allusion to the early séances brings up a rather interesting question. Reine declared more than once, at that time, that she saw her fluidic body disengaged and standing not far from her, while, at the same moment her physical body was lying back in the big chair. Where, then, was the centre of vision at that moment? It is she herself who answers

---

[97] Not that even this will avail. It may always be said that Reine had known the person, in her lifetime, or a friend of the person or a friend of the friend etc. No case is proof against the suspicion of the sceptical. There are on record examples of spirit identity that defy all rationalistic explanation. They have never yet convinced one who chooses to deny them.

me, saying that in those first séances her fluidic vision remained still in her physical organism, because her fluidic body was not yet completely disengaged. She perceived what was disengaged of her fluidic body, by looking at it from her material organism, and she saw her material body as she ordinarily did when she was awake, that is, as though she had opened her eyes and glanced down at her chest, her knees, her hands, etc. A fairly complete disengagement is necessary before the centre of vision passes into the fluidic body.

I have often remarked the importance that music seems to have in astral life, and it is relatively easy to understand how there might be possibilities for this art in the more subtle conditions of matter. But painting? What becomes of our pictorial art in the world of Spirits? Vettellini says that there is no precise analogy to the practice of this art in the Astral, but the faculties of a painter may, nevertheless, find expression there: *the creation of images and scenes*, for example, offers innumerable opportunities. But we cannot understand this exactly; it is beyond our conceptions.

ONE-HUNDRED AND SIXTH SÉANCE

February 12, 1914

S ince January 21, Reine has been very ill with *grippe*, and we have had only rare communications by the table, which, the day before yesterday, announced a short séance for today.

She sleeps rapidly. Vettellini comes at once and forbids all experiment today. I may ask only what is necessary for my work on the book.

I beg him to confirm his explanation of the flat materializations produced by certain mediums, and why they sometimes give the effect of being made of pleated paper.[98] He explains that these flat materializations require much less fluidic substance than those having volume, "and the medium, or rather the Spirit-Guide of the medium, chooses this method for that reason; it is a great economy of force. They are veritably images. As to the wrinkles and pleats, or the various other defects of formation, and even the deformations which may exist, they are due to insufficient materialization—to a lack of efficiency in the operator. These flat images are often thin as gauze, and there is nothing astonishing in the fact that they are sometimes wrinkled and irregular, or even that a bit of the border be folded back."

---

[98] See the photographs taken during the séances of Madame Bisson and *The Phenomena of Materialization*, Dr. von Schrenck Notzing (Eng. Trans., Regan & Paul, London, 1920).

What is Vettellini's opinion of the faculty, which certain mediums seem to have, of producing exact images of things seen by them in their ordinary daily life? For instance, the man's head that was photographed in a séance with Linda Gizzard, and which is the exact reproduction of one of Ruben's studies in the Louvre?

The Maître replies that this is perfectly possible. But I insist that in this materialization produced by Linda, the most trifling details of the study were discovered (affirmed by M. de Fontenay)—even the irregularities of the brush work. Is such a thing really possible?

Vettellini affirms that the created image—following an impression previously received by the medium—may conform in every respect to the original, and may reproduce the most insignificant details. "And this should give you an idea of how acute is vision, and how complete is memory, in the astral plane," he adds.

I remark that I have not been conscious of Vettellini's presence during the past few days. Why has he not come?—He has come as usual, but finding me physically too depressed, he would not take from me the fluid necessary to produce the slight manifestations I sometimes perceive.

March 9, 1914

As Reine has suffered from the séance of February 12th, we have followed the advice of the Guide without protest, and have abandoned all hypnosis for the time being. The table, only, is allowed to maintain contact between us. But the table has given some interesting points,—one of the really curious being the distinctive character of its movements, differing totally as the communicating force is Vettellini, Old Friend, my father, or another. When it is Vettellini who speaks, it taps noiselessly; it is gentle, regular, and rapid, without a break or a shock. Old Friend, on the contrary, announces his presence by a sudden lifting and a violent bang; then the blows fall,—sharp, impetuous and hurried. In the course of conversation, when they are both present, the movement of the one suddenly inserts itself in the movement of the other, exactly as an interrupting word cuts the phrase of a person speaking. It is extremely curious,—and inimitable. My friend A. who has several times assisted at a "table-talk" was as impressed as we ourselves by the spontaneity and surprise of it. As to my father, who has manifested three times by the table (the first and second times aided by Vettellini), his movement is again quite different; it is hesitating, awkward, and achieved with difficulty. He does not know how to stop in time, so that frequently we must note the letter preceding the one that he has designated,—revert to *f*, when he taps *g*, to *r* when he taps *s*, etc. Nicolo and Méhul have also come to say a few words, and each in his own individual style. I asked the cause of this variety of movement when high Spirits are speaking,—since we know that they do not operate for themselves but make use of inferiors for this irksome task. Vettellini explained that the operator expresses, by his movement, the nature of the influence which he himself receives from the Spirit who is employing him.

Amongst the different communications by the table I will mention those of February 16, 19 and 20, giving advice and directions as to the choice of a publisher. In the first place Vettellini announces that he will investigate this question himself. Then, three days in advance, he indicates the precise moment when I must go to see the publisher: "Friday, in the afternoon,—at three o'clock." Now I know that this publisher receives only in the morning; but my statement to this effect only provokes an imperative repetition of the order.

Accordingly, on the day and at the hour indicated, I present myself at the publishing house, merely to be informed that Monsieur X. is not there, that he never comes in the afternoon, that he receives only in the morning. (Ah, Vettellini!) Disappointed, I linger a moment, ... then turn to leave the shop, when another clerk calls me back. *By some unusual chance, Monsieur X. is in his office and receives me.*

Several quite definite predictions, touching political events and prominent people, have been given both by Vettellini and the old friend. None of these predictions have been realized,—which fact gives rise to a curious incident on March 4. Scarcely are we seated at the table when Old Friend arrives and announces that Vettellini is not coming.—Why? "He is displeased with Pierre."

Again—why? "Pierre is sulking. He is cross because the predictions are not realized. He resents it." This is interesting, for it is a fact that I have been feeling rather sore, finding it inexplicable that affirmations which are *spontaneous and reiterated* should not prove correct. At least I would have liked from the prophets an equally spontaneous explanation! And it is true—I have been sulking. *But my discontent was secret; no one has had the least suspicion of my state of mind.*

In the midst of Old Friend's vigorous and impetuous blows—which we try with all our power to moderate—the gentle tapping of Vettellini suddenly intervenes. Reine, who has been grieving over his absence, gives a cry of joy.—"Pierre, you ought to understand how *events written in the Astral may be modified.*" I protest that I do understand it, but that, on such terms, a prediction has nothing of the transcendental; it does not differ from a human opinion. Vettellini taps a few words of conciliation,—he knows how I have worked, he is pleased, he is very busy. "What about?" asks Reine.—"Preparing for the reception of the new teaching," is the reply.

On March 7th, the Maître speaks at length of my life and private affairs. I mention the name of the person to whom I intend to give my notes, for copying. The table moves nervously then strikes out the word "Fool!"—"Fool?—Who fool?"—"You!" flings back the table in a wild movement. This is unexpected, but perhaps not unmerited, and we all laugh. The Maître must be deeply stirred to abandon his gentle tapping.

A possible séance for March 11th is announced.

ONE-HUNDRED AND SEVENTH SÉANCE

March 11, 1914

O n arriving Reine tells me that she consulted the table this morning, to know if we could have the promised séance. For the first time it is the old friend who came to inform her, and the violence of his movement was such that the child was fairly frightened. The phrase spelled out was this: "Yes, a great séance today! A voyage,—a grand one! You will be glad."

And, in fact, the séance has been one of the most remarkable. During four long hours Reine has not ceased one instant to either transmit for Vettellini and Old Friend or to speak on her own responsibility. Never before has she attained this degree of lucidity. Indeed, as her Guide remarked, her astral state was almost equivalent to that after death. For example, she could clearly see her own precedent lives,—and mine, and Vettellini's—and describe minutely the physical and mental conditions and environment of each of them.

So much has been seen, described, scrutinized and analyzed in this séance, that it is impossible to write a detailed account; a volume would hardly contain it. I will note only the chief incidents in the order of their occurrence.

We begin at 2.30 p.m. In the obscurity Reine notices a quantity of little bluish lights all around me, but more intense than usual; and I have barely begun the passes when she sleeps. Presently she lifts herself in her chair, seeming to remark something unusual over my head. Gently she protests: "No, don't come like that. I can't allow it. Go away. Stay near him, if you want to; but you mustn't sit on him." She reaches out her hand and brushes an invisible something from my hair, repeating with emphasis: "No, no! You must not stay here.—On one side, if you like, but not on top of him!" I ask to whom she is speaking—"It's Paul who comes like that on the top of your head! I won't have it. It would make me take his fluid—which would do me no good. I won't have it!"

She sinks back in her chair, and I continue to magnetize her for about twenty minutes, when she suddenly starts forward and begins to speak. It is the old friend. I gather from her words that there is question of a voyage. "You're going to take me with you? ... Far? ... Across the ocean?" But the child is frightened at this prospect. She wants Vettellini with them, insists upon his presence.

He too arrives, and after a moment's talk together, off they start— all three of them.

From this moment Reine's enunciation becomes slightly automatic. I realize that her Guide has put her in a special state, that she may formulate aloud the impressions of her voyage as they succeed each other. And not only does she express all that she herself is seeing and feeling, but she repeats everything that she hears her two protectors say, so that we are able to follow step by step the unfolding of this truly strange adventure.

It is Old Friend who is Guide—and host; for we soon realize that they have reached the city of X., and that he has conducted them to the house that was his, and which still exists almost as it was in his lifetime. Reine's reflections have informed us of their crossing the ocean; of their passing over American country; and then suddenly, to her great amazement, of their arrival at water again! She dilates over its beauty—so blue, so endless, and so calm! She admires the home of their host, splendidly situated, with its big gardens and comfortable porches dominating the water from a high cliff.[99]

Now they have entered the house. Suddenly Reine's interest—and

---

[99] The description is exact. It must be understood that we gather this not from what Reine says to us—she is wholly unconscious of our existence now—but from the constant stream of words that fall from her lips, now addressed to Vettellini, now to the "Old Friend," and again to her repetition of all they say to her. She does not cease speaking.

certainly our own—becomes acute: Old Friend is no longer the beautiful blue flame that she knows so well. He is changing. Redeeming a vague promise which he gave us in a former séance (the sixtieth), he is materializing—assuming human form. He is a person now—an important person, with a commanding air; and he is receiving in his home and showing his possessions with great ease of manner,—authoritative and fascinating at the same time. Reine describes his physical aspect with remarkable precision. She sees him tall (he spontaneously avows that he has made himself look taller than he really was); full-bodied; full, strong cheeks; eyes sparkling with malice; a pucker at the lips giving a slightly mocking expression; magnificent hair, etc. He wears a frock coat with wide silk lapels, a low-cut waistcoat with fine buttons—rather showy—a high collar, up to his chin, and a big cravat, wrapped around and around, and whose points fall negligently under his chin.

All this is exact. But what is more remarkable is the prodigiously acute observation of the bearing of the man, his walk, gestures, manners, his whole way of being; even his voice, so vibrant and warm; even to the swift changes of its accent, from imperious to winning and caressing—when he chooses! Nothing escapes her.

My wife is deeply moved, for she clearly recognizes her old friend in this detailed description, in which the child seems to delight, and which he himself enjoys. Evidently he stands with complacency to be examined. When she mentions his hands—"so fine and well kept"—he makes her look again, insisting that she shall admire his nails—"my greatest vanity," he says (and my wife laughingly attests the truth of this statement).

Finally, when she has fully appreciated his royal manners and his captivating charm, he gives her the elements of another portrait: the man he was mentally and morally. He analyzes himself, says what he was, what he wanted, how he conducted his life and affairs. And this gives rise to many ejaculations, for the child is puzzled and quite disconcerted by the *finesse* of the man of business,—"But Old Friend ... do you really mean that? ... You said one thing ... and then you did another thing? ... What! ... You told your friends that you were going to buy that stock, that it was sure ... and then, off you went and bought something else in secret? ... *Well*! Ah? You must never let anyone know what you are going to do? No need to mix them up in your affairs ... I see.—But afterwards? They must have known you had ... misled them? ... It doesn't matter? Ah, yes! I see ...You said that you had changed your mind!" etc., etc.—The definition is complete.

And now they are inspecting the house: and here occurs a subtle scene, rather difficult to invent. Old Friend shows with just pride, a large, fine drawing room, spacious bedrooms, and his own private study, all substantially furnished in a style that excites my little model's naive admiration. Two or three observations prove that her vision is a real one. For instance, she is astonished to find herself suddenly in a small place, dark—almost like a closet, she says—that separates two fine big rooms. (This construction exists, in fact.) But after a time she remarks that he has not shown her the dining room. She would like to see that, too; it must be something splendid in so fine a house. Her host, however, does not seem particularly interested, ... calls her attention, rather, to the view of the lake. But Reine insists, and they pass into the room in question—Exclamation:—"Why! ... it looks ..." She hesitates. "But, Old Friend, it's all dark, I can't see anything. The window is closed.— Open it. I want to see." But the master of the house is already turning in another direction, and to the child's obstinate "Open the window. Let me at least glance at your room. It must be beautiful," he imperiously calls back: "Come out to the cliffs now!" And off he leads them!

(This curious incident is explained in a following séance when Old Friend, pressed by my wife, confesses that he had always been a little ashamed of the modesty of his dining room, which, it seems, was not in keeping with the rest of the house.)

And then we know that they are out on the cliff, contemplating the lake, and talking together with such prodigious reality that we seem to be right there with them. Reine grows more and more lucid. This view of the water brings back the souvenir of former lives passed in Italy and the Orient. She recounts to her two friends certain incidents in these lives; makes descriptions and comparisons. She recalls her life in Naples, in Capri, speaks of Sicily, describes in minute detail different aspects of Vesuvius.[100] In Capri she was familiar with a house in which Vettellini lived later on; she gives its exact situation. She also remembers various strange aspects of nature in these regions. She has seen the sea just like boiling water,—when the lava, pouring down the flanks of Vesuvius, was swallowed up by it. She mentions a complete absence of birds in that beautiful sky, etc., etc. Then she turns to the Orient and is astonished that Old Friend has never had the curiosity to go there since he became a Spirit.—"But why don't you go? It would

---

[100] Needless to say that in her natural state Reine does not even know the names of these places.

be so easy for you now! Ah, yes,—you like the Stock Exchange better.[101] Well, one of these days we must go together. I'll take you ... Oh, Egypt! I know it well!" And she reverts to the time when she was a "healer" in Egypt,—a healer of the soul and body. In that life she was with Vettellini. They were friends,—he, already more advanced than she, higher than she, protecting her (or rather him, for in that incarnation she was a man.) She remarks that, in the Orient, astral life is more perceptible because of the atmospheric conditions. The natives who are of fair evolution are constantly conscious of contact with the disincarnate.

And here again Reine exclaims (as she has more than once in the course of this amazing séance), that never will she be able to remember and transmit it all to Monsieur Cornillier. Vettellini reassures her, saying that he has made her talk aloud; but she only half believes him, says it is impossible that she could have said aloud in Paris what she is seeing and feeling in America! How could that be? She will go back and find out if it is true!

And back she comes.

I assure her that I have followed every step; and, conversation being established between us again, I take my share in it.

Following a reflection from Vettellini concerning my private life, I am brought to speak of myself and of various failings and weaknesses in my past—small meannesses and faults which I recall all too vividly, alas! Does Vettellini know about them? Does he know what I mean? It is Reine who replies: "Vettellini knows the most insignificant acts of your life, of Madame Cornillier's, and of mine. But he says that in spite of your failings you have always had a conscience, *and for those who have conscience, faults serve. By means of them we rise."*

I raise the question of responsibility, pointing out the evident injustice of an inequality in the initial tendencies of human beings. If germs start out from the absolute, unequal, possessing from the very beginning unequal capacities for reaction, how may people be held responsible for the strength, or the weakness, of their resistance to their environment? Vettellini answers:

"The apparent injustice of Destiny is corrected by the fact that the forces that drive a soul towards evil are always proportioned to the

---

[101] "Old Friend" explains that he has sought in the Astral—but on a higher plane—the satisfaction of the interests that prevailed in his earthly life. He has not tried to investigate questions which were indifferent to him then. He has not run about the universe in quest of new sensations. The great financial centers have been his points of interests.

resisting capacity of that soul. The responsibility of each being is deter-mined by his liberty and his degree of consciousness."

Again the talk turns to private matters, and then to the Spirit Paul who, it would seem, comes often to be with us, and who, though he has been in the Astral over a year, is still always in a kind of dream. "In fact," says Reine, "he does not seem to make it out. It is strange, he is less strong than he looked. When he was living he was considered rather superior because he gathered right and left from everyone; he got his brilliancy from others. It will take longer for him to find himself than seemed probable at first." I express the hope that at our death we shall be able to see a little more clearly. "Oh, we are already partly living in the Astral," she returns, "we are studying the conditions of life there—the different ways of being. We shall find ourselves at home at once."

And here she begins to speak of my past lives, which she seems to see very clearly, but her Guide cuts her short.

I ask how does Vettellini explain the animals that calculate, the super-intelligent animals, so to speak?—"The animal kingdom[102] (sub-hom-inal) is belated in its evolution. If we did not look out, the earth might come to an end before animals have achieved the evolution they were destined to gain here. They are actually being stimulated. Certain ones amongst them, sufficiently developed in reality to migrate to anoth-er planet for a superior incarnation, are forced to reincarnate in their old class on earth. It is, first of all, a means of hastening the evolution of individuals of their own race; but it is *also a means of attracting the attention of human beings*, that they, too, may help on this evolution, by their study, their interest and their care." As to the extraordinary faculty for counting and computing manifested by some of them, this is explained by the fact that the mathematical faculty is only another sense, so to speak, not an intellectual development. "The sense of num-bers exists just as the sense of smell exists; it has nothing whatever to do with conscious intelligence and evolution."

I return to a statement that has been made about human auras. Does the color blue predominate in proportion to the degree of evolution?—"Yes. In the beginning red predominates; then, gradually, it is equalized by blue, and finally, as evolution progresses, the blue imposes itself."

Another question: the point of attachment of the Spirit's fluidic cord to his dead body. In case of embalming, the brain is removed from the

---

[102] See in *Les Annales des Sciences Psychiques* the accounts about the dog of Mannheim (numbers of January and February, 1914).

skull and discarded; where, then, is the fluidic cord attached?—"It remains attached to the interior walls of the skull."—When the fluidic body is disengaged (during one's waking hours) does it stand preferably on the left side of the physical body as many sensitives attest?—"Yes,—because of the heart action, which would be affected if the fluidic body stood on the right."

One more remark. Old Friend announces that by his interest in our work, and his own contribution to it, he has acquired a new element of consciousness; his concepts are broader and he has passed into a higher sphere. I ask Vettellini how this passage to a higher sphere is effected. Is it a decision of the Spirit-Judges, a recompense awarded? Or is it, rather, an automatic classification resulting from a change in density?

The Maître replies that it is neither one nor the other.—"The passage to a higher sphere is accomplished by the mere fact of understanding what is higher. *One becomes superior the moment one understands that which is superior.*"

And here my account of the séance must close, with much still unexplained, and much not even noted. But I wish to affirm once more what I stated in the beginning: *Today Reine has seemed to see and understand everything.* She has analyzed her role in the work, the conditions of it, and our individual characters. She has revealed various aspects of life in the Astral and fixed, in a measure, the responsibilities of life on earth; and all this with a lucidity and an authority altogether remarkable.

Note:

One may seek the rational explanation of this visit to the house of the old friend. Was it a real visit? And if so, how is one to understand this story of a closed window which he refused to open; and other details, such as the furniture as it existed in his lifetime, but which has since been dispersed? Or, was it rather a series of images, created by the master of the house, to give Reine an impression of old existing realities? And, in this case, was not the whole voyage, then, an impression artificially created?—Reine's astral body remaining all the time in our little salon, where she was in hypnotic sleep.

According to the explanation given there was, as a matter of fact, an association of the two phenomena. Vettellini, Old Friend and Reine, did indeed go to America, to the city of X., and visited the house in which Old Friend had lived, which still exists the same in structure and arrangement, but without the furniture of his time. He then, by making use of the vibrations registered and preserved in the environment—by the walls, the floors, the woodwork, etc.,—reconstituted the appearance of his dwelling as it existed in his lifetime. The fact of being on the spot where he had lived so long, of finding effluvia and emanations still subsisting there and giving trace of different incidents in his life, enabled him to recreate, with more force than he otherwise could, the images he wished Reine to see. Had they stayed in Paris, in an absolutely foreign milieu where nothing of his own could be found, he could have produced only feeble subjective images for her, without reality. But in his own house he found all the materials needed for vigorous objective ones.

If the reader will consult the definitions, given at the debut of these séances, of subjective and objective images and materializations, he will readily understand the reason which determined the trip to America. They were indeed images that Reine perceived, but objective ones with a slight degree of materialization. To produce the phenomenon with ease and intensity, they were obliged to be on the spot.

See also in the eighty-ninth and ninetieth séances the passages relative to Reine's visit to A.'s house, escorted there by Vettellini. In that case the phenomenon was less complex, but of exactly the same nature as in this of the Old Friend's voyage: and a comprehension of the one leads to a comprehension of the other.

1915

This long and impressive séance—the 107th—completely exhausted the poor child, and Vettellini, at the following séance (which I undertook only when I judged her entirely recovered), imposed an absolute abstention from all research during several months. He had, however, brought with him that very day, so he said, two Spirits capable of furnishing the examples I so intensely desired,—Spirits of people unknown to us, who had lived and died in distant towns, and who were able to give proofs of identity which could be controlled. But he was obliged to warn me that the two or three séances that would be required for this experiment might gravely compromise the health of the medium, adding: "It is for you to decide. I will do all that is possible to protect her, but the risk is indeed great."

In face of this risk—which I myself could easily appreciate,—there was evidently only one thing to do: postpone the interview with these new witnesses of survival. But scarcely had I begun to acquiesce in the opinion of the Guide, when Reine straightened in her chair and, with great eagerness, adjured me not to let this occasion slip *no matter what ill might result for her*. With tears streaming down her poor little face, grown suddenly pale and thin, anxiously, and with a presentiment, no doubt, of what was coming, she implored me to put the experiment through immediately. But I could not yield to her pleading, my responsibility was too great. And then ... what? A few months of rest would, I perfectly well knew, only make my medium a better instrument of transmission, ... and Spirits—these or others—would always be at hand. Alas! "A few months of rest," brought us to *August 1914 ... brought us to the war.*

My research with Reine has been resumed, it is true, but in these tragic circumstances (and even for other reasons) its character has changed, and I cannot use the records to terminate this book. So then, I break off rather abruptly at this 107th séance, adding only some personal remarks as a conclusion to these first twenty-one months of my experimentation.

CONCLUSIONS

After a more or less serious examination of these notes, the reader will inevitably range himself in one of the three following groups:

1. The indifferent and the scoffers.
2. The interested (of different degrees).
3. The convinced.

The conclusions I have reached on the questions that have arisen in the course of my research, are addressed to those belonging to the second group only. With the rare members of the third group I have only to express cordial sympathy; and as to the indifferent and the scoffing, I have not the slightest hope of influencing them, for nobody ever convinces anyone against their will. As some wise man has said: "Opinions and beliefs are not the fruit of argument and discussion merely; the very closest reasoning is impotent to change a conviction wherein mysterious and indefinable sentiments enter for a large part." I would even add that facts themselves lose all weight when they do not awaken an echo of that something already known, of that something met before, which is intuition—that mysterious intuition which ceases to be a mystery as soon as we realize that it springs from a persistent memory of our past existences.

So I pass on with a polite bow to the indifferent, and a tranquil disregard of the scoffers. They have the right to their road as we to ours. At the end of the voyage each one will reconnoitre his position and take his bearings.

The following comments are therefore addressed only to those who may have been surprised and interested in reading these notes and who have the desire and the will to form a personal opinion: to the uninformed, or the misinformed; to those discouraged by unfortunate experiment; to the regretfully skeptical;—in short, to all who, realizing the fundamental and formidable importance of the question foresee the beneficent change that its solution would effect in our moral and social life.

Such persons will probably have remarked that in the long course of my experiments I have refrained from establishing a so-called scientific control over my medium. As a matter of fact, the intellectual character of the phenomena (finally predominating) did not lend itself to such control. But even at the beginning, when I was looking for physical manifestations, I did not observe the ordinary precautions of experienced practitioners,[103] and for the following reason:—

In the greater number of cases, such precautions are established for the sake of outsiders, in order to combat their constantly reiterated accusations of hallucination or fraud. The operator himself knows perfectly well that he is not hallucinated and that he is fully capable of judging the reality of the phenomena; but, at the same time, he wishes to be able to refute the accusation of the critics and to convince them. In fact, the value of scientific control, *considered as an agent of conviction or propagation*, is nil, and its futility has already been amply demonstrated. Scientists of the highest reputation—such as William Crookes, Professor Richet, and many others—have, in investigating such phenomena, surrounded themselves with every possible precaution in their laboratories, whether medical, chemical, or electrical. Never permitting themselves to express their personal opinion as men, so to speak, they have merely produced the testimony registered by their instruments.

What has been the result of such precautions? Abuse, doubts as to the sanity of the investigators. And *as men of science*—honored and admired up to that moment— they have immediately lost prestige.

---

[103] In the intellectual phenomena (descriptions, information, teachings, etc.) I even dropped all preoccupation as to the form of my questions as soon as I was convinced that my medium accepted no suggestion. "What was the color of Henry IV's white horse?" has often been my type of inquiry, merely because the type of Reine's reply has ever and invariably been, "Why, Monsieur Cornillier, Henry IV was afoot that day."

Thus, in the course of the last thirty years, students of the first order, investigators whose perspicacity and integrity are universally recognized, have made it their business to examine these phenomena by methods impeccably scientific. But what influence have they exercised thereby either upon their colleagues or upon the man in the street? None. They have convinced themselves, and that is all.

It is much, I admit, that such men have been able to acquire an absolute certitude, thanks to the reliability of their experimental methods. It is not, indeed, the use (often legitimate and valuable) of this impartially established testimony that I contest but the immoderate abuse of it,—an abuse actually provoked by fear.[104] Fear of criticism, fear of being accused of believing in table tipping, in ghosts,—in Spirits, even,—inspire such methods. They merely serve to diminish personal responsibility. In this way, it need never be "I"—it is always "the instrument."

One of the results—if not the only one—of scientific control by means of instruments has, however, undoubtedly been to rehabilitate the control of our senses (as Monsieur de Vesme has remarked) and to force auditory and visual sensations—until now so easily classed as subjective and hallucinary—to be recognized as objective and genuine.

These are the considerations which led me to believe that, having healthy senses in normal condition, a brain trained by my profession to exact observation, and having already made a serious study of the question, I might without fear experiment freely, and thus avoid restricting the development of my medium. For it must be held in mind

---

[104] Take for example the exaggerated control inflicted upon Madame Bisson's medium (Eva C.). Two emetics, one after the other, were imposed on that unhappy creature in order to prove to some irreconcilable sceptics that her "ectoplasms" were not fraudulently produced by means of white gauze. The ingenious suspicion was that *she might have swallowed some of this white gauze* before the séance, *regurgitated it* during the séance to produce her effects, and then *reswallowed it*, since her effects had to disappear. (And this in spite of the fact that the "ectoplasms" often sprang from the abdomen, the breasts, or the flanks). But scruple was pushed further. These ejections were submitted to the examination of a chemist. This chemist, in a long and detailed report, attested that his analysis had discovered meat ... mushrooms ... salad ... and various other alimentary products, but of the gauze not a trace! Was one single sceptic convinced by this barbarous treatment, these emetics, these gynaecological examinations (two in one séance)? Not one. See *The Phenomena of Materialization*, Dr. von Schrenck Notzing (Eng. Trans., Kegan & Paul, London, 1920).

that a medium is a sensitive plate easily troubled by the influence of suspicion or raillery, be it never so well dissimulated. The method, so much in favor just now, of treating the medium as a convicted impostor is distinctly prejudicial to the production of phenomena. And it is unquestionably to my confidence, vigilant and critical,—as it has ever been—that I owe the gradual unfolding of Reine's faculties and the results obtained: results which are, in a way, unique in the annals of psychology and which, I believe, are not to be explained away by current rationalistic arguments.

How, indeed, without recourse to transcendental causes, can one explain this long succession of phenomena, presenting themselves in methodical progression, with never an incoherence, and tending always to one end towards which all the efforts, all the experiments, all the teachings, converge? If we exclude the transcendental, what, we are obliged to ask ourselves, can be the source of this tenacious and reasoning will, so often in direct opposition to our own wills? Why these claims of identity, justified by convincing revelations, which express a psychology invariably characteristic of the personality announced? Whence proceeds this profound comprehension of beings and things, this ensemble of facts and ideas—predictions, visions, admonitions, teachings, etc.—this whole profuse documentation wherein the highest spiritual faculties and the most touching human sentiment find expression in turn? ... Assuming that the undeveloped brain of an ignorant young girl is the mighty creator of this gamut of human capacities, what a monstrous indictment of nature such an assumption entails! To have produced all this power, all these prodigious faculties, *for nothing*, is surely inconceivable! Can we reconcile the idea of such a marvelous organism, so magnificently equipped for the struggle of life, *with the absolute impossibility of its functioning except in the accidental and abnormal condition of hypnotic sleep?*[105]

Let us examine the arguments advanced to destroy the significance which I claim for my work:

First comes the simple artless deduction: persistent delusion. The book, I shall be told, is the product of a sick mind. Without taking this accusation too tragically, I would point out that my insanity implies that of my wife, that of my medium, and that of the five or six people

---

[105] The everyday life of little Reine is insignificant, even miserable; and there is absolutely no possibility of suspecting these faculties, whose employment would confer upon her a formidable power in our society!

who have assisted at several séances, and who have recognized their genuineness. But this is not all. I am only one insignificant observer. With this long series of experiments, I bring only a few stones to a monument that is already half erected. My madness makes madmen of all the others engaged in the work. It is no longer merely my modest person that is attacked; each one who holds this opinion and defends this philosophy becomes subject to the same charge.

This explanation, then, explains nothing at all. It is the cursory verdict of the ignorant and the lazy-minded. We may set it aside and come at once to the only criticism worthy of serious consideration—that of the scientists, specialists in these questions, who, while admitting the authenticity of the phenomena, deny their spirit-origin.

This is the only point of view which I accept to fight.

But here I must make a distinction. Even if Reine's hypnotic sleep is accepted as undeniable, her good faith as above suspicion, her disinterestedness as established, there still remains a vague and not very compromising insinuation of unconscious lies and inventions proceeding from an hysterical nervous condition. That is to say, Reine asleep, though honest, is capable of inventions and lies attributable to hysteria. Fortunately, however, Reine is not an hysterical subject. She is a normal little animal of clean constitution, with no organic weakness. Nor would hysteria, even were it established, prove anything; for what must be determined is the cause, *the generating force and source* of the phenomena, and not the special attributes of the instrument used in producing them. Hysterical or not hysterical, Reine does not create, she *transmits*; as is evident when studying the text and following the development of the manifestations. It is not a subliminal romance imagined by the medium that we have to examine; the problem before us is a collection of phenomena, some of them intellectual, some of them physical, but a collection that must be considered as a whole.

Personally, moreover, I must absolutely reject a method of explanation which, in order to gain a point, consists in arbitrarily separating phenomena that are closely bound together, which proceed from one and the same source, and which converge towards a definite proclaimed end. To my mind, it is quite inadmissible to accept as gospel truth those phenomena which could be classified under the familiar rubrics "thought-transmission," "mind reading," "psychometry," "secondary personality," etc. ... and to blandly deny the authenticity of all the rest! This method, though currently employed, seems to me altogether discreditable. Impartially presented, the question then resolves itself as follows:

Considering these phenomena as a whole, is it possible to find their rational cause in the known constitutive forces of a human being, without recourse to the existence of so-called disincarnate Spirits?

This is, unquestionably, the only ground on which discussion may be profitable.

From this point of vantage only two possible explanations remain to be refuted, explanations which are frequently and indiscriminately applied to all mediumistic revelations for the purpose of avoiding the admission of spirit-origin. They are respectively subconsciousness and telepathy.

What, then, is this subconsciousness? And what is this telepathy? In analyzing them, we must strip them of all the borrowed attributes which zealous advocates, over interested in their success, have conferred upon them.

For, adopting legitimately the old adage, "Nothing can exist in the mind that has not passed through the senses," it is clear that *for materialists or rationalists the subconscious is only, and can be only, the sum of impressions and sensations unconsciously received and unwittingly registered in the memory of a being.*

Under certain influences (natural or provoked sleep, accidental super-excitation, or pathological conditions), fractions of this unsuspected subconsciousness may suddenly be exteriorized, as are other facts which have been consciously registered by the memory. This is clear and simple and has been experimentally proved. It is perfectly admissible, for instance, that a child, playing in a public garden with other children, and all-absorbed in his game, passing again and again before two Chinamen engaged in talk, may, forty years later on, in a sudden crisis, recall and pronounce certain words of the Chinese language, unconsciously heard and registered at that moment. But—and this is most important—*he will not thereby have acquired the capacity of understanding and speaking Chinese.* Let us take another example: An individual is, we assume, taken to the Louvre to see a certain picture in the *Salon carré*. To reach it, he passes through five or six rooms, talking all the time to his companion. Consciously, he has not looked at one of the pictures on his way; nevertheless, his visual memory has, without his being aware of it, registered an infinite number of sensations received by his eyes as he passed through the rooms. And later—the following night, or ten years afterwards—the image of one of those pictures may come back to his mind so vividly that he will recognize it and be able to describe it.

Examples might be indefinitely multiplied, but the real point is as follows: *It is only the knowledge thus obtained that a materialist may rationally accept as pertaining to the subconscious.* All the rest is hypothesis and transcendental inference, extremely dangerous for the enemies of spiritualism to manipulate, for, logically, they lead straight to the theory of reincarnation. There is no escaping it, as has been demonstrated by Doctor Geley in his admirable book, *l' Etre Subconscient*, which should be read for a clear understanding of this question.

Now let us examine telepathy—taking care to remark the obvious spirit-origin and spirit-character of certain faculties which—quite unconsciously, without doubt—the skeptics confer upon it.

Telepathy is experimental or spontaneous.

Experimental telepathy begins with the voluntary transmission of thought. Its domain—so far as I know, at least—is extremely limited. In all the many and varied experiments, the transmission of a word, a number, or an image, is about all that has been obtained sufficiently often to preclude the possibilities of coincidence and chance. Demonstrated between two people trained and, so to speak, tuned in harmony, results may go rather further. Impressions of acts or sentiments (generally very vague) may be transmitted and may manifest themselves in the mind of the percipient by images, by obsessive words, or even by a change in his psychological state. A sufficient number of successful experiments has proved beyond all cavil the real existence of telepathic correspondence between two operators. But never, so far as I am aware, has the communication telepathically received been found to hold any intrinsic interest.

Magnetism and suggestion from a distance may also be considered as forms of provoked telepathy: and in this branch, as in the preceding one, the demonstrated results are meager.

Spontaneous telepathy, on the contrary, is rich in varied manifestations: visions, auditory phenomena, announcements of events already realized, or to be realized—often of great importance for the percipient but sometimes, too, of insignificant interest or urgency. It is marked at times by a curious symbolism, an evident design—whose origin in many cases, it must be noted, cannot be attributed to living beings.[106] But never, to my knowledge, has there been telepathic transmission of

---

[106] See Ernest Bozzano's book, *Les Phenomènes Premonitoires*, which proves with admirable logic the impossibility of excluding the spirit hypothesis in many cases.

long messages expressed in clear and precise terms, or a progressive series of complex communications, all tending to the realization of a pre-announced purpose.

We must bear in mind also that, in telepathy, the phenomenon must be *subjective*. The moment there is *objective sensation or material action* it can no longer be rationally defined as telepathic. It belongs to us—partisans of the existence of the fluidic body—and we alone can explain it without pilfering in another man's field.

The so-called retarded or deferred telepathy and relayed telepathy are hypotheses invented for the occasion and not susceptible of experimental proof.[107] The argument advanced for the first is based upon the

---

[107] For those unfamiliar with these terms I will give two examples:—

(i.) Retarded or deferred telepathy. When through a medium, or by direct impression, a person receives a communication purporting to come from an individual who died ten—or twenty—years ago, the communication giving evidence of identity sufficient to preclude its attribution to a living being.

The psychist who advances telepathy as an explanation of the phenomenon applies his theory as follows: Since it is demonstrated that the message communicated could come from none other than that person who died ten—or twenty—years ago, *it was before his death or at the moment of his death* that his brain unconsciously emitted the telepathic radiations of this message. These radiations immediately reached the brain of the percipient, and, unknown to him, were registered in his subconsciousness. And ten years later—or twenty—provoked by a determinating cause, the message suddenly comes to life in the consciousness of the percipient, or is read in his subconsciousness by a medium who reports it, but who mistakes its origin.

(ii.) Telepathy by relay. Madame A. dies in Paris. She had a very dear friend, Madame B., who, having left for Russia, could not be informed of her death. This Madame B. is a cousin of Monsieur C. who lives at Nancy and is interested in psychical research. In a séance with a medium, Monsieur C. receives a message purporting to come from Madame A.—whom he had not known—begging him to transmit the announcement of her death to Madame B., as well as particular details of her last days (details afterward verified).

The psychist who advances telepathy as an explanation of the phenomenon applies his theory as follows:—Madame A. *emitted before her death* the radiations of this message for her dear Madame B. who unconsciously registered them, and, quite as unconsciously re-expedited them to her cousin, Monsieur C., in whose mysterious subconsciousness, and all unknown to him, the message was inscribed, and where it remained

results obtained in post-hypnotic suggestion, but the fact that such suggestion necessarily implies a *suggester* seems to be overlooked.

As to the supposition—which for us spiritualists is a fact,—that the subject can, in order to get information, spontaneously enter into the consciousness or the subconsciousness of other beings, or into their ambiance even,—this is for those psychists who are materialists a most imprudent concession. First it is a dip into the transcendental, which they should most carefully avoid, and secondly it is a tacit and inevitable admission—or otherwise one falls into absurdity—*that a certain organized, conscious and voluntary something leaves the physical body to go in search of information.*

And this is nothing more nor less than the unwilling recognition of a *fluidic body* which is the key to the whole mystery!

(It is indeed in this way that Reine, voluntarily, or at my order, proceeds to make her observations. But she knows it and says so; just as she always knows and announces the origin of her communications. One has only to read my notes to realize that she had not the slightest embarrassment in admitting that it was imagination which provoked certain visions in the crystal ball, or that such and such a dream or incident was merely an echo of her conscious life).

To sum up, telepathy is a phenomenon based on the fact that a human brain can emit radiations—whose nature is unknown—which, when they encounter another brain in synchronic accord, provoke in that brain images, or subjective impressions; and this, at no matter what distance.

Beyond the limits of this definition we fall into hypotheses involving the implication of a transcendental element which leads the skeptics ... exactly where they do not care to go. They will inevitably admit it one of these days; but till that day comes we must not cease protesting against the fact that, in order to deny survival, they make constant use of arguments belonging essentially to the spirit-theory—merely investing them with a new name. This "camouflage" should impose upon no one capable of thinking for themselves.

And, moreover, telepathy and subconsciousness, rationally defined, offer an already vast field for materialistic speculation.

---

concealed up to the moment of his séance with the medium who discovered it, announced it, and falsely ascribed to it a spirit origin.

Verily, as Ernest Bozzano has written, "there is a scientific credulity comparable in all respects to the blind faith of true believers"!

To this subconsciousness and this telepathy there is still another hypothesis that must be added—a new one.

According to the conclusions of a psychist of value,[108]psychometry—which, until now, was supposed to explain only psychometrical facts—turns out to be a pass-key giving access to all the mediumistic phenomena. In these accounts of my séances certain precise examples of psychometry have been given; and it would be as well perhaps to content ourselves with them, lest this honest psychometrical key turn into a "jemmy"![109]

What efforts are made, what intelligence is spent, in these efforts to deny the evidence, to avoid admitting at once the truth that we shall certainly be forced to recognize later on:—*The existence of a fluidic body as the vehicle of the Spirit, its independence, under certain conditions, of the physical body and, in consequence, its possible continuity after death.*

What, we may well enquire, underlies this animosity on the part of so many scientific men? What do they find so detestable in the mere idea of survival?

I am inclined to believe that the fundamental cause may be found in an unconscious reaction against the oppressive burden that clerical obscurantism has riveted upon human intelligence during so many centuries. To such persons, the mystery of the transcendental seems to furnish new elements for a re-forging of those heavy chains which centuries of revolt and martyrdom have only just succeeded in breaking. In all sincerity they believe that it is their unfettered reason which prompts this skeptical attitude, whereas they are perhaps impelled to it by the mysterious echo of past anguish.

The work of Vettellini may reassure them.

---

[108] Arsène Denis, *Annales des Sciences Psychiques*, July, 1913.

[109] It must be remarked that the so-called psychometrical phenomena are clearly of a transcendental order. It is absolutely inadmissible that rationalists should find it normal and simple that a medium, in touching a ring that has belonged to someone no longer living, can describe that person as he was in life, as well as different scenes in his lifetime.

There is, moreover, an unfortunate abuse of this term psychometry which should designate only the power, possessed by some mediums, of analyzing the moral and intellectual faculties of a person by taking contact with an object belonging to him. But the greater number of so-called cases of psychometry are in reality clairvoyance.

In any case, the facts of my experience are set forth here impartially and carefully. I have warned the reader against the would-be explanatory theories so much in fashion. It is now for him—if he has the necessary interest—to form his own opinion through personal work. He should try to apply the so-called rationalistic explanations to many and various cases, controlling and verifying them by the different examples cited in my notes. But he must remember that the account given here of my researches is only one stone in the great edifice. Any number of works and endless records of personal experiences exist. Some of the highest scientific authorities have given their testimony. Whoever is interested, in the question must, however, study it for himself.

My task is finished.

P. E. C.

APPENDIX

NOTE 1.

Doctor N.—an avowed believer in reincarnation—having examined my notes, was good enough to put down certain objections that rose in his mind in the course of his reading.

Not being responsible for the information and precepts transmitted to me, I made no attempt to discuss these criticisms myself, merely reading them to the medium in hypnosis and writing down her replies.[110] And I give them here, because they complete and clear up some of the points in Vettellini's teaching.

1. Concerning the confidence to be placed in mediumistic communications. (Influence of the medium, the operator, the environment—conscious or subconscious. The inevitable (relative) return of the communicating Spirit to the psychological conditions which were his in his lifetime, etc.) Should not all transmitted communications be received with reservations?

Reply: "Generally speaking, yes. Vettellini has already given several reasons why no great confidence should be accorded to the majority of communications. First: superior Spirits rarely communicate; it is almost always the mediocre and ignorant who present themselves. Second: the medium frequently fails to understand, and so gives a false interpretation.

---

[110] As I read each of these observations to Reine, asleep, she seemed to listen a moment, then the answer came clear and precise.

"But in our case it is different. Vettellini is a highly evolved Spirit. He affirms only what he knows. If there are doubts, he points them out to you.—Then, too, he was preparing the ground a long time in advance, and little by little. He is not, and he cannot be, troubled by the conditions in which he places himself for communicating. His thought and purpose is absolutely clear and precise.

"As to myself, I may certainly transmit badly, and make mistakes at times, but only in details. If it were an important error Vettellini would surely see it later on and correct it."

"You may be absolutely certain, Monsieur Cornillier,—Vettellini affirms it again—that all the important communications which he has given are true. The doctor's objection is sound, but it does not apply to our experiments."

2. Concerning the moment of incarnation: It would seem, after certain experimentation, that fecundation is not always instantaneous. It is established that spermatozoa can live for several days and penetrate the ovule some time after coition.

Reine answers immediately:—"But certainly they can live for several days and penetrate a long time after! Only in that case there is no incarnation *because there is no Spirit present.* Coition is not the cause of fecundation, but it attracts the Spirit and provokes its capture. If no Spirit were present, a spermatozoon would penetrate the ovule just the same, but there would be no incarnation. In certain cases, even, a fetus may form, but one non-viable,—which would result in miscarriage or a still-born child."

I object that some artificial fecundations have nevertheless succeeded.—"Yes, but in that case it is because a Spirit who is conscious comes voluntarily to incarnate. It is a deliberate act, a personal decision, or one made in common with the great Spirits. But it is extremely rare. If artificial fecundation were regularly practiced, it is very seldom that a living child would be obtained."

3. Concerning the disengagement of the astral body. The operation of trepan, remarked on prehistoric skulls—chiefly skulls of children— was it not an empiric process for the purpose of creating mediums?—A practice of religious magic to facilitate the sortie of the astral body?

Reply: "Yes, Vettellini says that the doctor is right; it is correct. If complete and intact skeletons of that epoch could be found, significant and special mutilations of the hands and feet, made for the same purpose, would be also discovered."

4. Do Spirits see us, the incarnated? Do they read our thoughts? Without mediumnic intervention, do they come into our lives? The

doctor makes a strong protest against certain facts recorded that would seem to imply *this abusive and inadmissible interference.*

Reply: (Reine's voice is sharp.)—"Yes, yes ... and yes! Agreeable or not, it makes no difference! It is a fact—an exact fact. Spirits do—or they may—assist at our daily life and witness everything we do,—*everything*, you understand. Naturally, what they see and how much they comprehend, depends upon their evolution. They distinguish more or less clearly. Not all, for example, can read our thoughts. The presence of a medium gives certain ones amongst them a force and lucidity, which they have not yet personally acquired,—that is evident. But you may be sure of this: *there are witnesses for each and every act we commit.* No,—it isn't agreeable! But after all, when one stops to think ... it might be a big help to us. Just think of the things we wouldn't do if we knew someone were looking at us. What a lot of mean, miserable, little villainies we'd escape! And the crimes!—Without that sense of secrecy, how many would never have been committed! Ah! No, *it is a good thing*! And it would be well for all of us to remember that nothing that we do or think is secret: life would be purer."

5. Concerning the dualism, *spirit-matter.* It is not easy to accept. Why this planting of spirit in matter? It would be more logical to admit that spirit is in suspense in matter.

(In stating Doctor N.'s question to Vettellini, I add that I, too, was—and still am—profoundly astonished at his teaching on this point. I understand—or I think I understand—how spirit could be in suspense in matter, and develop towards consciousness through the successive reactions that it would oppose to this matter, and to its environment. But spirit, having from the beginning its own existence, outside of matter, is inconceivable to me.)

Reply: (After attentive listening on Reine's part.)

"Vettellini reaffirms it. And it is not his personal opinion alone. All the Spirits of his evolution agree upon the original independence of spirit and matter. You understand, or you do not understand,—that is another question. Vettellini has never concealed from you that his knowledge is only more extended than human knowledge; he has never pretended to penetrate the mystery of the Infinite. He tells you what they, the Spirits of his evolution, observe and believe they understand,—that is all. And we, incarnate, may have conceptions that are logical and just, as measured by the conditions of our existence on earth, but which have no value or reason in astral life. The point of view is different there; they have another comprehension.

"In any case, there was no error in my transmission. It is certainly Vettellini's opinion that *spirit and matter are independent and distinct from their very beginning.*"

6. Concerning Fate. The doctor is not satisfied. Fate is the result of evolution, the result of all precedent lives. It is created by us. Free will is above all the outgrowth of anterior lives. Fundamental inequality in Spirits is inadmissible; the inequality is evidently in the working out of evolutions. Evil is necessary; but how can we admit the original necessity of maleficent Spirits? Evil is the measure of the inferiority of a world. It comes from the struggle with the conditions of life, struggle for reproduction,—the thousand factors of strife and progress.

Vettellini can only reaffirm what he has already given on this subject at various séances, and without dogmatism, for that matter. Reine remarks that the intervention of maleficent Spirits is for the purpose of hastening evolution which, without the aid of these ferments, would drag along too slowly. They are factors of reaction, stimulants that accelerate the march towards consciousness, etc., etc. I did not note the reply in detail because all the elements of it are found in the records of the séances.

7. Concerning the apparition of the early Egyptian Spirits. Is it possible that they are not yet reincarnated? Is not the story an imagination of the medium, based on the souvenir of precedent lives?

Reine transmits:—"Time, so important a factor with you, signifies nothing at all in the Astral. Some Spirits remain disincarnated for centuries. It is neither long nor short,—neither much nor little. Certain conditions—and amongst these, embalming—prevent their reincarnating, or indefinitely retard it. Sometimes, even, it is a voluntary choice. Reine did not imagine the Egyptian Spirits. They inhabit, or at least frequent, the museum because the tombs, the statues, the thousand different objects belonging to their race and civilization, attract them there: and also because of the attention and admiration which these relics provoke. Certain Spirits are happy in that place and live there for this reason."

NOTE 2.

Suggested by séances following the one-hundred-and-seventh, and explaining why certain perfectly authentic mediumnic communications may be incoherent.

1. The majority of Spirits of slight evolution are not, after death, immediately conscious of their passage into the Au-Delà. (Especially if they were convinced materialists; or, again, if death was violent, or sudden.)

From the fact that the disengagement of their Spirit was effected unconsciously (either through coma, or by sudden shock), and because the relatively material density of their astral body retains them in our atmosphere where—vaguely and half-awake—they follow the course of daily events, there is nothing to destroy their conviction that they are still living. Strange as it may seem, they do not recognize that they are dead, and even deny it with obstinacy.[111]

This, then, is one of the first sources of incoherence in communications.

2. By their fixed and persistent ideas Spirits, unconsciously, produce images around them—illusions of which they themselves are the first dupes, and which also mislead the disincarnated souls in their environment.

A number of incidents given in my notes demonstrate that the intentional creation of images is of current use amongst high Spirits. But the unconscious production of them by inferior ones may easily be admitted since, in experimental séances, we have been able to observe that certain mediums in trance—that is to say, whose disengaged spirit is in astral conditions—produce unconsciously slight materializations that can be imputed only to a sort of projection of their thought. Moreover, the phenomenon of telepathy demonstrates that images, whether generated by the brain of the agent unconsciously (spontaneous telepathy), or voluntarily (experimental telepathy), are received and perceived as such by the brain of the percipient. Thus these phenomena, whose creation and reality we admit in our physical world, continue and develop perfectly naturally in the astral world.

---

[111] Personally, I have had several examples of these strange cases, but any number of them are recorded in spirit documentation. The most curious I know are given by Admiral Moore in the appendix of his book, *Glimpses of the Next State*. Nothing could be more dramatic than the dumbfounded astonishment of these people when they hear that they are dead!

This condition would seem possible only for such as Vettellini, classes in the first degree of evolution; but it can nevertheless exist, for a time at least, in more evolved Spirits, resulting from spiritual tendencies—an obstinacy in fixed opinions, a refusal to investigate, etc. *"But when one is dead one knows it!"* a certain Spirit under this error replied to me. *"I cannot admit that, being dead, I can see and hear. So then, I am not dead."* To convince this, logician I sent him to find his buried body. Then he understood.

And this is a second source of errors in communications that are quite sincere but which, as information, are no more dependable than is any other hallucination.[112]

3. In astral life Spirits of slight evolution seem as a rule to perceive only these image illusions.

From my experiments, astral vision would seem to develop with and correspond to the degree of evolution, and the disincarnate, whose condition maintains them in our terrestrial atmosphere, cannot take cognizance of the subtle ethereal substance of their superiors, who exist for them no more than they themselves exist for us.

And this is a third cause of error in spirit communications.

To sum it up: The revelation of death is always in proportion to the degree of evolution. It may be nonexistent, it may be perverted and deformed by the soul's condition.

NOTE 3.

Why violent death forces evolution in one who is stagnant and too attached to terrestrial life. (The reason holds equally, of course, in the case of catastrophes involving the death of hundreds or thousands—earthquakes, floods, wars, etc.)

In natural death, the Spirit disengages slowly, gently, sifting out like a mist from the entire surface of the body: *and the disengagement of the fluidic double is complete.*

In violent death, the Spirit escapes suddenly by the mouth, and the precipitation of the rupture is such that *the heavy and denser portion of the fluidic double is left in the body. This heavy and denser element contains exactly what constituted his terrestrial bonds,—his tendencies, tastes, habits, etc.,—which normally would have accompanied the Spirit in his astral life and would have persisted in his new reincarnation.*

To use an analogy, *natural death* is the tranquil moving of a tenant who takes his time, carrying with him most carefully all his furniture,

---

[112] I ask a disincarnate—a carpenter killed in an accident how he sees himself? He replies that he is in his working clothes and has his saw. He is hunting for work and does not understand why no one pays attention to him. A lady who has been in the Astral for several months declares that today she has put on her red dress and is wearing her jewels. Soon she will take to her furs, for winter is coming.

works of art, bric-à-brac and cherished keepsakes, to organize the future dwelling place with the elements and on the lines of the old one; so that he may take up again all his habits: whereas *violent death* is a sudden flight, as when caused by fire, which obliges the tenant to escape half stripped—carrying nothing with him. He must then begin all over again to make a new life and acquire new treasures.

NOTE 4.

Rectification of passages concerning the disappearance of our race.
(Séance twenty-third.)

According to Vettellini, the time required for the terrestrial evolution of a human Spirit is from four to six thousand years and implies from thirty to forty reincarnations with their intervals of repose. But there is solidarity in the groups ready for interplanetary migration. And, in order that the totality of the "swarm" that has come to earth from another star (to evolve in and by the white race) may, each and all, pass through the ordeals of their terrestrial cycle, a period of about twenty-five thousand six hundred years must elapse.[113] Our "swarm," in truth, did not fall to earth all at once—entire and complete. It is in series of overlapping waves that we are successively accomplishing our stage here.

Now a great number of the Spirits comprised in the first series are actually to be found in the French nation; and it is these, and these only, who—having no further need of terrestrial incarnation—will, in the course of the next three hundred years, definitely enter into the Astral, whence they will aid and influence the newly incarnated. Thus it is not the French race nor the French nation that must disappear with the end of a cycle, as Reine mistakenly transmitted: it is the first incarnated, the earliest settlers, so to speak, of the white race whose arrival on the terrestrial plane dates back approximately five thousand years.

This theory would explain the sloth in the progress of human society—the incomprehensible, despairing sloth! For the fact that Spirits who have reached the requisite degree of consciousness do not return amongst us (save for special works voluntarily accepted), and the fact that they are replaced by contingents hardly yet freed from animality, necessarily maintains our society at a low level of morality and consciousness.

---

[113] This period corresponds to the cycle of the precession of equinoxes.

But, as the cycle advances in its course, evolution will be more rapid; for the newly incarnated will find educational conditions ever superior to those of their predecessors. That is to say, they will find organisms more and more supple and sensitive, better endowed for acquisition by personal experience and more open to astral influence: and they will find also a more and more rational social organization, which will enormously increase and foster individual action and production.

NOTE 5.

Concerning the invasion of the Yellow Race. (Twenty-third Séance.)

In a subsequent séance in 1915, at a moment when the Eastern question seemed unlikely to give us any grave anxiety, I asked Vettellini if the vision which the medium had in February, 1913—vision of a redoubtable invasion of Europe by the yellow race—had not been misplaced by her in time: was it not the intensity of the image which made her associate the terrifying tragedy with the actual Western wars?—"No," is the prompt and decided reply, "Reine made no mistake. *It was to be.* But we have driven it back."

"Driven back," too, the appalling cataclysm that was predicted,—"driven back" it has been and still is by constant effort and action, for its realization now in the full swing of events would materially and morally impair our cause.

Moreover, one of these days, if circumstances allow, I mean to publish all that has been transmitted to us concerning the war and the astral efforts that were brought to bear to modify its course. Seen from the other side, the drama is even more formidably *grandiose* ... And whatever may be the verdict as to the value of my experience, I believe it will not be denied that no epic poet has surpassed in height and power of imagination the conceptions that have sprung from the ignorant unlettered brain of little Reine in hypnosis.

NOTE 6.

Certain statements made by the Guide in the course of these séances will astonish and displease simply because they upset our habits of thought, or do not correspond to the ideals born of our own desires. But one point in the doctrine will more than displease, it will violently shock; it will be declared inacceptable and absurd. It is that which affirms, first, that still-born children are always of high evolution; and second, that children who die after a few months or a few years—including those whose short existence is passed in degeneracy or idiocy—are, all and always, very evolved.

How is it possible to accept such a statement? How can we admit that a great Spirit finds a complement of evolution by shutting himself up for eight or nine months in an organism in process of formation? And, worse still, by supporting for several years the lamentable existence of a poor vitiated body, deprived even of the possibility of all psychical expression!

There is in this teaching, and in the affirmation that it is "general law," something so shocking to our earthly conceptions, that I could not possibly abandon the point without trying to get some rational understanding of it.

The result of my investigation is this:

First point. To begin with, it must be clearly established that *evolution is the product of knowledge acquired by personal experience.* One knows only what one has experienced. Beyond this, there is only belief. So long as you have not gone to Versailles, you will not know that Versailles exists: you will *believe* it, from your friends' reports, from your reading, but you will not *know it from personal experience.*

Very well, a Spirit, a great one, who has passed through the complete cycle of terrestrial ordeals, has, nevertheless—and inevitably—failed to acquire a precise knowledge of one of them:—*the incorporation into matter, the "fall" into the physical plane.*

It is, in fact, the general law that incarnation cannot be *consciously* experienced: for the whirl of vibrations has the effect of plunging into night any Spirit within the radius of influence. There is exception only for those who, having reached the limit of their terrestrial evolution, possess a consciousness of such power and temper that they can resist this effect. These, then, can *experience* the fundamental phenomenon of the incorporation of spirit in matter. They are capable of going through with it and following all its stages with entire lucidity. And after the experiment, *they know.*[114]

And now for the second point:

When very evolved Spirits come to reincarnate for only a few months, or a few years, it is with a view to acquiring an element of conscience, a

---

[114] It must not be inferred that all Spirits who have reached the term of evolution undergo this last incarnation. There are in the Astral equivalent ordeals which they may prefer.

"vibration" which is lacking; and in such cases they never incorporate themselves completely in their organism, never take absolute possession of it. Often, even, they do not bother to come and fashion it, leaving it a living substance *such as heredity has made it.*

For at this high degree of evolution the constraint of the body itself is not an essential condition of experimentation. The fact of being maintained by the fluidic line in effective contact with matter suffices for them to gain their final acquisition through and in the physical plane.

It is, then, precisely *because the Spirit is not in the body* that the conditions of that body are of no importance:—it is merely a buoy serving to hold up for one moment a luminous Spirit in the sea of substance.

NOTE 7.

Rectifying a communication (badly transmitted by Reine) as to the way in which Spirits perceive time.

(1921.) Repeated communications in the course of these last years have convinced me that, if the disincarnate have a notion of time differing from ours, they none the less perceive *duration* and *sequence* in events. Briefly, it is the *rhythm* of time that varies for them.

The well-known fact that a fainting or suffocating person can in an instant live over again his whole past, and that, in a moment's dream, events requiring years for their development may unfold themselves, this fact helps us to conceive the prodigious acceleration in the rhythm of time in certain states of being (disengagement, disincarnation), and to understand the reply Vettellini gave me some months ago: *"It took me the thousandth part of a second"* (to go to a far distant star), *"but a second for us is equivalent to years for you."*

On the other hand, if the doctoral assertion that "the past, the present and the future co-exist," has merely a verbal sense, it must nevertheless be recognized that very evolved Spirits have the power of taking a, so to speak, instantaneous view of the successive. For the past, it is a reconstitution based upon imprints or fluidic residue; for the future it is a foresight of images or a reading of signs announcing events in preparation, but always susceptible of modification. This instantaneous general view (*vue d'ensemble*) is, for our perception of time, tantamount to co-existence; but, in reality, it is merely a sort of astral cinematography.

NOTE 8.

Concerning the question of the fourth dimension.

(1921.) Despite all my efforts in the past seven years, I have not obtained the slightest demonstration of the reality of a fourth dimension, nor the feeblest sign of its employment in the various activities of astral life. On the other hand, I have acquired the conviction of certain modes of existence, conditioned by a different density which is ever progressively subtle. And, in my opinion, it is this phenomenon which gave rise to the theory of multiple dimensions, though superficially there would seem to be no relation between them. In short, I would say that, *experimentally*, we discover in the successive planes of astral life (attained through a medium), no indication whatever of an additional division in space that could be utilized by the disincarnated (the only ones, however, to benefit by it); but that we do remark that each successive sphere of evolution implies a more and more subtle density, giving the Beings who have obtained it a power of penetration into and passage through Space, which is not perceptible to those of inferior spheres whose density is heavier.

The End.

Paperbacks also available from
White Crow Books

Jesus of Nazareth with Simon Parke—
Conversations with Jesus of Nazareth
ISBN 978-1-907661-41-9

Thomas à Kempis with Simon
Parke—*The Imitation of Christ*
ISBN 978-1-907661-58-7

Julian of Norwich with Simon
Parke—*Revelations of Divine Love*
ISBN 978-1-907661-88-4

Allan Kardec—*The Spirits Book*
ISBN 978-1-907355-98-1

Allan Kardec—*The Book on Mediums*
ISBN 978-1-907661-75-4

Emanuel Swedenborg—*Heaven and Hell*
ISBN 978-1-907661-55-6

P.D. Ouspensky—*Tertium Organum:
The Third Canon of Thought*
ISBN 978-1-907661-47-1

Dwight Goddard—*A Buddhist Bible*
ISBN 978-1-907661-44-0

Michael Tymn—*The Afterlife Revealed*
ISBN 978-1-970661-90-7

Michael Tymn—*Transcending the
Titanic: Beyond Death's Door*
ISBN 978-1-908733-02-3

Guy L. Playfair—*If This Be Magic*
ISBN 978-1-907661-84-6

Guy L. Playfair—*The Flying Cow*
ISBN 978-1-907661-94-5

Guy L. Playfair —*This House is Haunted*
ISBN 978-1-907661-78-5

Carl Wickland, M.D.—
Thirty Years Among the Dead
ISBN 978-1-907661-72-3

John E. Mack—*Passport to the Cosmos*
ISBN 978-1-907661-81-5

Peter & Elizabeth Fenwick—
The Truth in the Light
ISBN 978-1-908733-08-5

Erlendur Haraldsson—
Modern Miracles
ISBN 978-1-908733-25-2

Erlendur Haraldsson—
At the Hour of Death
ISBN 978-1-908733-27-6

Erlendur Haraldsson—
The Departed Among the Living
ISBN 978-1-908733-29-0

Brian Inglis—*Science and Parascience*
ISBN 978-1-908733-18-4

Brian Inglis—*Natural and Supernatural:
A History of the Paranormal*
ISBN 978-1-908733-20-7

Ernest Holmes—*The Science of Mind*
ISBN 978-1-908733-10-8

Victor & Wendy Zammit —*A Lawyer
Presents the Evidence For the Afterlife*
ISBN 978-1-908733-22-1

Casper S. Yost—*Patience
Worth: A Psychic Mystery*
ISBN 978-1-908733-06-1

William Usborne Moore—
Glimpses of the Next State
ISBN 978-1-907661-01-3

William Usborne Moore—
The Voices
ISBN 978-1-908733-04-7

John W. White—
The Highest State of Consciousness
ISBN 978-1-908733-31-3

Stafford Betty—
The Imprisoned Splendor
ISBN 978-1-907661-98-3

Paul Pearsall, Ph.D. —
Super Joy
ISBN 978-1-908733-16-0

**All titles available as eBooks, and selected titles available in Hardback and
Audiobook formats from www.whitecrowbooks.com**

Lightning Source UK Ltd.
Milton Keynes UK
UKOW04f0828021017
310244UK00002B/437/P